Cognitive-Behavioural Therapy for Anorexia Nervosa

This book presents CBT-AN-20, a newly developed briefer form of cognitive-behavioural therapy (CBT) for anorexia nervosa, designed to treat individuals in 20 sessions, helping clinicians to offer effective therapy to more patients and enabling patients to move more quickly towards recovery.

This manual addresses the key CBT skills needed to deliver effective CBT-AN-20. It uses a combination of psychoeducation, nutrition, exposure therapy, and behavioural experiments to overcome starvation and to support essential weight gain/stability. It then details the skills needed to work with emotional factors and with body image issues. Importantly, it also stresses the meta-competences needed to work with anorexia nervosa – such as early change, motivational work, engaging with the "anorexic voice", and maintaining a working alliance that stresses change. Accompanying the text is a range of useful web-based materials to support the clinician reading the manual. These include checklists, psychoeducation materials, measures, and videos of skills in action.

CBT-AN-20's pragmatic structure supports its delivery by both experienced therapists and those newer to the field who are practising under expert supervision. This book is a "must read" for all levels of practitioners from all disciplines who work with eating disorders.

Glenn Waller is Professor of Clinical Psychology, University of Sheffield, UK.

Kamryn T. Eddy is Professor of Psychology, Harvard Medical School, USA.

Charlotte L. Rose is a Principal Psychological Therapist at STEPs Community Eating Disorder Service, Avon and Wiltshire Mental Health Partnership NHS Trust, UK.

Jennifer J. Thomas is Professor of Psychology, Department of Psychiatry, Harvard Medical School, USA.

Hannah M. Turner is a Consultant Clinical Psychologist at the Hampshire Adult Eating Disorder Service, Hampshire and Isle of Wight Healthcare NHS Foundation Trust, UK.

Tracey D. Wade is Matthew Flinders Distinguished Professor, Flinders University, Australia and Director of the Flinders University Services for Eating Disorders, Australia.

"A powerful new resource in the battle to reduce suffering from anorexia nervosa. This book captures a wealth of clinical and research experience from some of the world's leading scientist-practitioners in the treatment of anorexia nervosa. It offers a novel, shorter course of treatment that can help eating disorder clinics see more patients in less time without sacrificing efficacy; it also increases affordability of treatment. Numerous clinical tools are provided including downloadable resources and skills videos for clinicians. Highly recommended for all who treat anorexia nervosa!!"

Carolyn Black Becker, *PhD, ABPP, FAED, FABCT, FAPS, Professor of Psychology, Trinity University, Licensed Psychologist, USA*

"This much-needed treatment manual for anorexia nervosa, written by leading experts in the field, offers a unique blend of depth, detail, and clinical practicality. Its international perspective ensures relevance across diverse clinical contexts, while the clear, step-by-step guidance makes it an invaluable tool for both novice and experienced clinicians. Stand-out chapters on meta-competence, clinical skills, and adaptations for varied presentations support flexible application of the intervention. In summary, this book is an essential resource for any clinician seeking to enhance their expertise and confidence in treating patients with this challenging disorder."

Roz Shafran, *PhD, FMedSci, Emeritus Professor of Translational Psychology, UCL Great Ormond Street Institute of Child Health, UK*

"Written by clinicians with deep expertise, compassion, and dedication to sharing knowledge, this work reflects how far cognitive-behavioural therapy interventions for anorexia nervosa have come in real-world clinical practice. It challenges the assumption that longer treatment is always necessary and offers clear, practical guidance on open weighing, early nutritional change, working with the anorexic voice, and exposure – alongside compelling rationales for clients ("the why") and strategies clinicians can implement immediately ("the how"). Whether new to the field or a seasoned clinician, this is what a treatment manual should be – and what we continue to refine as science evolves."

Dr Bronwyn Raykos, *MPsych (Clinical) / PhD, Morgan Psychology (Director), Western Australian Country Health Service, Centre for Clinical Interventions, Australia*

"This innovative work by an international group of collaborators is an effort to develop a briefer and effective treatment for anorexia nervosa. The treatment model rests on various techniques rooted in functional analysis and designed to help patients approach their anxieties and behaviors in the context of a realistic and collaborative treatment relationship. At the same time, there is careful attention to the "anorexic voice" which needs to be heard, understood, and addressed. Overall, this comprehensive and innovative new work opens possibilities for patients and clinicians. The field should look forward to new studies of this potentially very useful intervention."

Stephen Wonderlich Ph.D., *Interim President, Sanford Research, Chester Fritz Distinguished Professor, University of North Dakota School of Medicine and Health Sciences, USA*

Cognitive-Behavioural Therapy for Anorexia Nervosa

A Clinician's Guide to CBT-AN-20

Glenn Waller, Kamryn T. Eddy,
Charlotte L. Rose, Jennifer J. Thomas,
Hannah M. Turner, and
Tracey D. Wade

Routledge
Taylor & Francis Group

LONDON AND NEW YORK

Designed cover image: Getty Images

First published 2026
by Routledge
4 Park Square, Milton Park, Abingdon, Oxon OX14 4RN

and by Routledge
605 Third Avenue, New York, NY 10158

Routledge is an imprint of the Taylor & Francis Group, an informa business

© 2026 Glenn Waller, Kamryn T. Eddy, Charlotte L. Rose, Jennifer
J. Thomas, Hannah M. Turner, and Tracey D. Wade

For Product Safety Concerns and Information please contact our EU
representative GPSR@taylorandfrancis.com. Taylor & Francis Verlag
GmbH, Kaufingerstraße 24, 80331 München, Germany.

British Library Cataloguing-in-Publication Data
A catalogue record for this book is available from the British Library

ISBN: 978-1-032-97657-0 (hbk)
ISBN: 978-1-032-97656-3 (pbk)
ISBN: 978-1-003-59470-3 (ebk)

DOI: 10.4324/9781003594703

Typeset in Times New Roman
by Deanta Global Publishing Services, Chennai, India

Contents

Acknowledgements

Writing this book has been a surprisingly enjoyable task. The process of sharing ideas, wrestling with practicalities, and collaborating on the best way to use our experience has helped us to bring together our recommendations about how to best work with patients who have anorexia nervosa. However, we all know that so much of our experience and inspiration has come from those we have worked with, our families, and our own mentors. Many friendships have developed from our shared time and effort. We are grateful to you all, and we wanted to thank you here. You have contributed to this book in so many ways that we cannot possibly explain them all – hopefully you know what you have brought to this endeavour.

Being CBT people, we thought that it would be best to have a nice, orderly list:

Our students and research team members, who have grown up with this process and who we know will go on to great things:

Heather Duggan and Lily Palmer.

Our clinical and research colleagues on this project:

Gillian Adams, Lauren Breithaupt, Kathryn Brigham, Helen Burton-Murray, Debbie Clay, Jessica Cox, Esther Dechant, Lizi Graves, Laura Holsen, Elizabeth Lawson, Liz May, Louise Melhuish, Madhusmita Misra, Jacqui Pearce, Mia Pellizzer, Jamie-Lee Pennesi, Marcela Radunz, Meghan Slattery, Jade Southron, Madelaine de Valle, and Yuan Zhou.

Those who have delivered the therapy and supported our learning:

Faizer Abdulaziz, Jill Bluff, Ashley Dunford, Louise Dursley, Rachel Ebbens, Cathryn Freid, Molly Gilbert, Irene Gould, Evelyna Kambanis, Rebecca Mueller, Olivia Ovington, Eleanor Ruchpaul, Sara Souissi, Chloe Webster, Samuel Williams, and Geena Yip.

Our own mentors and collaborators over the years:

Sarah Barnett, Anne Becker, Carolyn Becker, Sally Brook, Kelly Brownell, Rachel Bryant-Waugh, Susan Byrne, Sian Coker, Peter Cooper, Rick Cooper,

Zafra Cooper, Helen Cordery, Emma Corstorphine, Rachel Coupe, Mirin Craig, Jaime Delgadillo, Sarah Egan, Jane Evans, Christopher Fairburn, Pat Fallon, Nicholas Farrell, Debra Franko, Anthea Fursland, Phillipa Hay, David Herzog, Hendrik Hinrichsen, Aaron Keshen and the Nova Scotia team, Rachel Lawson, Daniel Le Grange, Philip Levendusky, Caroline Meyer, Victoria Mountford, Sandra Mulkens, Sanni Norweg and all at the STEPs Eating Disorder Service, Vartouhi Ohanian, Kate Osborne, Robert Peveler, Bronny Raykos and all at CCI in Perth, Katie Russell, Roz Shafran, Ulrike Schmidt, Lusia Stopa, Alex Sheffield, Madeleine Tatham, Kate Tchanturia, Stephen Touyz, and Janet Treasure. Special thanks to Myra Cooper, Susan Hart, Caitlin McMaster, and Matthew Pugh for their generosity in letting us use versions of their innovative work.

And our families and loved ones, why have kept us firmly grounded throughout:

GW   – Minnie, who grew up with this book, and never let it get in the way of a good walk.
KTE   – my family, Cathryn, Colby, and Logan; my parents, Gail and David; and my friend, Kelly.
CLR   – Ember, Nicolai, and Cai: for making me laugh, keeping me connected to the real and natural world, and bringing me coffee.
JTT   – Noah, Asher, and Aria.
HMT   – Fraser, for his endless support and encouragement, and for always having time to listen.
TDW   – Stephen, who never hesitates to provide the emotional and practical support that helps me get the job done.

Finally, a couple of names who we could not simply list without recognising their exceptional contribution:

- Jessica Beard, for all her work on education materials, the book's website, and the video demonstrations that you can access there, along with delivering CBT-AN-20.
- Kendra Becker, for all of her work as principal investigator of the Boston-based CBT-AN-20 trial, as well as her delivery of the therapy.

And of course, our patients, who inspire us to do this work every day by their own strength and willingness to trust us with their stories and their care.

If we have missed anyone, please let us know and we will apologise in person and try to make good in a future edition.

Glenn Waller
Kamryn T. Eddy
Charlotte L. Rose
Jennifer J. Thomas
Hannah M. Turner
Tracey D. Wade

Foreword

Welcome to this manual, designed to support clinicians in delivering cognitive-behavioural therapy (CBT) to patients with anorexia nervosa. CBT-AN-20 (20-session therapy, specifically for individuals with anorexia nervosa) has been several years in development. We have used our extensive clinical and research experience, working to ensure that CBT-AN-20 meets the needs of this clinical group. We have also been inspired to develop our approach over that time, as the evidence base has developed (e.g., the emergence of effective single-session interventions; feedback from patients on the need for more comprehensive psychoeducation; developments in approaches to understanding the "anorexic voice"). Our aim has been to bring clinical and research perspectives to bear on the complex issue of effective treatment of anorexia nervosa. Our evidence to date is related to making this therapy work with adults, but we also consider appropriate adaptations for younger people.

The background to the development of CBT-AN-20

In 2017, the National Institute for Health and Care Excellence (NICE) recommended that there should be greater attention paid to developing briefer, effective therapies for eating disorders, to enhance patient care and treatment availability. In 2019, the CBT-T manual (Waller et al., 2019) was published, showing that a brief psychological therapy (the "T" stands for "ten sessions") could be as effective as longer therapy for non-underweight individuals with eating disorders (e.g., Allen et al., 2024; Kambanis, Graver et al., 2025; Keegan & Wade, 2024a; Paphiti et al., 2023; Tatham et al., 2020). Over time, CBT-T has been widely implemented for such patients (e.g., bulimia nervosa; binge-eating disorder, other specified feeding and eating disorders). Its short duration has meant that more patients can be offered effective treatment, completing it in less time. Since its development, we have found that CBT-T can be used more widely than originally envisaged. For example, we have found that it can be used with adolescents (e.g., Hart et al., 2024), including being used when first-line therapies like family-based treatment (FBT; Lock & Le Grange, 2012) are not effective or viable (e.g., parents or the child not wanting or able to engage in family work).

CBT-T was deliberately targeted toward non-underweight patients, because their access to effective treatments was limited and they make up the largest proportion of the population with eating disorders. Anorexia nervosa patients were more likely to be offered treatment because of their medical needs and greater risk. Therefore, CBT-T was designed and targeted to make sure that the maximum number of people got access to the support that they need.

Differences between CBT-AN-20 and CBT-T

But what about those with anorexia nervosa? Now that CBT-T is widely implemented, we felt that it was time to turn our attention to the treatment of anorexia nervosa. We wanted to determine whether similar principles to those underlying CBT-T could be applied to CBT for anorexia nervosa – can we be as effective as 40-session CBT-ED for adults with anorexia nervosa (as currently recommended by NICE, 2017), but using a less resource-demanding version of CBT-ED?

If you are familiar with CBT-T, then you will recognise that there are clear overlaps with CBT-AN-20 (e.g., the phases of therapies, the core CBT skills needed). However, we do not regard this therapy as a simple extension of CBT-T. We do not consider anorexia nervosa as simply "another variant of an eating disorder, which just needs more time" – in short, anorexia nervosa is different enough from other eating disorders that it cannot be fully considered as part of a transdiagnostic syndrome. The dual challenges of low weight and ambivalence require a treatment that is qualitatively different from that of other eating disorders. So, rather than preparing a manual for eating disorders that includes working with underweight patients as a stand-alone chapter, we wanted to be sure that we provided a detailed protocol that was specific to working with underweight patients. Anorexia nervosa has some elements in common with atypical anorexia nervosa and with avoidant/ restrictive food intake disorder (ARFID), even though it also has important differences. Therefore, we also consider approaches to those two disorders in this book.

One last word – why did we call this therapy "CBT-AN-20"? We originally thought that "CBT-20" would be nicely complementary to "CBT-T". However, we realised that there was a danger that clinicians might see this as a 20-session alternative to 10-session CBT for non-underweight patients and just use CBT-20 as a license to extend therapy unnecessarily for such patients. We recognise that there can be a general tendency for clinicians to extend therapy without seeing any further benefit for the client (e.g., Beintner & Jacobi, 2018). With this tendency in mind, we encourage you to approach CBT-AN-20 as a shorter form of CBT-ED for anorexia nervosa (with a stress on some different skills), so that you can assess the outcomes of a more focused approach. In short, we decided that we needed to make the clear case that this therapy is devised specifically for anorexia nervosa – hence, "CBT-AN-20".

About the team

We are an international group of clinicians, researchers, supervisors, and trainers, all with extensive experience of working on solving the problems of understanding and treating eating disorders. We have all learned from patients' feedback over time. More specifically, in preparing this manual, we have been aided by the experiences of small groups of patients across multiple continents who have undertaken CBT-AN-20, and whose participation in qualitative research (Duggan et al., 2025) has helped shape the treatment protocol and resources.

Our work together is driven by the need to get better at working effectively with people who have eating disorders, with all the complexity and challenges that are seen in routine clinical practice. Several of us were involved in the development of CBT-T, which has led naturally to this book. The same approach has been used – collaboration to reach agreement about the best clinical skills that we can use for the treatment of anorexia nervosa. We fully and gratefully acknowledge how much we have learned from those colleagues who have provided informal feedback that has shaped our thinking on the development and implementation of CBT-AN-20, and we have identified them in this book's Acknowledgements.

How to use this manual

While there is a lot of content and material in this CBT-AN-20 manual that will be familiar to clinicians who have delivered CBT-T, there are key differences too. These include issues around motivation, working with the "anorexic voice", weight gain/maintenance skills, the importance of emotions in compulsivity, working with family and loved ones, and more. Critically, you will find clinical materials and psychoeducation in the Appendices of the book, also provided in downloadable form on our website (CBT-AN-20 website (https://sites.google.com/sheffield.ac.uk/cbt-an-20)). There are also links here to the videos that we have provided on that website, demonstrating these CBT-AN-20 skills in action. We suggest that you check on the website for details of videos and psychoeducation resources, as we will add to these as and when we think of ways of enhancing those resources.

Glenn Waller
Kamryn T. Eddy
Charlotte L. Rose
Jennifer J. Thomas
Hannah M. Turner
Tracey D. Wade

Chapter 1

Introduction

Before we detail CBT-AN-20 over subsequent chapters, it is important that the reader is familiar with the key literature on anorexia nervosa, and how it has informed the development of an anorexia nervosa focused CBT approach. This initial chapter will provide a grounding for Chapter 2 onwards.

1.1 Identifying anorexia nervosa

Anorexia nervosa is an eating disorder that is characterised by being underweight, restricted eating due to fears of loss of control/weight gain, and body image disturbance. Key diagnostic features in *DSM-5* (American Psychiatric Association, 2013) and *ICD-11* (World Health Organisation, 2022) include:

- Reduction in food intake, leading to very low body weight (relative to age, sex, and physical health);
- Pursuit of thinness and lower weight (whether stated as intentional or not, and whether or not one sees the pursuit as successful);
- Distortion of body image;
- Intense fear of gaining weight;
- Denial of seriousness of low body weight/lack of recognition of that severity.

Individuals can present with purely restrictive eating patterns (restrictive subtype) or with restriction-driven binge eating and purging behaviours (binge/purge subtype). The intervention is relatively similar, whichever the subtype. It is also similar for cases in which individuals exhibit persistent behaviour that interferes with weight gain but deny frank body image disturbance.

Of course, not all cases neatly fit diagnostic categories. There are several presentations (atypical anorexia nervosa [AAN]; otherwise specified feeding and eating disorder [OSFED]; unspecified feeding or eating disorder [UFED]) where the optimum treatment is likely to be dependent on the nature of the individual's clinical presentation or need (e.g., has an identified case of AAN lost a substantial amount of weight or not?). These cases need careful clinical consideration, as their outcomes might be different. For example, Keegan and Wade (2024a) found the

DOI: 10.4324/9781003594703-1

odds of having a good outcome from CBT-T at one-month follow-up were eight times less likely among patients with AAN than those with other disorders. This is an area where we need further evidence, but the length of CBT-AN-20 could give the clinician and patient long enough to work out what is happening with weight, agree an appropriate weight to work at/weight targets, and consider ways in which the patient can accept this (Keegan & Wade, 2024b). We will return to this clinical issue in Chapter 12, when we consider approaches to such cases.

1.2   Presentation of anorexia nervosa

Anorexia nervosa has a high rate of medical complications and a high risk of premature death (e.g., van Eeden et al., 2021), as detailed in Chapter 5. It has a very substantial impact on the quality of life of those with the eating problem and on their loved ones (see Section 12.3). Table 1.1 details key information that it is important to be aware of when working with anorexia nervosa.

1.3   Existing treatments for anorexia nervosa

Clinical care for anorexia nervosa needs close attention to the patient's medical and psychological needs. Such care can be difficult to implement fully, given that the individual is likely to value their eating disorder, making them less engaged with treatment. This lack of engagement can mean that there is conflict between the individual with the eating disorder, their family, and clinical services. Therefore, it is not surprising that anorexia nervosa attracts considerable attention in clinical and research terms and is typically treated in a multidisciplinary context. We clearly need more effective treatments for anorexia nervosa – particularly among adults. Among younger people, family based treatment (FBT) has the strongest evidence base (National Institute for Health and Care Excellence [NICE], 2017), though CBT for eating disorders is showing utility in supporting some cases where FBT has not been fully effective (e.g., Craig et al., 2019). CBT-AN-20 might be suitable in such cases, assuming appropriate parental involvement and support – we discuss this further in Section 12.3.

Clearly, our treatments need to be acceptable to patients, and to address the concerns about treatment that many patients can experience. Importantly, those therapies need to be efficient as well as effective – to be time-limited, so that scarce treatment resources can be made available to as many people as possible. Current recommendations for psychological therapies for anorexia nervosa can run to over a year of outpatient sessions (e.g., Fairburn, 2008). With limited treatment resources, it is important to determine whether briefer therapies can be as effective as longer interventions (NICE, 2017). In recent years, more focused psychological therapies for non-underweight eating disorders have been shown to be as effective as longer versions of the same therapy (Adams et al., 2021; Waller et al., 2018).

Table 1.1 Anorexia nervosa statistics

Domain	Key information
Prevalence	Anorexia nervosa is not the most common of the eating disorders. Lifetime prevalence estimates vary substantially, depending on methodology and sampling methods (e.g., Qian et al., 2022; van Eeden et al., 2021). The National Institute of Mental Health (NIMH: https://www.nimh.nih.gov/health/statistics/eating-disorders) suggests a lifetime prevalence for adults of 0.6% (female = 0.9%; males = 0.3%), which is substantially below the lifetime prevalence of either binge-eating disorder (2.8%) or bulimia nervosa (1.0%). However, community populations of youth show a 6.2% and 0.3% lifetime prevalence of anorexia nervosa in females and males respectively (Silén et al., 2020). Regardless of the true lifetime prevalence, anorexia nervosa requires a disproportionate amount of clinical effort and resources, due to the severity of the psychological and medical impact.
Comorbidity	Anorexia nervosa is commonly found alongside other psychological disorders. The National Institute for Health Research (NIHR) found rates of 56% comorbidity with other disorders – particularly anxiety (e.g., obsessive-compulsive disorder; social anxiety disorder) and mood disorders. This comorbidity rate is lower than for bulimia nervosa (95%) and binge-eating disorder (79%), though mood and anxiety disorders are also commonly found in those disorders. We note that being underweight is associated with a definite increase in the risk of suicidal behaviour, particularly death by suicide (Geulayov et al., 2019; Keshaviah et al., 2014). We also know that the binge/purge type of anorexia nervosa is associated with a significantly higher level of suicide attempts than restricting anorexia nervosa – 16.7% compared to 7.7% (Mandelli et al., 2019).
Age of onset	While anorexia nervosa is commonly represented as having its onset in early adolescence, it is important to note that the NIHR identified the median age of onset as 18 years (the same as for bulimia nervosa, but lower than for binge-eating disorder). It is estimated that 48.6% of anorexia nervosa onset is in early adulthood, compared to 51.4% onset in either childhood or adolescence (Grilo & Udo, 2021). So we should not get fooled by the "early adolescent onset" stereotype, allowing that many patients will have started their problem much later.
Recovery and response to treatment	Importantly, the longitudinal course of illness in anorexia nervosa can be protracted, with only about 31% of those seeking treatment in the community reaching recovery by 9 years, but this rate more than doubling to 63% at 22 years (Eddy et al., 2017). While this longer-term improvement argues against reducing efforts to help people to recover, it is a slower initial rate than for bulimia nervosa. Anorexia nervosa also has poor response to treatments. There are no drug or other medical interventions that have been proven to be effective for anorexia nervosa, and psychological interventions to date have had limited benefits (e.g., Solmi et al., 2021). While non-underweight eating disorders (e.g., bulimia nervosa; binge-eating disorder) have a higher prevalence, they are also more likely to respond to evidence-based treatments (e.g., Monteleone et al., 2022).

(Continued)

Table 1.1 (Continued)

Domain	Key information
Treatment-seeking	A key issue is whether the patient seeks help, which cannot be assumed to be the norm, given the high level of ambivalence that characterises eating disorders and that can delay or prevent treatment-seeking. NIMH figures suggest that only a third of those with anorexia nervosa in the USA ever seek help for their anorexia nervosa (about 10% lower than for non-underweight eating disorders), though they are more likely to seek help for other emotional disorders. Working with this ambivalence over treatment forms a key therapeutic task.
Predicting who will do well in treatment	The key message here is: don't try to predict. There are no clear predictors before treatment commences of who will do well in treatment, including chronicity of the disorder (Radunz et al., 2020). The firmest evidence points us in the direction of trying therapy to assess early response (Vall & Wade, 2015).

1.4   Why do we need a more focused CBT for anorexia nervosa?

A repeating theme in the field of eating disorder clinical practice and research (and among charities advocating for people with eating disorders) is the importance of accessing effective treatment for anorexia nervosa. First, is therapy available at all, or affordable? Far too often, the answer to these questions is "no". Second, is the therapy that is offered effective or not? Unfortunately, where the person can and does access treatment for their anorexia nervosa, they will often encounter either a therapy that has no clear evidence base (e.g., Tobin et al., 2007, von Ranson et al., 2013) or one that is of limited effectiveness (e.g., Solmi et al., 2021). This limited effectiveness of therapy cannot be accounted for by severity or duration of the disorder (e.g., Radunz et al., 2020). One option is to consider intensive treatments for anorexia nervosa (e.g., inpatient, residential, day patient), but the cost of such an approach is very high, with limited effectiveness (e.g., de Boer et al., 2023). Those factors have led to the recommendation that more intensive treatment should be reserved for focusing on nutritional and medical targets that will help the patient to benefit from outpatient treatment for their eating disorder (NICE, 2017). However, our outpatient treatments can be complex and costly relative to those for other disorders, resulting in the NICE (2017) call for briefer, effective therapies for eating disorders to make them cost-effective too. The result of having long therapies (e.g., 49.5 sessions is the mean number reported by anorexia nervosa patients who have experienced CBT – Cowdrey & Waller, 2015) combined with limited resources is that we have long treatment waiting lists for anorexia nervosa and for other eating disorders.

1.5   Are 20 sessions enough?

As with CBT-T, our goal in devising CBT-AN-20 was not to deliver a more effective therapy, but one that could be as effective as existing CBT for anorexia nervosa while taking far less time and fewer resources. After all, we know that patients with anorexia nervosa can benefit in part from even very short, single-session interventions (Fursland et al., 2018; Schleider et al., 2023), so 20 sessions should give us lots of opportunities to help patients to recover. That way, more people on the waiting list can get the opportunity to benefit from therapy. Such a development means that we can widen the options for adult patients with anorexia nervosa who could benefit from a briefer, 20-session therapy, adding a CBT-based option to the existing range of evidence-based therapies such as Specialist Supportive Clinical Management (SSCM; McIntosh et al., 2023) and the Maudsley Model of Anorexia Nervosa Treatment for Adults (MANTRA; Schmidt, Startup & Treasure, 2018). Our early findings support the benefits of CBT-AN-20 (Duggan et al., under consideration).

Effective psychological interventions for anorexia nervosa clearly need to be part of a wider treatment offering, as no one therapy has proven superior for this eating disorder (NICE, 2017; Solmi et al., 2021). When developing CBT-AN-20, we were also aware of the need to address the physical and medical risks of anorexia nervosa, as well as the biopsychosocial factors that maintain the disorder. Any therapy needs to be responsive to the current severity of the patient's anorexia nervosa. Patients with very low weight have salient medical and nutritional needs that make it highly unlikely that they will be able to benefit from a psychological intervention at that point. Therefore, as with CBT-E (Fairburn, 2008), we recommend CBT-AN-20 for patients with a body mass index (BMI) of 15–19. However, it is important to remember that patients below a BMI of 17 can show limited response, regardless of the therapy used (Wade, Allen et al., 2021), and that limited response might require us to plan care around as much early weight gain as possible (as well as responding to a lack of progress more robustly – see Section 7.7). Other factors need to be considered in determining the suitability of any therapy, of course, such as a comprehensive risk assessment and the level of starvation symptoms (see Chapter 5 for a more detailed consideration of suitability).

Of course, it could be asked whether 20 sessions of therapy can be enough for treatment of anorexia nervosa, if existing CBT for anorexia nervosa is recommended to last 40 sessions and regularly goes above that (Cowdrey & Waller, 2015). Here, we should consider the precedents of FBT, SSCM, and MANTRA, which are all recommended for anorexia nervosa over a similar shorter timeframe and with similar outcomes (NICE, 2017). With any of these interventions, our aim is to teach the patient the benefits of improvement and the skills needed, so that they can continue to improve over time even if they have not achieved full recovery during the therapy. Therefore, we can expect the impact of the intervention to continue after therapy has finished, over a follow-up period (the suggested follow-up period for CBT-AN-20 is six months – twice as long as for CBT-T – to allow time for the gains of therapy to come to fruition). That improvement will include key symptoms (e.g., weight, body image), but we particularly value seeing the long-term development of self-efficacy and enhanced quality of life.

We aim to work to a limit of 20 sessions (plus the one assessment session and three follow-ups), though we recognise the adage "rules break, principles bend". The augmentations that we detail below (particularly single-session interventions) are planned for the client to use between therapy sessions, rather than taking place in a standalone session. Within treatment, we also emphasise the importance of family involvement in supporting recovery. While this will normally involve significant others joining part of some sessions, where family involvement is very intensive, we would suggest including up to four additional family sessions to run alongside individual sessions. These can be offered either in parallel with or as an extension to individual sessions, whichever suits the patient and the clinical setting. Key issues commonly addressed include to:

- Support the family to collaborate with the individual in applying the therapy – reinforcing existing material rather than introducing new material. This could involve explaining to the family what CBT-AN-20 involves and why, helping them to reduce accommodation patterns (such as not keeping the patient's feared foods in the house, ostensibly to avoid the anxiety that the patient experiences, but limiting the possibility of change), and being available to support specific homework tasks.
- Help the family to manage the stress that they experience in coping with the impact of anorexia nervosa on their loved one and themselves.

As significant others tend to routinely join sessions when delivering CBT-AN-20 with adolescents, these additional sessions are rarely required, and the norm would be to include this work within the 20 sessions. We find that these additional sessions are most often used when working with emerging adults (18–25 years). This element of the intervention is addressed further in Chapter 4 (Section 4.16).

In keeping with the FREED programme (First Episode Rapid Early Intervention for Eating Disorders; Mills et al., 2024), we stress the importance of early intervention, wherever possible, to limit the damage across life domains. However, that early access requires a therapy that is effective and that is efficient enough to allow for good patient turnover. Hence, we see CBT-AN-20 as being a potential contributor to the suite of therapies that are offered within FREED (while duration of eating disorder does not determine suitability for CBT-AN-20). CBT-T is already offered to a large proportion of such patients in FREED services and is as effective as longer therapies for those with non-underweight eating disorders (Allen et al., 2024). We hope that CBT-AN-20 will merit similar levels of uptake in early intervention services and beyond.

1.6   Summary

There is a need for a briefer version of CBT for anorexia nervosa, where treatment duration is more in line with that of other evidence-based therapies. This drive reflects developments in the field for non-underweight eating disorders in recent years (e.g., Waller et al., 2019). That need has led to the development of CBT-AN-20 – a 20-session cognitive-behavioural therapy for anorexia nervosa. Early findings (Duggan et al., 2025; Duggan et al., under consideration) have shown that CBT-AN-20 has comparable effectiveness to 40-session CBT-E (Fairburn, 2008), and that it has a good level of acceptability to patients. This manual details how clinicians can implement CBT-AN-20, using examples of patient-therapist interaction.

This manual is supported by links to websites that contain useful tools; psycho-educational materials and clinical tools for patients, clinicians, and carers; video demonstrations of clinical skills; and a series of brief augmentations (single-session interventions) that can be used to facilitate CBT-AN-20. Whenever recommending the use of additional resources as homework, it is important that we become familiar with the resources ourselves to support follow-up discussions in subsequent CBT-AN-20 sessions. For example, a highly perfectionist clinician might struggle to be effective, particularly for a patient who is also highly perfectionist. Therefore, we should become familiar with the resources we recommend to patients, to benefit ourselves, our patients, and our work together.

Chapter 2

Overview of anorexia nervosa

In the previous chapter, we outlined the definition of anorexia nervosa, the existing evidence base for treatments, and the case for a more focused CBT for anorexia nervosa. In this chapter, we detail the functional analytic model that has informed the development of the CBT-AN-20 protocol. We also consider whom this treatment might be appropriate for, taking into consideration factors such as BMI and illness duration, as well as physical and mental health risk. Consideration is also given to when it might be appropriate to use CBT-AN-20 and when this approach might be used following another therapy or type of treatment.

2.1 A functional analytic model of anorexia nervosa

While several cognitive-behavioural models have been proposed for the treatment of anorexia nervosa (Garner & Bemis, 1982; Fairburn et al., 1999; Waller et al., 2007), the model underlying CBT-AN-20 draws largely on a functional analysis paradigm. This model is a generic one, informing our understanding of anorexia nervosa as a disorder rather than of the individual patient. Later (particularly Chapter 5), we will outline how we develop individual CBT case formulations of anorexia nervosa.

A functional analytic model is based on links between antecedent, triggers, behaviour, and consequences, which in turn determine the maintenance and development of the behaviour over time. One of the main tenets of this approach to understanding behaviour is the acknowledgement that behaviour is dynamic – constantly changing because of the interactions between an individual and their environment over time. As outlined in Waller (2017), this functional analytic approach to understanding anorexia nervosa makes several core assumptions:

a. The eating disorder makes sense in its context – the behaviour is primed by its antecedents (often a combination of genetic, biological, temperament, and environmental factors), is triggered by immediate circumstances (precipitating triggers), and is maintained by its consequences (including the emotional, interpersonal, and biological).

DOI: 10.4324/9781003594703-2

b. Genetic, social, behavioural, psychological, emotional, and biological factors can all play a role in initiating and maintaining anorexia nervosa.
c. The model is not tied to any specific theory. Consequently, it is a tenet of functional analytical models of psychological disorders that anybody *could* develop a disorder with the right combination of such factors.

The functional model underlying CBT-AN-20 has two important features. First, there is the recognition of the importance of the coincidental presence of a key set of risk factors and precipitating triggers that lead to restrictive eating. Second, the model stresses the changing role of maintaining consequences across the short and the long term.

2.2   How does anorexia nervosa begin?

The model stresses the coincidental occurrence of a core set of long-term antecedents that will be unique for each individual. Those long-term antecedents can include factors such as genetic/biological predisposition, family functioning, peer bullying and teasing, interpersonal problems, trauma, and sociocultural pressures. An overview of potential long-term antecedents is given in Table 2.1. There is a multiplicity of postulated antecedents (e.g., Barakat et al., 2023), which are relatively non-specific (i.e., can predispose to any psychological disorder), with no risk factors specific to anorexia nervosa yet identified (Solmi et al., 2021).

It is hypothesised that a combination of these factors leads to the development of a sense of low self-efficacy – one of the core features of anorexia nervosa. In the face of developmental challenges encountered when transitioning to adolescence and adulthood, this can be experienced as a fragmentation of one's sense of self. Negative core beliefs about the self, others and the world (e.g., "I'm worthless", "others are untrustworthy", "the world is overwhelming") become increasingly dominant over time, whilst strengths, values, and the potential to cope and thrive in life start to fade. In turn, this developmental pattern manifests in a strong need for control over some aspect of life as a way of coping with negative self-schemas, feeling better about oneself, or maintaining some degree of limited contact with others and the world.

Patients often, but not always, recount a specific trigger for the development of the anorexia nervosa – typically an event that drove the individual to begin restricting their food intake (e.g., sudden weight changes, such as gaining weight when starting at university and drinking/eating in a less healthy manner; losing weight following illness) – which is then reinforced by others' perceived or actual responses to weight or weight changes (e.g., teasing, criticism, bullying, or praise). Life stresses or transitions can also be immediate triggers (e.g., changing schools; exam stress; friendship and other relationship difficulties; breakdown of a romantic relationship; issues navigating gender or sexuality within contexts that might be hostile or unaccepting), particularly where the stressor precipitates a need for certainty and control. Many patients describe dietary intake as the one area where

Table 2.1 Long-term antecedents associated with the development of anorexia nervosa

Risk factor category	Clinical features
Genetic	Family history of anorexia nervosa, obsessive-compulsive disorder, depression, anxiety, neuroticism and metabolic (glycaemic) factors
Parental relationships	Parental focus on weight and dieting
Adversity and trauma	Childhood adversity, significant family disruption, childhood trauma (including neglect and emotional or sexual abuse), stressful life events Bullying – including cyberbullying Interpersonal difficulties
Personality traits	Anxiety sensitivity, harm avoidance, intolerance of uncertainty, perfectionism, obsessive-compulsivity, high self-criticism, shame, neuroticism, inflexible and overly detailed thinking styles, ineffectiveness and low self-efficacy
Comorbid conditions	Obsessive-compulsive disorder Social anxiety disorder Depression Neurodivergence
Social/environmental	Exposure to, and internalisation of, the "thin" ideal Early puberty development Peer teasing about weight Marginalised sexuality or gender Food insecurity

there seems to be a possibility of feeling completely in control, as other areas of life (e.g., social relationships or work performance) remain complex and dependent on the behaviour or judgement of others.

This pattern of development is referred to as the "ego-syntonic" nature of anorexia nervosa – where dietary restriction represents values that are in harmony with valued aspects of one's sense of self (Vitousek et al., 1998). In particular, dietary restriction is highly valued in society and therefore represents a pathway to building self-worth in individuals who value simplicity, control, and predictability. Such restriction conveys the illusory promise that a lower number on the weighing scales will equate to the person being more valued by others and feeling better about themselves.

A second core feature relates to perfectionism and the ability to relentlessly adhere to "the rules". Personality traits (including perfectionism, obsessive-compulsivity, and high self-criticism) can all arise through a combination of genetic predisposition and early experience. However, all of these factors can be central to the individual's ability to push past the body's attempts to communicate its needs (e.g., through hunger), and to adhere to the strict, detailed dietary rules associated with the task of weight loss, thus establishing a reinforcing cycle of restrictive eating and weight management.

2.3   What maintains weight-control behaviours?

The model distinguishes two processes – short- and long-term maintenance. Initially, the *short-term consequences* (e.g., weight loss, positive comments/admiration from others including via social media, an enhanced sense of control and self-worth) serve as strong positive reinforcers for further dietary restriction, as well as other behaviours, such as driven exercise. During these early stages the "buzz" of achievement can feel exhilarating and addictive, negative emotions are numbed, and life is reduced to a focus on one concrete issue rather than the many complex social, emotional, and identity issues that underlie the illness.

However, dietary restriction relatively quickly (particularly in adolescents) results in *long-term consequences*, which serve as perpetuating factors unless they are disrupted. These are the neurobiological changes associated with dietary restriction and starvation, including increased denial, rigidity, anxiety, depression, and obsessionality. These consequences all serve to keep the individual trapped in a progressively harmful relationship with the illness, which in turn leaves them less and less able to resolve the underlying social and emotional issues that led to the disorder in the first place.

These increasingly biologically embedded results of restriction result in changes to family dynamics, withdrawal from friendships, and disconnection from wider and previously valued domains of life such as work, study, and hobbies. These changes can serve to negatively reinforce the illness (i.e., through avoidance of associated anxiety). Additionally, the disconnection from support and from personal strengths and values (e.g., the ability to be self-compassionate) and physical deterioration (e.g., weakness, tiredness) reduce the person's capacity to overcome the illness. Cognitive and emotional changes (e.g., anxiety about being made to eat by others; fear of losing control due to bingeing) are natural consequences of the effects of starvation. Over time, further loss of support (e.g., the burden of illness on others, loss of interpersonal relationships, isolation) leaves the individual increasingly fearful of losing control; their identity becomes increasingly synonymous with anorexia nervosa as they sink deeper into the disorder.

It is also important to note that we often see a common desire to get back to that positive experience (i.e., the initial "buzz"). We need to stress to the patient that while this wish to go back is understandable, attempting to return to the early stage of the eating disorder is highly unlikely to be a realistic or sustainable solution (even if it were achievable), as losing weight last time did not tackle the real problems. It didn't leave the patient feeling better about themselves or more able to manage the challenges of life. Like chasing the initial high of an opioid addiction, no amount of compliance with the increasingly perfectionistic and critical demands of anorexia nervosa will resolve the underlying issues. Figure 2.1 shows

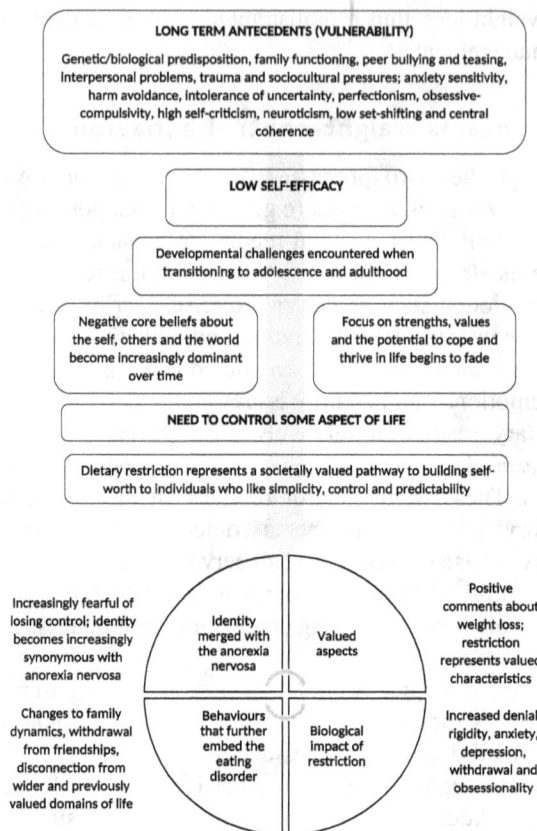

LONG TERM ANTECEDENTS (VULNERABILITY)

Genetic/biological predisposition, family functioning, peer bullying and teasing, interpersonal problems, trauma and sociocultural pressures; anxiety sensitivity, harm avoidance, intolerance of uncertainty, perfectionism, obsessive-compulsivity, high self-criticism, neuroticism, low set-shifting and central coherence

LOW SELF-EFFICACY

Developmental challenges encountered when transitioning to adolescence and adulthood

Negative core beliefs about the self, others and the world become increasingly dominant over time

Focus on strengths, values and the potential to cope and thrive in life begins to fade

NEED TO CONTROL SOME ASPECT OF LIFE

Dietary restriction represents a societally valued pathway to building self-worth to individuals who like simplicity, control and predictability

Increasingly fearful of losing control; identity becomes increasingly synonymous with anorexia nervosa

Identity merged with the anorexia nervosa

Valued aspects

Positive comments about weight loss; restriction represents valued characteristics

Changes to family dynamics, withdrawal from friendships, disconnection from wider and previously valued domains of life

Behaviours that further embed the eating disorder

Biological impact of restriction

Increased denial, rigidity, anxiety, depression, withdrawal and obsessionality

Figure 2.1 The functional analytic model of anorexia nervosa underpinning CBT-AN-20.

a formulation of this functional model of anorexia nervosa as a disorder, which can be personalised in the form of an individual "5Ps" formulation (see Chapter 5).

When understanding the individual case, we use an adapted 5Ps formulation as it allows for understanding of individual experiences, which we can discuss and agree with the patient and use to target their individual treatment needs. When personalising the individual formulation in this way, we find that it can also be extremely valuable to take a "helicopter view" when reviewing it, as this enables us to come together with the patient and say: "We get it, this makes sense". We can understand why the illness developed, and how that has led to the core functions that the anorexia nervosa is attempting to fulfil in the here and now. This formulation also allows for the individual's strengths – both outer and inner resources, such as an ability to problem-solve, honesty, a hard-working nature, compassion, courage, creativity, or a sense of fun – to be voiced, as these often get lost over time but are important to harness during recovery. Integrating a "strengths" focus to therapy helps construct or access a narrative about the patient in which they are competent, safe, and worthy without the anorexia nervosa. Expressing interest in specific personal strengths can positively reinforce and help to build upon self-efficacy, supporting the transfer of valuable prior learning from different areas of life (i.e., that challenges can be overcome with perseverance; that uncomfortable feelings pass without causing harm) to the task of recovery.

2.4 Who might be appropriate for treatment with CBT-AN-20?

It is important to consider which patients might be most appropriate for CBT-AN-20. We *generally* recommend considering this treatment for patients with a diagnosis of anorexia nervosa who have a BMI between 15 and 19, and who are experiencing the physical and psychological effects of starvation (see Chapter 12 for adaptations for those who are fully or partially weight restored). People vary substantially in their natural, healthy BMI range (or weight centile for height adjusted for age among younger cases), and BMI alone is a poor determinant of healthy physical status. The individual's healthy BMI range (often referred to as the "set point") typically falls somewhere within a range of 18.5–25. However, an individual's set point is likely to be influenced by genetics, ethnicity, sex, life stage, athletic status, and so on. Consequently, there is no "ideal" target weight that we can promise the patient who is eager to know it. One person with a BMI of 19 might be at a weight that works well for them, while another person might struggle emotionally, cognitively, socially, and physically at that same BMI. That latter person needs to be considered as functionally underweight (having a naturally higher set point than the first person) and would benefit from a therapy involving weight regain.

So, while BMI is a start point to guide decisions, the question for us as clinicians should be whether the patient is *functionally underweight*. The decision about which therapy to use should be determined by consideration of both objective and functional underweight status. CBT-AN-20 has been tested with individuals with a BMI of 15 or above, so any efforts to use it at a lower weight than that should be based on clinical presentation and discussion with the patient, and through careful consideration with the multidisciplinary team. Working with a patient at a lower weight in this way should be monitored closely, to determine patient safety as well as effectiveness. In Chapter 12, we will consider indicators of suitability in related problems, such as atypical anorexia nervosa and avoidant restrictive food intake disorder (ARFID).

CBT-AN-20 fits well with early intervention models (Brown et al., 2018; McClelland et al., 2018) as it emphasises the importance of early change as well as working with family members and supporters. However, it is important to note that whilst CBT-AN-20 is suitable for those in the early stages of their eating disorder, we do not consider duration of illness as an exclusion factor. This is particularly important to highlight given that illness duration is not a robust predictor of treatment outcome (e.g., Radunz et al., 2020), even in relatively brief CBT for eating disorders (Rose & Waller, 2017; Rose et al., 2021). We would instead advocate a "let's try it and see" approach.

A range of physical and psychiatric risks should also be reviewed when considering the suitability of CBT-AN-20. As a rule, patients must be medically stable with no active suicidal ideation. Prior or current active suicidal ideation or behaviours might indicate that the patient would not be able to safely tolerate the change required in CBT-AN-20, or early discharge resulting from this. Therefore, we would exercise caution in considering CBT-AN-20 for this cohort of patients, who might need a longer, differently focused approach. We do not exclude patients based on current or past self-harm, though such cases should be managed with a safety plan and risks monitored closely. This pattern of inclusion is discussed further in Section 3.7. Similarly, for those presenting with very rapid weight loss and associated medical risks, we suggest collaborative care planning for a period of stabilisation (i.e., making sufficient dietary change to prevent further weight loss and reduce risks), which might need to be supported by more intensive treatments, such as partial or in-patient treatment in the first instance, with CBT-AN-20 being re-considered at a later stage.

It is also important to consider social and safeguarding risks, given that factors such as homelessness or significant safeguarding issues (e.g., domestic violence) must typically take priority, and can negatively impact the patient's ability to actively engage in therapy until resolved. In such cases it can be more helpful to arrange appropriate support and agree that the patient will return to treatment after broader life issues have been addressed and recovery from anorexia nervosa becomes the priority.

2.5   Response to previous treatments

CBT-AN-20 can provide a useful next step following family-based treatments for adolescents with anorexia nervosa (FBT, Lock & Le Grange, 2012; FT-AN, Eisler et al., 2007, 2016). It can also be suitable for adolescents who might benefit from a more autonomous approach to recovery-oriented eating, those who report persistent rule-bound eating, or those with related body image–focused distress while remaining functionally underweight. We would also consider CBT-AN-20 where family-based treatments have been successful in supporting weight regain but severe functional impairment continues to exist, including overdependence on family to maintain nutritional intake and an ongoing need to build self-worth, life skills, and independence.

This treatment can also be appropriate for those who have had previous experiences of other therapies or previous courses of CBT. In such instances it is important to understand these previous experiences in terms of what was helpful and less helpful, and to consider similarities and differences. From the outset it is important to discuss the non-negotiables of CBT-AN-20 (i.e., weekly open weighing; self-monitoring; the requirement to increase dietary intake and restore weight) and how these compare to the patient's expectations, based on their previous therapy experiences. At the same time, it is important that the clinician should be honest, stating that there is no route to recovery from anorexia nervosa that does not involve physical recovery (including weight restoration), and that the sooner we make a start on these critical changes, the sooner we can help with the issues that are driving the anorexia nervosa. The aim is to allow the individual the best opportunity to actively engage in and benefit from this treatment.

In some instances, where the patient might not be sure if CBT-AN-20 is suitable, we encourage them to give it a try. We would also acknowledge that if during treatment they decide that now is not the right time to let go of their anorexia nervosa, we will respect that decision (whilst acknowledging that there may never be a perfect time). Depending on their needs, the result of not engaging in CBT-AN-20 might be that we encourage the patient to come back to treatment at a time that feels right for them (see Section 7.7). Alternatively, depending on need, we might recommend a more intensive treatment approach (e.g., day- or in-patient care). However, we would also stress that a shift to more intensive care does not mean that the patient could not re-start CBT-AN-20 after leaving that setting, as long as appropriate goals could be agreed at that point. Such issues and how the treatment can be flexibly adjusted to meet individual need are discussed further in subsequent chapters (particularly Chapter 12).

It is important to be aware that the relationship an individual has with their eating disorder changes over time and, as such, so do motivation and determination to recover. We aim to strike a balance between encouraging patients to make the most of this opportunity to recover and shortening the time that anorexia nervosa has an impact on their lives, while also encouraging them to return to CBT-AN-20 therapy if they need to do so at a later, better point.

2.6   Summary

This chapter has presented the functional analytic model that has informed the development of the CBT-AN-20 protocol. We have considered whom this treatment might be appropriate for, taking into consideration factors such as BMI and illness duration, as well as physical and mental health risk. Consideration was also given to when it might be appropriate to use CBT-AN-20 following another therapy or type of treatment. Now it is time to outline the therapy itself. The following chapters outline key meta-competences (Chapter 3) and competences (Chapter 4) that are crucial to the delivery of CBT-AN-20. Following that, we will outline the process of assessing and formulating the case (Chapter 5), followed by an outline of the therapy (Chapter 6) and a detailed account of the different phases of the intervention (Chapters 7–11).

Chapter 3

Meta-competences in CBT-AN-20

In Chapter 4, we will outline the CBT techniques needed to deliver CBT-AN-20 (e.g., how to use behavioural experiments) – the "competences" of the therapy. However, before we outline those techniques, in this chapter it will be important to consider the skills that are needed to allow us to be strategic and appropriately flexible when we are implementing the techniques of therapy. Such skills are called "meta-competences" and are applicable across different disorder-specific therapies (e.g., Roth & Pilling, 2007). Meta-competences allow us to personalise treatment while maintaining our focus on the core tasks and goals of the therapy. Such meta-competences can be generic across therapies (e.g., maintaining an effective working alliance) or CBT-specific (e.g., maintaining the clinician's focus on behavioural change).

In this chapter, we discuss evidence-based meta-competences that produce significantly better outcomes for patients (Wade & Waller, 2025a), enhancing the effective protocols. Meta-competences assist clinicians in adapting manualised CBT to the needs of each individual patient – knowing why and when specific skills are necessary to apply interventions in ways that address individual patient needs and circumstances (Campbell-Lee et al., 2024). In other words, meta-competences help us to be flexible in how we deliver therapy. We begin by considering why such flexibility is particularly necessary when working with patients with anorexia nervosa, before detailing the meta-competences that clinicians need to bear in mind when delivering CBT-AN-20.

3.1 Why do we need flexible approaches to therapy for anorexia nervosa?

In the first two chapters, we emphasised the difficulties of conducting therapy with patients with anorexia nervosa, in part due to the impact of starvation on cognitive functioning, and in part due to the highly ego-syntonic nature of the disorder (Vitousek et al., 1998). To the patient, the anorexia nervosa represents values that are consistent with their own and with those of society. Pursuing a lower weight is highly valued by the patient – a value that is reflected across many sectors of society. Working towards such weight goals is seen as representing competence,

DOI: 10.4324/9781003594703-3

health, self-control, and moral superiority. To individuals who value simplicity, control, and predictability, pursuing a lower weight can represent a pathway to building self-worth and self-efficacy.

Given this context, we need to maximise the effectiveness of the therapy skills that we outline in Chapter 4 and throughout the protocol. Developing our use of meta-competences allows us to get the most out of therapy for anorexia nervosa and other disorders. Despite the critical importance of meta-competences, we have found that many clinicians are unaware of them and of the evidence to support their use. *Hence, we encourage all readers, regardless of clinical experience, to prioritise the reading of this chapter before progressing to the disorder-specific competences in the following chapters.* It is important to remember that these generic meta-competences apply broadly across therapies and disorders, though we focus here on how they apply specifically to CBT and anorexia nervosa. Clinicians delivering CBT-AN-20 can play a vital role in advocating for a consistent and skilful approach to the implementation of these meta-competences across the multidisciplinary team.

At the heart of meta-competences is a focus on flexing the protocol to the patient (rather than vice versa), without losing track of where you need to get to. Where appropriate, CBT-AN-20 should be adapted to individuals and their different beliefs, experiences, and circumstances, across race, health conditions, disability, gender, religion, sexuality, age, duration of disorder, trauma experiences, and neurodivergence. Similarly, it can be adapted for those unexpected life events and crises that inevitably arise during therapy. The clinician can support the patient to manage these issues without losing sight of the shared goals, tasks, and timeframe.

The point here is that plans (i.e., a session-by-session manual or within-session agenda) are important, telling us how we might reach the goal if all remains predictable. However, when circumstances change, rigid adherence to a plan is not as adaptive or helpful as focusing on the goal. Our patients typically struggle with being flexible, so the clinician who displays thoughtful flexibility in therapy represents a valuable and powerful role model. As Jasper Fforde puts it in his book *Early Riser* (2018), when talking about the way that winter conditions can throw plans off track:

"Plans are all well and good in the Summer, but in the Winter it's wiser simply to have an objective".
"I thought we were meant to have a plan and stick to it?"
"Events move fast and you need on-the-hoof flexibility to ensure the plan doesn't get in the way of a good goal".

We discuss ten meta-competences in this chapter, previously outlined in Wade and Waller (2025a) and summarised in Table 3.1. We will focus on the clinical value of applying them to CBT for anorexia nervosa. Each is supported by evidence for

Table 3.1 CBT-AN-20 meta-competences at a glance

#	Meta-competence	What does it look like in clinical practice?
1	Firm empathy	The clinician does not wait until therapeutic alliance is established before commencing therapy – they immediately start introducing CBT techniques to the patient in conjunction with a clear rationale and evidence, and an empathic understanding of the challenges inherent in change.
2	Don't overestimate the patient's fragility	The clinician understands that they tend to overestimate the fragility of a patient, and that this clinician anxiety means that they are less likely to push for behavioural change. The clinician sits with their anxiety so they can help the patient *do* the CBT.
3	Prioritise early change in therapy	The clinician is highly motivated to work on early weight regain in therapy (first six sessions), as they know it is one of the best predictors of therapy outcome.
4	Measure symptoms at each session and share outcomes with the patient	The clinician uses measures of eating attitudes and behaviours and weight in each session to identify early change, sharing this with the patient, because it reduces therapy drop-out and improves treatment outcomes.
5	Utilise weekly sessions initially to maximise change	The clinician advocates for weekly sessions initially, sharing evidence with the patient that more frequent therapy is associated linearly with steeper recovery curves compared to therapy conducted every two or three weeks, or the deterioration expected with monthly appointments.
6	Do not assume that more complex therapy is required where there is comorbidity	The clinician "holds their nerve" in the face of comorbidity and starts therapy by focusing on one disorder, observing benefit in comorbid conditions. Where there is evidence of lack of early change, the clinician adapts the intervention or approach in response to the client's individual obstacles to change or develops an alternative primary target from the comorbid conditions.
7	Competence in adapting the protocol to the patient is better than rigid adherence	The clinician has a deep understanding of the therapeutic protocol and can adapt this to the patient's characteristics, avoiding rote application of the manualised therapy.
8	Respond to motivational stages of the patient	The clinician uses motivational enhancement techniques, weaving in frequent opportunities in each session for the patient to argue for change in order to promote behaviour change.
9	Collaborate with the patient to effectively set goals between each session	The clinician is proficient in effective goal-setting – considering obstacles that prevent the patient from achieving valued goals.
10	Prioritise both training and supervision/ consultation	The clinician knows that just reading the manual won't change what they do in therapy. Both training and supervision/consultation are required to change clinician behaviour in the therapy room. Supervision may also improve patient outcomes.

improving outcomes for our patients and helps us ensure that the disorder-specific protocol doesn't get in the way of a good goal (i.e., a meaningful, recovery-oriented goal that is shared between the patient and the clinician). It will be clear that these meta-competences overlap in how we apply them, but it is important that we understand the core of each of them.

3.2 Meta-competence 1: Firm empathy

> **Both adherence to CBT techniques and maintaining the therapeutic bond are required to produce a better outcome in therapy.**

Firm empathy (Wilson et al., 1997) is not a new concept, but one that is often poorly practised in the therapy room. It broadly refers to a judicious balance between adherence to disorder-specific CBT techniques and maintaining the therapeutic bond. When working in this way, the clinician will use the effective elements of CBT from the first session onwards, rather than waiting for several sessions until they feel that the patient likes and/or trusts them. We find the term "working alliance" (Bordin, 1979) to be more useful than "therapeutic alliance" or "therapeutic relationship", as it stresses both change and engagement. Bordin describes the working alliance as consisting of three components: (1) agreement on goals; (2) assignment of tasks; *and* (3) the development of the attachment bond. All three components are essential for change, emphasising the point that simply having a good relationship between clinician and patient is not adequate to help the patient recover (though it can feel appealing to both clinician and patient to focus on that attachment bond).

In CBT for eating disorders, the evidence is clear that bond development alone is insufficient for change. In fact, the data demonstrate that early improvement of patient eating disorder symptoms leads to an improvement of working alliance, and in turn, a better outcome of therapy for the patient (Graves et al., 2017). The finding that these reciprocal effects exist between early symptom improvement and therapeutic alliance holds true across depression, anxiety, and post-traumatic stress disorder, as well as eating disorders (Flückiger et al., 2020).

In other words, the patient and clinician might like each other, but if that is not in the context of shared focus on the tasks and goals of CBT, then that means that the patient is unlikely to change and benefit from therapy in the short or the long term. The longer you wait to start on change, the less likely change is to happen. *The clinician does not need to fear that an immediate focus on using CBT techniques will damage the working alliance – the opposite is true.*

Regardless of this robust evidence, many eating disorder clinicians fear damaging the alliance by immediate introduction of collaborative weighing and of the increased nutritional intake that is needed to promote weight gain in patients with anorexia nervosa. Careful attention to the early working alliance is required in this patient group, alongside introducing techniques that provide an opportunity for change. We find this combination works best when there are no surprises. Before therapy commences, the patient is presented with a clear description of the therapy and an explanation of therapy non-negotiables, which are accompanied by a clear rationale and engaging summaries of the evidence showing that these non-negotiables promote better outcomes for the patient. Geller and Srikameswaran (2006) advocate for non-negotiables to (1) be parsimonious (i.e., what is the least number required?); (2) recognise and validate patients' experiences (which is generally that all options on the table seem unattractive to them, but that those options are the only way to progress); and (3) provide options, even where this represents a very limited choice (e.g., starting the therapy immediately with weekly sessions, versus delaying the start of therapy until the patient is able to work weekly sessions into their schedule). Evidence suggests that allowing patients to choose preferred treatment modalities significantly improves outcomes for depression and decreases therapy dropout (Johnson et al., 2025). Incorporating meaningful choice of therapeutic elements for people with anorexia nervosa, however, is more challenging within the framework of non-negotiables. It requires a profound understanding of the therapy to enable choices that are consistent with the spirit of the protocol, and that maintain the meaningful shared treatment goals.

In being firm, the clinician needs to be authoritative and not authoritarian. While we accept that clinicians do not know everything, and that we certainly don't know exactly what will happen for our patients during therapy, we can make guesses informed by science and by our experience. We don't make specific promises about outcomes (e.g., never promise a very specific weight gain target, though a range could be useful), but use Socratic skills to work with the patient to solve problems and negotiate a strategy for figuring out what works for them and what does not.

3.3   Meta-competence 2: Don't overestimate the patient's fragility

> **Build self-efficacy in your patient: don't let your own anxiety stop you from giving the patient a chance to prove their ability to change.**

Working with patients with anorexia nervosa is necessarily associated with some anxiety on the part of the clinician, given the potentially serious consequences of the disorder. Effective therapy requires the clinician to continuously keep in check their belief that the patient is so fragile that any adverse events (e.g., criticism, rejection, or failure – or just being encouraged to change) will lead to catastrophic consequences. Meehl (1973) called this the *spun-glass theory of the mind*, based on the way that clinicians often fail to push their patients to change, for fear of damaging them (as if they were a fragile spun-glass Christmas tree ornament). In contrast, our mantra to the patient should echo Christopher Robin's message to Winnie the Pooh:

> **"You are braver than you believe,**
> **Stronger than you seem,**
> **And smarter than you think".**

Take care throughout each session to reflect to the patient the evidence showing their ability to change and rise to challenges. This can include their choosing to try treatment at this time; any changes they have made in therapy, particularly those made when the patient doubted their ability to make them; and any previous examples across all domains of the patient's life that might have occurred before therapy (e.g., "At the time you were trying for it, did you think that you could get into the college that you ended up going to?"). Similar to the way we look at protective factors in the patient's individual formulation (section 4.4), consider the patient's values, what they already do well outside of the eating disorder, the skills they draw on to achieve those things, and how that skill base can be used to reclaim their life from the anorexia nervosa.

Clinician anxiety about having an adverse impact on the patient or a negative impact on working alliance renders us significantly less likely to use exposure in therapy (Langthorne et al., 2023). However, in anorexia nervosa, as with many other disorders, it is exposure that will powerfully reduce patient anxiety over time and produce examples of behavioural change that can be stressed across therapy sessions to reinforce patient self-efficacy, leading to more change. At the top of the list of avoided exposure tasks in CBT for eating disorders is anything related to weight. This, of course, is problematic when doing CBT with a patient with anorexia nervosa. Clinicians not uncommonly justify avoidance of weight-related discussions by recognising that the cause of an eating disorder is unrelated to food. This truism and its dialectical relationship with increased nutritional intake being the pathway to recovery is captured humorously but pointedly in the book *Eight Keys to Recovery from an Eating Disorder* (2011) by Carolyn Costin and Gwen Schubert Grabb – two women who have recovered from anorexia nervosa. One chapter is titled "It's Not About the Food", dealing with the causes of the eating disorder. It is followed by a chapter entitled "It *Is* About the Food", which focuses on the need to change one's relationship to food to recover.

Given the widespread anxiety of many clinicians about using exposure in the early phase of treatment, *it is essential that clinicians use supervision or consultation to ensure their personal characteristics or prior (or lack of) experience does not interfere with the delivery of evidence-based therapy, for fear of "breaking" a patient whom the clinician perceives as fragile.* Use of supervision/consultation to manage clinician anxiety ensures that we do not deprive the patient of the chance to surprise themselves and us with their ability to change.

Weight recovery is an element of all evidence-based therapies for anorexia nervosa, regardless of the therapeutic orientation. However, it is crucial to recognise with the patient that weight gain is a necessary but not sufficient aspect of recovery from anorexia nervosa. Discuss with the patient the rationale for an early focus on improving nutritional health, in terms of (a) improving the neuroplasticity of the brain to form new connections in response to practising new behaviours and embedding them as habitual (see Appendix A.1); (b) improving the environment to enable epigenetic action that can turn down or off unhelpful genetic vulnerabilities that may sustain an eating disorder; (c) removal of control over food as a coping strategy, giving the patient active opportunities to learn and practice alternative and more self-nurturing approaches to coping; and (d) the delay that restriction places on addressing other (potentially more appealing) goals, such as working on improved body image, which is dependent on getting to a healthier weight. If the patient has experienced prior ineffective treatments, reflect on why previous therapies have not worked for them. Was there not enough emphasis on weight gain, or was it too exclusively about weight gain without attention to changing the behaviours and challenging beliefs involved in weight regain? Was the bigger contextual picture not attended to, due to a focus on control of food and weight? The patient needs to know that successful CBT will be an arena in which both the patient and clinician will have to spin more than one plate at a time. Successful CBT involves balancing change related to eating and weight gain with challenging behaviours and expressions of traits across the domains of life that could be currently supporting beliefs generated by the anorexic voice (see Section 4.9).

3.4   Meta-competence 3: Prioritise early change in therapy

> The clinician and patient can be highly motivated to focus on early change in therapy (first 8–12 sessions) if they recognise the evidence showing this is the strongest predictor of good therapy outcomes in eating disorders.

While this meta-competence clearly overlaps with the two described above, it is worth stating separately, given the evidence demonstrating the ethical imperative to provide active therapeutic components to patients from the first session of therapy. Early change in therapy for eating disorders, including anorexia nervosa, is the strongest predictor of a significantly better outcome for the patient, and is also the time when most of the overall change of therapy occurs. The evidence for this benefit of early change is very clear across eating disorders and other mental health conditions (see Beard & Delgadillo, 2019; Klein et al., 2024; Rose & Waller, 2017; Saxon et al., 2017; Vall & Wade, 2015; Wade, Allen et al., 2021).

To work collaboratively to achieve early change, we should explain its importance to the patient. Given the typical reluctance of patients to make early changes, the clinician also needs to engage the patient in psychoeducation about the nature of anxiety. In short, change in anorexia-related behaviours cannot be made without experiencing anxiety. Anxiety is a normal part of the process and will abate over time (see Chapter 4).

This early change in anorexia nervosa needs to include a start to the weight regain journey. It is important to discuss with the patient what might be expected as part of this process. Unless the patient has a much higher weight history (Meule et al., 2022), weight regain takes much longer than the patient will predict. The process is necessarily gradual, as restoration of major organs needs to occur and metabolic rate increases, and incidental exercise is also likely to increase as energy levels increase and social isolation decreases.

The exact number of sessions that comprise the window for early change is not set in stone, but the absence of any weight regain over the first six sessions is associated with significantly less likelihood of remission of the anorexia nervosa at the end of treatment. *To achieve such remission, it is important to push for change in eating and weight gain from the outset of therapy, rather than delaying.*

We find that clinicians can get caught up in the patient's anxious predictions about uncontrollable weight regain – particularly those new to working with people with eating disorders. We encourage the clinician to be open with the patient – making it clear that we cannot know the outcome of getting any specific patient to change their eating in particular ways, but typically the process is slow and controllable. While the ultimate target/healthy weight will be something that we cannot pre-determine, the patient should be able to get there in a controllable way once they have realised that increasing their intake does not lead to uncontrollable weight gain (indeed, such weight gain can eventually feel like a frustratingly hard slog for the patient who once feared it was all going to happen immediately).

3.5   Meta-competence 4: Measure symptoms at each session and share the information with the patient

> **Assessing eating and weight at each session and sharing this collaboratively and motivationally with the patient improves treatment outcomes.**

Measuring and sharing progress on a session-by-session basis is required to help us to *get better* at delivering effective therapy in the present and into the future. While knowing whether the patient has done well by the end of therapy is helpful in informing an evaluation of our effectiveness as clinicians, by this point it is too late to make use of that evaluation in the service of the patient.

We use brief measurement tools immediately before each session to identify whether the problematic symptoms that bought the patient to therapy are indeed changing. We share these results with the patient routinely in session, preferably in a graphical format, capturing change over therapy, communicating the message about progress, discussing ways in which the patient has made the change happen, and using that learning to explore how the patient and clinician can do more to enhance progress going forward.

Evidence is clear that measuring sessional symptom change in psychological therapies and sharing it with the patient is associated with (1) reduction in therapy drop-out; (2) improved treatment outcomes; (3) reducing the length of therapy; and (4) making less effective clinicians more effective (de Jong et al., 2021; Delgadillo et al., 2018; Delgadillo, Deisenhofer, et al., 2022; Janse et al., 2020). In addition to the weight/BMI chart shared with the patient in each session, we use the ED-15 as our session-by-session measure, addressing eating, weight, and shape concerns, along with disordered eating behaviours, over the past seven days. The ED-15 is freely available and can be found here: https://cbt-t.sites.sheffield.ac.uk/resources. Use of any more than one eating disorder measure weekly is not necessary and could become overwhelming for the patient. In short, *the way that the assessment of eating and weight is shared requires consideration, to ensure that it enhances collaboration between the patient and clinician and strengthens patient motivation.*

Collaborative sharing of progress data requires the clinician to help the patient link changes in eating and weight to behavioural and biological changes (e.g., fewer episodes of compulsive or impulsive behaviours; improved ability to be present in the moment with others rather than preoccupied by thoughts of food; improved mood and/or concentration; greater evidence of cognitive flexibility or central coherence; an enhanced sense of self when not being so controlled by the eating disorder; reduced binge eating). Focus on these unfolding long-term benefits will help the patient remain on-target with the immediate changes they are working on.

Motivational sharing involves checking the patients' progress against a bench-mark within the provision of clinical support (such as motivational enhancement, a process associated with significantly better outcomes in many disorders – de Jong et al., 2021). We highlight positive change (no matter how small), reflect on how the patient has made this happen, and think together about what this tells them about their strengths and abilities. When discussing lack of sufficient early change, explore what therapy-interfering behaviours are in place that are preventing change, the fears these behaviours reflect, and how those fears can be tested. If a therapeutic task cannot be done straight away, the clinician can acknowledge the distress but emphasise that the task will be returned to soon, to maintain momentum in therapy.

Supervision/consultation can be made good use of by reviewing progress monitoring, which in turn helps to keep therapy on track. We provide on the CBT-AN-20 website (https://sites.google.com/sheffield.ac.uk/cbt-an-20) a client tracker in Excel that summarises each patient's progress on one sheet, which can be brought to supervision or consultation each week (see list of appendices and resources).

3.6   Meta-competence 5: Deliver weekly sessions initially to maximise change

> Anything less than weekly sessions early in therapy results in suboptimal outcomes for the patient and eliminates the potential for early change.

We recommend that initial weekly sessions should be presented as a therapy non-negotiable, certainly over the first part of therapy, when change is so important for the patient to learn and develop self-efficacy. The evidence for this is compelling – weekly therapy is associated with steeper recovery curves, compared to therapy conducted with larger inter-session gaps (Erekson et al., 2015). Figure 3.1 is a stylised illustration of the results (reductions in distress) from Erekson and colleagues' analysis of the change trajectories over six sessions, based on 21,488 university counselling centre patients (54.9% female, mean age of 22.5 years).

You will notice that any session frequency that is less than weekly does not result in as much improvement as weekly sessions. Indeed, sessions once a month will see a gradual *deterioration* in the person's functioning, and sessions every three weeks produce very little improvement. A pre-therapy discussion about the rationale for weekly sessions may be needed, in terms of more rapid and enhanced improvement and cost-benefit. *If the patient is reluctant to commit to weekly sessions initially, they could be asked to choose between delaying therapy until they can commit to weekly sessions so they can get the most benefit out of therapy, or to prioritise weekly therapy to give it the best chance of success.*

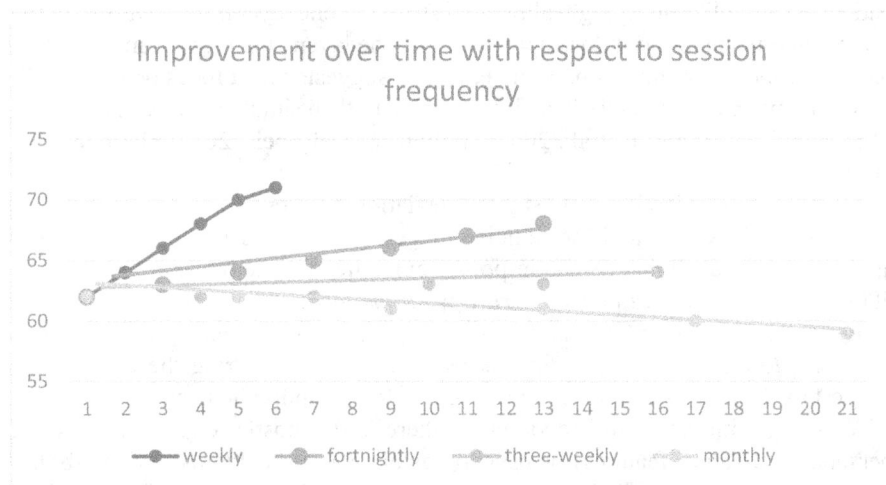

Figure 3.1 Improvement over time with respect to session frequency.

Ideally, we plan to start therapy when both the clinician and the patient anticipate being able to commit to weekly sessions without interruption within at least
the first 6 weeks. As therapy progresses, the occasional fortnightly session may
be necessary due to patient or staff absence. In the last part of therapy, spacing
sessions out might be indicated to enable sufficient weight gain and to assess the
durability and maintenance of change.

3.7   Meta-competence 6: Do not assume that more complex therapy is required where there is comorbidity

> **Start the therapy as per protocol even where there is comorbidity – if there is lack of early change, use evidence to make collaborative decisions about therapy augmentation or change.**

Meehl (1954) referred to "broken leg exceptions", where a relatively prominent
but evidentially irrelevant aspect of the patient's presentation is used by the clinician to reach the inaccurate conclusion that the evidence-based approach should be
dropped and that an alternative approach, not associated with evidence, should be
employed.

This is a common approach when comorbidity (one such "broken leg") is present in eating disorders, despite strong evidence to the contrary. A strong body of
evidence shows that the "one target at a time" approach benefits comorbid conditions and improves general quality of life (Cuijpers et al., 2023; Kindred et al.,
2022; Linardon & Brennan, 2017; Liu et al., 2023). This can be described to the
patient as being like stripping wallpaper – stripping one layer might remove all the
layers underneath, but if it does not remove all the layers, then work can take place
on the second layer and so on. Some evidence suggests that a focus on one condition at a time may be of *more* benefit to the patient than simultaneous consideration
of all conditions (Craske et al., 2007; Gibbons & DeRubeis, 2008; Shafran et al.,
2018).

Given the limited evidence to support deviation from protocol where comorbidity exists, and the potential for clinician judgement being used to choose "a more
appropriate therapy" that results in poorer outcomes for the patient (Grove et al.,
2000; Meehl, 1954), *we advise starting with protocol. Where obstacles to early
progress become apparent, introduce appropriate augmentations or alternative
treatment to address the specific obstacles* (always considering the evidence to
suggest the best augmentations or alternatives for the individual patient).

Working with eating disorders where there is diagnostic (e.g., social phobia,
personality disorder features) or psychological (e.g., perfectionism) comorbidity
has been outlined in detail elsewhere (Wade et al., 2024). In brief, while comorbidity at the point of starting therapy for eating disorders is not a strong predictor of

treatment outcome (Vall & Wade, 2015), it may prove to be an obstacle to early change. Working with any such potential roadblock requires starting the therapy as per protocol, while monitoring early change and any obstacles to it. In the case of insufficient progress (or, in some cases, deterioration), the clinician uses their understanding of the obstacle to collaboratively discuss either augmentation of therapy (Pennesi et al., 2024) or a change of treatment with the patient (again, using continued monitoring of sessional outcomes in the new therapy to determine whether it enhances progress or not).

A good example of this approach comes from a treatment study conducted by Chen and colleagues (2017). They offered weekly 20-minute sessions of guided self-help CBT to women who had eating disorders featuring binge eating. Patients not experiencing early change at Session 4 were moved to more intensive therapy (group and individual session of either dialectical behaviour therapy or CBT). Early responders continued guided self-help for up to 24 weekly 20-minute sessions. At 6- and 12-month follow-ups, outcomes indicated that gradual responders achieved similar outcomes to more rapid responders when moved to a more appropriate complex and intensive therapy.

A strategic, stratified response to lack of progress is required. Section 7.7 details how this process can be operationalised for CBT-AN-20. At the review of progress sessions in CBT-AN-20 (Sessions 6–8, and if necessary 12–14), where improvement is clear, we proceed as normal with CBT-AN-20. Where improvement is absent or limited, the obstacles to weight gain and the fear of weight gain need to be identified, and augmentation to therapy or a change in therapy needs to target this obstacle. For example:

- Where there are significant medical complications (diabetes, pregnancy, risk of re-feeding), a dietitian can be invited to offer sessions with the patient contemporaneously with therapy.
- The patient's perfectionism is holding them back as they repeatedly start each day adhering to an eating plan but abandon it when the first minor lapse occurs – augmenting treatment with CBT for perfectionism might be indicated.
- The patient is overwhelmed by a fear of not coping with strong emotion if they can't use restriction – concurrent skills-based work conducted in groups, including dialectical behaviour therapy skills groups or family therapy in-service that upskills families in helping defuse strong emotion, can sometimes be helpful.
- The patient continuously "talks themselves out of change" each time they leave the therapy room – consider drawing on mealtime support from significant others or visiting/online paid support staff, if appropriate. If this behaviour is linked with strongly held beliefs about eating "healthy" foods and eating cleanly that is linked to perfectionism, this might indicate a need for a more intensive "kick-start" to therapy using day patient or inpatient services that support the patient to do behavioural experiments with alternative eating styles.

When others are bought on board to augment therapy, it is important to remember that effective therapy is a case of pulling together rather than engaging in a tug of war. In situations when the treatment team will be broadened, very clear communication is required. Anorexia nervosa thrives on disagreements between those involved in treatment and support. Where parents and carers are working as collaborators, appropriate boundaries still need to be maintained and renegotiated as the patient moves to increasing self-efficacy and independence in managing their eating.

While short-term augmentation for eating disorder therapies is associated with better outcomes (Pennesi, et al., 2024), *we strongly advocate that the patient participates in only one individual therapy at a time.* Such work is intense and tiring, and any potential watering down or confusion between approaches is unhelpful.

Where there is deterioration in weight, it is dangerous to keep negotiating with the patient about continuing therapy. A family conference or multidisciplinary team meeting may be needed to discuss more intensive forms of intervention and the dangers of continuing in outpatient settings. In short, it is crucial to have a strategy for ending therapy if it is not working. In such cases, outpatient therapy can end even if the patient does not immediately agree to participate in more intensive treatment; the recommendation has still been made, and outpatient therapy does not need to be an indefinite holding place for the patient's ambivalence.

Obviously, there are some co-occurring life-threatening/therapy-interfering factors that need to be attended to before therapy commences (active suicidality, psychosis, addiction). These will be addressed outside of CBT-AN-20. Given we expect previous or current self-harm in around half our patients, we do not consider this a reason for not commencing therapy. We do, however, include it as one of the non-negotiables of therapy (i.e., the intent is to cease all self-harming behaviours, including lack of adequate nutrition). The rationale is that the clinician will be acting on the assumption that the patient deserves self-care, and the patient and clinician need to pull together in the same direction to get a good therapy outcome. We ask the patient to "act as though they deserve self-care" during therapy, even if they don't believe it at the time when they commit to this. We institute a safely plan for patients with any history of self-harm and regularly review its occurrence in therapy. Current self-harm usually signals the need to introduce alternative emotion regulation strategies earlier than they might be otherwise.

3.8 Meta-competence 7: Prioritise competent following of protocols over rigid adherence to protocols

> **The clinician has a deep understanding of the therapeutic protocol and can adapt it to the patient's characteristics, preferences, and situation, avoiding rote application of the manualised therapy.**

On reading a manual, many clinicians tend to stick to it rigidly, with a sense of such adherence being the best way to deliver evidence-based therapy. However, our patients are individuals, with different presentations, histories, support systems, and so on. Hence, the ability to personalise treatment without losing sight of the core philosophy and methods involved (an aspect of competence) has been clearly linked with improved treatment outcomes (Andersson et al., 2023; Delgadillo, Ali et al., 2022; Nye et al., 2023). Cohen, Delgadillo, and DeRubeis (2021) described three dimensions of personalisation. The first is the *timing of when personalisation decisions are made* in a patient's treatment pathway (e.g., before, during or after treatment). The second is the *level of intervention* (e.g., the intensity of treatment, choice of modality or techniques, or style of delivery). The third dimension is the *method of personalisation*, ranging from informal idiosyncratic personalisation to using a formal statistical model. Some psychotherapy manuals tend to stress the importance of rigid adherence, but the majority stress the need to personalise treatment, while maintaining the principles of the therapy. However, the evidence outlined above is clear. *Treatment that flexes to the patient's characteristics is significantly more efficacious and cost-effective than sticking to a one-size-fits-all protocol.*

For example, the length of the phases may be different by individual, with the phases introduced at different times and with different degrees of overlap based on the individual's presentation and progress. However, the clinician simultaneously needs to take account of the other meta-competences outlined here and ensure that they are not supporting the patient in anxious avoidance (e.g., waiting until they can perform a task "perfectly"), or reinforcing a message of client fragility. For example, initiating body image work earlier in treatment than prescribed by the manual because the patient has already made significant progress in weight restoration is an ideal use of personalisation, whereas avoiding self-monitoring records or weekly weighing (both core elements of CBT-20-AN) is not.

3.9   Meta-competence 8: Pay attention to motivation

> **We recommend motivational interviewing skills be used by the clinician as the default over the course of therapy, with greater use of motivational exercises where initial levels of motivation are low.**

One key strategy of motivational interviewing (MI; Miller & Rollnick, 2013) is to help the patient to "talk themselves into" change. This "change talk" should dominate each therapy session. The clinician needs to avoid provoking the patient to argue defensively for sustaining the problematic behaviour – "sustain talk". Magill and colleagues (2018) found that greater use of clinician MI-consistent skills was related to a higher proportion of change talk from the patient, and that change talk was related to reductions in unhelpful behaviour at follow-up. *We need to create opportunities for change talk and flip our therapeutic conversation to change talk when we notice sustain talk.*

In this context, Aesop's fable of the competition between the north wind and the sun is helpful to consider, teaching about the superiority of persuasion over force. In this story, the winner of the competition would be the one who most quickly stripped a passerby of their cloak. The north wind went first and directed mighty cold blasts of wind at the passerby. This resulted in the passerby simply clutching their cloak more closely to their body. The sun then took a turn, directing gentle beams at the passerby until they unfastened their cloak and let it hang loosely from their shoulders. The sun's rays grew warmer and warmer until the passerby became so heated that he pulled off his cloak, and, to escape the blazing sunshine, threw himself down in the welcome shade of a tree by the roadside.

Substitute the cloak with anorexia nervosa and you can start to see the implications of this parable. Anything that occurs in therapy to increase sustain talk will only serve to get the patient to hold on more closely to their anorexia nervosa. Motivational interviewing contends that the clinician behaviours that will typically cause this "holding on" behaviour and sustain talk are arguing, disagreeing, explaining without permission, directing, judging, criticising, blaming, labelling, warning, and (most damagingly) trying to persuade with logic. We have all experienced the imperviousness to logic of the brain that is overwhelmed by anorexia nervosa, alongside the starved brain's agility to find what seems like a good reason for maintaining the status quo. In the end, supporting the patient to participate in behaviour change and behavioural experiments is the only effective way to help them understand the benefits of change.

Warm and engaging persuasion is the way to increase change talk. Motivational interviewing lists the following strategies for achieving this: express empathy, develop discrepancy (between where the person is now and where they want to be, or between the values expressed by the anorexia nervosa and their own values), roll with resistance, and support self-efficacy. Reflective listening is an essential tool in promoting change talk. It involves listening carefully to the patient and then making a reasonable guess about what they are saying. The clinician then paraphrases the patient's comments back to them. Reflections become more effective in leading the patient to state the arguments for change when they offer a deeper interpretation or an unexpected twist to what the patient has said. An example would be the patient who says, "I don't think I can do this", followed by a reflection from the clinician along the lines of "It sounds like the anorexia nervosa has so eroded your confidence in your ability to change, that you have started to doubt whether you can ever do anything differently".

Freeman and Dolan (2001) make the point that it is natural and healthy for any individual to resist moving too far and too quickly beyond familiar patterns, even if those patterns interfere with functioning and cause distress. To prevent clinician resentment about the so-called "resistant patient", and to normalise this resistance, it can be helpful to hold in mind the ten stages of change described in Freeman and Dolan's (2001) revision of the classic stages of change model (Prochaska & DiClemente, 1992). The first stage (*non-contemplation*) is one in which an individual is not considering or even thinking about changing. While this can certainly be the presentation of many patients, we find that there is usually some problem that needs attention in their life (e.g., "Getting others off my back … they just always try to make me eat"), which can lead to an ongoing conversation about the need for change. The next stage (*anti-contemplation*) involves the process of becoming reactive and violently opposed to the notion of needing to change. This is common where the patient comes into treatment against his or her will, under duress or threat. The clinician will need to work hard to "come alongside" the patient and formulate shared goals for initial work with the patient (in CBT, this is commonly referred to as "working shoulder-to-shoulder, rather than head-to-head"). Following the familiar Prochaska and DiClemente stages of *precontemplation, contemplation, action planning*, and *action*, the Freeman and Dolan model has three stages pertinent to later relapse prevention in Phase 5 of CBT-AN–20: *prelapse, lapse*, and *relapse* (see Section 11.2). Our aim, of course, is to help the patient reach and remain in the final stage of *maintenance*, where the goals are to (a) fine-tune and adjust changes, (b) support growth, (c) encourage stability, and (d) help the patient be his or her own therapist even if future problems arise.

Anorexia nervosa is particularly associated with strong ambivalence about change or losing the positive aspects of the disorder. We suggest that the clinician:

- Routinely explore the reasons for not changing, to be able to understand the individual's fears – this can be a relaxed and open conversation, where we do not mistake stuckness as choice and are aware of the potent influences of biological starvation and anxiety.
- Consider initial level of motivation and use motivational work and exercises accordingly. Wade, Ghan, and Waller (2021) showed that less motivated people doing CBT-ED attained similar positive outcomes as more motivated individuals if they received early motivational work.
- Prefer the provision of positive reinforcement for change versus focusing on the grim reality of not changing and becoming permanently disabled and defined by that disability, unless it is part of the deliberate and strategic two-session disability training/honest conversations that we describe in Section 7.7.
- Routinely spend time discussing with the patient both the advantages of change and the fears of change (see Section 5.12). The former requires focus on changing the short-term positives of not eating versus the long-term benefits of change consistent with the patient's values and experiences (e.g., achieving big goals, developing quality of life, self-efficacy). The latter allows for the difficulty of change to be acknowledged, and responses to the fears can be formulated in such a way that enables the use of CBT techniques to test the veracity of these fears.

3.10 Meta-competence 9: Collaborate with the patient to effectively set goals between sessions

Optimising achievement of the collaborative goals set each week in therapy requires clear identification of *both* the desired outcome *and* the likely obstacles that will need to be navigated.

Most clinicians are familiar with goal setting, and use it, but may not be acquainted with the science associated with optimal approaches to goal setting. Evidence tells us that the use of mental contrasting ensures the most powerful impact of goal setting (Cross & Sheffield, 2019; Wang et al., 2021). This work, championed by Oettingen and colleagues (e.g., 2016), shows that thinking only about positive future outcomes decreases goal-relevant efforts, as well as the likelihood of goal achievement. In contrast, *after imagining a positive future, thinking about current obstacles that impede the realisation of wishes (i.e., mental contrasting) can transform people's positive wishes into binding goals, leading to a greater likelihood of behaviour change.*

In Table 3.2, we summarise the steps of effective goal setting as captured in the WOOP acronym (https://woopmylife.org/): Wish, Outcome, Obstacle, Plan. We also refer to the acronym many clinicians will be familiar with – setting SMART goals: Specific, Measurable, Achievable, Relevant, Time-based. A patient handout is provided in Appendix A.2 to explain the WOOP process. It is important to remember that goals need to be collaboratively developed over *each* therapy session (e.g., change in amount eaten) and reviewed in the subsequent therapy session. This goal setting occurs regardless of the patient's stage of change, but the stage of change will impact the type of goals and the extent of change with which the patient will experiment.

While the WOOP process is typically used for short-term goals, it is also important to balance discussion with longer-term goals. Typically, short-term goals dominate early therapy, and then discussion increasingly turns to longer-term goals when the patient has regained nutrition and can take a bigger-picture view. We are interested in what recovery looks like, and where the road to recovery could lead the patient in 12 months' time across the domains of life: social, emotional, physical, intellect, spiritual, community engagement, work and study, hobbies, and so on. How can the patient use their values to guide the decisions that they will need to make along the way and set goals to help them achieve their destination? Which values have been sidelined by the anorexia nervosa and which of these do they want to revive? Which values have been introduced by the anorexia nervosa and need to be jettisoned? Consideration of the issues that predisposed the person to develop anorexia nervosa will also need managing over the long term – how is this best done?

Table 3.2 The goal-setting process

Phase of effective goal setting	Description
Wish	*Imagine yourself looking ahead at the next week like a path stretching before you. At the end of this path is your wish about something that will be happening differently in your life. What is it? Formulate this as a SMART goal:* • *Specific – define what will be accomplished and the actions to be taken to accomplish the goal.* • *Measurable – what data will tell you that you achieved the goal?* • *Achievable – choose something you think is probably within your reach but will stretch you.* • *Relevant – choose a goal that maximises your progress against the anorexia nervosa.* • *Time-based – we are looking at a goal that can be achieved and measured over the next week.*
Outcome	*Imagine yourself achieving this wish. Picture the scene in vivid detail – how does it feel to have achieved this? What does it say about you as a person?*
Obstacle	*Picture a wall or barrier that appears on the path towards your wish. This wall represents something inside you – a habit, a fear, or a thought – that makes it harder to move forward. What words or images come to mind as you think about your main inner obstacle?*
Plan	*Formulate "if (the obstacle) then (I will)" plans. Having a few to fall back on is helpful in case the first one does not work.*

3.11   Meta-competence 10: Prioritise both training and supervision/consultation

> **Working with patients with anorexia nervosa tests the skills and resilience of even the most seasoned clinician – supervision or consultation is necessary to maintain a focus on goals and clinician mental health.**

Across the field of mental health, the push for ongoing supervision and consultation has been growing, regardless of clinician qualification and experience. Regular, appropriate clinical supervision or consultation is considered key to the ethics and performance of clinicians providing CBT (e.g., British Association for Behavioural and Cognitive Psychotherapies, 2022). For motivational interviewing and CBT, the evidence shows that training has a greater effect on clinician behaviour change compared to receiving no training or simply reading a treatment manual (Ragnarsson et al., 2024) – even a manual as excellent as this one! However, while training can provide clinicians with the knowledge and confidence to use exposure therapy, for example, it is insufficient to promote substantial changes in practice (Trivasse et al., 2020).

Training combined with supervision or consultation is more effective than training alone for changing clinician behaviour, with no differences found between face-to-face and online training (Ragnarsson et al., 2024). What is less certain is whether supervision results in better outcomes for the patient. There is evidence to show that trainees under expert supervision can provide as good an outcome for the patient as a more experienced clinician (e.g., Öst et al., 2012). Our stance is that even experienced clinicians will benefit from supervision or consultation, as will their patients. It is easy to get off track for many reasons, and having someone with the "bird's eye view" to discuss your cases with can ensure you get back on track quickly. This support feels particularly important in the case of anorexia nervosa, where the illness is often ego-syntonic, and where the patient is so capable and the illness so strong and persuasive the clinician can need additional support sometimes in reorienting and getting perspective. In each of our own teams in the United Kingdom, Australia, and the United States, we hold regular supervision and consultation meetings with our colleagues to keep our own therapies on track.

We stress here that supervision in CBT for eating disorders is not simply a matter of overseeing case management and professional development, as it can be in some areas of mental health treatment. We strongly recommend that supervision should be regular, focused on patient progress and outcomes, and delivered by a clinician who has expertise in both CBT and eating disorders. Indeed, supervision or consultation from a well-intended colleague who recommends an entirely different approach (e.g., supportive, psychodynamic) may even have detrimental effects on the therapy, as the response to certain clinical scenarios across different therapies may be diametrically opposed.

3.12 Final reflections: Holding our nerve

We conclude this section by collating summaries of our reflections and experiences of using and supervising trainees and colleagues in the implementation of these meta-competences.

- Combined teaching and supervising based on such meta-competences can have a profound impact on clinician and supervisor practice. In turn, those changes have a positive impact on how therapy is conducted and how patients respond to that therapy.
- In our supervision of trainees, we see what could be called an epiphany. Trainees arrive feeling very apprehensive and unsure about using firm empathy. Upon trying it once and seeing that the patient (a) does *not* expire in front of their eyes; (b) does *not* leave the therapy room in umbrage; and (c) *does* rise to the challenge, doing what is needed to keep therapy on track, those trainees are ecstatic. They revise their estimation of the patient as being fragile

and incapable, instead adopting the stance of firm empathy as their long-term approach to CBT with all their patients. Trainees now arrive for placement saying: "I want to learn how to do firm empathy". Many report finding the placement to be the first time that they have understood just how effective they can be as therapists, attributing that learning to the fact that they are using a protocol properly for the first time and to the symptom-focused nature of supervision.

- Other clinicians join eating disorder services somewhat apprehensively, expressing preconceptions regarding pessimism about patient recovery, or anticipating becoming bored of delivering the same treatment over and over. Gaining these meta-competencies supports clinicians to see that neither of those fears need be true. Relatedly, some patients who speak fondly of past clinicians recount experiences of receiving firm empathy – sometimes looking back on times where they'd felt angry about therapy non-negotiables, but with later recognition of those boundaries being crucial to their perspective of the clinician having saved their lives.

- The power of seeing patients recover is a huge motivator for clinicians to continue this work. What might at first feel like boring conversations about food and eating are often driven by the rigidity of the illness itself – those same patients who seem like shells (rigid, fragile, unemotive) tend to come to life when re-fed, when they start to re-engage with the world and others, and when their true selves come back. This return of the "real person" is enormously rewarding to witness and support.

- Our teams have sometimes been initially sceptical of using the ED-15 in each session as they were worried about patient burden, but it turned out to be a clinician concern rather than a patient concern. Overall, most patients have really liked seeing their progress and understanding their own role in the changes that have led to that progress.

- The clinicians who do well with both CBT-T and CBT-AN-20 are those who have lots of cases. We encourage people to work with lots of patients – you can't get to know a protocol and use it flexibly without using it across many different patients.

In short, it is entirely understandable that qualified and trainee clinicians can experience some anxiety about delivering a therapy such as CBT-AN-20, but trainers and supervisors can help them to face that anxiety and learn to be more effective clinicians.

Chapter 4

Introduction to the competences and skills needed for CBT-AN-20

This chapter addresses the competences necessary to deliver CBT-AN-20 – in other words, the CBT skills needed to deliver the therapy (e.g., implementing exposure therapy accurately). It complements Chapter 3, where we outlined the key meta-competences needed to deliver any therapy – the clinical skills needed to allow us to be strategic and appropriately flexible when we are following that therapy road map, so that we can personalise it without losing sight of the core and the goals of the therapy. In short, this chapter and Chapter 3 are key preparation for the core protocol in Chapters 7–11.

Here, we outline the key skills and competences that are going to recur throughout the CBT-AN-20 protocol, addressing the principles and practicalities of effective delivery of those interventions. Many of these skills (e.g., agenda-setting, maintaining a focus on early change, conducting exposure) will be familiar to any CBT practitioner, independent of the patient population treated. However, some will be applied in ways that reflect the core pathology of eating disorders (e.g., formulation, exposure to knowing one's weight). Finally, others will be specific to working with eating disorders (e.g., body image work, working with the anorexic voice).

4.1 Agenda-setting and review

A clearly agreed upon agenda/session plan supports the structure and coherence of CBT-AN-20 sessions. The agenda also acts as a link between the weekly sessions – based on reviewing between-session tasks agreed on the week before and identifying the steps to be taken in the week ahead. Skilful agenda-setting is based on collaboration with the patient. It should contain clear, prioritised topics that can realistically be covered in the available time (Blackburn et al., 2001). The approach to setting the agenda evolves over the course of CBT-AN-20. While it is helpful to formally write out the agenda with the patient in early sessions, this can become redundant later. Agenda adherence within the session also requires a degree of flexibility (Blackburn et al., 2001), in response to within-session developments (e.g., revelation of risk; positive change that merits positive reinforcement to enhance the chances of it happening again).

DOI: 10.4324/9781003594703-4

Some patients (and clinicians) might find the term "agenda" too formal, and prefer to use a different phrase (e.g., "session plan"). Whatever the term used, we find that physically writing out the agenda (i.e., with pen and paper, or on screen) with the patient at the start of each session early on supports collaboration. It helps to provide orientation to the treatment approach, which is particularly important in the early phases of CBT-AN-20. Indeed, we find that drafting an outline agenda for the following week at the end of the current session can help to get the next session off to a good start (even if it needs amending in light of developments over the week). As noted above, writing down the agenda might become redundant in later sessions (i.e., patient and clinician can easily recall their agreed agenda), but many patients and clinicians find that the written agenda provides a useful aide mémoire throughout therapy. A CBT-AN-20 agenda template can be found in Table 4.1.

Before setting the session agenda, two areas should be considered to ensure that the session can continue: reviewing the safety plan; and checking that the patient has prepared for the session by completing the necessary homework (food records and self-report measures – a food record sheet is available on the CBT-AN-20 website (https://sites.google.com/sheffield.ac.uk/cbt-an-20), but local versions can be used as long as they cover the same core material of date, time, and what was eaten/avoided). These tasks should become routine ones, which the patient comes to expect to attend to in confirming readiness for the session. This way, we reinforce the non-negotiability of these tasks, without which CBT-AN-20 cannot productively take place.

Table 4.1 Agenda/session plan template

CBT-AN-20 session plan (to adjust for the individual patient)
Preparation
- Safety check-in and planning.
- Checking whether homework has been done. Checking whether the patient has issues that they wish to bring to the agenda.

Main agenda items
- Review reflections/learning on any psychoeducational materials or other homework/ between-session tasks agreed in the previous week's session.
- Review of food records (process and contents, including exposure to dietary changes).
- Open, collaborative weighing.
- Weight regain/making sense of the current weight trajectory (supported by food records and self-report measures).
- Specific experience of challenge or success (chosen by the patient, from their food records).
- Discussion related to the relevant phase of therapy (e.g., managing emotional triggers, body image issues, working towards the ending).
- Patient's agenda items (optional, depending on whether the patient brings items – can be earlier if appropriate in context, though not at the outset, to avoid filling up the session).
- Planning/confirming next steps (homework), including dietary changes.

4.1.1 Starting the session

We recommend resisting the social impulse to begin the session by asking the patient how they are, or how their week has been. It is not that we are uninterested in this information, but that inviting dialogue in this way and at this point mirrors that of a social exchange and not therapy. Such an approach risks eliciting verbose and superficial responses, which are likely to delay and shorten the opportunity to make use of CBT-AN-20 in the limited time frame available. Instead, we might warmly greet our patients with a simple "Hello", "Welcome back", or "It's good to see you again", followed by stating something along the lines of "Let's check to see if you are ready to go ahead with your CBT session today, by checking in on your safety, and your food records". At this stage, we would also ask the patient if they had any items that they wanted to bring to the agenda today.

4.1.2 Reviewing safety

Safety is paramount throughout CBT-AN-20, as one would expect of any therapy for anorexia nervosa. New safety issues or issues in implementing previously agreed safety plans must always be attended to and should take priority over proceeding with the CBT-AN-20 session if necessary. Any new or unresolved safety issues (e.g., the patient becoming suicidal; medical instability; not attending for required blood monitoring; safeguarding concerns) should be addressed immediately. If the patient does not collaborate with this priority, outpatient psychological intervention (including CBT-AN-20) is not suitable, and the plan of care must be reviewed with the patient and the multidisciplinary team, focusing on risk management until stability and safety are established.

However, we find that patients more commonly collaborate on safety issues. Discussion about safety will typically be fairly brief, including checking that the recommended physical monitoring and review plan are being adhered to; considering any changes to treatment as a result; asking about any new physical signs/symptoms (e.g., dizziness, palpitations); and where there are any signs (e.g., patient mood appears low), asking about and elaborating upon suicide-related risk factors (e.g., hopelessness, change in interpersonal relationships, changes to mood, use of drugs and alcohol). If there are any such signs, the clinician should directly enquire about any known or new self-harm or suicide concerns. In contrast, as such risk declines, it becomes easier for the patient and clinician to focus on the core tasks of CBT-AN-20.

4.1.3 Checking on homework/between-session tasks

Next, the clinician enquires whether the patient is ready for the session with their completed food records and self-report measures. If self-report measures are completed via an online system, such as Qualtrics or RedCap, it is important for the clinician to check them before the session. The completion of diaries and measures can be positively reinforced through praise of efforts, even if only partially completed at first. When the patient doesn't appear to have attempted or returned the food records, the clinician should express concern about not being able to do CBT-AN-20 without such material. We recommend resisting any urge to jump into problem-solve this for the patient (e.g., explaining how to fill in a simple diary that the patient is highly likely to understand already). Instead, we share our dilemma with the patient. We communicate the conflict between our wish to continue with CBT-AN-20 and the impossibility of doing it fully without food records (e.g., not being able to understand the patient's weight later in the session). We might then ask the patient to help us resolve this dilemma, and what they would like to do. The aim is to allow the patient the opportunity to exercise their agency in preparing for future sessions.

We recommend remaining clear about the usefulness of food records in CBT-AN-20 as a means of building understanding and supporting change. If there are serious difficulties for the patient in completing such food records (e.g., obsessive-compulsive disorder interfering with monitoring), then we will work towards strategies for getting such records over the first few sessions. However, we advise the patient that if we are unsuccessful in helping them to prepare for future sessions with such records, we will need to bring CBT-AN-20 to an end and consider alternative approaches (e.g., discharge, risk management, an alternative treatment).

The patient arriving for a session without all completed self-report measures presents similar though less urgent problems, given the importance of feedback on change as a means of enhancing progress (Chapter 3). In the short term, we can ask the patient to complete the ED-15 at the start of the sessions, but not having measures of anxiety and mood at the appropriate points (start of treatment, review, end of treatment) means that the clinician and patient are limited in their understanding of progress (and that can contribute to unidentified difficulties in engagement, risk of suicide, etc.). Patients are less likely to complete psychometric measures if they feel like it is purely an administrative exercise. Instead, the completion of such measures should be positively reinforced by the clinician through their active in-session review. Their clinical utility should be communicated by the clinician expressing interest in the returned measures, sharing interpretation of scores (including graphs), and commenting on apparent changes.

4.1.4   The main agenda

We orient the patient to the task of setting or updating the agenda by saying something like: "Let's spend a few minutes agreeing about how to make the most out of the time we have together today". This agenda should include tasks that are relevant throughout therapy, as well as those that are relevant to the specific phase in CBT-AN-20, and patient contributions. These skills are addressed more fully across Chapters 7–11. However, the general agenda items should include:

- Reviewing tasks that were agreed upon in the previous session.
- Identifying any challenges or successful progress with the tasks of therapy (both between- and within-session), such as reviewing the whole week's records and developing energy graphs.
- Review of weight graphs and relating the consequent weight predictions to the patient's actual weight.
- Discussion related to the relevant phase of therapy (e.g., managing emotional triggers, body image issues, or working towards ending).
- Summarising and agreeing between-session tasks.

The patient is also invited to raise any concerns or additional issues they wish to add to the agenda, as detailed in Section 7.1.

4.2   Psychoeducation

The aim of psychoeducation is to help the patient to become informed, empowered, and engaged in facing the task of recovery from anorexia nervosa. We want the patient to be equipped with an understanding that they are not to blame for the illness, with the confidence to start eating more, and with the recognition that the time to do so is now. Psychoeducation is part of what makes formulation make sense and can be crucial in facilitating and motivating change.

Within CBT-AN-20, we recommend and provide a number of resources to augment therapy, including psychoeducation sheets, online resources and single-session interventions (SSI), which can be used in between sessions. These are included in the appendices to this manual, and they are outlined in Table 4.2, explaining how and when in CBT-AN-20 they should be used.

Psychoeducation forms a crucial element of CBT-AN-20. Topics include the short- and long-term effects of undereating, such as being underweight; the importance of early weight restoration; the growth mindset; nutrition and the brain; eating and epigenetic traits; the importance of carbohydrates; the anorexic voice; emotional and interpersonal problems; core beliefs; body neutrality; healthy distribution of fat; perfectionism; and the role and nature of emotions. Each of these topics is outlined within the assessment and core protocol (Chapters 5–11), and general written psychoeducational resources can be found in Appendices A.3–A.8 and online (weight regain; guidance on appropriate dietary intake; the role of traits such as perfectionism; starvation effects; long-term physical risks of anorexia nervosa; risks of compensatory behaviours). Other such psychoeducation material is identified in appendices linked to subsequent chapters.

We do not overwhelm the patient by providing them with all this psychoeducational information at once, but only when it becomes relevant to that individual during assessment and treatment. Furthermore, not all topics will be of relevance to all patients. So psychoeducation should be presented and utilised in a targeted, timely way. We also encourage patients to consider the storage system that they will use for the various psychoeducational materials that they will collect (along with other

Table 4.2 Resources for patients over therapy – how they can be used

Treatment phase	Material for the patient	How it should be used
Between assessment (or Session 0) and Session 1	Single-session interventions (SSIs)	We recommend use of the behavioural activation SSI, which can have a significant impact on dietary restriction; this may indicate that the patient is likely to have a positive early response to treatment.
Phase 1 (and then as needed over therapy)	Psychoeducation handouts (Appendices)	Curate use to what is relevant to the patient and getting them started on change as early as possible; the handouts addressing the advantages and fears of change, starvation effects, anxiety, the anorexic voice, growth mindset, and temperament will help the patient understand why change is so difficult, but also that change is possible.
From the progress review (Session 6), and then as needed throughout the rest of therapy	SSIs and brief interventions	Curate use to any key obstacles to progress noted in the reviews and over therapy – these are intended to be incorporated into the 20 sessions, so use parsimoniously. The patient should do most of the work out of session, with brief conversations in session about discoveries and implications for homework.

therapy documents). What is likely to best support their long-term recovery? While PDF resources don't have to be printed, having a physical ring binder or folder to hold onto and refer to can often be helpful, though others will prefer to store such material on their computer or device.

Introducing new psychoeducation topics to the patient is best supported by use of written information sheets for the patient to read through as a between-session task. Such core material for the patient can discourage them from looking at less reliable sources of information (e.g., online dieting and weight loss tips). The clinician skill in providing psychoeducation lies in timing, choosing wisely, and taking a collaborative approach (e.g., being relatively Socratic rather than instructive). We do not want to bombard our patients with more information than they can retain in one go. It is also important not to push information too hard at a point where the patient is not ready or does not want to hear it.

Psychoeducation can take different forms and is not confined to useful handouts or video examples. It can include apparently casual comments such as: "I will round your weight to the nearest 0.5kg/1lb before plotting it on the graph, because anything more precise than that is too small to be meaningful" (to encourage a less obsessional focus on weight). Repetition and revision support learning, so once a psychoeducational topic has been introduced, it is important that we refer back to it to prevent the learning from being lost (e.g., "Remember that we are rounding your weight to the nearest 0.5kg/1lb") and encourage the patient to re-read such material (with loved ones, where appropriate) between sessions.

We recommend starting with psychoeducation related to undereating, the need to restore weight, motivational issues, and working with the anorexic voice (across Phase 1 in particular). We then move to psychoeducation about emotion, temperament, perfectionism, body image, and so on across Phases 3 and 4. Psychoeducation supports formulation and sits before action, so we select psychoeducation based on which part of the formulation we plan to address next. Of course, if a patient requests psychoeducation early on that is related to a topic typically addressed later in CBT-AN-20, this can be provided as long as this focus does not result in avoidance of making the necessary dietary changes and weight restoration. Within some phases (e.g., working with maintaining factors), the psychoeducation handouts signpost patients to evidence-based programmes and workbooks. When discussing such handouts with the patient, it can be helpful to talk about any integrated signposting to ensure that the patient is aware of and encouraged to make use of the materials available.

Clinicians should aim to be "shoulder-to-shoulder" rather than "head-to-head" with patients in all areas of CBT-AN-20, and the task of offering psychoeducation is no different. Psychoeducation should be approached as an invitation, in which the clinician gauges the patients' interest in a topic and expresses clear interest in their perspectives, before offering information. All efforts on the part of the patient to read psychoeducational materials, retain this information, and apply it to understanding their own experiences (including the tasks of recovery) can be positively reinforced by clinician expression of curiosity, interest, and praise.

4.3   Planning dietary change for weight regain and stabilisation

Obviously, helping the patient to eat differently is going to be a key element in the successful treatment of anorexia nervosa, whatever treatment one is offering (e.g., Bulik et al., 2007). While the exposure, psychoeducation, and behavioural experiments in Chapters 7 and 8 outline methods used to encourage overcoming fears of eating in CBT-AN-20, it is critical for the clinician and patient to have an understanding of the amounts and types of food that are optimum for weight regain and stabilisation. Appendix A.3 provides psychoeducation for the patient regarding weight regain.

Part of this understanding of what is optimum is recognising that people differ in the number of calories that they will need to gain weight or to remain stable, both between individuals (e.g., different metabolism; different levels of weight regain needed to get to a healthy weight) and within individuals (e.g., number of calories needed at first might be lower than later on in weight regain, as metabolism changes; changing level of exercise). Therefore, any standard recommended meal template has to be seen by both patient and clinician as being a starting point, to be adapted according to the individual patient's physical response to what they are currently eating. There should be regular reviews of level of weight regain (Section 7.4) and of the changes needed when maintaining weight (Section 8.2), to inform shared planning about changes to dietary intake.

While there are other guides to eating healthily for anorexia nervosa, we recommend Hart and McMaster's *REAL Food Guide (Recovery from Eating Disorders for Life)* (Hart et al., 2025) – included in Appendix A.4 and on the CBT-AN-20 website (https://sites.google.com/sheffield.ac.uk/cbt-an-20). There is also a shorter version for your patients on the website. The *REAL Food Guide* recommends portion sizes for both weight regain and weight maintenance, which serves as the basis for that individualised dietary planning, based around impact on the patient's weight. It stresses the importance of eating "mechanically" (fixed timing; use of external cues rather than hunger/satiety cues), particularly early in treatment. It provides general meal plans based around weight gain and around weight maintenance (Tables 1 and 2 in the *REAL Food Guide*), and summarises the numbers of servings of carbohydrate, protein, fat, calcium foods, and so on (and what constitutes a serving in each case). It also addresses how to work with patients on a vegan diet.

We find that the *REAL Food Guide* is a valuable guide for clinicians and patients alike, providing valuable psychoeducation for clinicians who lack the nutritional knowledge and clinical skills of qualified dietitians, and it has a clearer link to evidence-based practice than many treatment manuals (e.g., McMaster et al., 2021). It also has the virtue of indicating when individuals should be considered for specialist dietitian support, including:

- Pregnancy/breast-feeding;
- Comorbid medical diagnoses that can impact on food intake/absorption (e.g., Type 1 diabetes; Crohn's disease; irritable bowel disease; allergies or intolerances due to Coeliac disease, cystic fibrosis, kidney disease, etc.);
- Medication that influences appetite, nutritional needs, or weight (e.g., novel antipsychotics; semaglutides);
- Weight loss or inability to gain weight when underweight (i.e., showing malnutrition/starvation signs, whatever weight they are at, even if they are above a BMI of 20);
- Consistent reluctance to engage with the wider range/amount of food that is recommended in treatment;
- Failure to engage in eating-related skills (shopping, cooking, etc.), despite clinical or family support for those skills.

Dietitians might also be involved where the patient wishes to engage in religious fasting (e.g., observing Ramadan or Lent). However, we also recommend asking the patient to discuss this with their religious guide, in order to understand that many religions do not regard fasting as being required when one has an eating disorder.

4.3.1   Summary

Planning food intake collaboratively with the anorexia nervosa patient requires a good understanding on the part of the patient and clinician alike of nutritional requirements. To ensure that this is viable, we recommend:

- Using the *REAL Food Guide* (Appendix A.4) as a starting point for understanding nutritional balance and for planning weight regain and maintenance (depending on the point in therapy);
- Working with the weight gain and weight maintenance food plans as appropriate (Appendix A.4 – Tables 1 and 2), encouraging "mechanical" eating to enable the necessary weight gain;
- Adjusting according to the individual's response as we progress through therapy (e.g., when weight is not rising as needed);
- Seeking specialist dietetic support where there are medical, physical, or behavioural reasons to do so.

4.4   Case formulation

In Chapter 3, we outlined a general *formulation of anorexia nervosa*. However, such understanding needs to be presented at the level of the individual patient's problem – *case formulation*. Case formulation is a crucial aspect of CBT-AN-20. In CBT-T (for non-underweight cases), there is no requirement to develop a case formulation for all patients, though one can be developed if the therapy becomes "stuck", and the reason needs to be understood. This CBT-T approach is based on our experience that formulations of behaviours (e.g., energy graphs) are sufficiently effective in explaining key features of the non-underweight eating disorders.

However, we recommend developing a case formulation when working with anorexia nervosa in CBT-AN-20, as there are many more ways in which the therapy can become stuck, making it valuable for the individual and their loved ones to have a clear, shared understanding of their problem from the beginning. Such understanding can engage the patient by explaining the need for the recommended changes, and by predicting the short- and long-term costs and benefits of making those changes versus remaining stuck in the anorexia nervosa. Furthermore, co-creating this shared formulation can assure the patient that the clinician understands and appreciates how hard – albeit necessary – embarking on this change-oriented treatment will be.

4.4.1   Key targets for understanding and formulating anorexia nervosa

Perhaps unsurprisingly, the CBT-AN-20 formulation of anorexia nervosa has some overlap with the formulation of the key elements of the pathology of non-underweight patients. As with CBT-T, the core elements of such cases (except for avoidant restrictive food intake disorder (ARFID), where the key issue is anxiety relating to different aspects of food intake – see Section 12.4) are:

- Fear of uncontrollable weight gain;
- Emotional triggers and their relation to (primarily) impulsive behaviours, including binge-eating;
- Body image disturbance.

However, it is important for the formulation of anorexia nervosa to address two further elements that are more prominent when working with underweight patients:

- Greater emphasis on starvation effects (including their impact on motivation, and the consequent impact of the "anorexic voice");
- Emotional factors and their relation to more compulsive behaviours, such as restriction and compulsive exercise.

It is important to consider whether one is formulating the disorder as a general case or the individual's personal manifestation of that disorder. Formulation of the general disorder of anorexia nervosa is detailed in Chapter 2 (Figure 2.1), giving us a generalised idea of what factors might need to be considered in explaining the development and maintenance of eating disorders. This is referred to as a *functional analysis*, because it is not dependent on any specific theory. However, when working to understand the *individual's* anorexia nervosa presentation, it is important to bring in theory to direct the therapy methods that are needed to help the specific patient. This leads us to the CBT-based formulation of the person in front of us. Of course, we cannot assume that all people with anorexia nervosa have the same pattern of problems – there will be differences between individuals in antecedents, triggers, symptoms, and maintaining factors. Therefore, we need to personalise the individual formulation to make it most effective.

4.4.2 The "5Ps" formulation applied to individual cases of anorexia nervosa

In CBT-AN-20, we personalise the formulation using the 5Ps template (e.g., Mcneil et al., 2012), where we work with the patient to understand:

- The nature of the *Problem* (the symptoms that the person experiences, such as starvation, restriction, and negative body image);
- *Predisposing* factors (the antecedents that make the anorexia nervosa more likely to emerge, such as genetics, engagement in appearance-focused activities such as gymnastics or dance, teasing about body shape and weight during childhood – even though these might be similar antecedents to those reported for other disorders);

- Precipitating factors (the triggers that can tip the vulnerable individual over into developing specifically anorexia nervosa behaviours. Those triggers can include such experiences as being criticised for weight, being praised for weight loss, changes in weight and levels of body scrutiny when starting in a new school or workplace and wanting to fit in, relationship difficulties, or other life stressors);
- Perpetuating factors (maintaining factors, which change over time in anorexia nervosa):
  - Initial perpetuating factors in anorexia nervosa are usually positive, providing the patient with a "buzz" as a result of their success in weight loss, leading to a short-term sense of control.
  - Later perpetuating factors in anorexia nervosa are negative, particularly the fear of losing that control over eating and life, making the person work even harder to keep their weight under control.
- Protective factors (internal and external resilience and strengths, such as family support, sense of self-efficacy, and other validating factors such as non-anorexic interests and hobbies).

When working with anorexia nervosa, the 5Ps model has a key advantage over other basic formulation templates that are commonly used in CBT (e.g., the five areas/hot cross bun model). It more easily accommodates change over time, particularly in terms of the perpetuating/maintaining factors, as the person shifts from their initial sense of control to a feeling of being out of control and panicked. It does not exclude the use of other, specific behaviour-focused formulations (e.g., energy graphs; Newton's Cradle), as outlined in the protocol chapters, but can be used to link to them as parts of the bigger picture. Appendix A.9 provides the clinician with a worksheet that can get the patient thinking about how all those elements might fit together, for subsequent joint working to get agreement and targets for therapy.

4.4.3   The process of developing an individualised formulation

As stated above, this approach has to be understood in terms of what matters for the specific person, and so this case formulation must be discussed and reviewed with the individual patient, as initiated here:

Clinician: "I think it is really important that we understand how your problem developed, by pulling together those parts of your history that seem to be relevant, including what was happening around the time that you first started restricting and losing weight. But it will also be important to understand what has kept the anorexia nervosa going".

Patient: "But do you really think it makes sense like that?"

Clinician: "Given what you have told me about your past, I am guessing that you initially found the anorexia nervosa pretty wonderful – like you were in control of things for the first time – but that that phase did not last, and now you have the feeling that you are desperately holding onto control. You have to try harder and harder, even though you have all these people on your back about wanting you to get well. Plus, your own body is starting to let you down too, feeling weaker and making you perhaps less likely to resist food".

Patient: "'Desperate' is a pretty good word for how I am feeling. But I am sure I can get back in control".

Clinician: "And if you could have, I am sure that you would have already. Let's see if we can make sense of what has gone on for you in the past, then what keeps the problem going. But I also want to see how your strengths might help you to get out of this hole, if you choose to do so".

Patient: "'Strengths?' Not sure that I have any of those".

Clinician: "You seem to be a determined soul. You are clearly hard working, and you have shown that you are bright by getting your degree. You have a family that is trying their best to support you, rather than supporting your anorexia nervosa. And you haven't run away from the offer of help here. Those sound like strengths to me, if we can just work out how you could use them to support your recovery and future life".

Patient: "So what do we need to do to make sense of all of this?"

Clinician: "We have a thing called the '5Ps model', which we use to understand what has led you to where you are, what triggered you into first restricting, what has kept it going and how that has shifted over time, and those strengths. All of that can make sense of your anorexia nervosa, and can suggest ways out of it. Happy to give that a go?"

Patient: "You will have to explain what '5Ps' means, but OK".

We aim to develop this formulation during either the assessment or during Session 1–2, commonly asking the patient to use the worksheet in Appendix A.9 for homework. In the session, we then use either the framework on page 2 of Appendix A.9 or the blank formulation in Appendix A.10 to reach agreement (see Section 4.4.4). We do so in the clinic room with the patient, during the assessment meeting (see Chapter 5) or Session 1 (see Chapter 7). Of course, if we complete the formulation in the Assessment, then it is important to revisit it at the start of therapy to monitor any change, just as we would recommend revisiting it to understand changes and "stuckness".

This formulation process allows us to check on the patient's understanding and pick up new information that the patient remembers as we go. It also allows the patient to consider the adequacy of their personalised model between sessions, so that they can suggest edits (which we usually find very informative additions or revisions). Furthermore, as with any formulation, as the patient moves through the disorder and moves through therapy, we should respond to those changes by updating the content of the formulation as treatment proceeds.

4.4.4   The 5Ps formulation itself

Having explained what the five Ps are (*Problem*; *Predisposing*; *Precipitating*; *Protective*; *Perpetuating*) and how they interact, we then develop a diagrammatic formulation to share with them. A blank version is provided below (Figure 4.1), in Appendix A.10 and on the website for downloading and use with the patient. The 5Ps model centres on:

• Identifying the *Problems* (e.g., restriction, starvation, binge-eating, negative body image);
• Understanding the way in which the early background factors (*Predisposing*) set the person up for the potential development of the problem;
• Identifying the triggers (*Precipitating*) that activate the eating and related behaviours;
• Noting *Protective* factors (e.g., supportive family, resilient aspects of their personality), which can be addressed and recruited to support recovery;
• Explaining the two ways in which *Perpetuating* factors serve to maintain the problem. In the short term, this is likely to be a product of positive

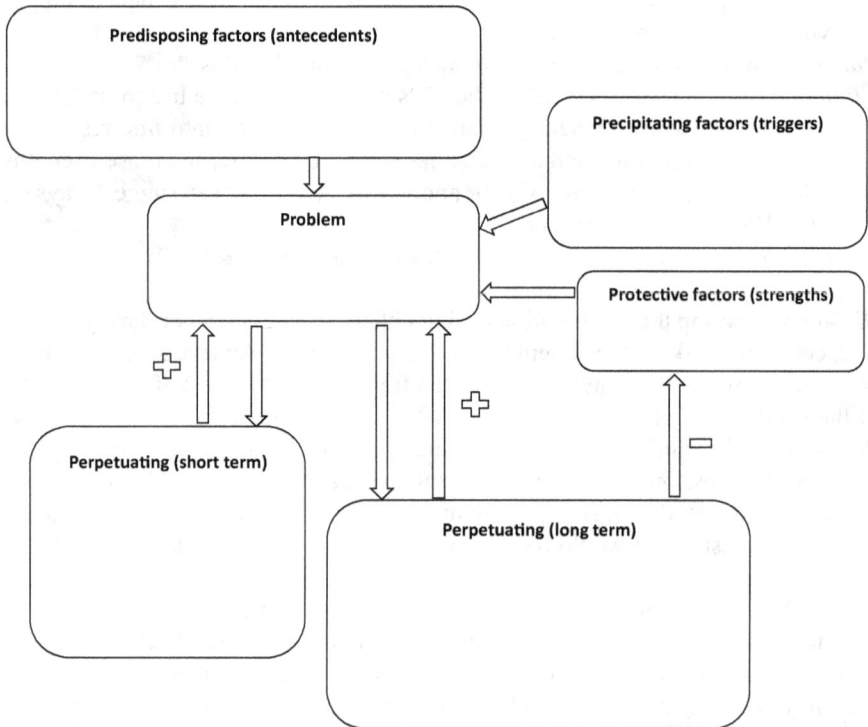

Figure 4.1 Blank formulation diagram, based on the modified 5Ps model that is used to understand anorexia nervosa ("+" indicates "enhancement"; "-" indicates "reduction").

reinforcement (feeling elevated by the outcomes of restriction); in the long term, the maintenance is likely to be due to negative reinforcement (where there is a fear of losing control).

Templates for this 5Ps model are given in Chapter 5, showing the general set of factors that can be drawn upon when putting together such a formulation (Figure 5.1) and an example of a 5Ps formulation as applied to an individual patient (Figure 5.2). We use such a personalised formulation to explain to the patient that the elements of therapy need to be ordered in a way that makes it possible to overcome the anorexia nervosa fully (e.g., overcoming starvation and working on weight gain has to come before it is appropriate and feasible to focus on body image work).

4.5   Writing to patients

Letter writing to patients is not a uniform procedure across services or clinicians. Although it is optional in CBT-AN-20, we encourage clinicians to put aside time to write to patients after the initial phase of CBT-AN-20 (usually between Sessions 6 and 8) and again at the end of treatment.

4.5.1   Early review letter to the patient

Evidence suggests that case formulation letters sent after the initial phase of treatment can enhance engagement and improve treatment outcomes (Allen et al., 2016). They are most likely to be effective where they give an overview of the development of the disorder, and they use a respectful and reflective tone. Therefore, in line with Allen et al. (2016), we suggest that formulation letters should:

- Reflect a collaborative and respectful stance;
- Include an overview of the development of the disorder;
- Make acknowledgement of some of the key maintaining factors; and
- Summarise the agreed way forward.

It is important to remember that our patients' recall of what was said in sessions can sometimes be inaccurate or incomplete, which is likely to be a result of the impact of starvation and anxiety, particularly in the early stages of treatment. In this context, a written summary can be a useful therapeutic aid. An example of a case formulation letter is given in Appendix A.11.

4.5.2   End of treatment letter

We find it helpful to write a reflective letter to the patient at the end of treatment to reinforce the benefits of therapy. The aim is to ensure that the patient has a concrete reminder of what they achieved in therapy and how. That allows them to review how far they have come and can remind them of the skills that they have developed in case they need to return to those skills during follow-up and beyond. We include an example of such a letter in Appendix A.12.

4.6   Collaborative weighing

While weighing the patient in each session is a key component in the treatment of eating disorders (Waller & Mountford, 2015), *how* patients should be weighed is a point of debate amongst patients and clinicians (Froreich et al., 2020). There are no clear data to support a particular approach, so we confine ourselves here to outlining what is required in CBT-AN-20.

In CBT-AN-20, we advocate "open collaborative weighing". Let's take the "open" bit first. Open weighing means that the number on the scales is shared with the patient. The rationale is that this provides an opportunity to modify the "broken cognition" that many eating disorder patients have – the irrational belief that consuming almost any foods will lead to exponential and uncontrollable weight gain. Additionally, like any behaviour that evokes anxiety, we consider exposure the most beneficial approach for the patient's long-term recovery. Most patients accept the need to be weighed openly from the beginning. Overall, however, it is true to say that some patients (and clinicians) prefer blind weighing, which involves the patient not looking at the scale reading (e.g., stepping on the scale backwards) and not discussing their weight explicitly in session. Open weighing represents a major challenge to many patients, who report that negative emotions and thoughts about being weighed often start the day prior to being weighed, impacting sleep and triggering urges to engage in compensatory (including restriction) and self-harm behaviours (Froreich et al., 2020). In the face of this distress, it is not surprising that many clinicians also prefer blind weighing. However, to use fully blind weighing means that the patient cannot learn that their weight is controllable.

Now let's look at the "collaborative" bit. This is the critical component of managing a potentially distressing situation well for the patient, so that it promotes learning and recovery. There are several important steps involved in this collaboration.

(1) The rationale for open collaborative weighing is shared with patient before therapy commences and is presented as a non-negotiable of therapy. The use of firm empathy is required, where the clinician acknowledges the initial high level of distress that might be expressed by the patient, but asks them to consider the benefits of such an approach.

(2) The patient has agreed that weighing only happens in session as a therapeutic task, and not to weigh themselves outside of session. Self-weighing outside the session usually represents a safety behaviour that will contribute to a growth in anxiety and weight preoccupation, interfering with therapeutic changes in eating.

(3) Weight is taken at the point in the session *after* discussing what the patient has eaten, after stressing the changes made, and after asking for their prediction of any weight gain.

(4) Overall, we consider the most transformative aspect of the open weighing to be plotting weight and body mass index trajectories over time on a "predictive weight chart" (see section 7.4, and Figure 7.2), which is shared with the patient in each session. In other words, looking at the number on the electronic scale is not required, as it is carried over to the graph and then discussed between the clinician and the patient. So, if the clinician is concerned that the "number on the scale" approach would be unhelpfully triggering of rumination over the session, particularly in patients who have OCD or are neurodivergent, then the openness of weighing can be ensured when we track weight on the chart instead. However, as the patient moves through CBT-AN-20, we should work with them towards being able to look at their weight on the scales, to enable them to do so following the therapy sessions and beyond follow-up.

(5) The discussion over the chart examines discrepancies between the prediction and the reality, and what such discrepancies mean. In this discussion, the clinician shows curiosity and works collaboratively with the patient to make sense of what has been observed. For example, the idea of uncontrollable weight gain can be questioned:

Clinician: "OK, this is really interesting. You described the last week as the being the first time in a while that you ate six times over the day at regular intervals, and you estimated that you ate twice as much as you normally do. So, you predicted you had gained 2kg (4lb). What we are seeing is that your weight actually decreased by 0.3kg (0.5lb). Not a huge change, but definitely not the big weight gain that you expected".

Patient: "How can that be? Are you sure the scales are correct?"

Clinician: "Do you remember what we discussed previously, about how hard it is to gain weight, even when you are at such a low weight? Can you remember the reasons for this?"

Patient: "Yes, you said that when I eat more, my metabolism would get more efficient".

Clinician: "Exactly. In the initial stages of eating more, your body gets more efficient at using the energy in the food and distributing it around to all the major organs that have been crying out for nutrition for some while – like the brain, the heart, and kidneys".

Patient: "I still think it is a bit of a fluke ... my extra eating will catch up with me next week, I bet".

Clinician: "That's a prediction that could be right or it could be wrong. That is why we will keep examining your weight trajectory over each session, so you know exactly what happens as you eat more. *In this way, you are in the driver's seat, not the anorexia nervosa.* Eventually, though, we do need the extra eating to catch up with you, to get you back to a body mass index that supports your nutritional health. We will just need to make sure that you gain that weight in a controllable way. Can we discuss a further increase to your nutritional intake this week that keeps us on track for that goal, given the evidence at the moment suggests that this is going to be a longer road than you predicted?"

We note that there are three skills illustrated in this dialogue that are used by only around six out of every ten clinicians delivering CBT for eating disorders, as reported by their patients (Cowdrey & Waller, 2015) – weekly weighing, introduction of regular eating, and exploration of beliefs about weight and eating. Clearly, clinicians find these matters challenging to address in therapy. We would all prefer to be talking about other things. We have found, however, that unless these issues are tackled consistently and collaboratively over therapy, the possibility for beneficial change over therapy decreases sharply.

4.7 Monitoring progress and outcomes

Monitoring progress and outcomes with the patient requires skill and competence on the part of the clinician. Patients with anorexia nervosa tend to struggle to be consistently and appropriately concerned about the effects of their undereating. We can easily find ourselves falling into the trap of colluding with the eating disorder by participating in a shared denial of the pressing need to make significant dietary change or celebrating very minor changes – such as eating half a banana rather than a quarter on a single occasion. Instead, our aim is to help the patient to become and/or remain sufficiently concerned about the impact of anorexia nervosa to continue with the ongoing task of recovery, and to encourage them with positive feedback about positive changes made. Explicit monitoring of progress supports this potentially challenging process, enhanced by the stance of firm empathy and by supervision or consultation from a clinician who understands eating disorders and the CBT-AN-20 approach.

The meta-competence of collaboratively measuring and reviewing symptoms was described in Section 3.5. In the present section, we stress what skills the clinician needs to make this happen in CBT-AN-20. Clearly, collaborative weighing (Section 4.6) and food records (Chapter 7) are critical examples of monitoring the patient's progress. However, we also monitor progress in CBT-AN-20 using session-by-session self-report measures. This ensures that we can collaborate openly with the patient throughout, based around a shared understanding of their mood, cognitions, and behaviours. We recommend the following minimum data set to be able to do well in therapy:

- Weekly – open weighing; eating disorder attitudes and behaviours (ED-15);
- At the outset of therapy, Session 6, Session 12, end of therapy, and all follow-ups – the above, plus height (in case of growth influencing apparent BMI,

in younger cases); eating attitudes (EDE-Q-7); depression (PHQ-9); anxiety (GAD-7); therapeutic alliance (WAI-SR); and self-efficacy (GSE).

The completed measures can be handed over on paper at the start of the session or submitted online if the local system supports that. Entering them into the Therapy Tracker (see website) can provide an illustration of progress that is very engaging for the patient and clinician alike. Whatever the case, we recommend discussing these measures with the patient when you meet them, so that you can review progress – what is working, what is not – and plan accordingly. Such immediate review promotes shared understanding and has benefits in terms of better outcomes (e.g., De Jong et al., 2021). The Session 6 and Session 12 measures should be used in the session to underpin the main review of progress points (see Section 7.7), to determine the benefits to date or to enhance engagement in change.

4.8   Stressing early change

In Section 3.5, we discussed the extremely strong evidence that early change in therapy, in the first 8–12 sessions, is the best predictor of a good outcome for the patient. In anorexia nervosa, this early change must invariably be assessed by weight increase. No other indicator has such strong predictive value – not stated motivation, chronicity, comorbidity, or the severity of the eating disorder psychopathology. This is important knowledge, to be shared openly and often with the patient, along with a collaborative discussion on how to kick-start the weight gain early in therapy. The use of the review between sessions 6 and 8, along with the countdown built into each preceding session and the use of the predictive weight chart, keeps this goal in focus for both the patient and clinician over the early stage of therapy.

4.9   Working with the anorexic voice

In recent years there has been a growing interest in the concept of the internal "anorexic voice" and its potential role in the development and maintenance of anorexia nervosa (Pugh, 2016; Pugh & Waller, 2017). We find that it is not uncommon for patients to refer to having an "anorexic part" or an "anorexic voice" when talking about their illness, and it can be helpful to think about this as one "mode" or "part" of their internal self, based on Beck's (1996) cognitive theory of personality modes (see below). For some, such a cognitive mode will take the form of a voice, whilst others find it more helpful to conceptualise an image of their eating disorder. The most important thing here is to go with what is most meaningful to the patient. A few patients find the "anorexic voice" so much a part of them that they do not find it easy to identify it as a part of their thinking, though we find that continuing to talk to the patient about it can result in recognition after a few sessions. Appendix A.13 can help to explain the "anorexic voice" to the patient.

The conceptualisation of the mind as consisting of multiple "modes" or "inner voices" has been well documented in the personality literature (e.g., Rowan, 1990). We find it helpful to draw on Beck's concept of modes as the basis of personality. Beck describes such modes as networks of cognitive, affective, motivational, and behavioural components, which together form integrated parts of personality (Beck, 1996). We all have many such modes within us – for example, our "social" mode might be dominant when out with friends, our "compassionate" mode might be activated by the need to help others, and our "focused" mode might be dominant when completing study or work tasks. In healthy individuals, these modes are likely to be integrated and intercommunicative, working together to process information from the outside world in a balanced way.

However, in those with anorexia nervosa, the "anorexic voice" or "restrictive mode" disrupts the relationships between the other healthier parts of the self, becoming the dominant information processing mode over time. This dominance makes it hard for other parts to have a voice, integrate, and thrive. For example, it might be hard to be in "social" mode and connect in friendships/relationships when suffering the physical effects of starvation or when the "anorexic voice" is constantly saying "You're fat". We often talk about the "anorexic voice" as being one element of the self that is struggling for control and domination over other modes. We find that it is important *not* to externalise the "anorexic voice" as this risks the patient viewing their illness as being something done to them that they are powerless to change (Vitousek, 2005). To avoid this, we talk about the "anorexic voice" as representing part of the patient's own self, rather than as being a discrete external entity (Mountford & Waller, 2006).

4.9.1   The changing nature of the "anorexic voice"

Within eating disorders, evidence suggests a complex relationship between the "anorexic voice" and the individual, whereby the voice is viewed as both protective and comforting, but also as controlling and intrusive (Tragantzopoulou et al., 2024). In the early stages of the illness, the "anorexic voice" is commonly seen as a solution – a way of addressing perceived difficulties related to self-worth, vulnerability, trauma, life transitions, or intolerable emotions. This drives a positive feedback loop, the individual becoming increasingly dependent on the "anorexic voice" as a way of feeling good about themselves and coping with daily life. However, over time the relationship becomes fraught – the "anorexic voice" becomes more hostile, critical, and omnipotent. Whilst initially offering a solution to the individual's problems, the "anorexic voice" ultimately comes to perpetuate the underlying difficulties by demanding increasing levels of disordered eating, which in turn makes it almost impossible for underlying issues to ever be resolved. Pugh (2020) summarises how the experience of the eating disorder "voice" or "self" [EDV/S] (referred to in CBT-AN-20 as "the anorexic voice") can pass through stages over time (Table 4.3).

Table 4.3 Time course of the "anorexic voice" (adapted from Pugh, 2020)

Stage	Description
1. Direction	The "anorexic voice" initially fulfils positive functions. Engaging with the voice is mainly positive, although contingent upon compliance, resulting in attachment. Internal dialogues are generally pleasant, and motivation to change the relationship is often low. Eating disorder symptoms start to emerge.
2. Domination	The "anorexic voice" is experienced as increasingly hostile and controlling. Internal dialogues are increasingly hierarchical, characterised by criticism, coercion, and control. The "anorexic voice" becomes increasingly powerful and dominant. Eating disorder symptoms escalate, although motivation to change may still remain low.
3. Disempowerment	The "anorexic voice" is experienced as punitive and overwhelming. The voice dominates internal dialogues and undermines self-esteem and self-efficacy. Individuals are more motivated to change their relationship with the "anorexic voice" but may doubt their ability to do so. Eating disorder symptoms may continue to worsen.
4. Defiance	Individuals begin to oppose the "anorexic voice". Power differentials begin to shift, generating strong push back from the voice. Internal dialogues are argumentative. Eating disorder symptoms may begin to improve, although setbacks and periods of disempowerment still occur (see stage 3).
5. Deliverance	The "anorexic voice" is weakened, the power differential now favouring the individual. Individuals are better able to "step back" from the "anorexic voice". More adaptive internal voices begin to emerge. Eating disorder symptoms continue to improve.
6. Disquiet	The strength of the "anorexic voice" weakens over time. Recovery from the eating disorder may be accompanied by feelings of anxiety or loss; individuals are sensitive to the voice returning and may miss its positive aspects. Intermittent "skirmishes" with the "anorexic voice" can occur.

4.9.2 Treatment targets when working with the "anorexic voice"

There are several possible treatment targets when working with the "anorexic voice". As mentioned in Chapter 3, this is a clinical technique that can be used throughout the CBT-AN-20 protocol. Targets might include building understanding of the functions of the eating disorder and identifying healthier ways to get these needs met; building motivation to change one's relationship with the "anorexic voice"; actively working to reduce the biological consequences (e.g., starvation) of the eating disorder through improving nutritional intake; and developing more assertive and adaptive ways of responding to the eating disorder (Pugh, 2020).

4.9.3   *Working with the "anorexic voice" using imagery, expressive writing, and dialogue-based methods*

We suggest using imagery-based methods (Mountford & Waller, 2006), expressive writing (Pennebaker, 1997), and dialogue-based methods such as chair work (Chua et al., 2022; Pugh, 2018; 2019). Imagery-based methods can support the patient in getting to know their eating disorder, and it can be helpful to invite the patient to consider generating an image or drawing of their eating disorder, thinking about its size, colour, appearance, tone of voice, personality, and motivations. While for some patients this will take the form of a "human-like" character, others might hold a more abstract image or voice in mind. A conversation with a patient in the initial stages of treatment might go as follows:

Clinician: "I'm aware that during your last session you spoke about your eating disorder as being like a voice in your head. It's not uncommon for people who develop anorexia nervosa to experience their illness in this way – it can feel like it has become part of their self-identity. Sometimes it can be helpful to think about our self-identity as being made up of many different parts, for example a social part, a kind part, a hard-working part, etc. We all have many different parts within us, and this is all really normal. Does that make sense?"

Patient: "Yes, but I think there is only one part in me and that's my eating disorder".

Clinician: "Sometimes, when the 'anorexic voice' gets really loud, it can feel like all the other parts have got lost, but I'm sure they are in there somewhere and I'm sure finding them will be an important part of your recovery. But I wonder if it would helpful if we started by spending some time getting to know the eating disorder part of you?"

Patient: "I think that would be really helpful. It just goes on and on in my head and never stops".

Clinician: "Can you tell me a bit about how you experience your anorexic voice?"

Patient: "I just have a raging voice in my head that constantly shouts at me, telling me I need to eat less. I have to calorie count everything and sometimes it's impossible to make decisions about what to eat. I just get so anxious about making the wrong choice. If I don't do what it says, I just feel terrible. It makes me feel awful, like I've totally failed".

Clinician: "That sounds really difficult, like it has a complete grip on you. It sounds very demanding and cruel, is it always like this?"

Patient: "Yea, sometimes I feel like I'm drowning, and I can't breathe. It's exhausting. If I ever try and ignore it, it just gets louder".

Clinician: "Sometimes our 'inner voices' or 'parts' can reflect our past experiences, almost like we've internalised someone or something from our past. Have you ever considered that?"

Patient: "Sometimes. I grew up in a family where doing well was really valued, my sister was so much more academic and sporty then me. Growing up, I constantly felt that I needed to prove myself, to be a certain way to be good enough. School was horrible. I was ostracised by my friends and a few of the boys bullied me about how I looked. So critical and negative. I felt completely unimportant and worthless. I just wanted to feel accepted and like I mattered".

Clinician: "I wonder whether some of those difficult earlier experiences have fed into your 'anorexic voice'?"

Patient: "I think so, I sometimes think I can still hear those boys shouting at me about how horrible I looked".

Clinician: "When you first noticed your 'anorexic voice', what purpose do you think it was trying to serve in your life?"

Patient: "To be honest, when it all first started, I think it was trying to help me. In the beginning it was amazing. The more I controlled my eating, the better I felt. It made me feel accepted, like I was finally good at something. I was the best. And it was always there, completely dependable".

Clinician: "It sounds as though initially it was really helpful, like a reliable friend. Life was hard – you constantly felt second best at home, and you had some difficult experiences at school, all of which feel like they had a huge impact on your self-esteem. Your eating disorder made you feel good about yourself, and feeling good about ourselves is a normal human need. You found a way to make it all feel better".

Patient: "Yes, it was that simple. I loved it".

Clinician: "Have things changed over time? What do you think your 'anorexic voice' wants for you now?"

Patient: "Over the past few years it has changed. It's got nastier, more critical and demanding. As I said earlier, it just feels relentless now, like I have no choice. Sometimes I hate it, but I also feel like I just can't let go. I don't know who I would be without it".

Clinician: "It sounds as though something that started as a solution has become the problem. It also feels that over time the eating disorder part of you has become more dominant and critical, less friendly. I wonder if the other parts of you have suffered as a result of this. How are the studies going?"

Patient: "It's tough. I feel tired all the time. It's hard to concentrate, and I feel like I have to constantly make excuses about why I can't go for coffee or lunch after lectures with others from my course. I can't face eating out, but I feel like it's so rude not to go. I think they know I lie, and I just feel awful about that as well".

Clinician: "It sounds like the eating disorder has become increasingly destructive, stopping you from doing many of the things in life that you enjoy. It also seems like it has started making you behave in a way that isn't really in line with your values, which just makes you feel even worse. At the start it was all positive – it made you feel good about being you, but it doesn't seem to work anymore. From listening to you, it feels like it's now completely controlling you. I wonder whether part of recovery is about learning to stand up to the 'anorexic voice' and looking at different ways in which you can feel good about yourself. Perhaps reconnecting with the other parts in you?"

Patient: "I love that idea and just thinking about it makes me feel excited but then I just think, I don't know if I can do this".

Clinician: "Recovery takes time and is hard work, there's no doubt about that. But from listening to you I can hear that there are strengths within you that the eating disorder has either taken advantage of, such as your determination, or has cut you off from, such as the social part of you that wants to go out with friends and have fun. I wonder whether through treatment you can start to stand up to your 'anorexic voice' and re-connect with your strength and interests, so that you can start living your life the way you want to, not the way your illness dictates?"

Patient: "The thought of standing up to it terrifies me, but I just want to get my life back".

Sometimes it can be helpful to draw on specific interview techniques, such as chair work, when exploring the "anorexic voice". A shortened version of the *Dialogical Interview Schedule for Eating Disorders* (DIS-ED, Pugh, 2019) is given below in Table 4.4 (see Appendix A.14 for a full version). More recently, chair work has

Table 4.4 Shortened version of the *Dialogical Interview Schedule for Eating Disorders* (DIS-ED, Pugh, 2019), adapted for the "anorexic voice" specifically

It can be helpful to think of interviewing the eating disorder voice as being like getting to know an interesting stranger at a party. Individuals are encouraged to discuss any questions or concerns about the process before the interview begins.   *Clinician: Shall I begin by explaining what we're going to do in a bit more detail?*   *Research suggests that many individuals experience an internal eating disorder voice. Other individuals describe experiencing not so much a voice, but rather a particular experience of themselves linked to their eating disorder – what we might call their "anorexic self" or "anorexic part". Internal voices and the experience of being made up of different selves, parts, or subpersonalities is very normal. The aim of this interview is to simply get to know your "anorexic voice" or "anorexic self" better. We can do this by asking your "anorexic voice" some questions. There are no right or wrong answers to these questions.*   *First, I will ask you some very general questions about your experiences of your "anorexic voice". Afterwards, I will ask you to change seats and to speak from the perspective of your "anorexic voice". Last of all, I will ask you to return to your origin seat and reflect on what your "anorexic voice" has said. Would you like to give it a try?*
PHASE ONE: Exploring experiences of the "anorexic voice"
Would it be ok if we begin by talking a little about your "anorexic voice"?   **Example interview question:**   • *Tell me about your experience of your "anorexic voice". What is it like?*
PHASE TWO – Dialogue with the "anorexic voice"
This involves the client speaking from the perspective of their "anorexic voice". Dialogues with the "anorexic voice" can be either direct (inviting the individual to change seats and speak as their "anorexic voice") or indirect (inviting the client to convey, in the third person, what the "anorexic voice" is saying).

(Continued)

Table 4.4 (Continued)

DIRECT DIALOGUE: *If you feel ready, I'd like to speak with your "anorexic voice" for a little while. All you have to do is change seats and speak as that part of yourself. Does that sound ok?*

INDIRECT DIALOGUE: *I'd like to ask your "anorexic voice" some questions. When I do, I'd like you to relay these questions to your "anorexic voice" and to let me know how it responds.* Irrespective of whether dialogue is direct or indirect, the client is asked to place a chair representing the "anorexic voice" somewhere in the room which feels appropriate and comfortable.

Before we begin, is there anything in particular that you would like me to ask your "anorexic voice" or things you'd like to know?

Sample interview questions for the "anorexic voice":
- *Tell me a bit about yourself. What's your role in this person's life? What do you do? (Function)*
- *What situations tend to bring you out? (Content)*
- *How about when it comes to eating?*
- *How about when it comes to the way this individual looks or how much they weigh?*
- *What do you tend to say in situations like that? (Content)*
- *When did you first come into this person's life? (Origins)*
- *What were your reasons for becoming a part of their life at that time? (Origins)*
- *Are you aware of any difficulties you might be causing this individual? (Relationship)*
- *Why do you do this for this person? (Intent)*
- *What are your fears and concerns about this person's shape/weight/eating? (Underlying concerns).*
- *What you think might happen if you weren't a part of this person's life? (Underlying concerns).*

PHASE THREE – Decentring from the "anorexic voice"

I'd like you to return to your original chair now. As best you can, leave your "anorexic voice" in the empty seat and connect with yourself again as you change chairs. [Individual moves seats]. Let's take a moment to separate from your "anorexic voice" by bringing attention to the breath. Find a rate of breathing that feels calm, soothing, and grounded. Do you feel a little more separated from that side of your self?

I'd now like to provide my understanding of what I have heard your "anorexic voice" share with us …

PHASE FOUR – Reflecting on the dialogical process

The final part provides an opportunity to reflect on the dialogue and their impressions of the "anorexic voice".

Sample interview questions:
- *What do you make of what the "anorexic voice" has said?*
- *What do you make of the "anorexic voice's" intentions/what the "anorexic voice" wants for you?*
- *How does that fit with what you want for yourself?*
- *Is there anything you would like the "anorexic voice" to know or understand?*
- *Is there anything you want or need from the "anorexic voice"?*

Adapted with permission and in collaboration with Matt Pugh, and based on Pugh, M. (2019). Dialogical Interview Schedule for Eating Disorders. Unpublished manuscript. Retrieved from: www.chairwork.co.uk/resources.

also been modified for online use, with suggested adaptions including introducing additional chairs into either the patient's space or the therapist's space or inviting the patient to re-position their seat as they move to speak from different parts of the self (e.g., when speaking as the "anorexic voice"). Moving around the fixed position of the patient's computer screen also allows for differentiation, the patient shifting their chair from one side of the screen to enact the "anorexic voice" before returning to the centre point. Alternatively, rather than moving seat, the patient might choose to move out and back into the frame of their webcam to indicate that they are changing role. Using the whiteboard function to depict different parts of self, using shape and size, or moving to different positions in the room within view of the webcam are also ways in which chair work can be adapted for online delivery (see Pugh & Bell, 2020 for further detail regarding tele-chair work).

Alongside dialoguing during sessions, we also encourage patients to complete tasks between sessions that will help them get to know their "anorexic voice". This might include keeping a reflective journal, holding some of the following questions in mind: When is it present? What makes it speak? What does it say – does it use any common phrases? What is it promising, and does it deliver? What is the need your eating disorder is trying to fulfil, and are there other options that might fulfil that need? Therapeutic writing (Pennebaker, 1997) between sessions can also help to reinforce conversations that occur during therapy. Other examples might include writing a letter to "Anorexia, my Friend" and "Anorexia, my Enemy" (Serpell et al., 1999) to support motivational and formulation work, or writing a "goodbye letter to my anorexia". Sharing these letters during therapy sessions can further strengthen their value. The overall aim here is to support the patient to better understand their relationship with their "anorexic voice" and to begin to see it as a loud voice but not the *only* voice. As clinicians, we can support this process further by drawing on other parts of self to support change, again using dialogue methods. This approach is shown in the example below:

Clinician: "I know that last session we agreed that you would start to include two snacks in your meal plan. I'm interested to hear how that has gone over the past week?"

Patient: "Well, after the session I went to the shop, but I just couldn't decide what to buy. My 'anorexic voice' was screaming at me, telling me how dare I eat more. It kept telling me that every snack I picked was too much. In the end I left with nothing".

Clinician: "It sounds as though your eating disorder was pretty angry with you?"

Patient: "It was in a complete rage. I just felt so crushed. It kept telling me I was lazy and pathetic; that I should be more self-disciplined. How would I ever succeed in life if I gained weight? I feel like recovery is something I really want, but every time I make a change it comes down so hard on me. It just makes me hate myself".

Clinician: "That sounds like a really difficult place to be, I can really hear how powerful and critical your eating disorder voice can be. Do you remember how we recently talked about all the other parts of you, many of which the anorexia has crushed or disconnected you from?"

Patient: "Yes, I think so".

Clinician: "I'm just going to pull out the drawing you did recently. Can you see, we put 'This is me' in the middle of the page and acknowledged that while anorexia is present, over here, there is so much more to you than your eating disorder. You were able to stand back and notice some of the other parts of you. You laughed when thinking about how competitive and determined you can be, and how you can stubbornly stick to a task even when the going gets tough and everyone else has given up! We also reflected on the fact that there is a fledgling part of you that wants to look after yourself – it wants to be kinder and more compassionate towards yourself, almost like a healthier part within you. I wonder whether we need to draw on these other parts to help give you the strength to stand up to your eating disorder. If you'd taken these parts to the shop, what would they have said to your 'anorexic voice'?"

Patient: "This feels weird, but I think the compassionate part would have said, 'Go on, it's OK to look after yourself, when you feel tired and hungry, that's your body trying to tell you it needs some food'".

Clinician: "And could any of the other parts join the conversation? What would they be saying?"

Patient: "Ummm, I think the determined part of me would be saying 'You can do it, just do it, you know anorexia just makes you feel worse, it's time to look after yourself, move on'".

Clinician: "And when the 'anorexic voice' pushes back, how might they respond?"

Patient: "Well, my feisty part has popped up now and its saying to my eating disorder, 'Hang on a minute, you don't have the right to rule here any longer, you're not in charge'. And self-care is chipping in again, telling me it really is okay to increase my intake because it will make me feel better and it won't be enough to make my weight shoot up – it's telling me to remember what we've discussed about how weight change works".

Clinician: "I wonder if we can turn this into an experiment? It sounds like one of the things your 'anorexic voice' keeps telling you is that if you increase your meal plan as we've discussed, your weight will shoot up, whilst the 'self-care' part is telling you that this isn't enough to make your weight change uncontrollably, but it might help you to start feeling a bit better physically. Is that how it feels?"

Patient: "Yes, the eating disorder feels like the stronger one though. I need the other parts to remind me that it's okay to look after myself. The self-care part of me is whispering … 'It's important to look after myself, your friends want you to get better too, they don't care about your size'. From reading the worksheets on how starvation impacts my brain and what we discussed about how weight changes, I know that putting in the snacks is unlikely to make me balloon. I just need to give it a go".

Clinician: "It sounds like drawing on these other parts could help you to start to stand up to your eating disorder, giving you a chance to discover the truth. Over the next week, if there are times when you find it hard to keep to your meal plan, how about stepping back from your 'anorexic voice' and asking yourself some of these questions: What does the 'self-care' part of me say I should do right now? Can my determined part help? Will obeying the voice help me to get better? What's my real need here? Do I need to ask for help from anyone? I know you're keen on journalling and it might be helpful to note and celebrate any times when the healthier parts of you win – no matter how big or small they are to begin with, noticing these times will help these parts to gain strength and stand back up in your life".

As we can see, dialoguing with the "anorexic voice" can be a useful clinical tool to building understanding, whilst also creating some dissonance between the patient and their illness. It can also be a powerful way to embed the idea that whilst the "anorexic voice" is the loudest voice, it is not the *only* voice, promoting the idea of choice – the patient can choose to listen to and behave in line with other, healthier parts of themselves. Sometimes we talk about how the eating disorder has turned down the volume of these other parts and they will need time and nurturance to regain their strength and positions. We also find that it can be helpful to return to therapeutic writing and dialoguing with the "anorexic voice" towards the end of treatment as this can be a powerful way of reflecting on progress made, as well as strengthening confidence in recovery. This value is shown below:

Clinician: "In last week's session we agreed that writing a 'good-bye letter to my anorexia' might be helpful for you. I know that writing is something you enjoy and I'm curious to hear how you got on with that?"

Patient: "Well, I was surprised at how emotional I found it".

Clinician: "How would you feel about sharing the letter with me today?"

Patient: "Yes, I don't mind. This is what I wrote: 'Dear Anorexia, You've served your purpose, my only regret is that we stuck together for so long. And I feel so sad about that. For years I thought I was happy having you in my life, but I wasn't really. I thought I needed you to feel acceptable, but I didn't, not really. I thought you were part of me – having you made me who I was, but I've realised that just wasn't true. I'm happier now that you've gone. I don't hear your voice anymore, not when I'm eating, not when I look at myself, and that's because you no longer serve any purpose in my life. Not eating used to make me feel in control, but now when life is stressful, I can think about why and just focus on that. Now that you've gone, I feel more in control. I no longer live in fear – I can eat more freely and have more choice. If I want to eat out with friends, I can. I can be kinder to myself. I can look in the mirror and know the changes I see are positive. I don't need to be critical and horrible to myself anymore, I'm just looking after myself and that's okay. I know that my family and friends would rather see me as happy and healthy. I feel like this is the real me, and I'm okay with that. You've served your purpose, you were good in the beginning, you really helped me out and part of me wants to thank you in a weird kind of way, but you changed. And now so have I. I feel like I've got my life back and I no longer need you now. It's definitely goodbye from me and I hope I never see you again'".

Clinician: "That's so powerful, I can feel just listening to you that your words come straight from the heart. When you wrote it, did your 'anorexic voice' have anything to say in response?"

Patient: "No, it was completely silent".

In line with findings from the evidence base (e.g. Jenkins & Ogden, 2012; Hormoz, Pugh, & Waller, 2019), we find that working with patients to understand and then change the way they relate and respond to their eating disorder voice can be a powerful way to support active change and recovery.

4.10 Working with temperament and common cognitive patterns

Perfectionism, avoidance of failure, self-criticism, shame, intolerance of uncertainty, harm avoidance, and inflexible and overly detailed thinking styles are often key in the formulation of anorexia nervosa (as detailed in Chapters 2 and 5), making them important targets to address when treating patients with CBT-AN-20. Even in the absence of comorbid obsessive-compulsive disorder or obsessive-compulsive personality, patients can exhibit repetitive, ritualistic behaviours in the pursuit of perfectionistic all-or-nothing standards. Perfectionism can also be associated with procrastination or avoiding any task that might end in perceived failure. It has been suggested that self-criticism is the active harmful element of perfectionism – a focus on perceived failure and a tendency to overlook and undervalue things done well. This selective attention can lead to a sense of defectiveness and shame. Intolerance of uncertainty leads to an over-reliance on guarantees in life and difficulty coping with unpredictability. Living a highly structured and ordered life and following rules can help our patients manage this intolerance. Harm avoidance is characterised by excessive worrying, pessimism, and being fearful and doubtful. Avoidance behaviours, including avoidance of food, can be used to reduce anxiety. Difficulty changing responses in the face of changing situations and a focus on detail (e.g., weighing or measuring in small, precise units) has been well-established as a key cognitive style in people with anorexia nervosa (Keegan et al., 2021). These cognitive patterns are typically addressed in Phase 3 of CBT-AN-20 (Chapter 9).

4.10.1   *Obstacles to getting started with assessment and therapy*

It is important to consider how these cognitive patterns manifest as barriers to initiating therapy. They can prevent patients from getting started with making the required dietary changes or completing the food diaries that are essential to CBT-AN-20. For example, the patient might repeatedly abandon their eating or self-monitoring plan when potential signs of failure occur; they might be very anxious about agreeing to commence therapy as they perceive themselves as too defective to do well; and they might utilise too much detail when using the self-monitoring and experience difficulty in recognising bigger picture patterns. As noted in Chapter 3, in these cases it is necessary to address these cognitive patterns and their consequences earlier on. Indeed, if there are early signs of such a slow start (e.g., lack of early change in previous therapies), then use of single-session interventions between assessment and Session 1 should be considered (see Table 4.2).

In practice, even when incorporated into the formulation early, the best course of action is simply to name and acknowledge the important role of the cognitive pattern(s) in the patient's anorexia nervosa, citing specific instances across different events observed in therapy, reassuring the patient that this topic will be returned to once the vital task of getting started with weight restoration is underway, unless it appears to get in the way of getting started. If this is the case, we recommend some psychoeducation (see Appendix A.5) and consideration of brief interventions focused on the obstacle with the view to increasing the patient's constructive engagement with therapy (see Appendix C). It may also be helpful to bring in significant others to support active change (see Sections 3.7 and 4.16).

4.10.2   *Addressing cognitive patterns to facilitate change during active therapy*

As detailed in Chapter 9, some patients who are not progressing can benefit from single-session interventions or shorter online interventions (interactive or static) to help challenge unhelpful cognitive styles (See Appendix.C). Core beliefs related to these cognitive patterns can also be addressed within the content of CBT-AN-20 sessions. This can be achieved in a variety of ways, including behavioural experiments (Chapter 8); chair work to support dialogue with the "anorexic voice" (e.g., Pugh, 2018) (Section 4.9); imagery rescripting (Section 4.13 and Chapter 9); and positive data logs (Chapter 9). Each can reinforce more helpful beliefs (e.g., "I am good enough"; "Most mistakes don't matter"). A vital CBT technique for illustrating the all-or-nothing thinking characteristic of many of these cognitive patterns, along with identification of a more sustainable middle way, is continuum thinking. Continua can be used in a variety of ways, which can involve a broad or targeted approach. We illustrate this with the example of perfectionism, below:

CONTINUUM THINKING APPLIED TO PERFECTIONISM

We sometimes start with a broad view of perfectionism, before potentially homing in on more specific targets. Using continua to illustrate and address the self-defeating nature of unrelenting, perfectionistic standards, we find it useful to draw a horizontal line across a landscape piece of paper, marking "0% = success/total failure" at the start of the line, and "100% = achievement" at the other end. Next, we invite the patient to reflect on what achievement or success means to them and invite them to list all their personal rules/standards for determining what would "count" as a valuable achievement, noting these under the corresponding part of the continuum (typically stating that only "100 % achievement" counts for anything). The aim is to identify perfectionism in as many domains of life as possible.

We might prompt our patients with questions such as those listed below, with each assessed on a corresponding continuum (with extreme end points):

- What are your requirements for determining success in school (or at work)?
- What does it mean to be a good friend/partner/parent?
- What do you consider a healthy diet to be?
- What would achievement as a runner/dancing/in yoga/at the gym/etc. look like to you?
- What would successful control of your body weight/shape look like?
- What do you consider to be the ideal way to feel about your body?

Having identified the broad range of unrelenting standards our patient is striving for, our aim is to validate just how exhausting (and ultimately impossible) it is to attempt to achieve all of these standards. We might warmly ask our patients: "OK, so as you find yourself to be human, and don't achieve one or even all of these standards, how do you evaluate yourself then? Do you then put yourself at 95% success, or do you find yourself being harsher than that?" Patients will inevitably indicate that their self-evaluation will sit at the "failure" end of the continuum. We might invite the patient to draw a vertical line cutting across the continuum, to indicate their personal "cut-off" for what counts as failure or success. We encourage the patient to recognise their dichotomous, all-or-nothing approach to achievement (where anything short of 100% typically equates to failure), prompting them to consider what actual total failure in each of the identified areas would really look like, and how this compares to where their actual capability might be. We also seek to normalise the everyday experience of mini-failures, expressing interest in whether the patient or anyone they know has ever failed at anything (driving tests, exams, relationships, etc.) and whether and how they survived this.

Of course, failure is upsetting, and some of our patients might have been treated harshly for failures of the past. It is therefore essential to support them in accurately evaluating the safety of failure in their current lives, in their current contexts, and with their current supports. Next, we elicit a detailed account of all the ways in which the patient has perhaps understandably *attempted* to avoid failure (avoidance and scrutiny of performance evaluation, their body, food, and relationships), enquiring about the helpfulness and consequences of these behaviours. We prompt the patient to consider how this avoidance and scrutiny affect their actual performance. We encourage them to identify what middle-ground, "good enough", reasonable, and sustainable standards might entail. As one athletic patient put it: "If I lower the bar, I might *actually* jump it, instead of simply beating myself up and hiding away in bed". Finally, we encourage the patient to begin putting into practice behaviours that are consistent with these fairer, more flexible standards. A similar continuum approach can be taken to re-evaluate perfectionist standards in one particular domain, allowing for a more detailed, zoomed-in approach.

Like other manifestations of perfectionism, compulsive exercise tends to serve the function of avoiding emotion and can be particularly relevant to anorexia nervosa. Compulsive exercise is often related to guilt, can be self-punishing in nature, and has similarities with restriction in that it involves denial and overriding of the body's needs (in this case, the need for rest and repair). Compulsive exercise compounds the physical risk from other eating disorder behaviours, and when linked to perfectionism can lead to a sense of the exercise also never quite feeling like enough. On commencing CBT-AN-20, we recommend contracting that patients should not increase their exercise and advise that part of CBT-AN-20 will involve navigating a new, individualised, healthy approach to exercise (e.g., building in flexibility, sociability, rest, and fun).

We also find it useful to consider with the patient how aspects of the cognitive pattern can be harnessed as a strength – for example, redirecting energy to achieving excellence rather than being perfect. It is important to differentiate perfectionistic strivings from pursuing high standards and excellence, where the latter is not intrinsically unhelpful. It is the *way* these high standards are approached and the *reaction* to failing to meet those standards that becomes unhelpful. When self-evaluation is overly dependent on striving and achievement, adverse reactions can include feeling more afraid to fail than most people, being self-critical, and worrying so much about doing something imperfectly that they become immobilised. Being somewhat intolerant of uncertainty and organising a life that has some predictability is also good for mental health, if there is plenty of space left for exploring the "roads less travelled" and taking up spontaneous opportunities on a regular basis. Having an eye for detail can be a very good thing in some contexts, say when building a bridge or editing a manuscript, or when redirecting focus away from self-criticism to the detail of what is happening every day that tells the person they are good enough. Using the "Make your temperament work for you" worksheet (Appendix A.5) with the patient can support this material well.

4.11   Exposure therapy

Exposure therapy (more properly, exposure with response prevention) is one of the most effective methods for addressing anxiety-based disorders, including the eating disorders. Indeed, exposure therapy is central to CBT for eating disorders, regardless of whether the individual is underweight or not. In this manual, we will address its role in treating anorexia nervosa. (Its use in non-underweight eating disorders is detailed in the CBT-T manual.) This section is particularly important for understanding the skills outlined in parts of Chapters 7, 8, 10, and 12, where exposure is widely used in CBT-AN-20.

4.11.1   The principles of exposure therapy

Anxiety-based disorders involve four major features. The *emotional* experience is one of fear of a negative outcome. In the case of anorexia nervosa, the fear is commonly of weight gain, loss of control of eating, seeing one's own body, and so on. The *cognitive* element is related to uncertainty and vulnerability (e.g., "What if that slice of cake makes me gain 2kg/5lb?"; "How do I know that the people at work don't think that I look huge?"), leaving the person unsure as to whether they will lose relationships, be injured, be attacked, and so on. The *physiological* element is based on autonomic nervous system reactions to threat, such as muscle tension, sweating, heart-rate acceleration, and urges to vomit and defecate (to allow blood to go to the muscles when needed, rather than being dedicated to digestion). Such biological reactions can be mistakenly seen as evidence of fullness (tense abdomen, rather than full stomach), resulting in loss of desire to eat. Finally, the *behavioural* manifestation of anxiety is seen in the use of avoidance and safety behaviours (e.g., refuse food; avoid emotional arousal; refuse to be weighed openly; avoid seeing one's own appearance by covering up one's body).

Of course, anxiety is a natural, adaptive response to threat, provoking us to fight, flee, or freeze, according to the nature of the threat. It becomes maladaptive when we overestimate the threat element and, in turn, have an inappropriately strong anxiety-driven response. For example, in panic disorder, that overestimation might be the belief that the physiological effects (e.g., faster heart rate) are more meaningful than they actually are (e.g., "I am going to have a heart attack"). Then, the use of safety behaviours (e.g., "I ran out of the room with all those people in it, and my heart rate went down") results in erroneous escape learning that simply enhances the overestimation (e.g., "Running away is the only way to stay alive") and precludes opportunities for new learning. (See Appendix A.15 for a psychoeducation handout to help your patient understand anxiety.)

Considering eating disorders, there are multiple ways in which the patient over-estimates threat and uses safety behaviours to escape that threat in the short term, but with the result that the perceived threat becomes even greater. For example, if the patient fears that they have a huge body, they are likely to avoid looking at it or to let others see it (e.g., dressing in baggy clothes; removing mirrors from home; keeping their camera off during online meetings). As with any phobic reaction, that pattern of avoidance becomes self-maintaining and worsens – not having seen their body for a long time does not reduce the patient's belief that it is huge, but it does make the individual more hypervigilant and more careful to avoid exposure to their own body (e.g., not going out for fear of seeing themselves in a shop window; avoiding intimate relationships). That sense of immediate safety (e.g., "At least I do not have to see what I look like") results in feeling even more vulnerable, but at the same time the avoidance also keeps the patient from testing or disconfirming their fears.

4.11.2   Exposure therapy in practice

Exposure therapy addresses anxiety symptoms directly, by encouraging the indi-vidual to expose themselves to the anxious situation (exposure) without avoiding it or running away from it (response prevention). Its immediate effect is to increase anxiety, but if the individual can be supported to tolerate that anxiety for long enough (usually 30-40 minutes), the physiological reaction declines (as the human body has only so much adrenaline with which to run away or fight). This process is known as extinction or habituation. Experiencing that decline in arousal means that the anxiety is reduced, and the individual learns that the feared outcome did not come true. This means that the primary impact of exposure therapy is on fear and anxiety. However, there is a secondary cognitive effect on the person, with the failure of the feared outcome to manifest itself resulting in reduced overestimation of threat. Finally, exposure therapy results in enhanced self-efficacy, as the indi-vidual learns that they can make effective changes in the world and to their life. For example, the patient who adds to their food intake might fear a substantial rise in their weight when they next get on the scales, but when that increase does not hap-pen, their anxiety about eating and being weighed is reduced, and they learn that new foods are not a threat in the way that they had believed. That gives them the confidence to eat other feared foods, and to address other fears (e.g., forming rela-tionships, looking at themselves in mirrors). On the rare occasion that their fears do come to fruition, the patient has the opportunity to practice new healthy coping skills with their clinician, to manage their anxiety in the longer term.

When working with eating disorders, exposure therapy can be used to address a number of impulsive and compulsive behaviours, including restrictive eating, purging, exercise, avoidance of weighing and record-keeping, body avoidance, and blocking of emotional reactions. These approaches will be detailed in Chapters 7, 9, and 10. Given the nature of anorexia nervosa, the balance is more towards reduc-ing compulsive behaviours, such as restrictive eating and compulsive exercise, where the effect of engaging in the behaviours is to prevent the emotional arousal being triggered. However, both impulsive and compulsive presentations should be considered, especially in cases of anorexia nervosa of the binge–purge subtype. Unlike work with those who are non-underweight (e.g., in CBT-T), cue exposure is far less commonly used in anorexia nervosa and will not be addressed here.

4.11.3 Approaches to using exposure

Many clinicians will be aware of the two traditional methods of exposure, helping the individual to overcome their fears of food, emotions, body image, and so on – graded exposure and flooding. (Systematic desensitisation is not considered here, as its emphasis on anxiety reduction means that is it much less effective, taking far longer to reduce anxiety.) *Graded exposure* is the more widely used of the two methods, and involves gradual approaches to the feared object, working through a hierarchy of feared situations leading to the maximum fear (e.g., starting with a quarter slice of bread, then a half-slice, and so on until eating an adequate quantity), each time allowing the fear to subside before moving onto the next step in the hierarchy. The common alternative to graded exposure is *flooding*, where the individual is asked to expose themselves to the feared object all at once, without passing along a hierarchy of fear. This approach is faster than graded exposure but can be more difficult for the patient (and for the clinician – see below). It is more commonly used in eating disorders where there is no way of gradually approaching the feared object – particularly in mirror exposure (see Section 10.8.2).

Over the past 15–20 years, there has been an important development in the field of exposure. In the anxiety disorders, there has been a shift towards adopting the *inhibitory learning* model of exposure – an innovation that has been taken up in the field of eating disorders (e.g., Cardi et al., 2019; Reilly et al., 2017; Waller et al., 2019). In this model, the emphasis shifts away from unlearning fear gradually, on a stimulus-by-stimulus basis, and instead stresses the learning of generalised safety. The generalisation of safety learning involves:

- Starting as high up on the individualised fear and avoidance hierarchy as possible;
- Maximising the feared outcome of exposure (so that when the feared outcome does not come true, the patient learns maximally);
- Varying the setting, timing, and context of the learning.

It is also important to note that prolonged exposure is less likely to be necessary when using the inhibitory learning approach, as the aim is learning general safety rather than unlearning specific fears (e.g., if eating toast at breakfast, then it is more useful to move straight on to cereal or fruit immediately afterwards, rather than to sit tolerating the anxiety that is specific to having eaten toast, as this way the patient learns that several foods are safe).

This inhibitory learning approach underpins the use of exposure throughout CBT-AN-20 (as it does for CBT-T), and will be seen throughout Chapters 7, 9, and 10 in particular. For example, if the patient needs to gain weight, then the most appropriate learning will come not from eating one core feared food (e.g., toast at breakfast), but from having a wide variety of feared foods in combination in different settings and at different times. The patient's learning about the safety of eating different foods is much quicker in this way than if multiple hierarchies have to be worked through. They learn that their weight goes up only slowly (e.g., 0.5kg/week) compared to their fear-based predictions (e.g., 3kg/week). Such rapid safety learning is usually surprising to the patient but provides substantial confidence that future exposure work can be achieved successfully (e.g., if the patient has learned that a "full on" approach to eating differently works well, their sense of self-efficacy is likely to be enhanced later when undertaking emotional work or mirror exposure).

In short, we can encourage the patient to take risks that enhance their fear as much as they can tolerate (e.g., eating a diverse breakfast from the start of therapy). That means that they then make very significant predictions about what the outcome will be (a more extreme prediction, such as "If I eat all that food then I will gain lots of weight – at least 3kg/7lb") – predictions that are far beyond any likely actual outcome. Then, when they see the actual outcome (e.g., weight barely changes), the challenge to their fears and beliefs is very strong, resulting in substantial learning and further behavioural change.

4.11.4 Clinician reluctance to use exposure

While exposure therapy is clearly an important part of therapies for a range of anxiety-based disorders (including eating disorders) and the inhibitory learning model informs therapies such as CBT-AN-20, there is a problem in its implementation, resulting in exposure being used far less often than should be the case. That problem is clinician implementation – our reluctance to use exposure therapy (Harned et al., 2013). That reluctance is due to negative attitudes about exposure, clinician characteristics such as anxiety, and/or clinician lack of awareness of this clinical approach (e.g., Becker et al., 2004; Deacon et al., 2013). Meehl (1954, 1973, 1986) describes clinicians as citing irrelevant characteristics (e.g., patient age or gender) to explain why we bypass the evidence base in this way ("broken leg exceptions"), attributing such actions to our desire to avoid distressing the "fragile" patient during the session ("spun glass theory of the mind").

There is clear evidence that clinicians' own characteristics (e.g., age, anxiety, experience) can have such influence (e.g., Langthorne et al., 2023; Speers et al., 2022), sometimes interacting with patients' characteristics (e.g., a particular reluctance to ask female clients to undertake exposure therapy). It is certainly the case that clinicians working with eating disorders are highly likely not to deliver an evidence-based protocol (e.g., Tobin et al., 2007; Waller et al., 2012). The issue of keeping clinicians on track is dealt with in detail in Sections 3.2 and 3.3, including the importance of training and supervision and the need for firmness as well as empathy when delivering treatment. Training and supervision (including "exposure for exposure therapists") are recommended to support clinicians' flexible use of skills, but such training and supervision should stress the need not to flex so far that we bypass essential work – particularly exposure therapy and other behavioural interventions.

4.12   Behavioural experiments

While exposure therapy addresses fear directly (having a secondary effect on beliefs, as the patient learns that their beliefs about the effect of the feared behaviour have not come true), behavioural experiments work directly on testing the patient's beliefs (having a secondary impact on fears, as the negative outcome does not come true). In CBT-AN-20, we begin with exposure therapy, as immediate work on cognitions is less likely to be effective while the patient is starved (less flexible thinking) or highly anxious (finding it harder to keep everything else stable while make the one change that is planned – for example, uncontrolled anxiety makes the patient skip a subsequent meal, so that the patient cannot learn that the planned change did not have the anticipated impact). However, it is important to remember that both exposure and behavioural experiments are likely to have a tertiary impact – enhancing self-efficacy – making it important to deliver them well. So, exposure therapy and behavioural experiments overlap conceptually, but behavioural experiments are more focused on delivering key cognitive changes, due to their more formal structure of generating alternative predictions that help the person to determine the impact of their eating and other behaviours.

Behavioural experiments integrate cognitive and behavioural aspects of CBT by planning behaviours that test out the beliefs and assumptions that maintain anorexia nervosa. Structured behavioural experiments become a key aspect of CBT-AN-20 from Phase 2 onwards, where they are used to challenge cognitions about food and the uncontrollability of weight gain (Chapter 8). Behavioural experiments are used to address the core beliefs underpinning interpersonal and emotional issues in anorexia nervosa in Phase 3 (Chapter 9) and are crucial to the body image work of Phase 4 (Chapter 10).

The aim of a behavioural experiment is to help the patient to change cognitions. We begin such work in Phase 2, so that there has been time for weight restoration to get underway and for the patient to become sufficiently cognitively flexible to be able to make good use of the intervention. Regardless of what type of cognition the behavioural experiment is designed to test, behavioural experiments follow a similar format, as detailed below. A behavioural experiment record is pictured in Figure 4.2 (see Appendix A.16). The behavioural experiment record helps the patient to learn the behavioural experiment process, and to build efficacy in designing their own.

The first four columns of the behavioural experiment record should be completed collaboratively in session, while setting up the experiment with the help

Belief to be tested (Rate belief 0-100%)	Experiment: What will I do to test the belief? When?	Prediction: What exactly do I think will happen? How will I know whether it has happened or not? (Rate belief 0-100%)	Alternative prediction: What else might happen? What have I got to gain? (Rate belief 0-100%)	Outcome: What actually happened? Was the original prediction correct?	Re-rate cognition: On balance, what is my view now? How do I rate the beliefs above in light of the experiment?	Plan: What can I do now to further test the belief?

Figure 4.2 Behavioural experiment record (adapted from Waller et al., 2007).

of the clinician. The latter columns should be completed as part of the homework of conducting the experiment. The fully completed record is then brought to the subsequent therapy session, where reviewing it together can support positive reinforcement of new learning and behaviours, problem-solving any challenges, and confirmation of the next steps. As illustrated in Chapter 8, the behavioural experiment should:

1. Follow the general structure of an experiment – the patient should be encouraged to try to keep everything else as stable as possible (not eating less, not compensating by exercising more, etc.), so that they can learn whether making the specific behavioural change (i.e., to their diet, their interpersonal behaviour, or their body-focused behaviour) has the predicted outcome or not.
2. Focus on the patient's current belief about the dangerousness of changing the eating disorder behaviour, suitably quantified so that it can be tested (e.g., instead of "Chocolate will make me gain weight", then "If I eat five 50g/2oz bars of that chocolate, then I will keep gaining 2–3kg/4–7lb in weight each week"; "If I express my disappointment to my sister, she'll never speak to me again"; "If I wear a skirt, everyone will laugh and stare at me"), and how strongly the patient holds that belief (e.g., "90% certain"). While we recognise that regaining 0.5kg in weight triggers anxiety for most patients, we typically use behavioural experiments to test the likely disproportionate beliefs and assumptions that are driving the anorexia nervosa (i.e., the "broken cognitive link" regarding a feared drastic uncontrollable weight regain), or the feared consequences of regaining weight (e.g., "If I gain weight, then I'll be so distressed that I can't do a day of work").

3. Support the patient to develop an alternative belief (e.g., "Given the number of calories in that chocolate bar and the number of calories that the books say I would need to regain a lot of weight, then maybe eating the chocolate bar will mean that I will not gain more than a hundred grams/a quarter of a pound or so"; "If I calmly express my disappointment to my sister, she might be annoyed but she'll probably forgive me"; "If I wear a skirt, some people might look, but most people probably won't care"), even though they do not rate that belief strongly (e.g. "Maybe 5%?"). It can also be helpful to prompt the patient to consider the potential short- and long-term benefits of finding out whether their feared consequence is accurate (e.g., "I'll get to participate in social eating, and eventually feel closer to others and have more fun"; "My sister may learn to appreciate my experiences and perspectives"; "I'll gradually begin to feel less self-conscious, and more confident").

4. Plan out how to test these conflicting beliefs, for how long, and how often – remember that an effective experiment might need to be repeated on a few occasions to rule out that the result is a chance occurrence.

5. Test out the belief behaviourally – for example, add the chocolate every day for one week while keeping the rest of intake stable, and see if there is the predicted massive jump in weight (i.e., over and above the expected weight gain that comes with the changes introduced in the concurrent Phase 1); plan how to safely communicate a specific emotional experience; or decide when and where to make the less body-avoidant clothing choice, and exactly how to evaluate the response of others.

6. Review the outcome with the patient, specifically attending to what it says about their belief.

7. Repeat with a range of related behaviours (i.e., feared foods; healthy expression of emotion; choice of less body image-determined actions).

The clinician needs to be Socratic throughout and should be careful not to undermine the experiment by excessively reassuring the patient – "We don't know what will happen, but your fear of this thing happening seems to be holding you back and keeping you stuck. There is only one way to find out if you need to be going to such lengths to stay safe, and that is to try something different to see if what you fear really comes true". As a result of such experiments, we expect to see a reduction in avoidance (i.e., of feared foods, or the body), or a healthier way of expressing emotion or relating to others. In turn, the practising of these new behaviours provides the patient with a greater repertoire of experience from which to continue to contribute towards less dangerous beliefs about food, others, feelings, and bodies.

4.13   Emotional work

Phase 3 (Chapter 9) addresses work with emotional triggers and maintaining factors in detail, outlining the role of CBT-AN-20 skills such as nutrition, psychoeducation, exposure therapy, cognitive restructuring (particularly in the form of attributional work and working with core beliefs), imagery rescripting, and developing counter-schematic behaviours. Therefore, this section focuses on the rationale for employing these different skills, to indicate where they are needed and where they are not. Additionally, you may wish to consider augmenting CBT-20-AN with an emotion regulation single-session intervention (see Appendix C) or use of the information sheet that suggests strategies for managing distress (Appendix A.23).

4.13.1   Core considerations in working with emotions in anorexia nervosa

We must consider the role that emotions can play in the development, maintenance, and treatment of eating disorders:

- *The role of starvation.* As will be seen in Chapter 9, clinicians should be wary of assuming from the beginning that the eating-disordered patient will need the skills outlined in Phase 3. While most of our patients will show some emotional issues when first referred, this might be due to starvation effects, resulting in low serotonin levels and emotional instability. Such biological factors can result in misdiagnosis (e.g., borderline personality disorder/emotionally unstable personality disorder), due to such mood instability and the resulting impulsive and compulsive behaviours. In such cases, simply reducing that starvation can reduce mood instability. Of course, reduction in starvation is not enough to deal with these emotional states for lots of patients, as is made clear in the case formulation (see Chapters 3 and 5). However, we cannot know whether there is a fundamental emotional problem unless starvation is reduced substantially – hence, Phase 3 should only be implemented where we are sure that starvation is no longer a concern (see Chapters 9 and 12).

- *Working with trauma versus working with trauma effects.* It is important to be clear about what we are treating. Many clinicians describe themselves as working with trauma. However, a traumatic event is not unusual in the lives of people who have no current psychopathology, as many people have resilience based on their past experience (e.g., the driver who has many years of driving experience before being hit by another car, and who can rationalise the problem as being the other driver's fault and unlikely to recur). Instead of "working with trauma", it is more important to consider the tasks of working with the impact of trauma, where present (e.g., PTSD; dissociation; behaviours that may provide some short-term avoidance or relief from difficult feelings or memories, while causing other problems including keeping the patient stuck). It is also imperative that we should use evidence-based approaches where they are available. The term "trauma-informed therapy" is often used – we would stress that CBT-AN-20 can also be trauma-informed, where necessary. The examples in Chapter 9 will demonstrate how the emotion-focused work in Phase 3 is directly relevant to the outcomes of traumatic experiences.

- *Nature of traumatic experiences.* While more obvious forms of physical and sexual abuse play a role in many cases of anorexia nervosa, it has been suggested that the more pervasive effects of emotional abuse, teasing, bullying, and neglect are just as impactful (McKay et al., 2021; Porter et al., 2020). Indeed, analyses that have looked at the overlap between different forms of trauma in eating pathology have shown that such emotional abuse effects might be the main causal factor behind the psychopathological effects of sexual and physical abuse (e.g., Kent et al., 1999). Such trauma effects can occur during childhood, adulthood, or both, and can be harder to recognise than the effects of more obviously violent trauma (for both patients and clinicians), potentially compounding the earlier experiences of invalidation. Therefore, we particularly consider the emotional abuse and neglect elements of trauma experiences at the relevant points in life, because addressing the consequences of those experiences gives us the best chance of helping the individual to develop healthier emotional and behavioural coping skills in the here and now. In Chapter 9, we stress this approach by paying close attention to the impact of emotionally invalidating childhood environments, as well as other childhood and adult experiences, all resulting in the development of maladaptive core beliefs.

- *Addressing impulsive versus compulsive behaviours.* Impulsive behaviours are commonly used to reduce intolerable emotional arousal (i.e., safety behaviours), while compulsive behaviours can serve to avoid the activation of those emotions in the first place (e.g., Waller et al., 2007). When working with non-underweight cases in CBT-T, the focus is primarily on the emotional factors that drive impulsive behaviours (e.g., emotionally driven binge-eating, vomiting, self-harm). In contrast, CBT-AN-20 has a focus on addressing emotional factors that result in compulsive behaviours (e.g., long-term restriction of eating, compulsive exercise, obsessive-compulsive symptoms). However, impulsive behaviours (e.g., binge-eating) are also found in anorexia nervosa cases at times, so also need consideration. Emotional factors that maintain such impulsive and compulsive behaviours are addressed in more detail in Chapter 9.

- *Timing of addressing underlying emotional factors.* Of course, the clinician is working with emotional issues from the very beginning of therapy (e.g., using firm empathy, supporting the patient to overcome anxiety; working with the patient to increase carbohydrate levels). However, the consequences of more trauma-related emotional experiences need to be addressed somewhat later – in Phase 3, where the biological factors have been largely resolved. It is important to remember (as outlined in Chapter 3) that clinicians can be keen to dive straight into addressing these more trauma-related emotional factors when working with eating disorders, because this "talking therapy" approach can seem more appealing than focusing therapy on eating and behavioural change when those are frightening for the patient. On the other hand, some clinicians prove reluctant to begin addressing the emotional factors that underlie any psychological problem, due to their concern about distressing the patient by doing so (e.g., Meehl, 1973). Either way, it is important to time emotional work appropriately – not starting too soon but not waiting too long. Supervision, consultation, and discussion with the patient can be the most valuable way of getting the timing right here.

4.14   Body image interventions

It is important to be aware of the wide range of factors that drive and maintain negative body image, and how to address them within a CBT framework. Indeed, within CBT-AN-20, body image work forms the whole of Phase 4. Its importance is simple to explain – the ubiquity of body image disturbance across those with eating disorders. Apart from those with ARFID (see Chapter 12), pretty much every patient whom we see is likely to have a high level of body dissatisfaction and body size overestimation. While this body image disturbance might reduce across the earlier phases of therapy in a few cases, it is highly likely that we will need to help the individual to improve their body image. Without such work, relapse into the eating disorder is very likely (e.g., Keel et al., 2005), and the patient's quality of life will deteriorate.

The specifics of working with body image in CBT-AN-20 are detailed in Chapter 10, providing clinical examples and techniques that can be mapped to the different beliefs, experiences, and safety behaviours that maintain negative body image. This section will address the "big picture" of work with body image – what are we aiming for, what can we do when, and what methods are going to be needed? Clearly, there will be overlaps with other skills that we address in this chapter – particularly in the use of methods such as exposure therapy, behavioural experiments, and working with the "anorexic voice". However, we want to help the patient to develop skills of strategic thinking when it comes to body image work.

4.14.1   Aim of body image work

The first consideration is what we are aiming to achieve with body image work. While we recognise the value of an approach that is centred on body positivity or body satisfaction, those are more sociocultural and developmental goals, dependent on a shift away from the Western thin ideal across media, other people's attitudes to body size and overweight individuals, and so on. Prevention work can go some way towards reducing vulnerability to such social factors if it is implemented early enough (e.g., Diedrichs et al., 2021; Becker & Stice, 2017). However, by the time that the patient reaches treatment for their eating disorder, negative body image is "baked into" the individual's problems. Furthermore, due to the same Western thin ideal for females and other factors (e.g., parental behaviour, teasing at school) that our patients experience, some level of body image dissatisfaction is normative, particularly among those living in Westernised cultures. Therefore, aiming to get the patient to a positive body image – something that is not achieved by most in society – might be an unrealistic target for patient and clinician alike. Here, it can be useful to engage the patient in understanding the difficulty of achieving full body satisfaction (e.g., asking "So what are we aiming for here? How many people do you know who are OK with their eating, but still not 100% satisfied with their body? And yet who are happy with life? Do you think that happiness with life could be a good place to be, regardless?").

Consequently, we recommend that clinicians should focus on *body acceptance* or *body neutrality* as the immediate goal of therapy, even if the ultimate goal of body satisfaction remains a future aspiration. In short, body acceptance can be defined as the individual being aware of their body without reaching unhealthy judgements on what it says about them, and hence being able to operate in the world without being constrained by their body image (e.g., not dressing to conceal their body; not focusing on what others might think about their appearance; not checking their appearance; etc.). We find that many of our patients make very substantial positive changes in this direction, with improvements in perception, feelings, and beliefs about their body, alongside changes in their body-related behaviours. We make sure that we do not promise body satisfaction per se, given the world that our patients live in, and they report understanding that the goal of body acceptance is more plausible. This outcome can be measured using various questionnaires (outlined in Chapter 10, Table 10.1), but the most rewarding aspect of body image work is when the patient's behaviours change, and they start to see the positive benefits of not being defined by their appearance. Such signs can be when the patient dresses differently, lets relationships develop, goes out with minimal preparation, and more.

4.14.2 Deferring body image work to the latter part of therapy

In evidence-based CBT for eating disorders, the majority of the structured, effective body image work takes place later in therapy, when issues of restriction, weight management, and eating concerns have been addressed. The same is true of CBT-AN-20, where body image is addressed in Phase 4. However, as will be seen in Chapter 10, that does not mean that body image should be an unspoken topic until that point in therapy. The patient is likely to be eager to get to this work from very early on in therapy. It is important to stress at the assessment that we acknowledge the critical nature of body image work, given its role in driving eating behaviours (e.g., "If I see myself as being huge, then of course I want to restrict my eating severely – anyone would"). However, we equally need to be honest that working on body image is only likely to be effective when it occurs later in therapy. In particular, we explain this as being related to the need to get the underweight patient to a stable, healthy weight range, where most of the body image interventions outlined here can be most effective at creating long-term change.

So, we defer the majority of the body image work from the beginning, despite our patients' common desire to focus on their body image before (or instead of) their eating and weight. The ability to engage the patient in waiting for this element of CBT-AN-20 is an important clinical skill, calling for firm empathy in abundance (see Chapter 3). We must be clear that we understand the patient's experience of body image distress and their desire to prioritise working on it immediately, while also maintaining the clear need to prioritise eating and weight, so that we are able to deliver most of the effective body image work later in therapy. However, that does not mean that we do not consider body image work from the outset, as will be seen below. Obviously, this might mean using Chapter 10 to address some material from Phase 4 before ending previous phases, but that is entirely compatible with the importance of flexing any therapy to the patient (see Section 3.2).

4.14.3 Early body image work

While the bulk of the effective body image work that we do will take place in the latter half of CBT-AN-20, there are several ways in which we address body image as a live topic earlier in CBT-AN-20. These will be addressed in Chapter 10, but they include:

- *Talking about body image in the assessment.* This includes normalisation of body image disturbance (not specific to eating disorders), and asking about any memories of how the patient's body image developed (e.g., teasing, praise for weight loss, social media) as part of the assessment and formulation process.
- *Demonstrating overestimation of body size in the assessment and Session 1.* This is a very powerful method (see Section 4.9) to use to help develop cognitive dissonance in the patient that we can work with to tackle their fundamental assumptions about why they have been acting so restrictively (e.g., "That is so weird. In my head ... in my eyes, I look so huge, like a blob. So, I diet and diet and diet, even though I never seem to feel thinner. But this doesn't make sense. Have I really been doing all this, messing up my life so totally, just because I can't see myself right?"). The results can be used to start developing a distrust in the accuracy of the "anorexic voice" and picked up as a theme over therapy (e.g., "Remember when you overestimated your body size – is this another example of the 'anorexic voice' trying to fool you in to believing something that isn't true?").
- *Psychoeducation.* As will be seen in Chapter 10, psychoeducation is a key element to working with body image. It can be used from early on to engage the patient in understanding the nature of their body, its nutritional needs, its negative responses to some of the safety behaviours that they use (e.g., bloating effects of laxatives), the way that weight can start being gained on the waist but redistributes over time, cultural influences, and more. This understanding can be evoked repeatedly as therapy progresses, to enable the clinician to support the patient to focus on the importance of preparing to enter Phase 4.

4.14.4   Body image work to reduce "stuckness"

As well as using some body image work during the assessment to lay the ground for therapy, more such work might be needed to assist progress in the first half of CBT-AN-20, particularly when the patient feels "stuck". For example, during the weight gain of Phase 1, the patient might feel that they have gained so much weight that others will be looking at them and seeing someone who is "grossly fat" (even though they are still objectively underweight). In such a situation, it can be worthwhile to repeat the body size estimation method referred to above to make it clear that the reason that they feel so much bigger is emotion-driven rather than because they are now objectively much bigger. Furthermore, we often find that conducting an intrapersonal survey (Section 10.7) can be very helpful here, allowing the patient to learn that others do not see them as having gained weight in the way that they fear. A behavioural experiment for body checking (Section 10.6.2) can also be used if uncontrolled checking is a safety behaviour that is keeping the patient stuck in terms of their willingness to eat enough for necessary weight gain (e.g., "I cannot eat any more because I can pinch my skin, and it is just horribly fat").

4.14.5   Skills used in addressing body image

These skills are detailed in Chapter 10 (Table 10.1). Therefore, they are simply summarised briefly here. We stress that these approaches are based on core skills that are used in CBT for many disorders, but are adapted here for specific body-related behaviours:

- *Psychoeducation and body size estimation* – used to assess and address the lack of knowledge that many people (not just those with eating disorders) have about their bodies, and that can maintain unhelpful body-related behaviours.
- *Addressing the "anorexic voice"* – here, we address the "anorexic voice" (see earlier in this chapter) to encourage the patient to treat this voice as an option, rather than as a command or definitive description of their body.
- *Imagery rescripting* – a cognitive approach to specific traumatic memories and underlying body-related emotions (e.g., shame due to having been criticised for their appearance as a child).
- *Changing the focus of exercise* – here, the aim is to encourage the patient to exercise for enjoyment, rather than to work on developing an unattainable "perfect" body.
- *Behavioural experiments* – these are used to address the cognitions that underpin behaviours such as body checking, body comparison, and reassurance-seeking. In each case, the individual is invited to test their belief that these safety behaviours are effective, versus the possibility that they are more harmful to body image.
- *Surveys* – a form of behavioural experiment, used to address the belief that the patient holds about other people's beliefs about them (e.g., "I know that they think I am fat, but they would never tell me so"), addressing the safety

behaviour of not asking those others what they actually think and other avoidance patterns (e.g., not going out of the house).
- *Exposure therapy* – used to address body avoidance (similar to phobic avoidance). This can be in the form of graded exposure but is most effective when used as flooding (particularly exposure to their own reflection in mirrors).

4.14.6 Considerations in addressing body image

When considering what we do and when we do it, it is important to consider why we are using the body image skills, as outlined here:

- Our focus is primarily on addressing behaviours and cognitive patterns that maintain the body image disturbance, given that the problem is likely to be long-standing, with its origins lying in pervasive cultural factors rather than specific events. So, we focus a lot of work on addressing the multiple safety behaviours that can maintain negative body image (e.g., checking, comparison, reassurance-seeking, mind-reading, avoidance).
- Individual patients will have different histories of body image development, maintenance patterns, and routes out of those maintenance patterns. Therefore, we pay close attention to the individual's needs. Two consecutive patients might both present with very negative body image, but one might be due to unhealthy levels of body checking and comparison, while another might be maintained by body avoidance, mind-reading, and reassurance-seeking. Consequently, Chapter 10 stresses that we use key skills (e.g., behavioural experiments, exposure, surveys) in a way that is shaped by the individual's presentation and formulation.

4.15 Relapse prevention and follow-up

In CBT-AN-20, as in CBT-T, towards the end of therapy we hope to see the patient having reached a healthier place, where cognitions, emotions, and behaviours are more stable, and a healthier sense of self is present in the patient's day-to-day life. It is important to emphasise to the patient that further strengthening of self-efficacy through continued active work on recovery is an essential part of the latter parts of CBT-AN-20 and throughout follow-up. The final phase in treatment is therefore longer than the comparable phase in CBT-T. It is important that the patient learns to practice skills and work on maintaining the benefits of therapy. As stated in Chapter 11, the key elements covered in Phase 5 are common to those found in CBT for other disorders:

- Positive feedback on the benefits of the work conducted so far, to support self-efficacy;
- The development of an effective therapy blueprint;
- Normalising eating, to ensure that the patient can continue to progress without therapy sessions;
- Engaging others in support of the patient;

- Working on returning to or developing a life without anorexia nervosa;
- Follow-up sessions;
- Referral for any outstanding problems.

At this stage, it is important to remind the patient of how much work they have undertaken to get to this point in their recovery, and to stress how that work has been done by the patient themselves, our role as clinicians having been to coach them along the way. It can be helpful to hold in mind some of the meta-competencies discussed in Chapter 3 – particularly meta-competence 2, relating to the importance of not letting our own anxiety get in the way of giving the patient a chance to prove that they can get better and stay better. Endings in therapy can be anxiety-provoking for both the patient (who is set to transition to self-therapy and follow-up) and the clinician (who might be concerned about a stalling of progress or relapse in the absence of weekly therapy). If the clinician feels a pull to "offer more sessions" or is feeling particularly anxious about a patient who is nearing the end of therapy, it is important to take these issues to clinical supervision. We find that talking through such issues can help support both the clinician and the patient to positively approach the transition to life beyond CBT-AN-20. Supervision can often remind the clinician just how far the patient has come, and that "perfect" outcomes (e.g., scoring zero on all the measures) are unrealistic and unnecessary, given scores in non-clinical groups. For example, a normal score (50th centile) for a non-clinical adult on the ED-15 Global scale is 1.75 for women and 0.90 for men (Tatham et al., 2015). If the clinician's thoughts about extending therapy do reflect limited change, then supervision can support useful planning, based around the possible alternatives that are addressed in Section 7.7 (Progress Review).

There are a number of important tasks at this stage in treatment:

- To highlight how far the patient has come by reflecting on the difference between how they were before therapy and how they are now;
- To identify the strengths and values that helped them to move on from their eating disorder;
- To encourage them to keep *actively pursuing* recovery; and
- To remind them that if their eating disorder should ever re-emerge in the future, they have a choice in how they respond.

An example of the type of conversations we have with patients is as follows:

Clinician: "I know that over the past week you've started to complete the Therapy Blueprint. Would it be helpful to spend some time today looking at the initial parts of that, perhaps looking back on how life was before you started therapy? I feel like the person sitting here with me today is very different to the person I met back in January – I wonder whether back then in the room with me was 95% anorexia nervosa and only 5% you? What do you think?"

Patient: "Yes, when I look back now, I can see how toxic my eating disorder had become. It used to constantly tell me how bad and disgusting I looked, and how I needed to work harder on improving myself by eating less and exercising more. It constantly picked out my faults suggesting areas where I could improve; lose weight, go to the gym more, be thinner, look different ... It was never satisfied".

Clinician: "It really was loud wasn't it, yet despite that, you've been able to do so much to change and move forward. What do you see as the main changes you've made?"

Patient: "Well, my eating is much better, and I've had several periods now, so I guess my body is telling me how much better it's feeling. I definitely have more energy. I know that eating regularly is really important, and I want to continue to push myself to by including new foods, I had a hot tuna and cheese wrap for lunch last week".

Clinician: "Sounds great. How was that?"

Patient: "I really liked it, I had it again the next day".

Clinician: "It sounds like you enjoyed it, and I know that continuing to build your food confidence is an ongoing goal for you – do you remember our conversations about practising things multiple times to reduce fear and build confidence? It sounds like you've really drawn on the determined part of you to keep pushing forwards with that. Well done".

Patient: "Yeah, sometimes I surprise myself, I just know I need to stick at it. I also know that criticising my body gets me nowhere and comparing myself to others can be a trigger – it just gets me into all that negative thinking, that I'm not as pretty, I don't look as good, and all of that, so I just need to stay neutral and kind to myself".

4.15.1   Staying well and building a future

Alongside using the Therapy Blueprint to guide conversations, we find it can be helpful to talk with the patient about what their "healthy self" looks like – how is life going when they are in "healthy mode"? This discussion takes us back to the modes that we were considering when tackling the "anorexic voice", illustrating those later stages outlined in Table 4.3; as the "anorexic voice" gets weaker and more adaptive, authentic modes become the main way the patient sees the world.

Here we are aiming to highlight the broad range of changes the patient has made during their recovery, directing them once again to notice their strengths, as well as the stronger connections they have with the other more valued parts of themselves and their life. Our conversations might look something like this:

Clinician: "Martha, I know we touched briefly on 'staying well' in our last session and how much of an active process this is. A bit like looking after a flower or plant; your health needs your care and attention to flourish. What do you think will be the important things for you to keep doing to stay well? How do you know when you are living life in 'healthy me' mode?"

Patient: "I think being in 'healthy me' mode involves accepting 'physical me' and appreciating my body more for what it does and what it can do, rather than constantly criticising it for not being good enough. I know I need to eat for health and stability, keeping it flexible, listening to my body".

Clinician: "Holding kindness and acceptance in mind when you think about your eating and relationship with your body sounds really important. Are there other things?"

Patient: "I think I've learnt that I can accept different versions of me – I can be calm and empathetic; talkative and social; or ridiculously competitive. But I can also sometimes feel insecure and that's okay. I just need to know what that 'part' of me needs to feel okay, and that means I need to listen to myself. I know my critical voice can still creep in sometimes, but I can stand back from it. I don't have to listen to it".

Clinician: "We've spoken, haven't we, about how recovery doesn't necessarily mean that life will always be easy and I'm sure there will be times when you feel insecure, that's normal. But I guess what you've shown yourself is that you can manage these times, as long as you draw on your strengths and the other more nurturing parts of yourself, as well as being more open with those you are close to in life".

Patient: "Yes, I think so. Also, since I've been going out more, I feel like my value and who I think I am as a person is based on so many more things. I know I still sometimes feel nervous, but I enjoy being with people so much more now. I used to feel so inadequate in relationships, but I just don't feel like that anymore".

Clinician: "It feels like connecting with others means you're having more fun! And I know that was one of your goals when you started therapy. And how about those emotions – do you remember us drawing out all those Newton's Cradles?"

Patient: "Yes, I know this is something I need to keep working on, but I think I'm getting better at noticing how I'm feeling – I can think about what the emotion is trying to tell me I need, and whether I can let it go if it's not helpful. Overall, my emotions are much more stable, far less overwhelming, and I know that if I feel sad, its ok, it won't last forever".

For some patients, it can be helpful to draw this out in a diagram or map, or even a collage, so pen, paper, and creative materials are always helpful here. Again, it's important to go with what feels right for the patient, and this is something they can work on between sessions as you move towards the end of therapy. Figure 4.3 gives an example of a diagrammatic explanation of the recovery picture for the client discussed above, Martha.

One important topic often relates to weighing outside of therapy. While the follow-up period offers an opportunity to experiment with phasing out weekly weighing and moving to more flexible weight-monitoring options, we find that an individualised approach tends to work best. This involves asking the patient: "What does healthy, non-avoidant but non-obsessive recovery-oriented weighing look like to you?" We encourage patients not to weigh in response to emotional triggers, but to consider having a set day or other external prompt and an upper and lower timeframe (e.g., "On a Tuesday; every 1–4 weeks; when I visit my mum").

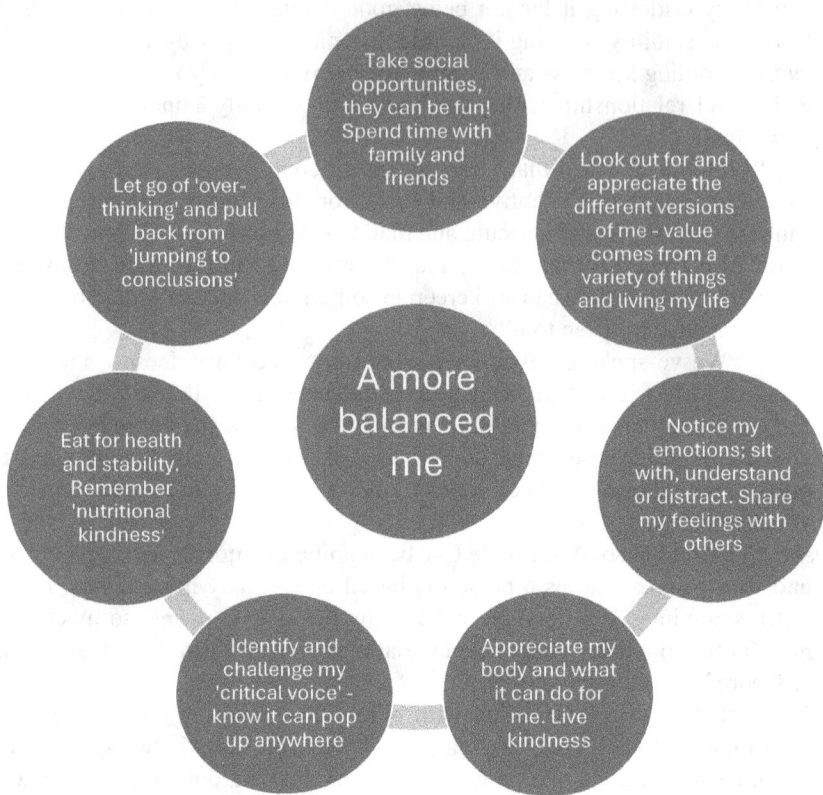

Figure 4.3 Martha's recovery picture.

This structure can be further phased out over time, as the patient comes to learn that their weight can be maintained well by eating appropriately.

4.15.2   *Managing the risk of relapse*

We always acknowledge that it is possible the "anorexic voice" will try to re-emerge in the future, and intermittent skirmishes with the eating disorder are not uncommon (Pugh, 2020). However, here we stress that we believe the patient now has the awareness and understanding to identify potential triggers and respond to their underlying needs in healthier ways. As mentioned in the protocol (Chapter 11) and when considering meta-competences (Section 3.9), we think about relapse as having three stages: *prelapse* (where the individual *thinks* about letting a healthy principle go, such as *thinking* about comparing themselves to others); *lapse* (where the person makes one behavioural slip, such as skipping lunch); and *relapse* (a full return to the eating disorder) (Freeman & Dolan, 2001). As part of the Therapy Blueprint, some patients might want to list their "vulnerable areas" – the initial signs that they might spot and how they can respond in a productive, self-protective manner. Again, this is an opportunity to reinforce learning and change, and to highlight strengths and self-efficacy.

Finally, we also emphasise the importance of drawing on others – we know that developing anorexia nervosa leads to social withdrawal, and it is important to openly acknowledge that many of the strategies for managing the initial signs of relapse will involve sharing experiences or drawing on the support of family and loved ones. For patients who have had difficulties believing they have been a burden to others, it is important to be clear that drawing on others doesn't constitute being a burden – it just means they are being a healthy human being. Table 4.5 shows Martha's relapse prevention plan, which she developed to identify and respond to risks of relapse:

Table 4.5 Martha's relapse prevention plan

When am I vulnerable?	What will I notice?	What will I do? My actions
Feeling anxious about eating a particular food.	I might try and avoid a food that I would really like (e.g. not sharing chips with my partner).	Remind myself that anxiety is just anxiety. It is okay to eat a range of foods. Continue to actively include a range of foods in my meal plan. If I feel scared, it means I need to have it. Anxiety feeds avoidance, not me! Ask for help from others.
Criticising myself about my weight and shape.	Looking in the mirror more, scrutinising my body, being internally critical about myself.	Remind myself to appreciate my body for what it can do. Stop engaging in behaviours I know are unhelpful. Revisit the Body Neutrality material.
Slipping back into compulsive exercise.	Feeling I *have to* exercise when I don't want to. Losing the choice.	Remembering that exercise has to be on *my* terms. Listen to my body and move in a way that feels good for me. Yoga rather than a run? Stay in tune with my body and be led by its needs. Act opposite to any unhelpful demands.
Increased self-criticism.	Being meaner and nastier to myself. Louder critical voice. Feeling sad and angry more. I notice increased expectations of myself; perfectionism kicks in.	Notice and push back – turn up the volume of the other parts – what would self-care say? What is the point in treating myself this way? Act opposite.
Feeling more emotional, lower in mood.	Being less able to pick up on emotions but feeling them more in my body. Not sharing how I feel with others.	Give myself some time, relax in my room, think about the triggers, ask myself, what do I need? If stressed about work, pre-plan and give myself time to relax. If lonely, make contact with others. Remember it's always good to share.

4.15.3   Ending letters

As in CBT-T, we find it helpful to write a reflective letter to the patient at the end of treatment to reinforce the benefits of therapy (see Section 4.5.2). An example is provided in Appendix A.12.

4.15.4   Conclusion

These final sessions in CBT-AN-20 are crucial for supporting the patient to continue to develop their life beyond the eating disorder. Our role here is to validate any anxiety if needed, but to foster a sense of independence within the patient. We aim to support the patient in developing their self-efficacy and a belief that they can live a healthier and more balanced life beyond anorexia nervosa.

4.16   Working with significant others

We have already said it, but it bears repeating – recovery from anorexia nervosa is hard work. For this reason, we suggest in the early stage of therapy that the clinician reviews with the patient any environmental resources they can use to help with this recovery. A major potential resource is the significant others in the patient's life – family, partner, close friends – whether this is targeted at immediate support, stress reduction, or developing age-appropriate independence. The value of engaging these people is well illustrated within the literature on anorexia nervosa (e.g., Pepin & King, 2016; Potterton et al., 2025; Treasure et al., 2007), supporting both the patient and the carers themselves.

When working with adults with anorexia nervosa, the way we work with significant others differs from the way we outline when working with adolescent patients (see Section 12.3). We suggest that the involvement of others is discussed with the patient, making them aware that up to four additional sessions can be utilised for meetings with significant other(s) if required. If parallel or extended sessions are to be offered, it is essential that the content is discussed with the patient first and they have agreed to what will be disclosed about their personal functioning, and the specific forms of potential support that will be discussed.

Many adult patients will not want to take up this offer, and it is worth exploring why this is so. Sometimes the response is informed more by the "anorexic voice", where the patient feels like they have already ruined other people's lives enough, or that they have been an intolerable burden, or that the other person simply won't be interested. In the end, however, it is up the patient as to whether they want to take up these joint sessions.

Even where the patient does not want a shared session with the significant other, it is still important to explore ways of communicating with significant others. It is also worth touching base on this issue later in therapy when the situation and the patient have changed, and a joint session might seem a much better fit.

There are four main options for involving significant others: (1) ask the patient to give the significant other information that is helpful outside of session; (2) conduct joint sessions with the significant other to provide psychoeducation about eating disorders and explore areas where it could be helpful for the significant other to step forward with specific forms of assistance; (3) conduct joint sessions with the significant other to provide psychoeducation about eating disorders and explore areas where it could be helpful for the significant other to step back from offering assistance; and (4) accepting Charles Dickens's maxim that "accidents will occur in the best regulated families" – in other words, some significant others are simply unable to offer assistance, or indeed are consistently unhelpful when it comes to the eating disorder, meaning that the clinical decision might need to be *not* to involve significant others.

Ask the patient to discuss topics with the significant other out of session   We emphasise that this is not necessarily a "second best option". Where the patient and therapist identify that the patient feels able to have necessary conversations with the family with support from the therapist, this is a good pathway to helping the patient increase their sense of self-efficacy. The following questions might help the therapist and patient understand the types of tasks that could be set up:

- What kind of patterns do you see in your relationships and in your communications with this significant other?
- What kind of things do you have difficulty talking to them about?
- What is it like for you to express anger or displeasure to them and how do you respond when they get angry with you?
- What do you do when you are under stress and how do you communicate with them in these situations?
- How well do you think this person understands you? What do they need to know about you?
- What would be the one most helpful thing they could do to support your ability to stop allowing the "anorexic voice" to call the shots in your life?
- What do you think they need to understand about the eating disorder that will be most helpful to you?
- How do you perceive the eating disorder has impacted this person and your relationship with this person? What aspects of your relationship would you like to revive?

It may be, however, that the patient is reluctant to experiment with different ways of relating to significant others. In such circumstances, the best that can be done is to ask them to share psychoeducation materials that they receive over therapy with the significant other, and for the clinician or patient to alert the significant other to psychoeducation materials available for carers (e.g., Treasure et al., 2007).

Joint sessions for stepping forward   This is probably most pertinent to young adults or people living with a partner or spouse. The structure of the first session is usually to give some general psychoeducation about eating disorders, including the treatment that they are receiving. This is followed by a summary of what the patient is experiencing. Finally, specific areas for more support can start to be explored, with a focus on small tasks that may be helpful. Throughout, there is ample opportunity for the significant other/s to ask questions and offer insights. The clinician must be prepared to step in actively if the conversation starts to turn to blame on either side, acknowledging the burden the eating disorder has placed on all members, and redirect the conversation to constructive problem-solving. Examples of helpful tasks can include the significant other sitting down to have meals with the patient on a regular basis if this has not been happening; the significant other preparing a shared meal once a week, with agreement on the ground rules of how this would be achieved without leading to arguments; shared an activity after eating to decrease the likelihood of purging or driven exercise; and situations in which the patient can contact them for encouragement, and a prepared "script" for offering such support.

Joint sessions for stepping back.   This is probably most pertinent to young adults who have undergone family-based treatment when younger, and where parents have continued to be quite involved in supervising their nutrition. Often both the family and the young person are highly anxious about letting go of the safety net. We advocate for gradual steps towards independence, acknowledging the previous hard work and anxiety but also explaining that the vicious cycle associated with such safety nets erodes self-efficacy and keeps anxiety growing steadily. Sessions can be used for generating specific goals accompanied by extensive problem-solving. The use of a behavioural experiment framework can be helpful in approaching these goals with curiosity and as information-gathering exercises.

No involvement of the significant other   This is probably the least common option. An example would be family members who have consistently made negative comments about the appearance of the patient over their lifetime, especially in relation to weight gain, despite knowing that they have an eating disorder. It may also relate to a family member who has their own mental health problems, which distracted the patient's past efforts to achieve recovery over many years. The work involved with the patient is to help them accept that they can no longer turn to this significant other for support. This might look a bit like the work involved in complex grief, where the patient says goodbye to the significant other as a source of support and is assisted to establish new social supports and attachments, or to get closer to existing supports. This does not (necessarily) mean that contact with the significant other is severed, but rather that their limitations are recognised, as are any aspects of the relationship that the patient continues to appreciate and wishes to retain. The work also focuses on not allowing the actions of the significant other to impact the decisions they make and the actions that they take with respect to their nutritional health. Ways to limit or respond to unhelpful contact with the significant other can be explored. It is useful to wrap all this work up with a therapeutic letter addressed (but not sent) to the significant other, where the following issues are explored:

- What specific interactions have formed an obstacle to recovery from the eating disorder?
- What does the patient continue to appreciate about the significant other?
- How will the relationship change moving forward?
- How will the patient counter any unhelpful interactions with the significant other – what they can say to themselves, what they have discovered about themselves that they can fall back on, and who they can rely on to be in their "cheer squad" as they travel their recovery journey?

We find it is helpful to discuss the structure of the letter in session, ensuring the patient is clear about the task. We ask the patient to write it for homework over no more than a 20-minute period, paying attention to any support required immediately after writing. Getting the patient to read the letter out loud in the next session is also desirable, with discussion about any new issues that emerge. If the patient feels unable to read it out, the clinician can ask permission to read it to the patient.

4.17   Summary

Chapters 3 and 4 have addressed the skills base of CBT-AN-20 – the meta-competences and competences that inform good, evidence-based practice. These chapters provide the foundation of the work that is needed throughout CBT-AN-20, while stressing that flexing to the patient's needs is more important than rigid adherence.

Now, it is time to outline the full protocol for the therapy. We will start with the importance of assessing the patient with anorexia nervosa (Chapter 5), and an outline of the therapy (Chapter 6). Then, we will detail the five phases of CBT-AN-20 (Chapters 7–11), where we explain how the skills from Chapters 3 and 4 should be applied to the individual case. Following that, we will consider adaptations that can be useful for those who might not benefit so well from the therapy without them (Chapter 12).

Chapter 5

Assessment of the patient and their needs

Your patient might already have undergone an assessment that resulted in their coming to you for CBT-AN-20. However, given the importance of considering current risk, motivation, and new information, and with developing an effective therapeutic alliance, a re-assessment at the outset of therapy ("Session 0") is required before the 20 sessions of CBT begins. That assessment and some of its elements (e.g., risk, formulation) will undoubtedly spill into the start of treatment, too.

It is always important to consider the generic formulation of anorexia nervosa from the outset of the assessment, so that it can be used as the template for a more personalised formulation that the patient can understand and in which they feel personally invested. Following that, the assessment should consider the following:

- Diagnosis and nature of the eating disorder;
- Weight status (objective and functional);
- Risk factors and management;
- Maintenance factors;
- Preparedness for the non-negotiables of therapy;
- Past therapies;
- Goal-setting;
- Confidence in and suitability of the therapy;
- Time limits of the therapy;
- Potential for family/loved ones to be involved;
- Possible pre-treatment brief methods of enhancing engagement and participation.

5.1 Case formulation process

While CBT-T does not usually require a case formulation in order to be effective, we find that CBT-AN-20 can benefit from a relatively simple case formulation to engage the patient, particularly by helping them to understand why the anorexia nervosa was so positive for them at first (and why they strive to get back to that early positive experience). While we use the same behaviour-level mini-formulations that are used in CBT-T (particularly energy graphs to explain physiological

DOI: 10.4324/9781003594703-5

Predisposing factors (antecedents)
Trauma history; Bullying; Family/societal modelling of perpetual dieting and thin ideal; Genetics; Perfectionism; Anxiety sensitivity; Harm avoidance; Low novelty seeking; Intolerance of uncertainty; Self-critical

Precipitating factors (triggers)
Teased about weight; Body changes in puberty; Lost weight through physical illness; Complimented on weight loss

Problem
Restricted intake of food; Starvation; Body image concerns; Fear of uncontrollable weight gain

Protective factors (strengths)
Family support; Caring partner; Personal traits

Perpetuating (short term)
Feeling in control; Able to reduce life scope to focus on one concrete issue rather than many complex issues; Succeeding at weight loss goals and feeling worthwhile; Avoidance of emotion

Perpetuating (long term)
Loss of friends and support; Failing at college and work; Weak; Body deterioration; Cognitive and emotional limitations (including 'anorexic voice'); Starvation effects – neurobiological changes that increase denial, rigidity, anxiety, withdrawal and obsessionality

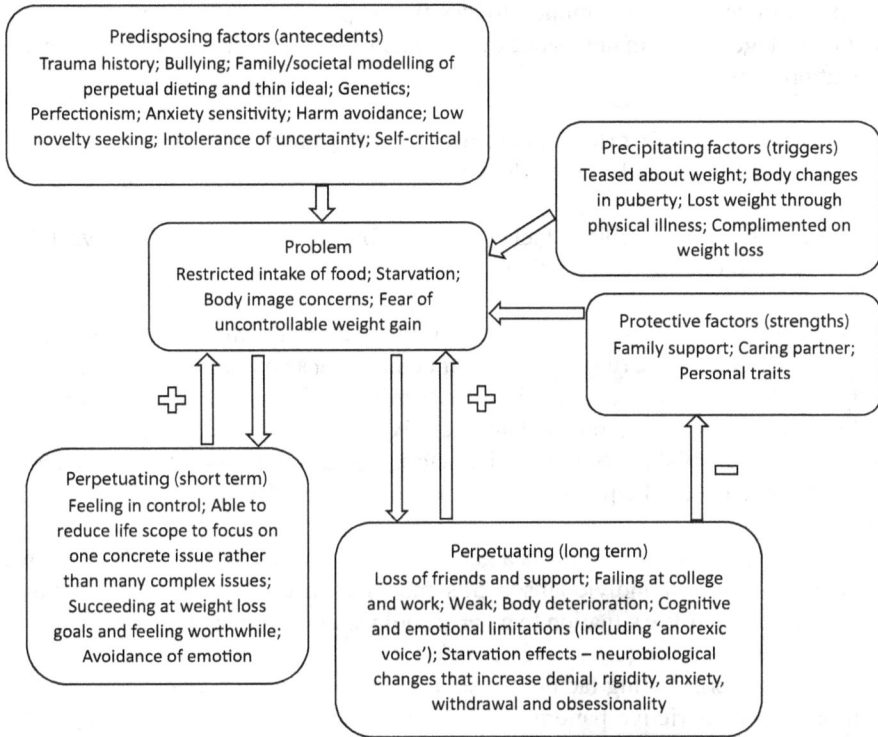

Figure 5.1 Generalised example of a modified 5Ps model of a case of anorexia nervosa, showing maintenance cycles that perpetuate the problem through positive reinforcement of the problem (i.e., the restriction is associated with feeling good in the early stages) and negative reinforcement of the problem (e.g., the problem is maintained by avoidance of difficult feelings in the later stages), alongside the reduction in protective factors over time. ("+" indicates "enhancement"; "-" indicates "reduction").

factors and the Newton's Cradle model to explain core belief activation, as detailed in Chapters 7 and 9, respectively), we find that a variant on the 5Ps model (See Section 4.4.4: *P*redisposing, *P*recipitating, *P*roblem, *P*erpetuating, and *P*rotective factors) provides a useful structure for building a collaborative understanding of the eating disorder. We use the structure in Figure 5.1 (see blank template in Appendix A.9 or A.10) to engage the patient in explaining and making sense of their own individual problem, how it has developed, what maintains it, what the pros and cons of anorexia nervosa have been over time, and what would be necessary to leave it behind. This formulation should be done with the clinician who will be conducting therapy with the patient, to ensure a shared language in understanding and adapting treatment over time. At every session, it is important to work with the formulation on the table for the clinician and patient to share and review.

This variant of the 5Ps model divides the perpetuating factors into the earlier and later stages in the maintenance of anorexia nervosa, so that the patient can see the rationale for:

- Feeling great at first (lots of control of the self, others and the world);
- Feeling terrified and a failure later (hanging on desperately, not feeling in control at all);
- Dreaming of being able to feel great again (but feeling unable to achieve it – or why would they be here in therapy?).

This model also allows us to focus with the patient on the protective factors/ strengths that they have (e.g., support from others; sense of humour; kindness; persistence), so that we can consider how these might be built up or revived over time (adding to coping skills, rather than exclusively focusing on taking away negative experiences of starvation, isolation, etc.). Across CBT-AN-20, this strengths-focused approach can help to engender hope and direction as the patient progresses through therapy.

For example, Figure 5.1 shows a generalised set of factors that might be drawn upon to develop an individualised 5Ps model of a case of anorexia nervosa, depending on their life situation (e.g., at school vs. living alone) and how long they have had the disorder (e.g., long enough for substantial physical deterioration). Note that the perpetuating factors are split into two – the positive experiences that reinforced the restrictive patterns at first, and the fear of negative consequences that currently maintains the problem. The formulation also demonstrates how the longer-term negative consequences of the anorexia nervosa can reduce the protective factors/strengths that initially allowed the person to maintain their restrictive eating initially.

Drawing on that generalised model, the following example (Figure 5.2) shows a more specific example of an individual's 5Ps model. In this case, the pattern shows details the factors that are relevant to a college/university student in their early 20s, who has had anorexia nervosa for four years.

Of course, if the eating disorder is of more recent onset (e.g., an adolescent whose eating disorder is only six months in duration), the balance of short- and long-term perpetuating factors might be very different, demonstrated by different motivational patterns. In Figure 5.3, we provide an example formulation for Arlo, a 16-year-old non-binary youth with a more recent onset of anorexia nervosa. However, one can still use this formulation to develop a "what is going to happen longer term if you maintain your eating disorder" scenario for the patient to consider.

Once the initial formulation is agreed upon with the patient, it should be reconsidered at appropriate points in therapy (e.g., if weight gain is proving difficult) to review progress, update the formulation, and direct therapy. It should also be used to structure the wider assessment, as outlined here.

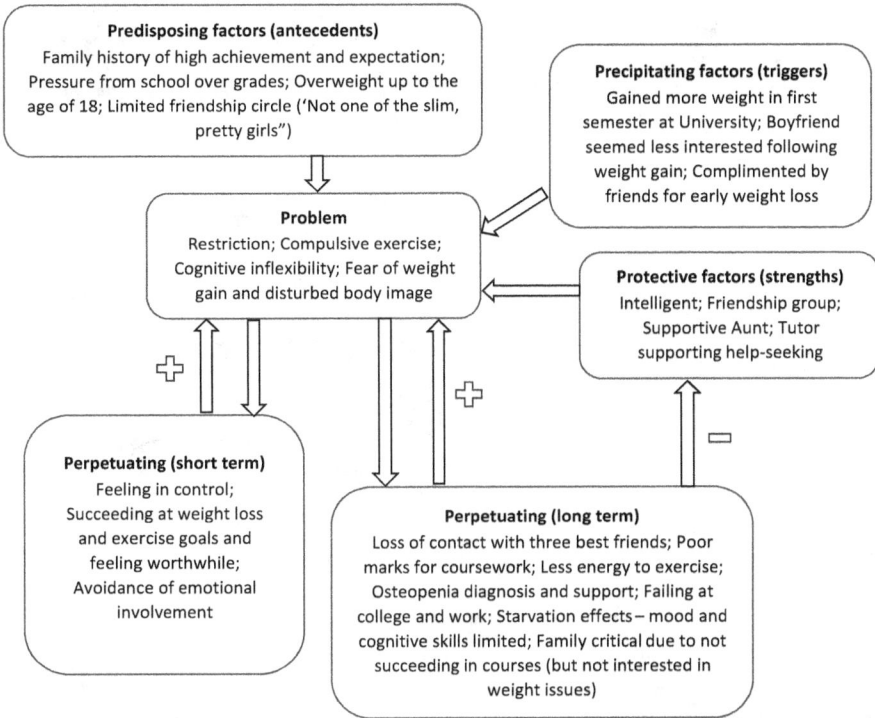

Predisposing factors (antecedents)
Family history of high achievement and expectation; Pressure from school over grades; Overweight up to the age of 18; Limited friendship circle ('Not one of the slim, pretty girls")

Precipitating factors (triggers)
Gained more weight in first semester at University; Boyfriend seemed less interested following weight gain; Complimented by friends for early weight loss

Problem
Restriction; Compulsive exercise; Cognitive inflexibility; Fear of weight gain and disturbed body image

Protective factors (strengths)
Intelligent; Friendship group; Supportive Aunt; Tutor supporting help-seeking

Perpetuating (short term)
Feeling in control; Succeeding at weight loss and exercise goals and feeling worthwhile; Avoidance of emotional involvement

Perpetuating (long term)
Loss of contact with three best friends; Poor marks for coursework; Less energy to exercise; Osteopenia diagnosis and support; Failing at college and work; Starvation effects – mood and cognitive skills limited; Family critical due to not succeeding in courses (but not interested in weight issues)

Figure 5.2 Individual example, using a modified 5Ps model to explain the development and maintenance of her anorexia nervosa. ("+" indicates "enhancement"; "-" indicates "reduction").

5.2   Diagnosis

As established more widely (e.g., Clark et al., 2018), patient outcomes can be enhanced if the service uses diagnosis or problem descriptors to ensure understanding of the patient's problems. Diagnoses of AN(R), AN(B/P), AAN, OSFED, and ARFID can ensure that the therapy is appropriately targeted and not used inappropriately where other factors can account for the patient's symptoms (e.g., loss of weight tied to loss of appetite in depression). The same is true when considering the behavioural, cognitive, and emotional patterns in the individual case (e.g., is the problem purely restrictive or does it involve bingeing and purging behaviours?). Such information might indicate whether the best therapy for that individual is CBT-AN-20, CBT-E, CBT-T or CBT for ARFID (CBT-AR). A lot of that decision-making will depend on weight status (or, in the case of CBT-AR, the centrality of body image concerns to the formulation).

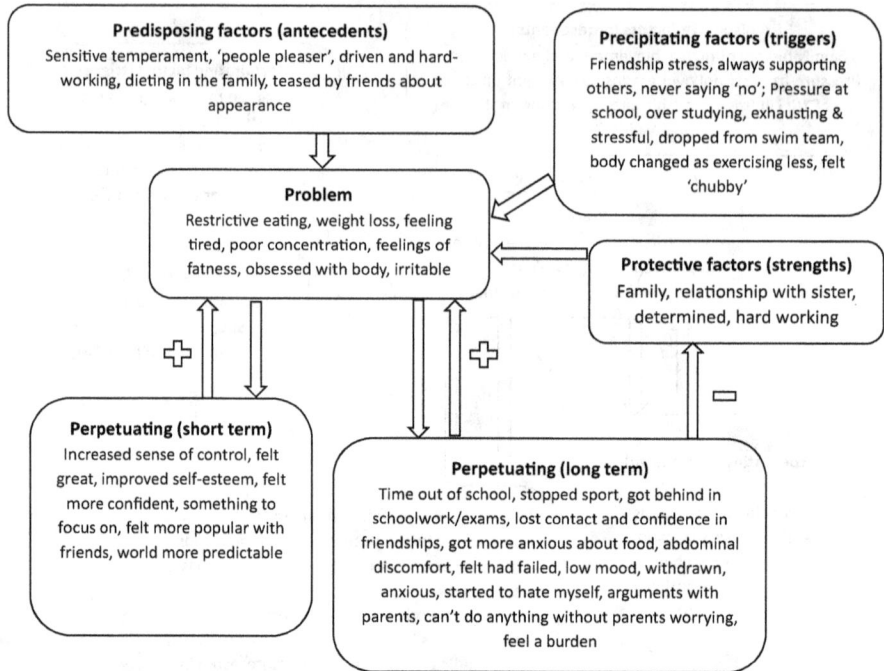

Predisposing factors (antecedents)
Sensitive temperament, 'people pleaser', driven and hard-working, dieting in the family, teased by friends about appearance

Precipitating factors (triggers)
Friendship stress, always supporting others, never saying 'no'; Pressure at school, over studying, exhausting & stressful, dropped from swim team, body changed as exercising less, felt 'chubby'

Problem
Restrictive eating, weight loss, feeling tired, poor concentration, feelings of fatness, obsessed with body, irritable

Protective factors (strengths)
Family, relationship with sister, determined, hard working

Perpetuating (short term)
Increased sense of control, felt great, improved self-esteem, felt more confident, something to focus on, felt more popular with friends, world more predictable

Perpetuating (long term)
Time out of school, stopped sport, got behind in schoolwork/exams, lost contact and confidence in friendships, got more anxious about food, abdominal discomfort, felt had failed, low mood, withdrawn, anxious, started to hate myself, arguments with parents, can't do anything without parents worrying, feel a burden

Figure 5.3 Individual example (Arlo, 16yrs) using a 5Ps formulation. ("+" indicates "enhancement"; "-" indicates "reduction").

5.3 Weight status

A key issue is whether the person is underweight, either objectively or functionally. Objective underweight is often taken as being below a specific threshold (e.g., body mass index [BMI] < 18.5; a particular weight for height, adjusted for age among younger people). However, we should not get caught up with the idea of a "good" or "safe" BMI, when functional weight for height is also important. We should always stress that a BMI = 18.5 is at the end of a bell curve, and most people will not be at a healthy weight if their BMI is that low. It is more useful to stress that the patient needs to consider that their own healthy body weight is likely to be somewhere within a higher range, to be determined experimentally during therapy. People vary substantially in their natural BMI (or weight for height adjusted for age), and BMI can be affected by ethnicity, gender, athletic status, and so on. One individual with a BMI of 19 might be at a weight that works well for them, while another person might struggle emotionally, cognitively, socially, and physically at that same BMI. That latter person is *functionally underweight* (e.g., maybe they have a higher set point than the first person; maybe they have a much higher muscle mass) and would benefit from a therapy involving weight gain. So, the question for the clinician should be whether the patient is *functionally underweight*, and the decision about which therapy to use should be determined by the answer to that question (alongside the issue of diagnosis – Section 5.2). CBT-AN-20 has been tested with individuals with a BMI of 15 or above, so any efforts to use it at a lower weight than that should be based on clinical characteristics and monitored closely to determine whether it is effective or not. Across a range of therapies, an entry BMI < 17 is associated with fewer people achieving remission at the end of outpatient therapy for anorexia nervosa (Wade, Allen et al., 2021), though this finding has not been tested with CBT-AN-20.

5.4   Managing risk

Risk should be monitored over therapy, whether immediate or longer term. The Academy for Eating Disorders medical guidelines (2021) and the Medical Emergencies in Eating Disorders (MEED) guidelines (Royal College of Psychiatrists, 2022) are useful summaries of what clinicians should look out for, and it is important that these should not be seen as "someone else's concern". There should be agreed support for the clinician from a medical practitioner who monitors and addresses physical risks from anorexia nervosa (e.g., low BMI/weight for height for age) and any associated issues (e.g., diabetes, low mood) throughout CBT-AN-20.

More immediate risks (those that are life- and health-threatening) should be addressed within the assessment session (delaying the therapy if appropriate, of course), and monitored for stabilisation or improvement over therapy. Other risks (e.g., long-term bone deterioration) should be used as part of the pros and cons needed to motivate the patient to engage in therapy, as well as being addressed directly and through weight regain. The common risks and key skills needed to address them are summarised in Table 5.1.

5.5   Predisposing and maintenance factors

As shown in the 5Ps model above (Figure 5.1), the perpetuating factors that maintain anorexia nervosa are important to understand, alongside the predisposing and precipitating factors that explain the origins of the individual's eating disorder. The assessment should consider both predisposing and perpetuating factors, including temperament (e.g., perfectionism; intolerance of anxiety; emotional inhibition), which were part of how the problem developed but which can impede therapy if they are not considered. As suggested in Section 4.10.2, some of those characteristics can be reframed as potential allies to escape the anorexia nervosa (e.g., using a desire for achievement to develop meaningful goals for the future). In subsequent chapters, it will be made clear how those temperament factors (see Figure 5.1 for a wider set of possible factors) can be addressed in CBT-AN-20. As is commonly the case in CBT, initially we focus primarily on current maintaining factors (e.g., starvation, avoidance of close relationships). This does not mean that we do not

Table 5.1 Common risks in anorexia nervosa, and the necessary clinical considerations. Use the MEED or AED guidelines for detailed recommendations.

Risk type	Clinician actions within CBT-AN-20
Psychiatric risks	
Suicidal and self-harming thoughts and actions	Monitor and formulate mood and suicidal thoughts regularly/weekly. Plan for safety with the patient (e.g., actions to take, people to contact, emphasis on protective factors). NICE (2022) stresses that it is important not to rely on assessment tools and scales to predict suicidal or repeated self-harm behaviours or to determine who should or should not be offered treatment. Similarly, the guidelines stress that we should not create global risk categories for such behaviours, or use them to determine whether treatment is offered.
Risk to others	Consider issues of anger, particularly when considering trauma-based factors in the origin of anorexia nervosa. Arrange a review of safety in activities that could harm others due to anorexia nervosa (e.g., at work; ability to drive safely; childcare), and of other factors (e.g., financial problems).
Comorbid disorders that interfere with engagement	Consider which disorder is the most prominent (commonly the anorexia nervosa, due to starvation and mood effects), and focus there initially.
Medical risks	
Monitor and address urgent threats to life and health	Observe the patient and ask about risky physical states (e.g., heart rate; physical weakness; fainting; lapses in consciousness; drug and alcohol use; purging and exercise levels). Evaluate the risk of re-feeding syndrome, arranging with the relevant medical practitioner to monitor medical signs and manage risks at the assessment stage. Weighing the patient within therapy is critical, rather than relying on others to do it (see APPG report, 2019). Arrange medical monitoring (e.g., electrolytes; blood glucose; ECG; blood pressure) and appropriate responses (e.g., electrolyte replacement; hospitalisation). Clinicians should be clear that such medical monitoring is beyond their skill base, and should contact the relevant medical professional to undertake such work (providing key information to inform that medical work – e.g., https://cfih.com.au/wp-content/uploads/2017/01/Outpatient-Medical-Monitoring-for-Eating-Disorders-in-Adults.pdf; https://meed.org.uk/)
Monitor and develop safety in the case of important but less urgent threats to health	Check on or arrange bone scans; monitor weight (considering norms for different groups to evaluate potential risk); balance diet to meet bodily needs. Again, these tests should be undertaken and interpreted by a medical professional, or in collaboration with a dietitian where appropriate.

address past experiences, but we focus on them only if they are impeding progress in therapy.

5.6   Preparedness for the non-negotiable tasks of therapy

Treatment non-negotiables are mandatory treatment components (Geller & Srikameswaran, 2006) that need to be discussed before treatment starts. They need to be provided with a clear rationale and evidence and applied consistently over therapy. Examples of some non-negotiables in CBT-AN-20 include recording food intake, open weighing, early change in terms of reducing dietary restriction, weekly sessions in the early phase of therapy, and doing agreed therapy tasks between sessions. Such preparedness issues being considered, the start of the therapy itself can be seriously compromised or simply delayed, which is problematic given that early change is so critical (see Section 3.4).

During the assessment session, we ask the patient about what they have eaten recently, to get a general picture relating to severity of the anorexia nervosa, risk, and so on. However, we recommend that the patient always be asked to record their food intake ahead of the first active therapy session, so that Session 1 can be focused on dietary change for weight regain from the start. To facilitate such recordings, in the assessment session we negotiate how the patient would like to keep such records (e.g., app, phone, pen-and-paper diary).

The patient should be *weighed openly* in the assessment and at each session thereafter (access to reliable scales is essential, of course), so that the patient is aware of their weight and can link it to their eating (see Section 4.3 and Section 4.6 and Phase 1 of therapy). The patient is typically asked to look at the scale during the process. If they are reluctant to do so (e.g., saying that they find the numbers on the scale too fixating), then the clinician can present the figure to the patient as part of the weight chart that they draw up at each session. We have found that many clinicians avoid open weighing at the assessment for fear of distressing the patient or their family, but that avoidance maintains the patient's distress and builds up later problems for the clinician when the patient declines to be weighed but still expects therapy to be effective (see Waller & Mountford, 2015). Supervision and consultation can be key to keeping the clinician and patient on track with the evidence-based approach, while retaining patient-centred flexibility about how this element of therapy is delivered.

Finally, the assessment should openly address the need for *changes in eating*, stressing the need to make such changes from the beginning of therapy (or even before therapy starts, in some cases) to improve physical health, brain functioning, mood, and so on. If the patient is reluctant to monitor intake, to engage in open weighing, or to eat differently, then knowing that fact at assessment can allow the clinician to stress work on motivation and on the non-negotiables of therapy from the outset of therapy (see Phase 1, Chapter 7).

An issue that can be a concern for clinicians is if the patient expresses reluctance to engage with the necessary dietary change due to religious reasons such as fasting. In such cases, we stress the key importance of self-care. Our experience has been that asking the opinion of a religious authority whom the patient respects can be decisive in ensuring that the patient engages in treatment fully at this stage.

5.7 Discuss past therapies and expectations of CBT-AN-20

It is important to consider what was involved in previous therapies, and why they were ineffective or why the patient relapsed (e.g., lack of an evidence-based approach; lack of engagement in part or all the therapy on the part of the patient). Given how many patients value previous therapies that may not have been effective, it is important to discuss those previous therapies with the patient as foundations on which we can now build, using CBT-AN-20. In contrast, some patients will have no prior experience of therapy. In those cases, it is valuable to ask them what they understand about treatment, providing an opportunity to orient them to how therapy works and their active role in the process. For example, the patient might need help in understanding that while out-of-session tasks are vital, such work is different from being assigned homework by a teacher at school (in particular, therapy homework is about learning skills for integration into life, rather than one-off tasks). Concerns and barriers are actively invited into the therapy process, so that the clinician can offer help to the patient in troubleshooting solutions to getting on track and consider any adaptations that might be required.

5.8 Goal-setting

We should calmly accept that the patient's motivation to change is limited or conflicted and normalise any ambivalence. Use of visual scales to assess motivation to change and confidence in their ability to change (see Section 5.9) can assist in making this a matter-of-fact discussion. The reasons for ambivalence (e.g., the patient seeing anorexia nervosa as their only identity) can be used to inform goal-setting and to address lack of engagement (Vinchenzo et al., 2022). One issue behind such poor engagement can be that the patient has felt unheard, misunderstood, and unsupported in the past (e.g., being told that they are "not underweight enough" to merit treatment). They might also recognise their reliance on their eating disorder to manage difficult feelings, problems, and relationships in their life. Finally, and importantly, many patients with anorexia nervosa derive a sense of identity or "specialness" from their eating and feel a sense that their identity is being removed in therapy, with no alternative being offered.

One technique that we have found helpful is to point out the negative outcomes of sticking with anorexia nervosa in terms of identity. We ask the patient to consider whether they can see how people have come to identify them with anorexia nervosa, rather than who they are as a person. Using ideas outlined in Section 4.9, we frame treatment as being about re-connecting with those other, valued parts of their self-identity (e.g., caring nature, sense of humour, competitiveness, being focused). We stress that no parts are inherently negative, but that some have become too dominant or hostile, and others might be engaged at the wrong times (e.g. being detail-focused when thinking about meal planning; letting concern about how others see the person get in the way of socialising). The aim of treatment is to support the patient to become the "conductor of their own orchestra", able to guide and manage all parts of self in a way that enables them to live in a healthier manner. Many patients are able to use this metaphor to see how the anorexia nervosa has disconnected them from their sense of self, allowing the clinician to work with them in setting valued goals that the patient can work on in therapy.

5.9   Confidence in and perceived suitability of the proposed therapy

It is important to consider the patient's confidence in and perceived suitability of treatment at the assessment (regardless of whether this is an initial course of treatment or in the context of previous unsuccessful therapies). These beliefs are rated using simple Likert-type rating scales. If the scores are low on those scales (e.g., 3 out of 10), we address the reason for lack of confidence/perceived suitability at this point (e.g., considering whether previous therapies did or did not involve the level of planned change that we discuss in CBT-AN-20). We stress that there is never going to be a perfect time to recover, and that it is more important to consider whether this is a good enough time to change. We also discuss who can support the patient (family, partner, work, etc.).

5.10   Stressing the timing of the therapy

The assessment should stress that therapy is time-limited, and that continuation past six sessions is subject to demonstration of measurable and substantial progress by that point (or over the next two sessions – Section 7.7). We particularly address the need for the patient to show that they are on track for necessary weight regain (adjusted for the patient's likely needed level of weight gain). Such targets should be individualised to the patient's current weight and weight regain planning (see Phase 1) and should be developed through supervision and consultation with the patient's medical provider. Using this "try it and see" approach, the patient can be encouraged to view therapy as an opportunity to seize the moment, and to see if they can start to shake a little free of the grasp anorexia nervosa has on their life. We also discuss timing in terms of initial ability to commit to weekly sessions.

5.11   Involvement of family and loved ones

We give the option for the patient to invite key family members or support people into the assessment, so that they can understand the focus of treatment, and potentially adjust their level of support to increase its chances of success. This support might involve making plans for what foods will be available in the house, who will shop and cook, or (for families who have been very involved) handing over the task of weighing (and discussing weight) to therapy. We often find that a clear collaborative agreement about what sort of concerns should be communicated between families and services can help build trust and confidence in the treatment plan. A CBT-AN-20 information sheets for carers is provided in Appendix A.17 to facilitate such discussions. Further detail related to working with significant others is provided in Section 4.16.

5.12   Consider the potential to encourage pre-therapy change

We also recommend that the clinician should use the evidence that assessment can play a role in early change, certainly where there might be a delay between assessment and treatment, but even where there is no such delay. We suggest using a single-session intervention (SSI) between assessment and start of treatment to increase retention and kickstart some change before Session 1. This approach can increase a sense of self-efficacy (e.g., psychoeducation about the physical and psychosocial consequences of eating disorders, an understanding of factors maintaining their eating disorder and goals to work on before treatment – e.g., Fursland et al., 2018; a behavioural activation SSI – e.g., Wade & Waller, 2025b). Even relatively simple contact pre-therapy can result in better retention in therapy (e.g., Keegan, Waller, Tchanturia & Wade, 2024). We also use an exercise to address motivation, which can improve outcomes for the less motivated – the "Advantages of Change, Fears of Change, and Reponses to Fears" worksheet (Cooper et al., 2001; see Appendix A.18).

5.13   Summary

This chapter has considered the elements needed for an assessment that will facilitate engagement in CBT-AN-20. Those elements have included consideration of risk and its management, the nature of the eating disorder, and the patient's readiness to engage in change. Importantly, we have also outlined a way of formulating the patient's case within the framework of the 5Ps model. That formulation has the benefits of being adaptable to the individual's history, maintaining factors and strengths. Critically, it allows us to help the patient to understand how the initial positives of anorexia nervosa inevitably give way to the longer-term negatives over time. This understanding of the case allows us to flex CBT-AN-20 to the individual patient, without losing sight of the core tasks that need to be addressed in order to make the therapy effective. Following an outline of the structure of CBT-AN-20 in Chapter 6, we will progress to detailing the different phases of the therapy (Chapters 7–11).

Outline of CBT-AN-20

The structure of CBT-AN-20 is linked explicitly to the competences and meta-competences outlined in Chapters 3 and 4, and to the needs of the individual with anorexia nervosa. It is structured in overlapping phases, such that at times, more than one phase of CBT-AN-20 can be delivered in parallel. At times, we will return to a phase that began earlier, where necessary to consolidate progress (e.g., revisiting the need for weight gain where progress on that front slips). While CBT-AN-20 has many similarities to CBT-T (e.g., focus on early dietary change; use of an inhibitory learning approach to exposure therapy; similar approaches to body image), CBT-AN-20 has some key differences to CBT-T, over and above the longer duration of the therapy. These include being informed by an anorexia nervosa–specific formulation, which is used to engage the patient in early change; the use of behavioural experiments to teach weight maintenance; working with the "anorexic voice"; a later review point (to allow time for substantial early weight gain); and more of a focus on emotional triggers of compulsive behaviours, rather than simply impulsive behaviours. These differences from CBT-T are all detailed in this chapter.

When working with anorexia nervosa, it is natural to think about multidisciplinary team (MDT) involvement. The support of a multidisciplinary team (particularly dietitians, family physicians [GPs], family therapists, peer support workers, psychiatrists, psychologists, medics, occupational therapists, and more) helps us to ensure that we can work safely and effectively. Such a team supports holistic consideration of the patients' needs. Involvement of multiple members of the MDT must be balanced against not overburdening the patient, as determined by patient needs–led prioritisation of which professions are best to provide direct clinical consultation, and which are best supporting through consultative roles. It is also important to have coherence in the general team approach, supported by use of the 5Ps formulation and eating disorder meta-competences. We do not consider the direct involvement of other members of the MDT to be part of the CBT-AN-20 itself. Therefore, we would not reduce the number of CBT-AN-20 sessions if the patient needed additional dietetic support or medication reviews, for example. Such MDT input would run alongside CBT-AN-20, as required.

DOI: 10.4324/9781003594703-6

Remember that this is a therapy developed for individual outpatient use. It might be possible to use it within more intensive treatment settings, but the evidence for that is not yet available. NICE (2017) recommends that more intensive treatments should be used in preparation for the move to outpatient care, so CBT-AN-20 could be started when it is clear the individual is on their way out of more intensive care settings and heading towards active therapy in an outpatient setting. Where the individual has fully regained weight (e.g., in intensive care settings) but still has substantial anorexia nervosa cognitions and behaviours, then the clinician could use CBT-AN-20 by moving to the later phases more quickly (e.g., if weight maintenance has been well-internalised by the patient). In cases where much of Phase 1 (weight regain) has taken place in a higher level of care, the remaining interventions of CBT-20-AN (Phases 2–5) remain important. For example, since higher meal energy density/variety is associated with significantly *lower* odds of eating disorder relapse (Sala et al., 2023), Phase 2 behaviour experiments with feared foods might be especially relevant. Similarly, since poor body image is associated with significant *higher* odds of relapse (Keel et al., 2005), Phase 4 body image interventions take on even greater importance once weight restoration has been achieved. Such decisions will depend on the progress in the individual case but should include building the individual's confidence in the maintenance of their nutritional health, both in terms of weight and eating. Alternatively, the patient who has regained weight already might be considered as more suitable for the shorter timeframe of CBT-T (e.g., if the clinical team identifies that eating cognitions and low weight are no longer problems, but that body image remains a substantial concern). These scenarios are expanded upon in Chapter 12 (Section 12.1).

6.1   Phases of CBT-AN-20

Most patients will need most of the following phases, as outlined over the next five chapters. However, remembering the importance of flexing the therapy to the patient, if a particular phase is not needed, then it is not implemented (e.g., the emotion work of Phase 3 might not be required once starvation effects are addressed). Similarly, not every patient will need the clinician to address every skill in a specific phase (e.g., most patients might require only two or three of the body image methods in Phase 4).

The skills and meta-competences needed to deliver the phases of CBT-AN-20 have already been outlined in Chapters 3 and 4, and the necessary assessment elements have been detailed in Chapter 5. Chapters 7–11 explain the necessary phases in CBT-AN-20. Those phases are:

1. Dietary change and exposure for weight regain (reviewed formally at Session 6);
2. Behavioural experiments (modifying cognitions) to introduce new foods, and to help the patient to maintain weight between periods of weight regain;
3. Addressing emotional triggers and maintaining factors in anorexia nervosa;

4. Body image work, using a range of techniques that map onto what the patient needs to enhance body acceptance;
5. Ending and relapse prevention.

These phases appear in this order because addressing body image work is likely to be premature if the patient has not gained enough weight early on, and because the reduction of starvation in Phase 1 and learning about how to maintain weight in Phase 2 are prerequisites for the cognitive and emotional flexibility needed for later stages. However, the duration of each phase will depend on the speed of the patient's response, so session numbers linked to each phase (see Figure 6.1 and Chapters 7–11) are broad guidelines rather than specific directives. We provide a Therapy Checklist for the clinician to monitor their delivery of therapy across the stages (Appendix A.19). That checklist should not be taken as a rigid guide to what should be done in each specific session. Instead, it is designed to alert the clinician and supervisor to any gaps in what is being delivered for the individual patient, and prompt review of whether this is clinically indicated or otherwise.

6.2   Structure of CBT-AN-20

Figure 6.1 shows the overall structure of CBT-AN-20, demonstrating the approximate points over the course of therapy where the different phases are likely to be implemented. The initial (re)assessment session/s (Chapter 5) are used to determine suitability of CBT-AN-20 for the individual. Thereafter, the overall length of the intervention is 20 sessions over 20 weeks (although the latter half of therapy can be stretched by offering fortnightly sessions if time is needed to achieve weight gain/maintenance and to consolidate skills), plus three follow-ups, at one, three,

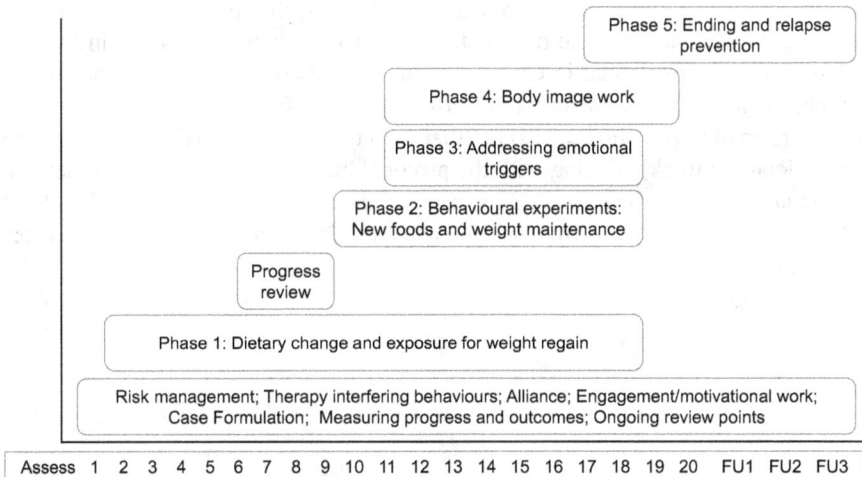

	Phase 5: Ending and relapse prevention
Phase 4: Body image work	
Phase 3: Addressing emotional triggers	
Phase 2: Behavioural experiments: New foods and weight maintenance	
Progress review	
Phase 1: Dietary change and exposure for weight regain	
Risk management; Therapy interfering behaviours; Alliance; Engagement/motivational work; Case Formulation; Measuring progress and outcomes; Ongoing review points	

Assess 1   2   3   4   5   6   7   8   9   10   11   12   13   14   15   16   17   18   19   20   FU1 FU2 FU3

Figure 6.1 Structure of CBT-AN-20.

and six months post-treatment. Progress is reviewed formally at Session 6 (see Section 7.7), though we measure and respond to measures weekly (see Section 3.5). We also recommend an informal review at Session 12 to ensure that the progress by Session 6 has been maintained and built upon.

As noted previously, these phases are intended to be delivered for long enough to suit the patient's needs, requiring the clinician to adapt based on the patient's responses to treatment. The phases will routinely overlap, as it is normal to tackle more than one topic in a session (e.g., starting work on emotional triggers, while coming back to maintaining positive changes in eating pattern), and to expand the impact of therapy using between-session work on more than one skill at a time. Involving significant others will be individual to the patient's needs and might occur at different time points across treatment (see Section 4.16).

6.3 Summary

In this brief chapter, we have provided an overview of the *structure* of CBT-AN-20. Over the next five chapters, we detail the *content* of the different phases of CBT-AN-20. Critically, we need to stress again that it is competence in delivering the therapy that is crucial – not rigid adherence to the protocol (see Section 3.8). Competence is defined as the use of core skills, but adapting those skills as the therapy progresses to fit the patient, rather than applying the protocol without responding to the patient's individual needs. It is important that we flex the therapy to the individual patient, but without drifting so far from the core tasks that we render the therapy ineffective.

Following the next five chapters, several specific variants are considered in Chapter 12 (e.g., working with younger people), but all are based on this core protocol. Because anorexia nervosa is physiologically maintained, the goal of weight gain is key and cannot be bypassed. However, the route to motivating and encouraging the patient to eat differently might vary substantially from individual to individual. As explained in Chapter 3, clinical supervision/consultation from a clinician who is familiar with eating disorders and CBT (whether one-to-one or with a group of peers who are also familiar with the intervention) is critical to keep the clinician on track, sticking with the protocol but delivering it in ways that suit individual patients. Appendix A.20 is a summary of the nature of CBT-AN-20 to help the patient to process what will be needed of them to enhance their chances of success.

Chapter 7

Phase 1 (Sessions 1–19)

Dietary change for weight regain and exposure therapy

This phase runs for as long as is needed throughout CBT-AN-20, to allow enough time for the necessary weight regain. Early weight regain is an important part of this element of treatment, giving momentum to the patient's progress, and this fact should be stressed from the assessment onwards. As an indicator, Wade, Ambwani et al. (2021) have shown that where the starting BMI is lower, at a mean of 16.42, a BMI increase of 0.51 points over the first six sessions of therapy is a predictor of better clinical outcomes from anorexia nervosa. Where the starting BMI is higher, a mean of 17.42, Wade and Allen (2021) indicate that a mean weight regain of around 4kg over the first 13 sessions of therapy predicts better outcome. This level of weight regain needed can be used as psychoeducation to support dietary changes that will give the patient the best possible start in therapy. Of course, regaining even more before Session 6 is likely to be even better.

If the patient makes the necessary weight regain and learns to maintain their weight (Phase 2) earlier, then the focus of therapy can shift to Phases 3–5. Otherwise, those phases can run in parallel with Phase 1 and 2, meaning that emotional and body image work can be managed alongside the weight regain and maintenance tasks.

While sessions can be run online, we advise that this use of online work should be minimised, as getting a reliable and valid weight can depend on the patient being in the clinic. If sessions must be online, then the patient should have their camera on, which is more akin to normal in-person interaction. Barriers to being visible can be explored (e.g., most video platforms include a function to hide the view of self). If online sessions are necessary, it is critical for the initial weight to be taken in person (e.g., at the physician's office) before the patient begins taking their weekly weight at home during teletherapy sessions, with regular in-person meetings to ensure that the weights being reported are accurate. If there is uncertainty about the accuracy of home weight readings, remote therapy sessions should not be made an option, to ensure patient safety.

DOI: 10.4324/9781003594703-7

7.1   Setting the agenda for the session

In each session throughout CBT-AN-20, it is important to set an agenda with the patient (see Section 4.1), though this might become less detailed towards the end of therapy. Monitoring and responding to risk should be on that agenda every time (see Table 4.1), as should addressing therapy interfering behaviours and maintaining an effective working alliance, with items related to these added where appropriate. In Phase 1, the more specific agenda items should include reviewing progress: reviewing food intake records (in whatever form works for the patient – see Section 5.6); weighing the patient openly to demonstrate links between weight and eating; changing diet to enhance nutrition and to expose the patient to anxiety about uncontrollable weight gain; preparing to address other targets later in therapy (Phases 2–4); planning eating changes and other homework; and discussing points that the patient wishes to bring to the session.

We should be responsive to the patient's experiences and life issues. This material is often related to quality of life issues that can be fed back into motivation work by considering the advantages of change, fears of change, and responses to fears (Appendix A.18 (e.g., "I am worried that my parents are going to nag me about not eating at my mother's birthday party, so I am not sure that I can go".). This avoidant response by the patient can be considered with them in terms of the short-term benefits versus long-term losses that could follow from deciding not to go. Similarly, the patient will often bring issues about emotional issues and body image, which allow the clinician to stress the importance of improving eating promptly so that treatment can progress to Phases 3 and 4.

As noted above, it will also be important to maintain progress during therapy by updating the agenda from session to session, adding items that are relevant to the specific phase of therapy and relevant tasks. This approach also helps to manage session pace and ensure good use of time. The final agenda item to be added is always that of planning or confirming eating changes, assigning psychoeducational materials, and other homework tasks for the week ahead. Each of the standard agenda items are described more fully below and in future chapters.

We review progress on the agenda at the end of the session, supporting plans for the next meeting. This helps us to set a provisional agenda for the next session, while the tasks of therapy and the plans for next time (e.g., what between-session tasks will be reviewed) are fresh in the mind of the clinician and the patient. We expect to focus less on some issues over the course of Phase 1 (e.g., decreasing the need for discussion about weight regain; diminishing influence of the "anorexic voice"). However, weight regain and experimentation should remain on the agenda, especially when linked to the behavioural experiments in Phase 2. So, leave a few minutes to prepare the agenda collaboratively with the patient (incorporating their agenda items), and then it can be ready on the screen or on paper as you walk into the therapy room next time, while allowing for adjustments as necessary.

7.2   Starting the clock

Session 1 is the point in therapy where we start the clock. We remind the patient from the beginning that therapy will last up to 20 sessions plus three follow-ups. However, we initially make it clear that there is a first countdown to Session 6, when the review will determine whether it will be helpful (for patient and clinician) to continue beyond that point. It is worth noting that qualitative analysis (Duggan et al., 2025) has found that the time limitations on therapy are generally not remarked on negatively by patients, except where they have previously had (but not responded to) much longer therapies. It can be more common to see clinicians who express concerns about shorter therapies, even though the evidence to date (Duggan et al., under consideration) has shown similar outcomes from 20- and 40-session CBT for anorexia nervosa.

Over the first sessions, it is important to remind the patient about the Session 6 review as a point where we really want them to breeze through it. This means reminding them of the need to change early (considering a weight regain of at least 1–2kg (2.5–5lb) over that time as a promising start – see above); focusing on the positives of recovery; and stressing our belief that this is achievable for them, rather than making the review feel like a threat. This process is likely to mean validating and containing distress, without backing off from the importance of such change for the improvement of their wellbeing:

Patient: "You mean that I only have six sessions of therapy, then?"
Clinician: "Actually, I would rather that you had all 20 sessions, if you need them. I am just saying that early change is so critical – especially weight regain – that if you're not able to show that vital early change in your eating and weight, then it will be important that we review how effective this treatment is likely to be for you".
Patient: "But what if I cannot change my eating and gain all that weight? Do I get kicked out?"
Clinician: "We will review at Session 6 and see what options we have. Being discharged until you are ready to actively engage in recovery is one possibility, certainly, though we would want to give you the best possible chance of getting on track, if you want to try – up to a couple of extra sessions to give you a chance to start making those changes, if you are willing. But we would have to end therapy after those extra two sessions if you still are not changing".
Patient: "So how can I do this – stay in therapy and get well?"
Clinician: "Well, we do not wait until Session 6 – that is lesson number 1. We work from today to give you the maximum chance of regaining those 2.5–5lb over the coming weeks, so that the review is a simple session, where I say 'Well done – let's keep going' and you commit to the other changes that are going to be important in your recovery".
Patient: "What do I need to do straight away, then?"

Clinician: "Let's talk about how your body works, what food you would need to get you to that level of weight regain, whether we need to cut back on your exercise level, and how you are also going to need to learn to slow your weight regain down in future, to feel in control".

Patient: "That sounds like a lot".

Clinician: "If you mean that it sounds like a lot of work, then you are right, but you have these sessions and the whole week to work on it. But if you mean that it sounds overwhelmingly scary, then I would agree that it is going to feel scary at times, but I have seen so many people manage this level of weight regain and then go on to do well, and I do not see why that could not include you".

It is also important in the first session to reiterate the rationale, evidence, and need for the non-negotiables of therapy (See Section 5.6 e.g., keeping safe; weekly therapy sessions; completing homework), using the relevant psychoeducation sheet to reinforce this learning (see Appendix A.20). This reminder allows the patient to understand that this therapy is very much focused on change for their benefit, however tough it will be at times.

7.3   Getting body image onto the future agenda

It is also useful at this early point in therapy to disrupt the patient's certainty regarding their body size, to limit their terror about what we are asking them to do with their eating. Almost every patient with anorexia nervosa will overestimate their body size, often very substantially, but will believe that their perceptions are correct.

To give the patient feedback on their tendency to overestimate their body size, we use a method that we commonly employ in CBT-T – a body size perception challenge. Using Blu Tack/Post-it notes on the wall, we ask the patient to estimate their current size (e.g., width of waist, or navel to spine, according to the patient's concerns). We then get accurate measures by asking them to stick Blu Tack/Post-it notes while standing in position at the wall, against the contour of their body. Our experience is that patients' estimates of their actual size are always substantially larger than their actual size. For people with anorexia nervosa, sometimes the width of waist assessment is accurate but the navel to spine is vastly overestimated, so it is worth doing both estimates. We use that disparity Socratically, encouraging the patient to consider whether the overestimations serve a function (e.g., supporting the urge to restrict). We also display a compassionate curiosity about how it feels to be basing decisions in their life on a misperception rather than reality, with consideration of how this must distract from addressing real-life problems. We also speculate about the reliability of the "anorexic voice" and in what other ways it may be perpetuating erroneous information. We encourage the patient to repeat their estimates for homework, to show them how strongly they still overestimate, even in the face of having seen the evidence. This exercise allows us to stress two things – first, the need to continue to strive for change, even while the "anorexic voice" is "shouting" about how big they are (see Section 4.9, and the formulation in Figure 5.1); and second, how important it will be to get through the early stages as quickly as possible, so that they can get to the body image work in Phase 4, as that is clearly going to be very important for them (see online skills video on https://sites.google.com/sheffield.ac.uk/cbt-an-20/videos).

7.4   Dietary change for weight regain and exposure therapy

At the assessment and from the beginning of Session 1, it is important to place weight regain firmly on the agenda. This focus is explained directly to the patient (reduction of starvation; reduction of any binge/overeating episodes; physical safety; cognitive and emotional stability), backed up by psychoeducation materials supporting what we tell the patient in-session. For example, Appendix A.1 provides a psychoeducation sheet on the growth mindset, the nutrition needed to help the brain form new neural pathways, and the role of eating in epigenetic changes that reduce genetically driven unhelpful traits. It is also important to summarise the evidence that this early weight regain is a powerful predictor of a good outcome of treatment.

7.4.1   Energy graphs

Two tools are very helpful in personalising the importance of eating differently at this stage. While reviewing the previous week's food monitoring, we will draw *energy graphs* (Figure 7.1) showing the difficulties that starvation can bring relative to normal functioning. First, we draw out a healthy energy graph, to show how carbohydrate levels are particularly important for maintaining normal function (along with the need to get calories and nutrients from a wide range of foods). Appendix A.21 provides a psychoeducation handout on the importance of carbohydrates (as used in one of the single-session interventions outlined in Chapter 5) to support the patient's understanding of the importance of this element of a broad dietary intake, which will support in their understanding of energy graphs. Blank energy graphs are provided in Appendix A.22, with enough for the patient to be able to review their carbohydrate levels between sessions (over eight days).

- The first energy graph (Figure 7.1(1)) is essentially psychoeducational – "If you were at a healthy weight, this is how a normal diet, complete with regular carbohydrates every few hours, would keep you in the 'comfort zone', where your brain works properly and your body functions healthily".
- The second energy graph (Figure 7.1(2)) "shows how a restrictive diet like yours, with very low-calorie intake and very little carbohydrate, leaves your body and brain unable to cope in the short and long term – your body has to shut down all those energy-demanding things, like thinking straight, socialising, physical tasks, growing bone, and more. Even if you can do some things

1. Healthy energy graph, showing how a regular food/carbohydrate intake provides sufficient energy at a normal weight

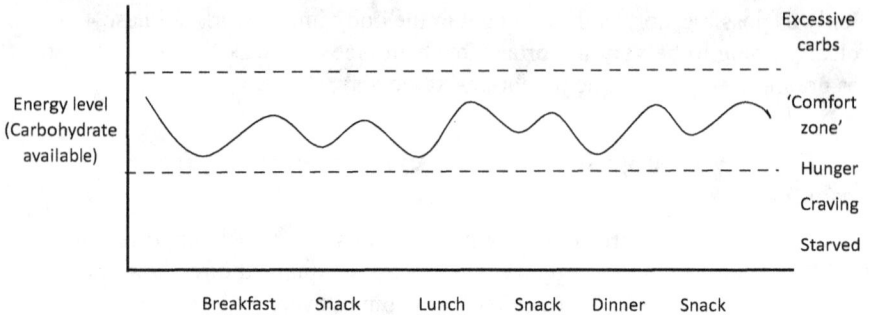

Energy level
(Carbohydrate
available)

Excessive carbs

'Comfort zone'

Hunger

Craving

Starved

Breakfast   Snack   Lunch   Snack   Dinner   Snack

2. Restrictive energy graph, showing how an inadequate carbohydrate intake affects the body's ability to function

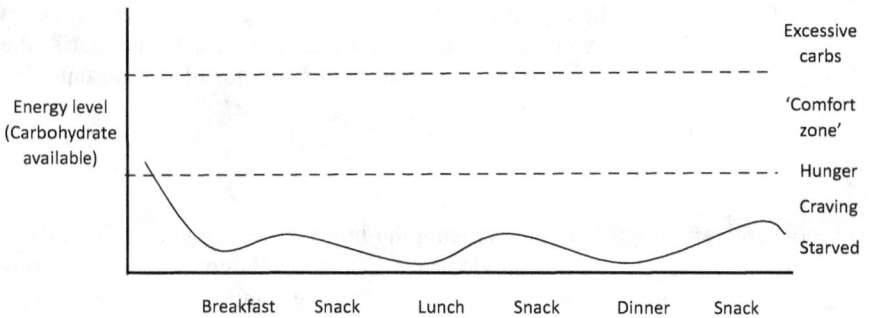

Energy level
(Carbohydrate
available)

Excessive carbs

'Comfort zone'

Hunger

Craving

Starved

Breakfast   Snack   Lunch   Snack   Dinner   Snack

3. Restrictive energy graph, showing how the body and environment trigger perceived or actual overeating in response to starvation and food cravings

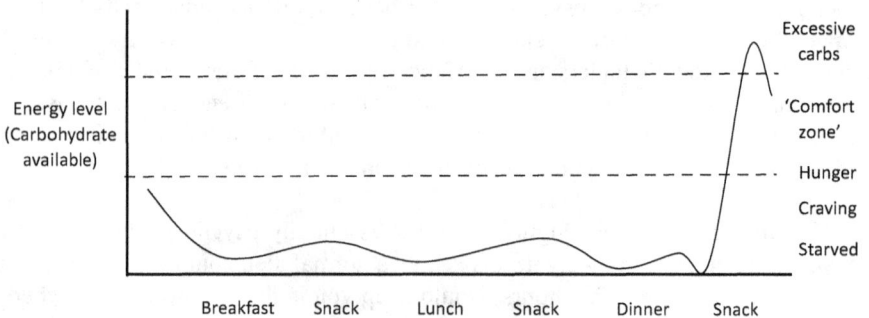

Energy level
(Carbohydrate
available)

Excessive carbs

'Comfort zone'

Hunger

Craving

Starved

Breakfast   Snack   Lunch   Snack   Dinner   Snack

Figure 7.1 Energy graphs in anorexia nervosa.

now, many will become harder and then impossible in time, as you lack the energy that food would give you".

- The final graph (Figure 7.1(3)) shows what happens when the individual cannot maintain the restriction (whether due to internal or external pressure to eat) – "So you restrict because your anorexia nervosa tells you to, but your body fights back and you end up feeling like you have lost control of your eating, so you eat more than you wanted to, and end up doing something like vomiting or exercise to feel in control again, only that ends up with you feeling worse physically and mentally, and puts you at risk of further binge eating".

We draw out the first graph and, based on the patient's food records, whichever of the other two is applicable now. Indeed, we might draw out all three, to show 1) what we are aiming to help the patient achieve; 2) what the problems were when the patient was simply restricting (to overcome the belief that this was a perfect time in their life); and 3) how the problems of restriction are likely to tip over/have tipped over into binge/purge behaviours (see online skills video on https://sites. google.com/sheffield.ac.uk/cbt-an-20/videos).

The point that we need to make to the patient is that the effects of starvation are partly about the *immediate energy level* that they have (especially how much carbohydrate they are eating intentionally), and partly about the *long-term effects of being seriously underweight*. Both of those deficits need to be addressed in order to counter starvation effects before social, emotional, cognitive, and physical problems can be overcome. That means eating both to function on a day-by-day basis and for weight regain. So, the balance of foods (especially carbohydrate) needs to be appropriate, and the amount of food needed to regain weight is going to be far higher than they are used to eating or believe they need to eat (see Section 7.4.3 for guidance on the amount and types of food needed). The stance needed is that "the medicine for most of your problems is food, and you need an extra dose of the medicine to overcome your problems until you are healthy". The patient can be reminded at this stage that their anxious predictions about "catastrophic" weight gain can and will be tested each week for their accuracy:

Patient: "But I don't want to gain weight too quickly".
Clinician: "Well, that makes sense. It is like a deep-sea diver coming back to the surface – they have to come up slowly and with rests to acclimatise, otherwise they are likely to get 'the bends', where their body cannot cope with the sudden pressure changes, and they suffer serious pain. We don't want you in that situation, do we? Just like we don't want you stuck down there forever".

7.4.2 Predictive/cumulative weight gain chart

The second tool that is needed to review and challenge patients' beliefs about their progress is a *predictive weight chart*. We chart the patient's weight on a tracker that creates a graph (see website) to share with the patient. The y-axis can be based on BMI (as per Figure 7.2) or regular weight readings (e.g., 0.5 kg/1lb). We also add

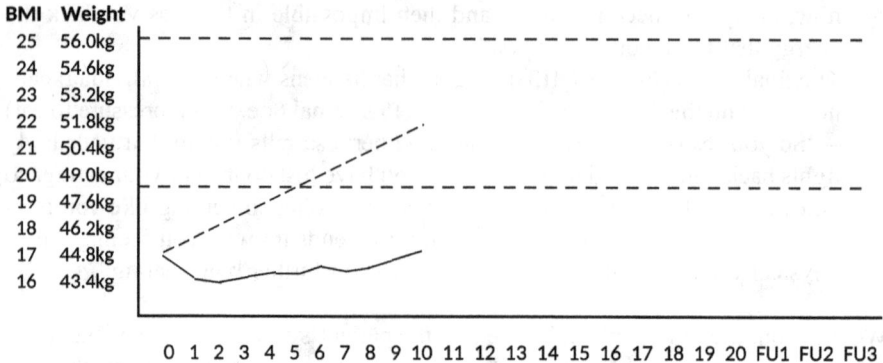

Figure 7.2 Cumulative weight chart, showing feared weight gain vs. actual weight gain in anorexia nervosa.

in the patient's predicted weight gain per session on a second line on the graph. As an example, Figure 7.2 shows the patient's actual weight across the first half of therapy (the solid line), showing a slow change due to the level of effort over time needed to regain weight. In contrast, their predictions week on week (the dashed line) accumulate to a far higher prediction of weight. This weight chart helps the patient to see that their schema (large, uncontrollable amounts of weight gain) conflicts with the data (slow weight gain), testing their cognitions and assumptions in an overt way that takes time for them to process.

Weight is taken in the session *after* discussing what the patient has eaten and stressing the changes made (e.g., "I know that you haven't eaten the planned meals every day, but that is so much better than your eating last week. So much more carbohydrate. Good for you".) to ensure that the weight regain prediction is as high as possible, due to the patient's raised anxiety levels. Because the patient is fearful of uncontrollable weight gain in the early stages of therapy, that second line always shows a rapidly increasing cumulative weight prediction (i.e., if they predicted a 3kg/7lb weight gain this week, then add 3kg/7lb to the second line, regardless of any objective weight change). That chart (see Figure 7.2) is used to explain to the patient that "While you have been predicting that your weight would shoot up out of control, your actual weight is going up much more slowly, even though you are taking all those risks with your eating. What do you think it would take for your weight to *actually* go up in the way that you are predicting?" That can lead to experimentation with eating (see Phase 2) that encourages the patient to learn that the weight regain needed for health requires a long, hard slog, rather than being a matter of simply eating a tiny amount more. It is useful to make clear that when the two lines start to run parallel, this indicates that the grasp of the anorexia nervosa has weakened, and the patient is now listening to their body and what it needs rather than the punitive voice of the anorexia.

For clinicians who have experience with testing weight predictions in CBT-T, it bears emphasising that whereas the broken cognition in non-underweight eating disorders is that engaging in regular eating will lead to substantial weight gain, in the case of CBT-AN-20, substantial weight regain is actually the expected outcome. What differs between the two therapies is that in CBT-AN-20 the broken cognition is that regular eating will lead to *uncontrollable* weight gain on a very steep trajectory that continues indefinitely (e.g., 2–4kg/5–10lb per week for months or years, rather than the persistent hard work on behalf of the patient that results in steady and predictable 1–2lb/0.5–1kg per week gain, with intermittent periods of weight maintenance, that the CBT-AN-20 clinician is prescribing over 20 sessions of therapy). As clinicians, we know that uncontrollable weight gain in anorexia nervosa is very unlikely, as longitudinal data suggest that >90% of individuals who have recovered from anorexia nervosa at 22-year follow-up achieve a body mass index in the normal (rather than overweight) range of 18–25kg/m^2 (Murray et al., 2017). However, from an inhibitory learning perspective – and from our clinical experience – simply sharing these statistics with a patient is no substitute for them engaging in real-time learning using their own personal weight graphs, as we describe here.

Please note that we ask the patient to predict their weight twice in the session, but only one of the predictions is used to chart weight:

- Beginning with Session 1, at the end of the session, we plan initial eating changes (e.g., "Each day for the coming week, try adding two slices of toast at breakfast, add a bun to your veggie burger at lunchtime, and have a portion of rice or potato with your evening meal"), and then ask the patient to predict their weight gain as a result of these changes. If the patient predicts substantial weight gain (e.g., "It will go up by at least 2kg/5lbs in a week"), then we can be confident that the patient is making a prediction that is highly unlikely to be achievable. If the prediction is small (e.g., "Oh, that probably won't do much to my weight – maybe I will gain 200g/0.5lb?"), then we know that we should be encouraging the patient to eat even more (e.g., "Oh, well if making those changes feels okay, I wonder if we could take it a step further and also include a snack or two each day") until the patient expresses greater anxiety about weight gain. This means that the exposure element of the intervention is likely to overcome the patient's anxiety about eating and weight gain (see online skills video on https://sites.google.com/sheffield.ac.uk/cbt-an-20/videos).
- From Session 2 onwards, we review food records, emphasising how much the patient has added and how they feel about the food that they have eaten (even if they did not eat all the food that was planned). When their anxiety is raised, we ask them to predict their weight gain again, to enhance their feared amount (e.g., "Well, I know I said that it would go up by 2kg/5lb but now that I am thinking about it, I think it will be more – at least 3kg/7lb, maybe 4kg/9lb"). At this point, we use this post-diary prediction to complete the cumulative

weight gain element of the weight tracker, and finally we weigh the patient. This second weight prediction is used because it encourages faster learning by the patient that they overpredict substantially, based on an inhibitory learning approach to exposure (see online skills video on https://sites.google.com/sheffield.ac.uk/cbt-an-20/videos).

- It is important to emphasise that the clinician should ask the patient to predict relative weight gain each week, rather than absolute weight (i.e., the patient should frame their prediction as having "gained 2 kg/5lbs", rather than "weighing 50kg/110lbs"). This will enable the clinician to add the relative gain each week and thus leverage the cumulative aspect of the graph that is so crucial for inhibitory learning to take place.

7.4.3   How much to eat, and how quickly to add to the patient's diet?

Clearly, weight regain is a primary outcome variable when treating anorexia nervosa (Bulik et al., 2007), and carbohydrates should be a core part of the eating plan. The following should be explained to the patient, their families/significant others, and other professionals, so that the plan of action makes sense, and they can engage with it. While nutrition for weight regain is important, remember that the introduction of more food (and carbohydrates in particular) will introduce anxiety. It is important to frame this for the patient as the exposure therapy element of the intervention, where they can learn that if they tolerate that anxiety for long enough (e.g., not restricting or purging after eating), then the fear of weight regain will decline as a natural extinction process.

7.4.4   How much weight regain is needed?

The answer is very likely to be that *we do not know*, and that this question can only be answered by working on it jointly during therapy. Therefore, we need to be honest with the patient that we do not know and validate the understandable anxiety arising from uncertainty here. Otherwise, the patient will tend to fixate on whatever weight or BMI figure we first give and will be very unhappy if that turns out not to be an adequate amount of weight gain, and we then try to reset the target. And if we do try to calm the patient by providing an early estimate of necessary weight regain, our estimate is likely to be on the low end of possible necessary weight regain, as we try not to scare the patient. It is more important to help the patient to roll with the uncertainty, in order to approach the "So what weight would I have to reach to be OK?" question in a Socratic manner (see online skills video on https://sites.google.com/sheffield.ac.uk/cbt-an-20/videos):

Patient: "So what weight would I have to reach to be OK?"

Clinician: "Honestly, I have no idea. That is one that we will need to work out together across therapy. Everyone has a natural range of weights where their body operates at its best, but I'm not sure what yours is. Even you and your family cannot remember what weight you were before you started to lose weight, and back then you were much younger, compared to your adult self now. The only way to find out what works for you is to experiment and work it out as you go along. For example, we could try an interim weight of 56kg, which would give you a BMI of 19.5, but gaining that 7kg might or might not be enough to get your body working properly again. So we would need to review as you got towards that weight, and decide whether we needed to up that target, so that your starvation symptoms were sorted properly".

Patient: "But can't you just work it out? You are the expert, after all".

Clinician: "An expert knows when they do not know, and how to find out. And an expert also knows when it takes two to work out the answer. That means you and me working together to find it out over the next few months".

7.4.5 How quickly should we ask the patient to regain weight?

NICE (2017) suggests aiming for a weight regain target of 0.5kg(1lb)/week, which is a good target in terms of seeing measurable weight regain. In the first few weeks, that level of weight regain can seem scary for the patient, so over the first six weeks of CBT-AN-20 we aim for at least the 1-2kg (2.5-5lb) that we discussed earlier as a good starting level of weight regain. Of course, some patients will gain more, and that is even better. After that, we discuss the 0.5kg (1lb) weekly target. That is likely to mean eating around 500kcal more than the patient is currently eating to maintain their low weight, spread across the meals and snacks of the day. The number of calories needed will vary with the patient's BMI, metabolism, compensatory exercise level, use of bingeing, and so on, so make sure that you explain that the rate of weight regain is also a matter for experimentation, and that exact calorie counting is only going to generate anxiety. Of course, measuring the rate of weight regain should allow for natural weight fluctuations, so reviewing overall progress every few weeks is more meaningful than getting caught up with lower or higher levels of weight regain on a weekly basis.

7.4.6 How quickly should we start weight regain?

In a word – immediately. Many clinicians will wait until after the first few sessions before they focus on weight regain, for fear of pushing the patient too soon. However, the importance of early change (see Section 3.4) has already been explained and applies here just as much as for any other therapy for any other disorder. So, it is important to push for changes in eating that will result in weight regain from the very beginning of therapy. If the patient compares this approach unfavourably with previous treatments, just remind them that the previous therapy might have started talking about weight regain later (if at all), but ultimately did not help the patient to leave the anorexia nervosa behind fully (they are still in therapy, after all), so it is worth trying this different approach.

In keeping with the principles of inhibitory learning, we stress the importance of substantial early change in eating, to determine how much the person can eat and drink before they regain any weight at all (i.e., "Losing weight was hard work, and so is weight gain"). As explained above, especially because we weigh the patient after reviewing their week's eating, their expected weight gain is likely to be far greater than the reality, as demonstrated in their weight chart. This "maximum expectancy violation" means that the patient can learn far more quickly and robustly that their weight is not shooting up as predicted than if we had adopted a slower approach to weight regain, making their future weight predictions more accurate.

7.4.7   But what about re-feeding syndrome?

Many clinicians are reluctant to push for early or substantial weight regain, because they fear that the patient will suffer from re-feeding syndrome. Some guidelines suggest that this should only be considered as any risk if the patient's BMI is below 16, if there is precipitous weight loss, if there has been little or no nutrition over more than five days, if bloods are abnormal prior to feeding, or if there are complicating factors around alcohol or drug abuse, including insulin, chemotherapy, antacids, or diuretics. Such cases are rare but important to identify and test more fully. It is relatively straightforward to plan with a family physician (GP) to arrange blood tests for the key electrolytes of phosphate, magnesium, and potassium, and this should be done and monitored from the assessment stage via medical practitioners (see Table 5.1, including https://meed.org.uk/) to ensure that the clinician is confident about proceeding with the dietary change necessary to address the risks of undereating (with dietitian support as appropriate to plan dietary intake and associated micronutrients provision, if the physical signs indicate a risk of re-feeding syndrome – e.g., below BMI = 16; phosphate disturbance).

7.5   Working with the patient's reaction to weight regain targets

In Section 3.9, we addressed the motivational issues that are strong in anorexia nervosa – particularly the benefits and fears related to change and the role of the "anorexic voice" in magnifying the fears – and how to address these fears. These are more formally considered at Session 6, when reviewing progress. However, for some patients, they are likely to come up as soon as change is suggested or when it is first tried. Therefore, it is important to consider the potential therapy-interfering nature of such patient responses when they arise during these first few sessions. Revisiting the benefits and fears of changing and the responses to these fears can be used to encourage consideration of whether anorexia nervosa is working for the individual. Revisiting the formulation can also help to clarify the underlying need(s) that the patient is trying to get met though sticking with the eating disorder. Just as importantly, where the individual experiences strong fears about change or resentment towards the clinician for encouraging such change, it is valuable to talk about the experience of the "anorexic voice" and how it reflects internal thought processes rather than any external controlling influence (see Section 4.9, and the formulation in Figure 5.1). We discuss how the "anorexic voice" is shouting out only one option about how to live, and contrast that with the "authentic" person, whose long-term development and needs are being halted by the patient's short-term acceptance of that "anorexic voice"'s guidance. It can be useful to explore with the patient whether the "anorexic voice" represents an underlying need on their part (e.g., "You are too fat" might reflect an underlying feeling of sadness and a need to connect with others, which is the underlying functional need that the voice is trying to communicate).

7.6   Remainder of each session in Phase 1

In addition to all the above, there are three further elements to Phase 1, whether delivering it alone or running it in parallel with other phases.

Considering the patient's material on the agenda is considered in Section 4.1, where we stress the importance of responding to the patient's experiences and life issues.

Homework/between-session tasks relating to Phase 1 will focus on changing eating in order to regain weight. It should be stressed that you know that this will not be easy in the short term ("If it were easy, you would already be doing it"), but that you firmly believe that eating more and regaining weight will benefit the patient in the medium to long term (e.g., more able to think flexibly; stable emotions, linked to feeling less anxious and depressed; better social engagement; stronger; better physical health; enhanced quality of life; rediscovering who they are and living the life they want). From the beginning, stress that the braver the patient is, the sooner they can regain weight and (just as important) learn to maintain their weight. This early work will give them longer to work on emotional factors and body image and could ensure ending treatment successfully even before 20 sessions have elapsed.

Setting the agenda for the next session is best commenced at the end of each session, when the tasks of therapy and the plans for next time (e.g., what between-session tasks will be reviewed) are fresh in the mind of the clinician and the patient. Over the course of Phase 1, we expect to focus less on some issues (e.g., less need for discussion about weight regain; less influence of the "anorexic voice"). However, weight regain and experimentation should be on the agenda, especially when linked to the behavioural experiments in Phase 2. So, leave a few minutes to prepare the agenda collaboratively with the patient (incorporating their agenda items), and then it can be ready on the screen or on paper as you walk into the therapy room next time, allowing for collaborative adjustments as necessary.

7.7   Progress review (Sessions 6–8)

At Session 6, we review the patient's progress, looking for the early change that indicates potential to do well in therapy (having emphasised the need for such pre-review change throughout therapy so far, of course). The marker of progress at this point is that where the patient has changed their eating enough to have started the process of reliably regaining weight (at least 1–2kg/2–5lb – based on Wade, Abwani, et al., 2021), rather than an up and down pattern that suggests an overall trajectory of a straight or downward line. We also hope to see a change in eating attitudes and greater energy levels by this time. While in CBT-T we can identify such positive change within four sessions, in CBT-AN-20 we find that six sessions is more appropriate, as it allows the clinician and the patient to see a positive trend in weight regain beyond normal fluctuations, and allows time to respond to the individual's dietary requirements for weight regain (in particular, if the patient has made changes in intake that are not resulting in weight regain, then the clinician can advise increasing that intake further in good time for Session 6).

If the patient is doing well at this stage, then the review is a relatively brief matter, and we can immediately resume the work of weight regain in Phase 1. Obviously, however, that is not the only possible outcome – a substantial number of patients show limited or no progress. There are two other common outcomes when the patient is asked about reasons for not having progressed by Session 6:

- The patient states that they have decided that they do not want to change. For example, the patient might be attending therapy because it gets other people to back off from pushing them to change (e.g., parents, school, family doctor). This is typically the patient who routinely neglects to undertake therapy tasks in between sessions.
- The patient states that they have been trying, but that making actual behavioural change feels impossible in the face of the "anorexic voice" that they experience whenever they try to leave the anorexia nervosa behind.

Clearly, we should respond appropriately to whichever pattern of response we are seeing at Session 6. However, that does not mean that we should give up if the patient has not changed at this point, as explained below. So, the review period might all be finished within just a few minutes or might need to run across Sessions 6–8, depending on the patient's motivation and the level of that "anorexic voice" (see Section 4.9 and below).

In short, this progress review can take three distinct paths, depending on the patient's responsiveness by Session 6. Those paths are illustrated in Figure 7.3.

The key questions to ask early in Session 6 (after setting the agenda, monitoring risk, reviewing food intake, getting the patient's weight regain prediction, and taking the patient's weight) are:

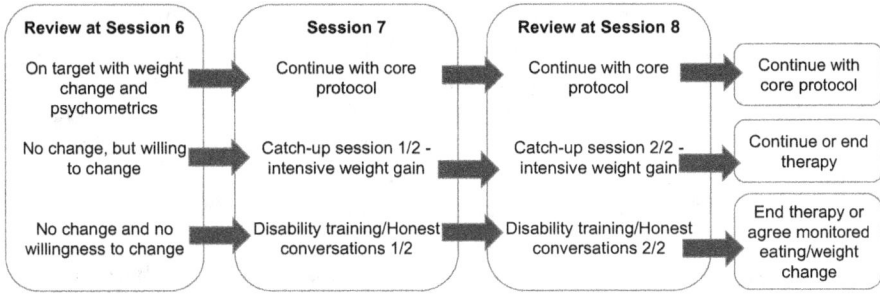

Figure 7.3 Routes through Sessions 6–8, depending on the patient's early response to treatment.

- Is the patient making big enough changes in their nutritional intake?
- Is the patient's weight rising at a satisfactory rate (at least 1–2kg/2–5lb or a corresponding BMI increase by this point is a good rate of change)?
- Are there signs of reduction in starvation symptoms?
- Are the patient's scores on the psychometric measures progressing in a positive way (even if they worsened when initially making dietary changes, as often happens)?

Of course, the clinician might notice a lack of active engagement earlier than Session 6 (e.g., if the patient's weight starts at the lowest recommended level and continues to fall). In such a case, the clinician might need to use the following skills in Path 2 or Path 3 before reaching Session 6. Supervision or consultation is an important means of supporting clinical decisions of this sort. It is potentially useful to consider the use of single-session interventions (see Table 4.2) as homework between sessions to support more intense focus on change and speedier progress.

7.7.1   Path 1 – On target

If the answers to all the above indicate that the patient is well-engaged in positive change, then the review is likely to take just a few minutes. The patient should be praised for how well they have faced their fears so far and reminded of just how far they have come in a short period of time. It is helpful to reflect on what it was in them that helped them achieve this change (possibly amending the "Protective factors" element of the formulation to incorporate those strengths – Section 5.1) and how these traits and abilities can be used for further change. This positive reinforcement should be authentic – we need to remember that the patient would have walked away from the anorexia nervosa a long time ago if change were easy. Of course, this praise should be followed by a reminder that there is still a long way to go, but that the patient has made a great start. Reminding the patient that such early change brings them closer to being ready to work on their emotional/body image issues can be a particularly positive message, also serving to reinforce the work the patient is doing, as they are often more motivated to work on the emotional/body image issues than the weight regain itself. Then the clinician can get back to the tasks of Phase 1, foreshadowing the weight maintenance learning of Phase 2 if appropriate at this stage in the process (see online skills video on https://sites.google.com/sheffield.ac.uk/cbt-an-20/videos).

It can also be reinforcing to revisit the Advantages of Change, Fears of Change, and Reponses to Fears (Appendix A.18), to see how reasons for change have expanded and how the fears have diminished, and whether there are further responses to fears that the patient can use moving forward. The remainder of Session 6 can then be focused on extending the eating changes to deal with weight regain and nutrition needs, while stressing the exposure element to keep the anxiety about the uncontrollability of weight (re)gain coming down. Session 7 and 8 are a continuation of Phase 1 for this group of patients, aiming to move to the first weight maintenance point in Phase 2.

7.7.1.1   But what if the patient is not making such progress at this early stage?

Some patients will not be making active or adequate changes in their eating by Session 6 (e.g., never committing to change for fear of weight regain). Rather than giving up on such cases at this stage, the clinician should try one of the other two options – Paths 2 and 3. These are short-term motivational efforts (Sessions 6–8) to engage the patient in change, to get them back on track with their eating and therapy overall.

7.7.2   Path 2 – Eager and willing to change, but feels unable to do so

The second path through the review process is one where the patient is eager to change, seeing the anorexia nervosa as hampering their life, but experiences major difficulties in doing so between the sessions. In such cases, it is very common to find that the patient is experiencing strong pushback from the "anorexic voice" (see Section 4.9) when they try to eat. While that "anorexic voice" might be audible to them during the therapy sessions, they usually do not find it as dominant as they do when they are facing the food, resulting in restriction or very restricted, "healthy/orthorexic" eating rather than eating the necessary food.

At this stage it is worth revisiting the exercise with the patient, using the Advantages of Change, Fears of Change, and Reponses to Fears worksheet (Appendix A.18). The bottom of the page provides a prompt for a short summary comment: "Putting it all together – what can I say to myself to help myself move forward in overcoming the anorexia nervosa when times get tough?" This exercise will provide you and the patient with a clear overview of key obstacles.

In Section 4.9, we detailed ways of addressing this anorexic voice, treating it as reflecting an extreme cognitive hypothesis that excludes other beliefs (e.g., "That food will make you fat"), rather than being one hypothesis out of several (e.g., "That food is unlikely to actually make me fat, whatever my first fears, but is likely to help me to feel healthier in many ways"). We also laid out ways in which that anorexic voice could be challenged, to allow the patient more flexibility in trying out behavioural changes.

At Session 6, if there is no appreciable change in eating patterns or weight, but the patient states that they really want to change but they do not feel able to, then we ask about the possibility that the reason for this is that the "anorexic voice" is getting in the way. With Beck's (1996) personality mode model in mind, we remind the patient that we regard the "anorexic voice" as reflecting one mode of thinking ("Anorexia is my only friend – the only way that I can feel in control of my weight, my emotions, my life"), but that it has become predominant, pushing other ways of thinking into the background (e.g., "This way of eating restrictively is really damaging my health and my quality of life – I would rather be getting on with friends, my relationship, my job, and more"). We use analogies to explain how that one way of thinking can take charge of life – for example, the workaholic mode:

Clinician: "Think about people who you know who are so obsessed with their work that they turn down every other opportunity to mix with people, go out, enjoy themselves. They know that all those other options exist – but the workaholic mode takes charge, stopping them trying out other ways of living. The only way for that person to enjoy life is going to be if they relegate the work mode to 'just one of the options that I could take up, but I don't have to'. It seems like the anorexic mode is currently preventing you thinking of the options, and thinking about your options is what we need to help you to do".

As Mountford and Waller (2006) have pointed out, experience of a therapy that challenges the anorexic mode's status quo of being in charge can shift that voice from being a calm, "best friend" to being angry and threatening (e.g., "You cannot listen to that therapist – you will be weak and pathetic and fat if you do, and then no one will care about you, and you won't even have me as your only friend").

7.7.2.1 Providing a rationale for the difficulty in eating and challenging the voice

To counter the influence of the "anorexic voice", we ask the patient to talk about the way that the "anorexic voice" operates, summarising in terms of the personality modes model (e.g., "It appears to be one way of thinking that becomes predominant over a long time, and that keeps you pinned down by promising to be your best friend and make you feel good"), and how that voice becomes less of a friend and more insulting and hostile when the patient tries to change their eating (e.g., "So when you try to do the homework that we have planned, the voice becomes hostile and abusive, so that you will back off from eating, in order to stop the shouting"). Then we explain that the only way out of anorexia nervosa is to challenge that voice, to tolerate the anxiety caused by the "abusive" anorexic voice, and to identify how "standing up to it" (i.e., eating as per the homework) will result in a weakening of the "anorexic voice". We stress that the "anorexic" voice might never go away completely ("This thing called the 'Western thin ideal' pretty much guarantees that for most people"), but that with recovery, the "anorexic voice" will fade down to just being another option, which the patient is free to ignore so that they can work on rebuilding their health and a good quality of life (see online skills video on https://sites.google.com/sheffield.ac.uk/cbt-an-20/videos).

Obviously, the prospect of standing up to that bullying voice is going to be daunting for the patient, but we recommend that they use Sessions 6–8 to push back against the "anorexic voice" by eating as prescribed, so that they learn that the voice does not have control over their choice to recover. To support this, we will use imagery (Mountford & Waller, 2006) or related schema-level imagery- and dialogue-based methods such as chair work (Pugh, 2018, 2019) to assist the patient in challenging the "anorexic voice", stressing its actual impotence if they choose to ignore it. The aim is to help the patient see that the "anorexic voice" once felt like their best friend (hence their attachment to it), but that the voice has moved to being more of a toxic way of managing their lives (see Section 4.9).

When faced with the patient who is experiencing the urge to stay with their anorexia nervosa, a key element of motivational interviewing can be valuable – "*Siding with the negative*". In short, it is important to roll with defensive responses rather than oppose them. Taking up the negative side of the argument will often bring the patient back to a balanced or opposite perspective.

This approach to motivation and addressing the "anorexic voice" requires consideration of the self-criticism and perfectionism that can influence the pros and cons that the patient perceives (see Section 4.10 for further details on how we implement these skills, and Section 2.1 regarding how perfectionism and self-criticism can be stressed in the formulation of anorexia nervosa). As mentioned in Section 3.7, it is sometimes appropriate to integrate a short augmentation to therapy to address specific barriers to change, and it might also be helpful to revisit support from significant others at this point to explore whether family or loved ones are able to actively support change if not already involved (see Appendix C for short augmentations to therapy, and Section 4.16 for working with significant others).

7.7.3   Path 3 – No interest in active change or engagement in the active elements of therapy

Regardless of any early stated motivation to change versus staying with the status quo of being controlled by the anorexia nervosa (see Section 3.9 and above), many patients with anorexia nervosa still regard restriction and weight loss as being more important goals than recovery or believe that recovery is possible without weight regain. Their actual motivation might have been to be *in* therapy rather than to *do* therapy, as being in therapy would allow them to reduce pressures to change and eat differently (e.g., from parents and referrers). By Session 6, it will be apparent to the clinician if the patient is committed to actual change, or if their stronger motivation is to being in therapy without changing.

Waller (2012) recommends that early motivational statements are best treated as a manifesto – statements that serve a function that is different to the words spoken (e.g., "I really want help with getting well again" might mean what is stated, or it might be a statement that is intended to get the person into therapy but with no desire to change). While initial levels of motivation are a good indicator of active engagement with treatment for eating disorders, traditional motivational interviewing has minimal benefits (e.g., Dray & Wade, 2012; Fetahi et al., 2022; Knowles et al., 2013; Macdonald et al., 2012; Waller, 2012).

Rather than simply giving up on the patient at this stage (or reducing the requirements for changes in eating and weight, to the point where therapy is unlikely to work), we use "disability training" (Waller, 2012) in such cases. This approach is perhaps better labelled for the patient and carer as having "honest conversations" about the prospect of future change in light of the lack of change to date, and the likely negative outcomes that will result and how to minimise them. It involves the clinician making it clear that they know that they cannot force the patient to change and agreeing to spend a couple of sessions wrapping up therapy. The tone of these conversations is important. The clinician may express their concern for the patient's future wellbeing, and curiosity about whether the patient struggles to feel or sustain that concern for themselves. It is also important to avoid assumptions about what the patient "should" want for the future, as sometimes anorexia nervosa might be implicated in avoiding developmental milestones and societal expectations that the patient has conflicting feelings about. The clinician offers to plan with the patient to allow them to minimise the negative outcomes of their anorexia nervosa – training them to cope with their functional disability due to their decision to stick with the anorexia nervosa (see online skills video on https://sites.google.com/sheffield.ac.uk/cbt-an-20/videos), for example;

Clinician: "We already saw how the eating disorder has impacted on your physical state, your ability to think, your emotions, your social life and lots more. If you stick with the anorexia nervosa, you are going to keep seeing deterioration, of course, so I suggest that we used these last couple of sessions to plan for your 'crash landing' – to make it as soft as possible, given your decision to stick with the anorexia nervosa".

Patient: "Does that mean you are giving up on me?"

Clinician: "No – I am just being honest and saying that your decision not to change means that no clinician can make you recover, and we don't want to start getting into a tug of war. I just want to make sure that you are not too badly stressed by the changes in your life. If we cannot build up your coping skills by getting you healthier, then let's work on helping you to navigate the stresses in your life as you go forward".

Patient: "What would that look like?"

Clinician: "Well, let's look at what you find hardest that we can help with. For example, you have said that you feel guilty about not spending time with your friends or accepting their invitations. So perhaps you could give some thought to whether it might be possible to sustain something of the social connections that are clearly important to you, within the limitations of what you may be able to contribute towards if you continue to become more tired and frail. And you said that you feel bad about having been on sick leave from your job as a teacher so many times and for so long over the last four years. So how about changing to doing some voluntary work, so that you only have to work on the days you can face it. Less rewarding, perhaps, but something like working in a local shop or volunteering would let you take it much easier and feel less guilty".

Other reductions in potential stressors can be very powerful (e.g., "Giving up on your desire to be a mother, as your anorexic body cannot provide that, but aiming to be a favourite aunt"; "Moving back in with your parents, so that they can make sure that you are safe, rather than running the risk that you would be very ill with no support"). Of course, these are presented as some way in the future, but as inevitable consequences of the current decision to continue with the anorexia nervosa rather than make active changes in eating behaviour. For homework following Session 6, we ask the patient to take home and add to a list of future quality of life issues of this sort, and we use Session 7 and the homework from that session to work on how to "soften the crash landing" for as long as possible. We stress how the patient's authentic identity can be forgotten by those around them, so that friends and family only see the patient as "the anorexic person", where others do not remember or address the person who they were without the anorexia nervosa. Therefore, it can be helpful to encourage the patient to have a conversation with their family now, stressing that the real person is still there, though asking the family to lower their expectations of what the patient can do in terms of change, thus softening their landing as their anorexia nervosa becomes more prominent and all-pervading in everyone's lives.

The way that one presents disability training/honest conversations will vary with the age and experience of the patient. In the case of a patient who has many years of experience of the constraints to life that accompany anorexia nervosa, it is relatively easy to find examples of experiences and lost opportunities that can be so prominent in their life (e.g., social isolation, regret, loneliness, estrangement from family, spending holidays alone, being unemployed), and to link them to the decision to stick with the anorexia nervosa. In contrast, younger patients with relatively brief experience of the eating disorder might be less believing that it will have such constraining effects on their lives. In such cases, in order to elicit change talk, the clinician needs to focus on future "disability", considering the adverse impacts of anorexia nervosa that they are likely to experience (physical, educational, social, familial, and emotional). An immediate example of things going wrong in their life can be seen in the fact that the young patient is being pushed into spending time in therapy, for example:

Clinician: "I appreciate that you do not think that these negative outcomes will apply to you and your life. After all, you still have the friends and family support that must be so important. And school is keeping an eye on you to make sure that your exams do not suffer too badly. I wonder if that support feels the same now as it used to even a couple of months back?"

Patient: "Well, I know that it is a bit more focused on me and my eating than it used to be".

Clinician: "Well, there is always the danger that those who love you become more fixated on you as someone with anorexia nervosa, rather than the real you. And that is good in some ways – it shows that they care, and that they do not want you losing out on your education any more than you have to. However, I know that some people in your position find that level of attention more and more intrusive over time. Does that ring any bells for you?"

Patient: "I wish that everyone would leave me alone, I know. That has got worse lately".

Clinician: "Even to the point where they are all pushing you to come and see a therapist – I am pretty sure that this ramping up of the demands is not your favourite thing to be doing for the foreseeable future".

Patient: "Well, no, not really. How can I get my life back on track if they are being so intrusive and if I have to come to therapy?"

Clinician: "Good question. Let's think about how you could get life back on track, then".

Where the patient pushes back (e.g., "But I don't want to give up on my job/ school"), then we need to be very sympathetic but to stress that we are powerless to change the patient's trajectory given their current choices (e.g., "Well of course – I don't imagine anyone would want that. I am just helping you to see the inevitable outcomes of your decision to stay on your anorexic track, so let's get back to planning for that future").

Of course, our aim is to highlight those long-term costs of anorexia nervosa, making them feel more real to the patient. We want to hear the patient pushing back, and to respond appropriately (with some "constructive scepticism", designed to get the patient to push back harder and plan more productive changes):

Patient: "What if I wanted not to have to give up on my friendships or resign from my job?"

Clinician: "I am sure that you don't want either of those things. But I don't have the power to stop them happening. The only thing that would allow you to avoid them would be to eat more and leave your anorexia behind, and you have been very clear that you are choosing not to do that".

Patient: "But I *am* choosing to give up the eating disorder. I have been coming here and doing my food records, haven't I?"

Clinician: "You have indeed been coming along, but there is still no actual change in your weight – no sign of leaving your anorexia nervosa behind. All we can really learn from that is that coming here and filling out food records is not moving you out of starvation. The missing element is the extra food that your body needs but that you have not been adding into your diet".

Patient: "Well, what if I ate some more?"

Clinician: "Eating 'some more' is not going to do it. It would have to be a lot more to make a difference to your nutritional health, as we have talked about for all these sessions so far. Just eating a bit more would scare you and still not get you out of this long-term future".

Patient: "All right then – I will show you that I can eat enough to get out of this. I don't want that life where I have to give up on everything that I want for myself".

Clinician: "Well, if you are determined, we could add a couple of extra sessions, so that you can show that you are serious about eating enough food. But it would need to be a meaningful amount of food, as you are already about a third of the way through therapy and you have a lot of catching up to do. If you do not make the changes, then we will need to bring therapy to an end".

In that circumstance, you should continue the therapy, on a session-by-session basis at first, monitoring changes in eating and weight. In many cases, the result is that the patient does start the work of necessary weight regain, and therapy can get back on track. However, if the patient remains unengaged in the tasks of eating and weight regain, then CBT-AN-20 should end. The patient can be considered for an alternative approach, but the failure to engage with therapies is likely to be generalised and therefore appropriate alternative interventions might be those that are more intensive (e.g., day programme; inpatient treatment). Of course, it is important to end CBT-AN-20 with the offer that the patient can return to start again when they are tired of the consequences of anorexia nervosa that we have been discussing. In this case, discuss with the patient the need for ongoing medical monitoring as part of the disability plan, and communicate this to the medical practitioner involved.

Finally, it is important to note that patients can fit into the disability training/ honest conversations category even if they have been making consistent small changes (e.g., adding half a piece of toast to breakfast, adding milk to their tea at morning snack), but realistically these changes have not been sufficient to result in meaningful weight regain. A patient who regains 0.5kg/1lb over six weeks might indeed be trying very hard in their mind, but unfortunately their anorexia nervosa is pushing back even harder. Since past behaviour is the best predictor of future behaviour, continuing the therapy for 14 weeks on the same trajectory of weight regain would result in a further regain of just 1kg/2lbs, and hardly seems worth the patient's efforts in doing between sessions tasks and attending sessions. It is important to remember that the decision to move to disability training/honest conversations is *not* an overall judgement on how hard the patient is trying, *nor* the patient's worthiness to receive treatment, but rather a realistic assessment of whether the therapy is actually helping them and whether they are able to make big enough changes to move the needle on their eating disorder at the present time.

7.7.4   What if there is a response to Paths 2 or 3, but then the patient slips back into inaction?

This is not an unusual outcome and reminds us that we should be reviewing progress continually rather than relying on the Session 6 review alone. We expect motivation to wax and wane over treatment, particularly as weight starts to increase. For example, the patient might eat better and regain weight after Session 8 but return to restriction around Session 11. In such case, there is nothing to stop the clinician from returning to disability training or working with the "anorexic voice". However, this needs to be negotiated as something to be done briefly (and often alongside other tasks), so that the patient can focus on it for a short enough time to be able to return to the remaining tasks of therapy (e.g., weight regain; body image work).

7.7.5   What if Paths 2 and 3 end in no improvement in therapy engagement?

If the patient needed help to get back on track (e.g., through a short therapy augmentation, such as working on perfectionism; through additional support from loved ones; through work on the "anorexic voice"; or through disability training/honest conversations, as detailed above), then we aim to have them back into active change by Session 8. However, it is important to remember that some patients will not have engaged in this way. Rather than perseverating with a therapy that is not working, it is important to acknowledge with the patient that it is not working for them at present, and to stop CBT-AN-20. Otherwise, the patient is simply "in therapy" rather than "doing therapy" and will go on to learn that therapy does not work for them. Better to give the message that the therapy might work for them in the future, but only if the patient engages with it fully, making changes in their eating and in other areas of life.

As detailed in Chapter 3, it is important to have a strategy if therapy is not working, to avoid that sense of learned helplessness and personal defectiveness on the part of the patient (e.g., "I cannot do anything to change") or the clinician (e.g., "This patient cannot ever change"). There are several options as to how one might end the CBT-AN-20 at Session 8, with the choice being determined by several factors (risk; pressures from family; service model):

- *Strategic disengagement* (Geller, cited in Waller, 2012), where the patient is discharged from therapy with the very clear message that they are welcome to come back and start CBT-AN-20 (or another evidence-based treatment) again when they are ready to engage in the necessary changes, starting with inter-rupting restrictive eating. We ensure that risk is managed in routine services moving forward as part of ensuring patient safety. We acknowledge to the patient that they might have to wait until their quality of life has deteriorated before they are ready to engage in therapy fully in future, and we hope that they will keep monitoring that quality of life (with assistance from a medical practitioner, family, and loved ones), so that they are ready to return to therapy as soon as possible.
- *Stepping up intensity* might be the optimum approach at this time, especially if the patient has a recent history of low weight and weight loss (before and during therapy), as the combination of high risk and starvation might require day- or in-patient treatment.
- *An alternative evidence-based therapy* might be sometimes considered (e.g., MANTRA, SSCM, CBT-E, focal psychodynamic psychotherapy, integrated trauma-focused approaches) if the formulated reason for the lack of progress in CBT-AN-20 indicates that a different therapy is more likely to be effec-tive (e.g., the patient's interpersonal issues appear to have been instrumental in precluding this therapy supporting the patient to change). Care should be taken to avoid colluding with the tempting idea that a different approach would negate the need for weight restoration as part of recovery from anorexia ner-vosa. We should give careful consideration to whether the existing barriers to recovery are likely to be specific to CBT-20-AN, or whether they will apply equally to other therapies. In any of these eventualities, we do not rule out the possibility of change, or that CBT-AN-20 might be appropriate for this patient in the future. However, if weight has been gained (e.g., due to sub-stantial binge-eating), then the better option might be CBT-E or CBT-T. If we believe that CBT-AN-20 might be suitable in the future (even if it is relatively soon after this course of therapy is now planned to end), then we stress that we would need the patient to demonstrate that they are coming back to "do therapy" next time, rather than just to be "in therapy" again. In short, as part of the agreement to re-commence therapy, we would be clear that we would expect to see the patient eating enough (including adequate carbohydrates) to achieve some weight regain over the first 2–3 sessions. If this is not manifest after those early sessions, then we would aim to end therapy, on the grounds that the patient was not in a place to actively work on recovery.

This explanation to the patient should be reinforced by a therapeutic letter to the patient to remind them of their progress in therapy, as well as what would be needed to have a stronger chance of a positive outcome in future. That letter should go to the referrer and other health professionals involved in the case, so that they are aware of the transparent decision-making process that has led to this early end of treatment.

Finally, if the patient stops making progress after successfully passing the Session 6 formal review, it is reasonable to repeat this review process to determine whether the patient can be re-engaged in active change. This could happen at any point, but the additional data collection at Session 12 (see Section 4.7) is a natural point for the clinician and patient to discuss whether progress has slowed to a degree that therapy is being threatened.

Chapter 8

Phase 2 (Sessions 10–19)

Behavioural experiments to challenge cognitions about food and uncontrollability of weight gain

Behavioural experiments are important in addressing the beliefs of our patients. However, in CBT-AN-20, they are used for different (though overlapping) purposes to those in CBT-T. In CBT-T, behavioural experiments are used to support the patient with learning that they can eat specific feared foods, once the general anxiety about food intake has subsided during Phase 1. This use of behavioural experiments is also found in CBT-AN-20, helping the patient to learn that their weight does not jump up with more healthy and diverse eating patterns, and that they do not binge if they eat a feared food. However, behavioural experiments have a second role in the case of anorexia nervosa. With underweight patients, we also use behavioural experiments to teach the patient that their weight regain can be controlled. In short, within CBT-AN-20, behavioural experiments are used with anorexia nervosa cases to:

- Introduce new foods/feared foods where there are specific beliefs about that food (e.g., fear of excessive weight regain; fear of loss of control and overeating). This skill can be used to broaden dietary intake from relatively early in therapy, especially if that enhances calorie intake to promote learning from controlled weight regain;
- Teach the patient the skill of *weight maintenance* – learning that weight regain is controllable and can be stopped part way through therapy, so that the patient can be sure of being able to stop such weight regain when they get to a healthy weight, rather than drastically overshooting any planned target. This element of therapy can begin when the patient has made substantial progress towards a healthy weight range, and then returned to later in weight regain, so that the learning is reinforced.

8.1 Introducing new foods

Where we start with this use of behavioural experiments is dependent on anxiety reduction due to exposure and weight regain in Phase 1. Though it is a good plan to aim for starting around Session 10, earlier is certainly possible if the patient is making good progress with weight regain and introducing feared foods. The aim

DOI: 10.4324/9781003594703-8

of the behavioural experiments is to let the patient learn that specific feared foods do not cause massive weight gain (e.g., eating chocolate) or induce loss of control eating (e.g., opening a pack of cereal and feeling unable to stop until it is all eaten).

The aim of a behavioural experiment is to help the person to change their cognitions. To achieve this, the clinician should make sure that the patient understands that they need to:

- Be eating enough that they are sufficiently cognitively flexible, emotionally stable, and physically safe from urges to overeat (hence this intervention happens in Phase 2 rather than Phase 1);
- Follow the general structure of an experiment – that they should try to keep everything else as stable as possible (not eating less; not compensating by exercising more; etc.), so that they can learn from the specific change in their diet and whether or not it has the predicted outcome;
- Focus on their current belief, suitably quantified so that it can be tested (e.g., "If I eat three 50g/2oz bars of that chocolate, then I will gain 2–3kgs/4–7 lbs in weight"; "If I open a pack of cookies/biscuits with the plan of eating just one, then I will lose control and eat them all"), and how strongly they hold that belief (e.g., "90% certain");
- Work with the clinician to develop an alternative belief (e.g., "Given the number of calories in that chocolate bar and the number of calories that the books say I would need to regain a lot of weight, then maybe I will not gain more than a hundred grams or so"; "If I eat an hour before the cookie so that I am not too hungry, then I should be able to eat just the one"), even though they do not rate that belief strongly (e.g. "Maybe 5%?");
- Plan out when to do this, for how long, and how often – remember that an effective experiment might need to be repeated on a few occasions to rule out that the result is a chance occurrence;
- Test out the belief behaviourally (e.g., add the chocolate every day for one week and see if there is the predicted massive jump in weight, over and above the expected weight gain that comes with the changes introduced in the concurrent Phase 1):

Patient: "I know that it takes a lot longer for me to gain weight than I had thought. But I absolutely know that if I eat that chocolate every day, then my weight will shoot up. At least a couple of kilos over the week".

Clinician: "You might be right. I don't know, given how the calories do not look like they would add up to that much weight gain. But you are an individual, so I cannot say for sure. How certain are you about that belief that your weight would go up by two kilos, and how about the alternative possibility – that it would not result in that sort of weight gain?"

Patient: "Well, probably 90% versus 5%".

Clinician: "And how long would you need to try it out to be sure which belief was right?"

Patient: "Probably two weeks. I suppose that would tell me which was right".
Clinician: "Sounds like a good plan to me. Let's put that into a worksheet to get it all clear".

Where the fear is of loss of control (e.g., "if I open a pack of cookies/biscuits, I will just eat them all"), then it is important to remember that this should be tried about an hour after the last meal, to ensure that the patient is not simply likely to binge due to extreme hunger. The fear of loss of control can be tried out in vivo during a clinical session, but it should then be extended to different contexts (e.g., at home; with other people rather than the clinician; when alone) to ensure wider learning. This should be explained to the patient as a need to conduct most behavioural experiments (and exposures) outside of the clinic, so that the learning is more robust and appropriate to the settings that are most relevant to the patient.

- Review the outcome with the clinician, and what it says about their belief;
- Repeat with a range of feared foods.

The clinician needs to be Socratic throughout – "I don't know what the chocolate will do to your weight. Maybe it will go up as you predict, maybe it won't. But there is only one way to find out, and that is to try it". As a result of such experiments, we expect to see a reduction in avoidance of those feared foods, a more diverse diet, and a lowering of the fear of uncontrollable weight gain (see online skills video on https://sites.google.com/sheffield.ac.uk/cbt-an-20/videos).

8.2   Learning weight maintenance skills

Much of the clinical and research focus of working with anorexia nervosa is about the importance of teaching the patient *weight regain skills* for recovery, given the central role of being underweight in social, physical, emotional, cognitive, and quality of life domains. However, it is also important to teach the patient *weight maintenance skills* over the course of therapy. These are the skills that enable the patient to be confident that they will be able to maintain their weight when they reach a functional BMI, rather than fearing that they cannot stop the weight gain. In other words, they need to believe that the weight regain that they make is not just a long slog, but that it is controllable, to overcome that core fear of uncontrollable weight gain that underlies so many eating disorder behaviours. Otherwise, there is the high probability that the patient who has worked so hard to regain weight will not feel confident about their ability to control staying at that weight and will restrict after therapy in order to feel safe (e.g., the loss of weight following in-patient treatment vs. outpatient treatments for anorexia nervosa – Crisp et al., 1991).

Again, we are addressing beliefs in this circumstance using behavioural experiments. We encourage patients to regain weight quickly enough from the beginning that they can take at least one deliberate "weight maintenance" break (more, if time permits), to test their belief that their weight will go up out of control even if they reduce their eating. We do not want the patient to lose weight at this stage, but we want them to learn what happens to their weight if they reduce their "weight regain" intake to a more "weight maintenance" level. For example:

Clinician: "Here we are at Session 14. I know that you had a hard time getting going with weight regain, and we had to spend a couple of sessions after the Session 6 review working on that anorexic voice. But you have been doing well since then. Your weight has been going up about half a kilo/1lb per week, and you are on your way to that first interim weight target. We have also started on those body image issues. How does that feel to you?"

Patient: "Well, it feels good in theory, and I am glad that the body image work is getting going, but I am just scared that I will never be able to stop the weight gain, and that I will end up restricting again".

Clinician: "I can totally understand that fear. Do you remember way back, early in therapy, when I said that this might happen – you would be scared that the weight regain that you needed would be uncontrollable? And do you remember what I said would be important around this time?"

Patient: "You said that I would need to learn how to keep my weight stable, but that we should do that as we went along, rather than at the end".

Clinician: "Sounds like it is time to do that now, so that you feel confident that you can maintain your weight when you get to your healthy range. What this would involve would be another one of those behavioural experiments, but this time testing your belief that your weight will carry on going up, even when you try reducing your eating, so that the scales might be expected to stay around the same reading for a week or two. What do you think we could try taking out of your weight regain eating plan to make that happen?"

Patient: "Maybe the evening snack? It always feels like I have to make time to fit that in rather wanting it".

The behavioural experiment here is similar in structure to the previous one, but in this case, it centres on testing the patient's beliefs about what will happen to the patient's weight if an amount of food is withdrawn from their intake temporarily. It should be noted that the clinician might also fear that cutting food intake at this stage might mean that the patient suddenly loses a lot of weight and goes back to the beginning, with this clinician belief resulting in being hesitant to get the patient to experiment in this way. Therefore, reviewing the plan of therapy in supervision or with their consultation team can be an important factor in getting the clinician to try this element of CBT-AN-20. The supervisor can remind the clinician of the importance of this learning for the patient, and review that the patient is doing well so far and could regain the weight even if any were lost during the experiment.

The steps will be along the following lines (see online skills video on https://sites.google.com/sheffield.ac.uk/cbt-an-20/videos):

1. Ask the patient to predict what will happen to their weight if they carry on eating as they are (i.e., weight regain diet), and how strongly they believe that ("100% sure that I will keep gaining 0.5–1kg/1–2lb per week").
2. Ask them to predict what will happen to their weight if the reduce their intake by 500kcal per day ("80% sure that it will go up by at least half a kilo/1lb per week").
3. Ask for the alternative belief if they reduce their intake in that way ("In theory, I suppose it might stay about the same for a week, but I am not really very confident about that – say 20%?").
4. Work out a timeframe – maximum two weeks, as there is still more time needed on weight regain.
5. Test out which belief is most accurate (and the shift in confidence ratings) and stress the value of learning that eating at a normal healthy level clearly is not linked to the expected uncontrolled weight gain (or to unmanageable weight loss).

Of course, there is the danger that engaging in weight maintenance by cutting back on food intake might trigger the "anorexic voice", leading to the patient trying to reduce food intake even more, resulting in weight loss. This should be stressed as a potential negative outcome when planning the weight maintenance period:

Clinician: "Now, when you first cut back on food to learn how to stabilise your weight, there is a risk that it will re-awaken that anorexic voice, and you will be tempted to cut back even more and go back to weight loss. So we have to make sure that you do not go beyond the planned reduction, and we monitor your weight very carefully. Slowing your weight gain or stabilising your weight would both be fine – you can learn from those. But losing weight – we immediately need to get your intake up again. Does that make sense?"
Patient: "Totally – even when you said that we might try cutting down, there was a bit of me that was excited that maybe I would lose some weight too, even though the logical side of me was saying that I know that my body and brain are not back to healthy yet".

So the clinician should be prepared to respond positively to the patient's efforts if they stick to the planned reduction:

Clinician: "OK – you are two weeks into your weight maintenance phase, and you have done really well. Your weight had been going up by about a pound/half a kilo per week, but now it has been stable for one week, and gone up very slightly in the second week. What does that tell you about your abilities?"
Patient: "I am still surprised that I can pretty much stop the weight gain like this – especially as I am eating so much more than I was before I came to treatment.

But it does make me feel calmer when I think about having to eat more again to get to a healthy weight".

Clinician: "Well, you are doing a great job here, so time to get back to eating for weight regain?"

However, the clinician should also be ready to reestablish the planned eating pattern if the patient's "anorexic voice" takes over and drives weight loss:

Clinician: "Well, your weight has dropped for two straight weeks since we started with the plan for weight maintenance. Looking at your diary, you have dropped off more than the dessert and snack that we agreed, so that would explain the weight loss. The question is why you have reduced so much more than we planned. Any thoughts?"

Patient: "I suppose it is that anorexic voice. Every time I think about eating less, I just get excited and eat even less than that. That part of my head just goes 'Well, why not – you would be so much better if you just lost a little bit of all that weight you have put on'. So I ate a bit less, then a lot less".

Clinician: "That could mean that we tried the weight maintenance too soon, and that you need to be further along with weight gain before you can do that – at a point where the anorexic voice is not so strong. Or you could try one more week of weight maintenance now, where you focus on fighting the anorexic voice so that you learn that you can do it. What do you think?"

In short, working with the patient's ability to manage their weight might mean a return to focus on the "anorexic voice". We need to work alongside the patient to remind them that weight maintenance is an active element of therapy – not simply a "turning off" of weight regain – which can result in lifelong benefit.

8.3 Summary

You might previously have used behavioural experiments to address patients' beliefs about the introduction of new foods. In contrast, behavioural experiments to maintain weight might not be a skill that you have used previously. However, this method can be very powerful for addressing the beliefs about uncontrollable weight gain that the patient has experienced for many years, and the safety behaviour of severe restriction of intake.

Chapter 9

Phase 3 (Sessions 12–19)

Emotional and interpersonal triggers and maintenance

Most individuals with anorexia nervosa will have emotional and interpersonal issues when they begin therapy. In some cases, those problems will fade with the direct benefits of eating more healthily (e.g., adequate carbohydrate intake to stabilise mood and enhance cognitive skills). In others, a reduction in the extent of emotional and interpersonal difficulties is a product of the individual's enhanced ability to socialise and reductions in interpersonal conflicts around eating. This early pattern of reduction in emotional and interpersonal issues in response to eating differently (e.g., Arai et al., 2025; Turner et al., 2016) means that the clinician cannot be sure at the beginning of therapy whether emotional and interpersonal factors will resolve without therapeutic intervention. While the early formulation and working with the "anorexic voice" are likely to support the patient to understand the emotional and interpersonal issues that underlie their anorexia nervosa, working directly on these issues from the beginning of therapy is likely to be of limited benefit, due to the impact of starvation and the need to focus on eating and weight regain from the outset of therapy. Therefore, remaining emotional and interpersonal issues are usually addressed in the latter half of CBT-AN-20 (around Session 12 onwards, though earlier might be appropriate depending on progress with eating and weight), when the person is more adequately nourished. However, those elements are only tackled if they are still a problem at this stage in therapy.

At this later stage, traits that are associated with core beliefs and that were included as predisposing factors in the conceptualisation at the assessment are still likely to be present. Repeating key assessment measures at this time can help understand how improved nutrition has impacted these and what further work needs to be done. This work may be started in CBT-AN-20 or there may be an agreement that it will be picked up by another clinician after work on the eating disorder has been completed. It is important to acknowledge that reversal of starvation is not a miracle cure for all the problems faced by the patient, but that it does allow them to see more clearly which issues still need to be faced and managed differently to previous attempts, when the eating disorder became a solution or coping strategy. Reversal of starvation also gives the patient increased capacity to deal with these issues more successfully.

DOI: 10.4324/9781003594703-9

9.1 Aims and strategy in working with emotions and interpersonal issues in CBT-AN-20

Our aim is to support the patient to develop a healthier sense of self and more positive relationships with others (e.g., not focusing on the "sick role" of being someone with anorexia nervosa), based on a more functional understanding of and response to emotional experiences. Some of the approaches here are similar to those used in CBT-T. However, while the focus in CBT-T is more on addressing emotionally-based *impulsive* behaviours (e.g., binge-eating; purging; self-harm), CBT-AN-20 is more likely to be focused on the emotional and cognitive roots of *compulsive* behaviours (e.g., restrictive eating; compulsive exercise; checking). In other words, anorexia nervosa is more likely to be associated with primary avoidance of emotion, whereas non-underweight eating disorders (e.g., binge-eating disorder; bulimia nervosa) are more likely to involve using safety behaviours that reduce the experience of an emotion once it has been triggered.

Where it is appropriate to engage in Phase 3 (i.e., when starvation effects can be ruled out), CBT-AN-20 has the key strategy of modifying the negative core beliefs (i.e., schema-level beliefs, which are resistant to modification) that are associated with such emotional and interpersonal difficulties. This involves addressing, identifying, and modifying core beliefs, along with encouraging the individual to experiment with replacing the pro-schematic behaviours that they use (e.g., avoiding other people; prioritising others' needs over their own; exercise; self-comparison with others; perfectionist behaviours) with counter-schematic behaviours (e.g., engaging with other people; exercising for health and body appreciation, resulting in experiencing an unintended reduction in anxiety; reduction in social media use to reduce negative beliefs about the self and others; allowing oneself to be "good enough" rather than perfect).

9.2 Psychoeducation regarding emotional and interpersonal issues

Many individuals with anorexia nervosa have difficulty in identifying these emotional and interpersonal issues, often because they have spent years avoiding such experiences. In some cases, this is more characterological, particularly where there is neurodivergence (e.g., autistic spectrum conditions) or alexithymia. Sometimes, the reasons for being poor at recognising and responding to emotions are experience-based (e.g., where the person has experienced neglect, other trauma, and/or an invalidating emotional environment). In either case, the pro-schematic behaviours that the person uses (behaviours that are in keeping with one's negative beliefs – e.g., avoidance of others) worsen the ability to engage with other people and to understand or express emotions, which in turn, reinforces the reliance on eating disorder behaviours. Psychoeducation materials relating to emotional/interpersonal problems and core beliefs in anorexia nervosa are provided in Appendices A.24 and A.25 to assist the patient and those around them in identifying when these issues present problems for the individual, limiting their progress in treatment. There is also a single-session intervention on emotional regulation in Appendix C.

One key issue is that patients with eating disorders are sometimes poor at identifying emotions for a number of reasons. While this difficulty in identifying emotion could be related to neurodivergence issues (see below), it can also be related to the fact that both impulsive (e.g., bingeing) and compulsive behaviours (e.g., restriction) can reduce awareness of and, in fact, dull emotions. Where the clinician suspects such a limitation, we recommend using flashcards that identify emotions and core beliefs by name, explaining how they might be related to the patient's experiences and underlying core beliefs in a specific situation (see Appendix A.26), to assist the patient in developing their ability to identify emotions. Other tools (e.g., an emotion wheel or an emotion tree – in which a collection of figures on a tree each visually represent a different emotion) can be useful in making sense of behaviours and expressions, where the individual lacks words to describe their feelings.

9.3   The experience of neurodivergence

Issues around neurodivergence exist along a continuum and vary substantially from one patient to another, so psychoeducation here is usually an exchange of information and experiences between patient and clinician. From the beginning, we should consider with the patient that such a diagnosis is more likely to be reliable if it was present from childhood (or if it emerges from dialogue with those who knew them during childhood) and before the onset of anorexia nervosa, as the impact of starvation can have profound emotional and social functioning. It is not a good idea to rely on such a diagnosis made in the midst of starvation (Thomas & McPherson, 2025). Rather, it is important to monitor the patient's emotional and interpersonal skills as they regain weight and add to their carbohydrate intake. Where there are clear issues of neurodivergence, they require discussion with the patient, given the differences in patterns of neurodivergence (e.g., some patients who meet criteria for neurodivergence will find it hard to understand emotions and/or other people's perspectives, while others are more skilled in these domains). We advise discussion with the patient (and their loved ones, where consent to do so) and adjusting the approach that we use accordingly. For example, we often find that a focus on behavioural change rather than cognitive/emotional approaches is more effective in such cases, but that should be discussed as part of the process of mutual learning.

9.4   Emotional issues

Where there are emotional issues post restoration of healthy eating patterns, then we need to help patients to develop some basic understanding of why they find emotions so difficult to process or understand and why their emotions are relatively negative. A first aim of this psychoeducation is to let the patient get past the feeling of being somehow "broken" in this respect. The second aim is to understand their pattern of attribution for their perceived emotional difficulties, as their tendency to internal attributions for negative events and experiences makes it hard for them to see that they might not be to blame. Such attributions (cognitive process) need to be considered and addressed in CBT-AN-20, alongside the patient's core beliefs (cognitive content), as detailed below.

To understand cognitive content and process behind the emotional issues in such cases, we use psychoeducation about the origin and nature of core beliefs (relatively unconditional schema-level beliefs) and any invalidating environments or experiences over childhood or adolescence. Each is related to different patterns of traumatic experience, often over an extended period of time, and we need to make it clear to the patient that we are not holding them responsible for such trauma, but that we need to understand their experience to formulate their emotional difficulties and the maintaining pro-schematic behaviours in the present.

9.4.1   Invalidating childhood environments

Here, we draw on Linehan's (1993) model to explain the processes that lead to and maintain unhelpful emotional patterns. We explain that emotions are a natural response to the environment and provide motivation to act in ways that will satisfy the person's needs (e.g., "If I am lonely, then reaching out and making contact with friends is a good way of feeling connected and less lonely"). However, we point out that many individuals grow up in environments (including home, school, religious settings, and friendship circles) and within dominant cultures that have rules, values, and expectations about appearance, relationships, and expression of emotion, all of which might be difficult or impossible to conform to. Within such contexts, emotional responses are often treated as unacceptable, leaving the individual to find more solitary ways of attempting to manage affect. The resulting perception of unacceptability/dangerousness of emotion and the associated attempts to control emotion can be carried into later life – for example through eating disorder behaviours, self-harm, or compulsive behaviours. Linehan identifies three types of invalidating environmental response to emotion that mean that the individual grows up unable to identify or respond to emotional experiences:

- "Typical" – emotions are treated as unacceptable and are discouraged, however valid they might be.
- "Perfect" – while shows of positive emotion are encouraged (e.g., happiness), negative emotions are discouraged, as the emphasis is on presenting the family or setting in the best possible light.
- "Chaotic" – expressions of emotion are met with negative or unpredictable responses (e.g., threats of violence). This form of emotional invalidation is often associated with an environment characterised by mental health issues, substance abuse, and so on.

This lack of ability to identify and respond to emotions (e.g., not identifying anger) means that the individual is not able to meet the needs behind the emotion, resulting in the use of a behaviour that avoids or suppresses the emotion (e.g., compulsive exercise to avoid experiencing the anger long-term and across settings, or self-harm to close down awareness of or indirectly express the emotion when it arises in specific situations).

This inability to process emotion in a functional way is often associated with physically or sexually traumatic experiences, though the core element is the emotional/neglectful/misattuned element of the patient's childhood experiences. Regardless of the nature of the traumatic background, we explain to the patient that it is the consequent emotional invalidation that explains the way that they respond to emotions in the here and now. It can also be important to stress to the patient that their familiarity with emotionally limited relationships can explain why they sometimes settle for adult relationships that are unemotional, as they can experience a partner who expresses emotions (albeit in a healthy way) as being hard to understand or even threatening. Of course, settling for an unemotional relationship can feel safer, but has the longer-term effect of maintaining their emotional limitations and precluding escape from the need to use emotionally blocking behaviours.

Finally, we stress how such an emotionally invalidating environment can be associated with the development of a number of core beliefs, alongside those developed out of other aspects of their background (see Chapter 2). In particular, using the Young (1994) suggested list of core beliefs, we stress the way that an emotionally invalidating childhood environment is very likely to result in a long-term belief that emotions are not valid, and hence in behaviours that reduce the risk of expressing genuinely experienced emotions. This is an "emotional inhibition" core belief. (see online skills video on https://sites.google.com/sheffield.ac.uk/cbt-an-20/videos)

9.4.2   Core beliefs

We explain schema-level core beliefs in terms of the more elaborate taxonomy used by Young (1994), rather than the more generalist core beliefs used by Beck (2005) or Cooper et al. (2004), as the greater range of core beliefs in Young's taxonomy allows for a more individualised description of the inner world and emotional/behavioural reactions than the other models (see Appendix A.25). However, our intervention is based on addressing those individual cognitions and their maintaining factors, often using behavioural experiments, continuum thinking (see Section 4.10.2), or ongoing evidence logs, rather than using the more elaborate schema therapy detailed by Young et al. (2003). We do this due to considering the length and limited evidence for schema therapy for eating disorders (e.g., Simpson & Smith, 2019). We also consider the utility of using some elements of chair work (e.g., Pugh, 2018), as this approach can help the individual to develop their healthy self, supporting them to thrive as they regain the strengths that were lost as the individual became more immersed in anorexia nervosa.

While many of Young's core beliefs are less relevant to the eating-disordered population, several routinely emerge when we consider the history and current experience of patients who need to work on their emotional states after enhancing their nutritional status. We find that asking the patient to complete the shorter Young Schema Questionnaire (YSQ; Young, 1998) or the "life traps" questionnaire in Young and Klosko (1993) helps them to see their personal pattern of core beliefs, even when they cannot routinely discern them against the background of their long-term experiences and pattern of self-blame. Appendix A.26 includes a flashcard that the patient can use to identify their own schema-level cognitions. It details the core beliefs that anorexia nervosa patients commonly report, along with brief explanations of the kind of childhood experiences that can sometimes lead to the development of such beliefs. We divide the beliefs between those that are central to the person's invalidating emotional experience (resulting in negative attributions and beliefs about the self, the world, and others) and those that are compensatory (allowing the person to cope with those negative beliefs as they function in the world – akin to what Beck describes as "Ways of Coping").

The central and compensatory beliefs that we routinely find in such cases are clearly related to the patient's experiences. for example:

- *Central beliefs*: Abandonment – the belief that others will never remain in one's life; Defectiveness – I am broken and unable to be repaired; Vulnerability – I am at risk of harm at all times; Mistrust – I cannot trust other people, as they will abuse me; Dependence – I need others around me at all times to make sure that I am OK; Emotional deprivation – Nobody is going to be there for me emotionally; Failure – I am unable to succeed in anything.
- *Compensatory beliefs*: Emotional inhibition – It is not safe to express or experience emotions; Perfectionism (unrelenting standards) – I am only acceptable if I work extra hard to get everything right; Self-sacrifice/Subjugation – Others will only want me around if I do everything that they want; Social isolation – I am only safe if I stay away from other people.

These can be discussed more easily in the context of the patient using the core belief flashcard (Appendix A.26) and the shorter YSQ to identify the patient's own cognitions (see above). This understanding feeds into the formulation of emotional triggers and maintenance, and into the interventions detailed below.

9.5 Interpersonal issues

It is important to understand whether the patient has interpersonal issues resulting from their eating disorder, so that these can be brought into the patient's understanding (given that they might be so used to such problems that they do not notice them or attribute them to others being intolerant or excessively demanding). While there are several measures of interpersonal problems, these are mostly generalist and tend to have very limited links to eating pathology. Therefore, we recommend using the 15-item *Interpersonal Relationships in Eating Disorders* scale (IR-ED; Jones et al., 2019; Lego et al., 2024). This measure helps to identify *food-related isolation* (e.g., preferring to eat alone to avoid conflict), *avoidance of body evaluation* (e.g., avoiding other's scrutinising one's body), and *food-related interpersonal tension* (e.g., others pushing the person to eating differently). Feeding this back to the patient can be useful in alerting the patient to the need to recognise and address such issues, rather than effectively ignoring them. It is important to stress to the patient (using Appendix A.24 for psychoeducational support) that these interpersonal difficulties might have been caused or exacerbated by the anorexia nervosa, but that the way out of them is to change behaviours to re-establish positive relationships with others (i.e., counter-schematic behaviours, such as contacting friends and family who have been avoided for months or years). Rebuilding social confidence will take time, and so it is important to encourage the patient to take multiple opportunities for social connection. This encouragement also gives the patient the opportunity to notice value-based behaviours in others, such as social invitations being reciprocated by new friendships, over time. Wade and colleagues have developed a brief intervention to reduce social isolation (Appendix C), which we recommend trying during Phase 3, where the patient has lost a lot of social and interpersonal links in this way.

9.6   Formulating emotional and interpersonal issues in anorexia nervosa

In explaining the role of emotions and interpersonal issues in anorexia nervosa and how they relate to the anorexic and other behaviours, we formulate around emotional and interpersonal issues using the "Newton's Cradle" model. This model is the same as that in CBT-T, but here we are more likely to be addressing relatively compulsive behaviours (e.g., restriction; compulsive exercise). Figure 9.1 shows the Newton's Cradle model as we would draw it out for an anorexia nervosa patient whose main behavioural manifestation is to restrict eating to prevent the experience of anger, based on past experiences and the development of core beliefs around abandonment and worthlessness.

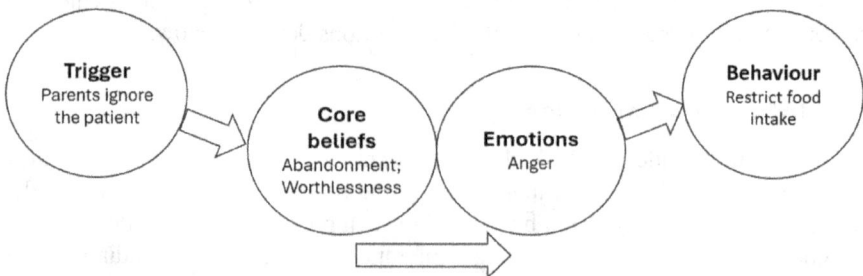

Figure 9.1 Newton's cradle model in anorexia nervosa.

In this model, we explain that the patient will be aware of the trigger and of the behavioural response but might not see them as connected or might treat the behaviour as inexplicable. This lack of any clear causal link in their head is a result of not understanding how the core beliefs (abandonment and worthlessness) and the emotion (anger) might explain that link (even if the patient is aware of those cognitions and emotions at all). We explain that the principle behind this model is that avoidance/safety behaviours are not simply directly linked to a trigger event (e.g., an interaction with one's partner results in restriction), but that the trigger activates core beliefs (both central and compensatory), those beliefs activate the emotion, and the behaviour is a response to that intolerable emotional experience. Within CBT-AN-20, the goal is to identify and target the core beliefs, so that the situation can be addressed in a less destructive way (e.g., tackling the trigger in an adaptive way, rather than using behaviours such as restriction or exercise to avoid experiencing the emotional state). As an example:

Patient: "I really don't know why I didn't eat my meal that evening *[Behaviour]*. I know that I needed to, I knew what I was going to eat in the plan, and I cooked it for me and my partner, but I just didn't eat it when he did".

Clinician: "So what was going on in the run-up to that mealtime? Let's check your diary on that. If you were going to eat at 7pm, when would you have started cooking?"

Patient: "I started at about 6.15pm. I cooked enough for him and me, but he was going on about his day at work, and did not ask about my day at all, even though I had a horrible day with my manager on my back".

Clinician: "So it sounds like he was not noticing you *[Trigger]*. What emotion do you think that would trigger if that had happened to your sister?"

Patient: "Well, it is odd that you say that, because she does have that sort of problem with her girlfriend – always a bit self-obsessed. She just gets really angry, and I can see why".

Clinician: "That makes sense. So do you think that you might have the same reaction – same circumstance, same emotion? What might tell you if you were angry?"

Patient: "Well, I try not to let things get to me, but yes, I suppose that I could have been angry. I know that I was very physically tense, and my appetite just went".

Clinician: "That certainly could fit with anger as your emotion at the time *[Emotion]*. So if we look at that Newton's Cradle model, it sounds like the trigger was your partner not paying attention to you, anger might have been the emotion, and not eating was your way of coping with that emotion, maybe because it lets you feel in control again? That leaves me wondering which of those core beliefs might have been triggered by the lack of attention and might link to your feeling of anger. Looking at that flashcard of core beliefs and their definitions, what do you think might have been going on in your head while you were cooking that evening?"

Patient: "Well, the one that makes most sense to me is that 'worthlessness' belief *[Core belief]*. I know that is not really how he sees me all the time, but it just makes me feel how my Dad used to make me feel".

Clinician: "If it feels that way to you, then let's go with that belief in the Newton's Cradle model. But can I just check whether there are any of those more compensatory beliefs that might be relevant too, in that situation?"

Patient: "Hmm. Looking at the list, maybe the one that we talked about a lot last week, when we discussed how I coped with my Dad ignoring me. Where I tried to do anything that I could to get him to notice me helping out – that 'self-sacrifice' belief *[Core belief]*".

Clinician: "Again, that could make sense in the model – a combination of feeling like you want to do your best for everyone but still feeling like it is not enough to make you worth noticing. How about if you spend next week using your diary to look out for whatever situations makes you angry – that tense feeling and the loss of appetite – and the thoughts that the situation triggers in you? If it turns out that you are right, then we should see a regular pattern emerging. If there is such a pattern, then we can look at recognising and challenging those worthlessness and self-sacrifice beliefs, so that you can respond to your emotions in a way that does not mean beating yourself up by not eating".

Having identified the emotional and interpersonal issues that drive the behaviour, it then becomes important to teach the patient how to tackle the central and compensatory core beliefs. This will start in the clinic but needs to be practiced for homework in the real world, using both cognitive and behavioural methods (particularly encouraging counter-schematic behaviours and correcting attentional bias).

9.7   Interventions addressing emotional/interpersonal triggers and maintaining factors

Unlike CBT-T, where the focus of emotional work is primarily on links to impulsive behaviours, CBT-AN-20's emotional and interpersonal focus is largely on links to compulsive behaviours – particularly restriction and compulsive exercise. These behaviours are hypothesised to serve the function of suppressing awareness of and dulling emotion and are reinforced by the individual not experiencing those emotions and associated interpersonal difficulties (e.g., "If I go for a long run, I can focus on that [rather than experiencing the loneliness that I fear]"). However, as with all avoidant and safety behaviours, the individual feels worse in the long term due to not resolving the emotional or interpersonal problem, leading them to use more of their avoidant behaviours.

Table 9.1 details schema-level CBT methods that can be used in addressing core beliefs and the resultant interpersonal difficulties that the person is experiencing in the here and now. These methods are mostly well-known CBT techniques, which are widely used when addressing negative automatic thoughts and conditional beliefs (e.g., Kennerley et al., 2016). They include diary keeping, data logging, Socratic reasoning, psychoeducation, surveys, and behavioural change. These are all methods that can be used successfully with core beliefs, whether with eating-disordered patients or others. These techniques are given in more detail in existing resources (Padesky, 1994; Padesky & Greenberger, 1995; Pugh, 2018; Waller, Cordery, et al., 2007; Waller, Kennerley & Ohanian, 2007; Young, 1994), but key ones will be considered here.

From the outset, it is important to stress the role of adequate nutrition and the reason that we do not try to work with these issues until the patient is adequately nourished (particularly having an adequate carbohydrate intake, even if not fully weight-regained). For example, in an early therapy session:

Patient: "I do not see why I have to start by eating differently and gaining weight. We already did that formulation, and it showed that I restrict because of how I was emotionally and sexually abused when I was young, so why don't we start with how that makes me feel and act?"

Clinician: "Remember that Minnesota study? The way that those people were so emotionally and socially unable to function? The problem there was that they were starved, just like you are now. That meant that even making sense of their emotions would not have been possible, never mind helping them to deal with their emotions and their social functioning more appropriately. It is clearly really important to help you deal with your emotions and with other people better, so that you do not need the anorexia nervosa, and you are not at risk of losing weight again. However, the only way that we can work on that is to get your eating straight first. So, the sooner we do that, the sooner we can get you ready to deal with your emotions and with other people".

When it is time to start Phase 3, we encourage the patient to familiarise themselves with the psychoeducation materials on emotions and core beliefs (above), to ensure that they are familiar with the necessary ideas. Where perfectionism is a large element of the patient's problem, we direct them to specific psychoeducation on the origins and the maintenance of perfectionism and its role in eating disorders (see Appendix A.5), as well as brief, single-session interventions to support challenging perfectionism (see Appendix C).

9.7.1   *Working with the patient's attributional style*

The overall aim is to assist the patient in changing their negative attributional pattern, shifting blame for negative and traumatic experiences (e.g., abuse, emotional invalidation) away from the patient and onto more appropriate targets (e.g., in a trauma-related case where CBT-AN-20 is suitable, helping the person to see that the responsibility for childhood abuse or abandonment was not theirs, but belongs with the adult who abused or abandoned them). The negative attributions are

Table 9.1 Schema-level techniques addressing core beliefs underpinning interpersonal and emotional issues in anorexia nervosa during CBT-AN-20

Element of therapy	Technique	Target
Preparation for any necessary schema-level work	Use an evidence-based CBT-ED: Where nutrition and exposure are key initial elements.	Adequate nutrition and reduction in emotional instability and cognitive inflexibility
	Reading of self-help guide: identification of own patterns of thinking and maintenance processes (e.g., Young & Klosko, 1993). (See Appendices A.25 and A.26 for psychoeducation materials).	Education regarding schema content (core beliefs) and processes (avoidance; compensation)
Cognitive and behavioural work	Use an evidence-based CBT-ED: Focusing on behavioural change in eating behaviours (especially reduction in restriction) in the first 4–6 sessions. Continuum thinking: To overcome black-and-white beliefs about who one is, based on a schema (e.g., "I am a completely bad person"). Followed by behavioural experiments (e.g., "John will be nice to me if I do X, Peter a bit less nice, and Suzanne will be horrible") to test the dimensionality of beliefs. Chair work can be valuable here (Section 4.9.3).	Reduction in starvation, reducing the intensity of core beliefs and emotional instability Overcoming dichotomous thinking
	Positive data logging: Diary used to identify positive experiences (e.g., successes, noting the positive behaviour of others towards them), which previously had not been noted because they were not schema-congruent. Following identification, the patient can use behavioural experiments to determine whether there are ways of enhancing the level of positive experiences.	Better identification of positives as normal part of one's experiences and life, allowing the individual to take greater control by engaging in positive experiences.
	Prediction log: Diary used to identify erroneous beliefs about future events, to overcome schema-level certainty about the self, others, and the world; followed by behavioural change, to determine whether changing one's actions can lead to even more positive experiences.	Reduction in belief that negative events are the norm and building a sense of control over the world into the future.
	Historical review: Review the individual's history and present to identify patterns of schema development and maintenance. Identify typical patterns of behavioural/interpersonal avoidance that maintain the problem belief, and experiment with changing those behaviours.	Show that beliefs made sense at the time and in the context that they developed (e.g., trauma), but that they are no longer applicable, given changes in context (e.g., abuser lacks real power now).

(Continued)

Table 9.1 (Continued)

Element of therapy	Technique	Target
	Review assumptions regarding the origins of specific core beliefs: Using Socratic approaches, consider alternative explanations for the origins of core beliefs, to shift from internal to external attributions for negative events in life. This can be followed by using surveys to discover how others attribute negative events in their lives. Chair work can be valuable here.	Attributional shift for general patterns of events in life (self-blame turned to blaming others or circumstances).
	Using others as a reference point: For example, where the person blames themselves for having been abused as a child, asking whether they would conclude that a child of theirs was to blame if they were abused. Of course, it should be acknowledged that their own self-blame was due to their having made sense of experiences in the only way that they could at the time and may have been needed in order to limit the danger at that stage in their life. This recognition can be followed by asking the patient to talk to others about how they process positive and negative information for themselves and for others. Again, chair work can be used to make this use of other as a reference point feel more concrete.	Allowing the person to understand their own self-defeating biases as being unfair on themselves, and that external attribution of responsibility (to the abuser) is appropriate.
	Pie charts regarding self-worth: Identification of patterns of overvaluation of body shape and appearance.	Allows the person to understand that they have value in other aspects of themselves.
	Imagery rescripting: Aiming to allow the individual to access memories that were laid down in a less verbal format (e.g., because of being very young at the time) from an adult, more verbal perspective.	Attributional shift for specific events in life (self-blame turned to blaming others/holding others to account).
	Counter-schematic behaviour: Allowing the individual to test their assumptions and attributions directly against the newly developed beliefs and attributions.	Learning that other ways of understanding negative experiences are viable, showing that the individual's emotional experience is valid and does not need to be masked using compulsive or impulsive behaviours.

usually internal ("it's my fault"), global ("it is something that applies to all aspects of my life"), and stable ("this is how it has always been, and it will always be this way"). Thus, our goal is to help the patient to change their attributions in one or more of those aspects, and to reinforce such changes with counter-schematic behaviours. We aim to get this attributional work underway as quickly as possible within Phase 3, so that the patient and clinician might review the history of the patient's invalidating/traumatic childhood in Session 12 and be exploring attributional patterns in Session 13 (see online skills video on https://sites.google.com/sheffield.ac.uk/cbt-an-20/videos).

As an example, let us consider a patient – Lucy, aged 34, with a 16-year history of restrictive anorexia nervosa with compensatory exercise and occasional vomiting. Based on historical review conducted with Lucy herself, we concluded that she grew up in an emotionally invalidating environment. Developing a schema pattern of emotional deprivation and a compensatory pattern of emotional inhibition and perfectionism made sense in that context, because it allowed Lucy to predict her world and not to expose herself to further emotional trauma. The cost was that she needed to find other ways of coping with her emotions, such as restriction and exercise, with occasional vomiting when the distress became too immediate to avoid. In such a case, our goal is not to attempt to overcome or change Lucy's beliefs about what happened, but to help her to challenge whether those beliefs remain applicable (e.g., Lucy may have needed to blame herself for the lack of emotional support when she was young in order to protect her relationship with her caregiver, but does this belief continue to serve her, and what are the costs of this belief?). In Lucy's case, we used a historical review regarding the origin of her beliefs and data logging. These methods helped her to conclude that her experience when younger was not due to her "deserving" the emotional invalidation (i.e., internal negative attribution). Rather, we established that:

- Her mother and father were unable to connect emotionally with other people (i.e., changing the attribution from "internal" to "external").
- Her current relationship was not emotionally invalidating, and she has some supportive friendships (i.e., changing the attribution from "global" to "specific"). In fact, it could be seen that she would be at risk if she kept using her old style of emotional inhibition.
- Her parents remained emotionally invalidating throughout her adult life, too (i.e., the attribution remained "stable", but because it was no longer seen as her fault or relating to her wider life, then she was able to view that stability as being a consistent element of her parents, rather than being about her).

This change was sufficient for Lucy to be able to accept that her partner and friends could be trusted to be emotionally supportive and that she could express her emotions safely with them, though we used continuum thinking to ensure that she could see how some of those people were better at handling emotions than others.

However, it was also important that Lucy was able to say that she would not trust her parents to be supportive, but that that was their issue rather than hers (external attribution).

9.7.2   Imagery rescripting

Where this relatively cognitive approach is not sufficient to shift attributions, we employ *imagery rescripting* methods (e.g., Waller et al., 2019) to enhance the necessary cognitive changes. In such cases, the memories are usually stored in an "encapsulated" way (e.g., Hackmann et al., 2015; Wild & Clark, 2011), where they are relatively unprocessed. They are stored in more emotional and perceptual format, and not open to relatively cognitive, logical exploration and challenges. As with PTSD, social phobia, and personality disorders, imagery rescripting can be a powerful way of addressing such encapsulated beliefs in those with eating disorders, because it accesses the emotional/perceptual elements of the memory, then allows the memory to be accessed via more cognitive, logical processing. Imagery rescripting requires that we explain what is going to happen to the patient during the previous session, so that they understand what they are agreeing to, followed by an entire session dedicated to rescripting a specific, highly pertinent memory (i.e., one that the patient sees as being a memory with strong emotional and interpersonal elements, which well represents the way in which the patient sees themselves as responsible for that experience, without being a pre-verbal developmental experience, such as an infant memory).

Let us consider another illustrative example – Carmel, who is an 18-year-old woman. Considering Carmel's experience, she believed firmly that it was her fault that she had been insulted about her intelligence and appearance by her stepfather and her mother from her early years. She believed their statements that she had deserved it because she was "chubby" and "stupid", and she felt high levels of shame. Her core beliefs were focused on defectiveness and fear of abandonment, which she coped with by developing perfectionist beliefs and behaviours to compensate for her flaws. This manifested as extreme efforts at weight control, though without feeling that she ever managed to look thin (despite being at a BMI of 16.3 at the start of treatment). The beliefs were very fixed and resistant to Socratic questioning. Therefore, imagery rescripting was suggested to Carmel, and she was asked to come up with a specific memory to work on next time.

At the next session, Carmel explained that the big, representative memory for her was when she was aged five, and her mother picked her up from school. She remembered vividly how her mother had pointed out how slim and pretty all the other girls in the school were, and how disappointed she was with Carmel. Carmel remembered this as being very distressing, as she believed herself to be ugly and worthless. The imagery work followed in two parts, each of about 15 minutes:

1. *Original image.* Carmel was asked to describe the index event, as though it was happening in the here and now. This started with coming out of the school

building and seeing her mother at the school gate, excited to talk about her day in her new school, then reaching her mother and being told how plain and chubby she looked compared to all the other children there. She was asked to take her time describing the experience, detailing as much perceptual and emotional material as she could (e.g., colour of school uniforms; the weather; feeling of the grass as she ran over it; excitement at the prospect of talking about her new friends; feeling of upset as she listened to her mother criticising her and telling her that her stepfather agreed). At the end of the description, she was asked to say who she thought was responsible for her mother being so negative in her description, and Carmel replied that she was to blame herself, because she was such a disappointing child (i.e., a negative internal attribution).

2. *Rescripted image.* Immediately afterwards, Carmel was asked to re-run that image as though it was a movie she was watching, but this time to bring her adult self into the image at the critical point (which she saw as when her mother started to criticise her outside the gate), and for the adult self to do whatever was necessary to support young Carmel. The aim of this rescripting is to open up the emotional/perceptual memory, but to allow the adult Carmel to bring a logical/cognitive perspective to the memory to challenge that emotional/ perceptual memory. Following bringing in her adult self, Carmel was able to challenge her mother, calling her "a pathetic parent, who was entirely selfish and who had no right to call herself a mother, given how horrible she was to young Carmel". She described pushing her mother out of the way, giving young Carmel a hug, and telling her that she was going to take care of her until her mother could be a decent parent. After this, Carmel was asked to come out of the image, and to say again who she thought was responsible for how her mother had behaved. On this occasion, Carmel was very clear that it was her mother who had been totally responsible (i.e., external negative attribution).

Through this imagery rescripting, Carmel was able to see that her mother and step-father were the reason that she had always felt worthless and that she had to strive so hard to feel even marginally worthwhile. This cognitive change was followed by a substantial reduction in her shame, and more of a belief that she would be acceptable if she were a more normal weight. In some cases, it is easier for the patient to start by inserting another person into the rescripted image (a wise and compassionate figure) instead of their older self, but we encourage the patient to move toward inserting themselves as early as possible to promote self-efficacy (see online skills video on https://sites.google.com/sheffield.ac.uk/cbt-an-20/videos).

9.7.3   The role of perfectionism in maintaining anorexia nervosa

As in Carmel's case, a particular schema-level target can be perfectionism. In clinical cases, perfectionism manifests as extreme efforts to avoid failure or criticism.

As outlined in Section 4.10, case formulation shows that perfectionism is an important clinical target, along with the internalised criticism and shame that individuals like Carmel experience. Again, we recommend that clinicians should use evidenced resources, worksheets, and diaries to address perfectionism (Appendix C).

9.7.4 Counter-schematic behaviours

Following the emotional and cognitive work of re-attribution and imagery rescripting, it is important to underscore that the former attribution pattern was not helpful. We discuss "counter-schematic" behaviours that the patient can use in the here and now to demonstrate that they are able to function more effectively in the world if they trust in the new pattern of thinking (rather than maintaining their old pattern of pro-schematic behaviours, such as avoidance of other people).

In Carmel's case, we agreed that she should try talking to her friends about their childhood experiences of their first day at school and how their parents had reacted, and that she should ask her two elder sisters how their mother and stepfather had treated them (as opposed to her previous pro-schematic behaviours of never asking any of these questions, for fear of finding that she would find her beliefs reinforced). At the next session, Carmel reported herself amazed. First, her friends' parents had not commented on their appearance unless it was to compliment them on how they looked in their new school uniforms. Carmel was very clear that there must have been something wrong with her mother not to be like all the other mothers. Second, her two sisters (who Carmel had always seen as being very pretty) each reported that their mother and stepfather had been "cruel" and "nasty" about their appearance, too. Carmel reported that she could now remember seeing that happening to her sisters sometimes but had not understood until now how this reflected a pattern in her mother's and stepfather's behaviour that was about *them* rather than being about the children. Her eldest sister suggested that this was about the two adults being "obsessed" with each other and finding the three daughters to be "in the way". Carmel found these new perspectives stopped her from blaming herself and let her feel closer to other people (see online skills video on https://sites. google.com/sheffield.ac.uk/cbt-an-20/videos).

Of course, we need to consider the patient's experiences and characteristics. For example, if Carmel were an older person, her parents might be deceased, and she might therefore find it difficult to think badly of them. Such thoughts might be hard for her, due to triggering feelings of unresolved grief. In such a case, that grief might need to be addressed before other emotions can be worked with.

9.8 Summary

Where appropriate, emotional and interpersonal issues should be formulated into the individual case and should be targeted accordingly. This focus gives the patient the opportunity to learn that their self-criticism and compensatory behaviours (e.g., emotional inhibition; social isolation; perfectionism) are not necessary. The focus is on attributional work, to let the patient stop blaming themselves, and particularly to reduce the belief that externally directed emotions (e.g., anger) are more appropriate than internally directed negative emotions (e.g., shame). This change in self-blame allows healthier emotional and interpersonal functioning, meaning that restrictive and other compensatory behaviours (e.g., compulsive exercise) are less necessary, so that normalisation of weight and eating behaviours becomes possible. Imagery rescripting and counter-schematic behaviours are powerful tools, especially where more Socratic approaches are less effective.

Clinicians often consider schema-based approaches to therapy as requiring a long time. However, that is not always the case, particularly where we engage the patient in substantial review and experimentation between sessions (the notion of CBT as a 168-hour a week therapy). For example, in Lucy's case, this process took approximately three weeks, running in parallel with her Phase 2 work on weight maintenance experiments and with her initial Phase 4 body image work. Had imagery rescripting been needed, that could have required a further session, though early identification of her difficulty of reattribution could have meant that the same three-week envelope was needed.

Chapter 10

Phase 4 (Sessions 12–20)
Body image

Body image work in CBT-AN-20 is similar in nature to that in CBT-T, though with some additional considerations relating to weight restoration and starvation effects. While it is important to support the patient to identify their own body image–related goals, a key goal of this work with anorexia nervosa is to help the patient to achieve a greater level of body acceptance while at a healthy weight. Some body image work can be done during weight regain to facilitate the individual tolerating that weight change. However, it is important to revisit the topic when the person has achieved a functional weight in order to prevent relapse (e.g., Keel et al., 2005). This work can be done in parallel with the other phases of therapy, with multiple agenda items and homework tasks.

10.1   Preparation for body image work

It is important to consider the probability that the "anorexic voice" will get louder during this treatment phase as body image distortion is directly challenged. The "anorexic voice" is likely to be activated strongly to defend the belief that being thin is important and the only acceptable way of being and, in turn, that it is important to continue engaging in body-related behaviours (e.g., checking). It is particularly likely that the "anorexic voice" will focus on perceptions of "virtuous" body-related behaviours in the context of social media messages about thinness and social trends in eating (e.g., "clean eating"; "whole healthism").

As a prelude to body-image work (and often throughout the early part of that work), it can be important to discuss with the patient their personal values and choice. In particular, is this (over)focus on body image consistent with where they want to be expending their energy, or are there other life goals that they would like to achieve, such as happiness? For example, we have worked with an anorexia nervosa patient who was a cancer researcher. When she found herself engaging in body image checking, body image rumination, and so on, she reminded herself that "I could literally be curing cancer right now", which helped her stop the behaviours and re-focus on her recovery goals.

It can also be helpful to encourage the patient to consider how they might respond to the "anorexic voice" when it comes to body image. We ask them to

DOI: 10.4324/9781003594703-10

question that voice – do they believe it? If so, how does believing it help or hinder them in their recovery? We encourage the patient to consider how they can change their response to the "anorexic voice" in a way that will turn down its volume over time.

Usually at this stage, with the "anorexic voice" starting to amplify again but where the patient has experienced some of the benefits of recovery, we pose the two-choice challenge. We agree that they have the choice to return to a lower weight but that it will be accompanied by a return of the eating disorder. Alternatively, they can choose to be a higher weight than they desire, but without the eating disorder. Weighing up the pros and cons of each pathway is usually very helpful for the patient to clarify their choice and then inject new energy to focus on recovery.

10.2   Choosing body image interventions according to the nature of the maintaining factors

A number of approaches to the treatment of body image are available to the clinician in Phase 4, depending on the pattern of body image problems that the patient presents with. That pattern of expression of body image problems is often apparent from the beginning of therapy, though the focus can shift with weight regain, and some patients become more accepting of their bodies as a result of the changes in the earlier part of CBT-AN-20. The treatment approaches that can be used and their targets are detailed in Table 10.1, along with a potential timeframe (subject to individual progress in therapy, of course) and specific measures that can be used to assess progress and outcomes.

As always, we recommend measuring specific change and relating it to the interventions used to target the individual's body image issues. Of course, overall body image should be considered in progress and outcome measurement too– e.g., the body image–relevant scales of the relevant measures routinely used in CBT-AN-20, namely the EDE-Q7 (Grilo et al., 2015) and the ED-15 (Tatham et al., 2015). Additionally, measures such as the Body Image – Acceptance and Action Questionnaire (Linardon et al., 2019) and the Body Satisfaction Questionnaire (Cooper et al., 1987) could also be used. Such measures can be targeted on specific aspects of body image or more global issues, such as body image flexibility (BIAAQ) or neutrality (see Appendix A.27 for psychoeducation on body neutrality).

10.3   Psychoeducation

Psychoeducation about body image can be based on information sheets (e.g., Appendices A.27 and A.28, Appendix B, and the CBT-AN-20 website (https://sites.google.com/sheffield.ac.uk/cbt-an-20)), discussion with the patient, and physical demonstrations. It can be started relatively early in treatment. For example, patients often lack awareness of some fundamental body-related information, such as the role of fat in the body and set-point theory, and might need to have such information explained in the session. Backing that up with information sheets can

Table 10.1 Potential factors maintaining negative body image, linked to what CBT methods are helpful, when they can be used, and specific measures to determine progress and outcome

Maintaining factor	Intervention to use if the maintaining factor is present	When to implement this method (unless clinical indications suggest otherwise)	Examples of specific measures that can be used to measure progress and outcome
Lack of accurate knowledge of one's body or bodies in general (including depersonalisation); Experiencing difficult emotions as "feeling fat"	Psychoeducation; body size estimation; awareness of emotional impact on body image	From early in therapy; reviewed at the start of Phase 4, with a fresh body size estimate, further psychoeducation, etc., as necessary	Body size estimation
Non-specific negative body image/negative critical self-talk	Working with the "anorexic voice"/body neutrality	Use during early weight regain; reviewed at the start of Phase 4	–
Hurtful memories related to body shame	Imagery rescripting	Start of Phase 4	Body Image Shame Scale (BISS)
Excessive exercise to change body appearance/composition	Cognitive work on the problems of perfectionism; experimenting with exercise for positive goals	Start of Phase 4	
Reassurance-seeking	Behavioural experiments	Start of Phase 4	–
Body checking	Behavioural experiments	Start of Phase 4	Body Checking Questionnaire (BCQ)
Body comparison	Behavioural experiments	Start of Phase 4	Body Comparison Scale (BCS)
Mind-reading	Surveys	Use during early weight regain if stuck; early-mid Phase 4	Fear of Negative Appearance Evaluation Scale (FNAES); Social Appearance Anxiety Scale (SAAS)
Body avoidance	Graded exposure	Mid-Phase 4 (when weight restored)	Body Image Avoidance Questionnaire (BIAQ)
Body avoidance	Full exposure (flooding)	Late in Phase 4 (when weight restored)	Body Image Avoidance Questionnaire (BIAQ)

be very useful for the patient. However, it is important not to be more definitive than is appropriate. For example, where a patient is concerned about the way in which fat is being laid down in their body as they regain weight:

Patient: "My weight is all going on around my belly. If this carries on, I am going to end up like a ball".

Clinician: "Plenty of people worry about that at this stage, but mostly the early fat that you need goes on around your belly, then later it shifts to your bottom and your chest, where it more naturally sits".

Patient: "So how long before I look more normal again?"

Clinician: "I can hear that experiencing your body changing feels scary and hard. Lots of people struggle with this. Would you like to try to figure out whether there's anything in your response that might be magnifying your perception of just how much your body is changing? Or can I help you to think about how to manage upsetting feelings while in this difficult process of finding out what your healthy body might eventually look like?"

Within CBT in general, the best path is honesty ("I don't know, but there is a way of finding out"). Rather than trying to come across as "the expert" who knows everything, we show greater expertise when we can tolerate our own uncertainty, to help the patient learn to tolerate theirs. This can be supported with psychoeducation about the way that bodies distribute fat during weight gain, and how that distribution changes over time (e.g., El Ghoch et al., 2014; Mayer et al., 2009), but often we find that a simple biological explanation is well received by the patient (e.g., "Many of our organs are in the abdomen region, and they are most in need of nutrition for sustaining life, so it makes sense that your body will be trying to protect those organs by sending nutrition there".).

At the start of Phase 4, it is also important to revisit the introduction to body image that was outlined in Phase 1 (Section 7.3). At that point, we detailed how we use body size estimation to demonstrate that the patient is likely to have a very distorted body image (e.g., overestimating their size by 50%), to encourage them to work on the earlier phases of therapy so that they can get to Phase 4. We recommend obtaining a new size estimation when we begin Phase 4, to determine whether this is still a big issue, and an indicator that body image is still worthy of attention in therapy.

10.4 Addressing the role of the "anorexic voice" to establish body neutrality

This return to the topic of body size overestimation also illustrates that the patient needs to keep focusing on the rational and caring voice, and not the critical "anorexic voice". Addressing this need requires consideration of how negative body image can be driven by the defectiveness core belief that is experienced by so many of our patients, in combination with that more compensatory perfectionist thinking pattern. Some of those beliefs are addressed using imagery rescripting (Section 10.5), and improve as a result of the positive changes that are used to overcome behaviours such as body avoidance. However, we find that encouraging body neutrality (treating the body as something that does not need to be judged or to contribute to our self-worth) is a valuable start to body image work. We use psychoeducation (Appendix A.27) to explain body neutrality to the patient, along with practical strategies that can support this way of thinking about oneself. In addition, we recommend that our patients should undertake a specific single-session intervention (Appendix C) to support them with reducing their negative body focus with a more neutral one.

10.5   Imagery rescripting

This technique has already been addressed in relation to emotional/interpersonal issues (see Section 9.7.2). When it comes to body image, we use the same principles (helping the person to bring an adult cognitive/logical perspective to challenge an encapsulated emotional/perceptual memory, commonly developed in childhood or adolescence). This approach is particularly pertinent when working with body shame, based on memories of specific early experiences (e.g., teasing about pubertal development, criticism of one's size or weight, etc.). The process is derived from Pennesi and Wade's (2018; Zhou et al., 2020) protocol, which has demonstrated effectiveness in enhancing body acceptance and reducing other eating disorder concerns.

Delivering this form of imagery rescripting is detailed in full in Pennesi and Wade (2018), and is explained for the patient in Appendix A.28. It can be conducted in the clinic or online and requires ongoing rehearsal by the patient outside of session. The work with the clinician consists of three stages over 20–30 minutes, addressing a single event from the patient's history, while the homework is likely to take about 10 minutes per day, focusing on different past experiences each time. For example, Michael (aged 22) recalled being teased for being "flabby" by his classmates on the day that he started at a new school (aged 11) and felt ashamed every time he thought about this experience. His anorexia nervosa was driven in part by an effort to avoid feeling so ashamed, but in spite of his weight loss and consequent low weight, he was still concerned that he was too big and had a distorted perception of his current size. Michael's in-person rescripting consisted of the following steps in a session:

1. Developing an image of that key experience. Recount (or write down) the experience of being teased from the perspective of his 11-year-old self, including details of what he could see, hear, smell, and so on in the image. He was asked to focus on his emotional experiences and to describe the thoughts, physical feelings, and behaviours that went along with the sense of bodily shame that was so prominent for him.

2. Describing that image from his adult perspective, focusing on how the young Michael was teased and his feelings at that time.
3. Returning to the image from the 11-year-old's perspective, repeating the first step. When getting to the point where he was teased, he was asked to pause the image, and to bring in his adult self to support the young Michael, to defend him in a compassionate way.

Following this, he was asked to state how strong his body shame felt now, and to say where he attributed the blame for the teasing (to himself, or to those who teased him). Having brought in the adult logical/cognitive perspective, his response was to blame the children who teased him, and to report greater body acceptance.

To reinforce this in-session change in attributions and shame, each day Michael was asked to rehearse the Stage 3 imagery for homework, and to select other early memories of unpleasant body experiences where he might have been ashamed or embarrassed by his body (this could be the event described in the clinic session, but he was encouraged to think of other experiences to generalise the learning). Then he was asked to imagine the event, but bringing his wiser, compassionate adult self into the image, to support his young self practically and emotionally. Throughout, he was asked to write down the experience, then would continue writing the next stage, describing what was said and how the adult self defended the young Michael, including details of what was said, what the young Michael was feeling, and how the adult Michael supported young Michael's worth. These summaries were reviewed at the next session, and the improvement in Michael's body acceptance was explicitly linked to the work that he had been doing to bring in his adult, compassionate perspective. Ultimately, these new statements could be transferred to Michael's mobile device, or recorded, where he could see or listen to them wherever he was (see online skills video on https://sites.google.com/sheffield.ac.uk/cbt-an-20/videos).

10.6   Changing the focus of exercise in relation to body image

In anorexia nervosa, exercise is often motivated by a strong desire to lose weight or control body shape, and for some, it can become compulsive. For some, this compulsive exercise will represent a manifestation of perfectionism. In such cases, the individual might undertake competitive exercise (e.g., "I can run farther than anyone else at my gym"). However, that competitive element usually becomes internally oriented, with the patient becoming driven to beat themselves (e.g., "I can run farther than I did yesterday") and to change their body (e.g., "If I run instead of studying, I can lose the fat on my thighs"). This pattern of compulsive exercise is not pleasurable and is inevitably unrewarding (as goals keep shifting and are never achievable in a satisfactory way – e.g., higher running targets; thinner thighs). Therefore, the compulsive exercise results in *poorer* body satisfaction, as the perfectionist element of thinking will never allow the patient to feel that they have been successful in achieving those ever-changing goals. Indeed, excessive, compulsive exercise is commonly associated with bodily harm in anorexia nervosa, due to bone deterioration, cardiac dysfunction, muscular weakness, and so on. Furthermore, it might have been involved in maintaining low weight. These harms make the goals even less achievable (e.g., increasing risk of fractures; being banned from dance school), resulting in poorer body acceptance. Compulsive exercise can also become a form of self-punishment, driven by guilt and fear of the consequences of non-compliance (e.g., "If I don't go to the gym, it means I've failed/I'm not good enough/I'll get fat/I can't let myself eat").

Therefore, to address this element of body dissatisfaction, we ask the patient to focus their exercise on achievable, positive goals. Once the patient reaches and sustains adequate nutrition, this can involve stressing the value of limited exercise for physical health and functionality of the body, linked to relevant health guidelines. For example, the Australian NHMRC guideline on adult exercise (see Appendix B) recommends at least the following:

- Each week, adults should do either:
  - 2.5 hours of moderate intensity physical activity – such as a brisk walk, golf, mowing the lawn, or swimming;
  - 1.25 hours of vigorous intensity physical activity – such as jogging, aerobics, fast cycling, soccer, or netball;
  - An equivalent combination of moderate and vigorous activities.
- Include muscle-strengthening activities as part of your daily physical activity on at least 2 days each week. This can be:
  - Push-ups;
  - Pull-ups;
  - Squats or lunges;
  - Lifting weights;
  - Household tasks that involve lifting, carrying, or digging.

This outline contrasts to the driven, unrewarding compulsive exercise that many patients with anorexia nervosa have undertaken. While it might seem like an alien concept now, we stress the value of the patient returning to a focus on activity for fun and social connection (e.g., going for a short Parkrun with neighbourhood friends), rather than body-focused exercise (e.g., running until they collapse, in the hope of feeling better about their body). The overall aim is to support the patient to re-connect exercise with health and wellbeing.

10.7 Behavioural experiments

Behavioural experiments were addressed earlier (Phase 2), but are important when working with body image, too. Three body-related behaviours that can maintain the anorexia nervosa and that can be targeted using behavioural experiments are addressed here – checking, reassurance-seeking, and comparison. In this context, reassurance-seeking can be seen as very similar to body checking, but while body checking is about appraising one's own body, reassurance-seeking is about assessing others' appraisals of one's appearance. In each case, the behaviour is maintained by the short-term gains, but these are followed by long-term negative effects on body image. Body comparison can be to themselves (e.g., "How does this outfit look today compared to last year at this time?") or to others (e.g., "How does my body size compare to theirs?"). Again, body comparison can sometimes have a short-term benefit of reassuring the individual ("Well, at least I look better than that person", but that short-term benefit is not always achieved (especially given their own distorted body image), and the long-term consequence is likely to be poorer self-esteem and body image. Of course, body comparison manifests very strongly in the context of social media use, where comparison with often "idealised" or digitally enhanced/photoshopped images is all too easy.

The aim of the behavioural experiment intervention for each of these body-related safety behaviours is to test the patient's belief that the safety behaviour is an effective, positive means of coping with negative body image. The clinician asks the patient to test that belief against the alternative (that the behaviour is positive in the very short term but negative in the long term). This is done by encouraging them to change their behaviour and see which belief turns out to be accurate. Unless the prediction relates to weight (which needs longer to account for fluctuations and to allow weighing to take place in session), such experiments can usually be carried out in a week (e.g., three days of testing the current belief; three days of testing the alternative, adaptive belief).

In each case, the steps in the experiment would be:

- Identify the patient's current belief behind the safety behaviour (e.g., "Acting that way makes me feel calmer and better about my body");
- Ask the patient to rate the strength of that belief (looking for a strong belief at first – say 80%–100% certain);
- Identify an alternative belief (e.g., "Acting that way makes me feel calmer and better about my body in the short term, but makes me feel worse in the long term");
- Ask the patient to rate the strength of that alternative belief (this time, expecting a much less confident rating – say 0%–20%);
- Plan an experiment to test the two beliefs and a timeframe (e.g., "Try the behaviour every time you can for the next three days, rating your feelings about your body each time that you use the behaviour and then rating your feelings about your body and your mood at the end of the day. Then for the next few days, try reducing that behaviour as much as you can – rate your feelings about your body after you resist the behaviour, and then again at the end of the day. If your existing belief is right, then you will feel great about your body at the end of the first three days, and terrible about it at the end of the second three days. On the other hand, if the alternative belief is right, then you

will feel worse at the end of the days when you use the behaviour, and much better on the days when you do not use it".);

• Review the outcome at the next session, and plan for further reduction in the strength of the beliefs in the safety behaviour or move on to other aspects of body image.

If the outcome of the behaviour is weight-based, then the process is likely to take longer, given the potential for weight fluctuation. Otherwise, a week of explicit work on the behaviour followed by further work on it for homework over a few weeks is usually sufficient for learning while other body image targets are addressed.

Considering these three safety behaviours individually:

10.7.1 Reassurance-seeking

Three forms of reassurance-seeking are commonly seen in relation to body image – *active*, where the individual actively seeks the reassurance of others (e.g., "Do I look OK like this?"); *passive*, where the patient presents in a way that they hope will bring them unasked-for positives (e.g., "Will they say that I look thin if I wait for them to notice that I have lost weight and dressed like this?"); and *paradoxical*, where they act in a self-critical way (e.g., saying to others that "I just know that I have put on weight") in the hope that those others will tell them that they disagree. By their nature, the passive and paradoxical forms of reassurance-seeking are often less immediately obvious. For example, one of our patients expected others to comment on how little she ate or on her body (e.g., "You're too thin").

In each of these manifestations of reassurance-seeking, the target is addressing the underlying belief that reassurance-seeking is effective. However, in common with the impact of reassurance-seeking in other areas (e.g., depression and anxiety, Joiner et al., 1999), the alternative belief can be expanded to include the likelihood that excessive reassurance-seeking will result in other people avoiding or getting irritated with the patient in the long term (the patient will probably have experience of friends and others dropping out of their lives in this way).

10.7.2 Body checking

Here, the patient is likely to engage in a range of common checking behaviours (e.g., repeatedly using a mirror, weighing themselves, or scrutinising body parts for evidence of fat), as well as more idiosyncratic behaviours (e.g., testing their body against specific clothes, pinching their skin). Again, the target is to challenge the belief that body checking is an effective way to enhance body image and/or to reduce anxiety about body image. One point to consider is that it is possible to mis-label what looks like body checking. The person might appear to check their body (and describe their behaviour as such), but if they check very quickly then withdraw, that can be an example of phobic avoidance. In such cases, exposure work is the appropriate course of action (see Section 10.9.2). If the patient is misinterpreting the meaning of their body checking as "proving" that they have gained an unacceptable amount of weight, then it can be important to remind the patient that the best way to know whether weight is actually going up at that excessive rate is to go back to linking food intake with what the weight chart actually shows, compared with their predictions.

10.7.3   Body comparison

In this case, the patient routinely compares themselves visually with others or with past versions of themselves. As a result of their negative perception of their own body, this is very commonly a behaviour that results in "upward comparison" (e.g., relative to someone whom they regard as thinner than they imagine themselves to be), resulting in poorer body image most times. It is important to explain to the patient that comparison is maintained by the infrequent occasions when they see someone who they believe they look better than ("downward comparison") – an example of intermittent reinforcement. The beliefs tested need to stress just how bad the person feels after sustained comparison with others. A key example of this is the role of social media use, where it is important to explain just how people's use of social media means that it is highly unlikely that one will see many "real" body representations, resulting in an overwhelming level of upward comparison and negative body image. Experimenting with reducing/stopping social media use is useful, if the individual is prepared to try this (see online skills video on https://sites.google.com/sheffield.ac.uk/cbt-an-20/videos).

10.8   Surveys

Surveys are an "observational" behavioural experiment focused on the specific safety behaviour of "mind-reading". They are derived from the field of CBT for social phobia, where the core cognitive issue is fear of negative evaluation by others. Surveys address the more specific body-related cognitive pattern of *fear of negative appearance evaluation* or *social appearance anxiety*, where the individual is afraid that others are judging their appearance negatively. When it comes to body image, this fear is associated with the primary safety behaviour of never asking other people what they think, for fear of confirmation of that belief. It can also be associated with secondary safety behaviours, such as avoiding other people, dressing unobtrusively, overpreparation of appearance when forced to mix with others, and excessive use of alcohol in social settings.

Surveys of this sort are normally conducted in the early to middle part of Phase 4. However, they can be used earlier in CBT-AN-20 if they help to "unstick" the patient's progress (e.g., if the anorexia nervosa patient has regained some weight, but is convinced that they have ballooned in size and that others are appalled at how fat they have become). Surveys usually involve the following steps:

- Identify the patient's general beliefs about what others will think of their appearance and explain how fear of negative appearance evaluation and the associated safety behaviours are likely to operate and maintain their poor body image.
- Ask the patient to provide one or more photographs that they believe highlight the aspects of their body which will trigger negative judgements by others.
- Based on the provided photograph(s), ask the patient to generate questions to ask other people, and to make specific predictions about what other people will say about their appearance. Something between six and ten questions is a reasonable number to aim for.
- Ensure that the predictions about what other people will say give the maximum opportunity to disprove (as well as prove, of course) the patient's belief. Dimensional predictions (e.g., "They will rate me 9 out of 10 on fatness, and no-one will go below an 8") allow the patient more leeway to learn that they are wrong, compared with simple "yes/no" questions. Similarly, questions that allow other people to prioritise what they see (e.g., "What are the first three things that you notice about the person in this photograph?") allow the person to learn that their fears about what people focus on can be contradicted by completely different outcomes to what they expect (e.g., "I notice that nobody said that you have a fat belly, even though you thought that 90% of people would stress that"). Such responses to the survey can be equally surprising when they are comments on positive aspects of the person that are not to do with shape or weight (e.g., "She has a lovely smile and is really stylish. She looks really friendly"), because those comments tap into wider values and point out strengths in the individual.
- Give the resulting survey/questionnaire (anonymised as appropriate) to a group of people, to collect their responses. This can be done on paper or electronically. The patient will often be reluctant to show it to anyone who they know, so clinical colleagues make a good starting group. However, some patients will dismiss this option as being unhelpful because, for example: "They are clinicians and have to be nice about other people". In such circumstances, it can be useful to discuss options with the patient (e.g., clinicians have asked other student or staff groups who are not seen as so "nice" or have asked passers-by to do the ratings). Such discussion can sometimes result in the patient realising that they would be better "biting the bullet" and asking people whom they know.
- Go over the results with the patient, and review what others' opinions say relative to the patient's original thoughts.
- If the patient is convinced that their original belief was wrong, then a further survey can be developed, or they can be asked to engage in some

counter-schematic behaviour for homework (e.g., going out with friends, rather than avoiding doing so).

- If the patient is not convinced that their original belief was wrong (e.g., "Well, they were clinicians, so they have to say nice things" or "The questions/photo were the wrong ones to make my point"), then the clinician should be Socratic, agreeing that this is a possible explanation, and asking the patient how the survey should be revised to overcome that problem (e.g., getting a different group to complete the survey, preferably provided by the patient, to enhance their likelihood of believing the outcome next time round).

Unlike surveys used for individuals whose body mass indices fall in the over-weight or obese category, such surveys used with individuals in CBT-AN-20 rarely address stigma (e.g., "People will see that I am too fat to be a suitable parent"), but this possible route should not be ruled out completely.

Three types of survey are useful in such cases:

a) *Personal survey*: This is based on a single image of how the patient looks at present, using the steps outlined above. This is the most commonly used survey (see online skills video on   https://sites.google.com/sheffield.ac.uk/cbt-an-20/videos).

b) *Intrapersonal survey*: This is based on comparison of how the person looks now compared to at other times. For example, if the patient has regained some weight (e.g., starting at BMI = 16.2, currently at BMI = 18.1 but still functionally under-weight and needing to regain more), they might believe that others saw them as "chubby" at BMI 16.2, and that they are now seen as "horribly fat" at BMI = 18.1. Hence, they might be reluctant to regain any more weight because of this belief about what others think of their body. Such anticipated beliefs might be about topics such as: "People will think that I was really successful/in control when my BMI was 16.2, but not now that I am at a high BMI (18.2)"; or "People will think that I was much more friendly and approachable when my BMI was 16.2". That way, the patient can learn that a low BMI does not carry the person-ally valued qualities that they assume. A survey at this point in weight regain (e.g., during Phase 1) can result in a freeing up of that willingness to regain more weight when they realise that others rate their earlier photo as showing that they looked "dangerously skinny" before, and "unhealthily thin" now. Similarly, they can learn others saw them as "extremely fragile, unapproachable and out of control" before (BMI = 16.2), and that they look "very fragile/unapproachable/out of control" now (BMI = 18.1). Thus, they can understand that others did (and do) not value the same attributes that they value themselves, challenging their perception of their body and encouraging further weight gain (see online skills video on https://sites.google.com/sheffield.ac.uk/cbt-an-20/videos).

c) *Interpersonal survey*: This form of survey tests the patient's beliefs about how others rate their appearance compared to how they rate the appearance of important people in their life (e.g., "If people look at me with my friends, they will always see me as much fatter and uglier than them"). A survey asking others to rate both the patient and their friend(s) is a useful way to challenge that belief. We discourage comparison based on the appearance of celebrities and unknown people (e.g., others on social media), explaining that their images are unlikely to be a realistic representation, and that we have no idea of whether those are happy people or whether they are accepting of their bodies (see online skills video on https://sites.google.com/sheffield.ac.uk/cbt-an-20/videos).

10.9   Exposure with response prevention

Exposure with response prevention addresses a final (but very important) safety behaviour – where the individual avoids their own appearance (e.g., does not look in mirrors, wears baggy clothes). Exposure work of this sort is widely evidenced to be a very powerful way of enhancing body image, with collateral impact on a range of related issues, such as mood, body checking, and quality of life. However, it requires the patient to tolerate their anxiety during the exposure process (e.g., looking at their reflection in a mirror) without using their avoidant safety behaviour (e.g., looking or walking away). As explained in Section 3.3 (discussing the "spun glass theory of the mind"), exposure therapy also requires the clinician to tolerate their own concerns about distressing the patient without reducing the demands of the exposure (e.g., not ending the exposure early due to the patient being upset). When using exposure therapy for body image, it is important to use the inhibitory learning approach (see Section 4.11) to ensure rapid and resilient safety learning. Psychoeducation about anxiety (see Appendix A.15) can be used to prepare the patient for exposure therapy, and supervision/role plays are helpful for supporting the anxious clinician.

However, while exposure therapy is a valuable approach for working with eating disorders, in CBT-AN-20 any exposures for body image are scheduled towards the end of therapy. This is because the patient needs to be at a healthy weight/BMI before exposure is a viable approach, so that they can function well in the world. This approach (particularly mirror/screen exposure) is likely to leave the patient more satisfied with their current weight, so they need to be at a healthy level before they lose motivation to change.

There are two forms of exposure therapy related to body image – graded exposure and flooding. We do not recommend the historical third approach of systematic desensitisation (where the person learns to relax during exposure work – e.g., concurrent relaxation, mindfulness, medication), as this is less effective and takes a very long time, due to the dampening down of the anxiety and hence the level of anxiety reduction driven by habituation/extinction. Both graded exposure and flooding are more likely to be effective if they are used in an inhibitory learning framework. In such a framework, the level of anxiety is enhanced to maximise expectancy of negative predicted outcome (and hence subsequent expectancy violation), and where the patient is encouraged to develop the skills through practice in a range of settings. However, graded exposure will take several sessions and is limited in the breadth of its impact (e.g., can be used for encouraging smaller changes, such as wearing less concealing clothing). In contrast, flooding can be used in the form of mirror/screen exposure, where its effects are much quicker (one or two sessions) and wider than graded exposure (e.g., can be used for helping the person to extinguish their fear of looking at their whole body). Fortunately, at this later stage in therapy, the patient has already learned to trust the clinician more when we recommend exposure therapy. Therefore, it is usual to recommend full mirror/screen exposure to address body avoidance unless the patient rejects it outright, in which case it is important to stress to the patient that they are limiting their chances of full body acceptance due to their likely maintenance of body avoidance behaviours (as explained below).

10.9.1   Graded exposure

A graded exposure approach to body image has some utility, but relates to more specific facets of body avoidance, so is less likely to be used than the flooding approach of mirror/screen exposure. In graded exposure, a hierarchy is developed around body avoidance. For example:

Clinician: "So, you are concerned that if you wear fitted clothes, your body will look unacceptable. What would you say was your go-to safety behaviour in that situation?"

Patient: "I suppose it is wearing baggy clothes, so that I can cope with seeing my body and being around other people".

Clinician: "Remember when we used exposure therapy to help you get through your anxiety about eating new foods. How could you apply that here?"

Patient: "Well, I suppose that I worked my way up from the less scary to the more scary foods, and then I learned that the anxiety got more tolerable and I could go on to the scariest foods".

Clinician: "So how could we apply that here? Helping you to get more able to wear clothes that show your body more clearly?"

Patient: "I suppose that the obvious way would be to wear less and less baggy clothes, so that I could get used to the experience of what my body really looks like? But I haven't worn clothes like that since I was about 14".

Clinician: "You know, sometimes the obvious way is the best one, and you have clearly learned how exposure works. So let's firm up what you would need to do".

Patient: "First, I would have to come up with a set of clothes that were more and more fitted – I could borrow some from my sister or buy some. Then I would work my way through from the safest to the scariest".

Clinician: "So, for homework you could see what your sister could lend you, and rate them from safe to scary on that 0%–100% scale that we used before. But remember that the higher up the 'scary' scale you start, the faster you will learn. And you might try the clothes out in a 'safe' place, like your sister's or your bedroom, but you will benefit far more if you then get out into the world in those clothes".

Patient: "That sounds scary – can I just wear the fitted clothes, but under a coat?"

Clinician: "That would be a classic safety behaviour, wouldn't it. Just like going out in the fitted clothes but then changing clothes straight away".

Patient: "I suppose so. I know that didn't work when I tried eating a little bit of a scary food then threw the rest away. I just stayed scared of it".

Clinician: "And so …?"

Patient: "OK. I need to try the new clothes until I feel calmer and get used to them in lots of different places. Then step it up to the next level of 'fittedness' and do the same again".

Clinician: "Brilliant. You really have learned a lot. Time to give it one more go, so that you get more comfortable with your body, and you get to stay OK with your body. One last thing to remember, though – don't start right down at the bottom of your 0%–100% scale. If your sister has clothes that are not going to be very scary to wear, then don't bother with them. Start with something that is definitely going to make you anxious to wear out in public – maybe around a 50% anxiety level. You will learn a lot more quickly that way".

Note that the emphases here are on reinforcing the patient's learning so far and generalising of the core skills of exposure; making the work ecologically viable (e.g., using sister's clothes rather than spending on a hierarchy of increasingly tighter clothes); and the inhibitory learning skills of starting high up the hierarchy and generalising the skills into different settings. Once the process has started in everyday life, we find that the patient needs little support beyond review and positive reinforcement for their progress in the real world. Of course, graded exposure can be followed by mirror/screen exposure, if there is wider body avoidance to address (see online skills video on https://sites.google.com/sheffield.ac.uk/cbt-an-20/videos).

10.9.2   Mirror exposure/flooding

Flooding is a more rapid way of achieving reduction in avoidance, though it requires the patient and clinician to tolerate relatively high, sustained levels of anxiety while it is in progress for the first time (approximately 30–40 minutes in the session). Most importantly, we use flooding in the situation where the person needs exposure to their whole body (rather than partial exposure). Crucially, this includes most cases of body avoidance, including times when apparent body checking (e.g., inspecting one's face in the mirror) is followed by the safety behaviour of hiding from the mirror, or where the mirror is covered so that the whole body is not visible. In short, graded exposure is highly unlikely to be effective where the issue is whole-body avoidance. This is when we use flooding, in the form of mirror exposure (although this can also be delivered online, via the computer screen). This approach usually requires two sessions towards the end of therapy, with the latter overlapping with the start of Phase 5, as well as substantial practice during homework to ensure strong safety learning.

Two considerations are important before detailing the use of flooding/mirror exposure. First, the COVID pandemic taught us that, like many other skills, mirror exposure can be done online without a mirror. This adaptation requires the patient to use their computer screen and webcam to view their body. They will need to stand back far enough (with no screen filter/effects turned on and their image pinned to be the main one on the screen) that they can see themselves in the screen close to full length, while being able to use the microphone and speakers to communicate with the clinician.

Second, a practical issue. It might seem obvious that a full-length mirror is necessary for such work in the clinic. However, many clinical services have formal or informal policies that mean that the clinic does not have mirrors, some only have them in specific rooms, and many clinicians turn mirrors to the wall in order that the patient should not catch sight of themselves. The lack of mirrors for such work limits patients' chances of recovery and should be rectified. In fact, the hiding of mirrors is an effective way to maintain the patient's anxiety about their bodies (a form of accommodation by the clinical service), while the open presence of mirrors, by contrast, provides a form of exposure in itself, as the patient habituates to simply seeing a mirror in the room.

Once the necessary resources are in place, the patient needs to be oriented to what is going to come, so that they understand the practical and the emotional demands. The mirror exposure is likely to take up to 40 minutes. This means using the final part of a session (e.g., Session 16) to explain what is coming next time, explaining its potential benefits and the similarity to the exposure work that the patient has already done earlier in therapy. For example:

Clinician: "Remember that we said that when you were at a good enough weight to be able to function long-term, we would be able to do some of the really powerful body image work? Well, you have now got to a point where your body and brain seem to be working well, and the last step is that one of getting your body acceptance to a level that will let you stay well".

Patient: "What does that involve?"

Clinician: "You have already done good work on your worries about what other people think about your appearance and all that body comparison that you were doing. However, you are still overestimating your body size. The remaining problem is that you are still using that safety behaviour of avoiding looking at your body, and that is keeping you afraid of what you really look like".

Patient: "But what can I do about that?"

Clinician: "Remember when you were really reluctant to eat anything that you were scared of? Well, we addressed that by getting you to face your fear and actually eat that food, until the anxiety faded. What does that suggest?"

Patient: "You mean that I would have to look at myself and get used to my body? That definitely sounds scary. Though I have to admit that I have often wondered why you have that mirror here in the office".

Clinician: "Well spotted. Just having the mirror here can make you worry about it, but I suspect that that worry has gone down over the past few months while we have been meeting".

Patient: "I suppose it has – it is just part of the furniture".

Clinician: "That is the idea. So, when we start you looking at yourself in the mirror next week, you are part way there already. Because we need your anxiety to come down a long way, this is likely to take 30–40 minutes, so we would start after checking in on your risk and food diaries and use the rest of the session to give you long enough to learn the benefits of the exposure. Just make sure that you are wearing fitted clothes, so that when you look in the mirror then you can see what your body looks like".

As indicated, following this preparation in Session 16, the next session gets the mirror exposure going very quickly, to ensure sufficient time for the exposure to be effective, and for the patient to learn that their anxiety becomes far more manageable.

There are multiple ways in which exposure therapy can be delivered effectively (e.g., pure exposure, guided exposure, methods based on cognitive dissonance, different forms of dress, focus on positively regarded body parts, and focus on body functionality). The key element is the exposure itself, with the patient monitoring the fall in anxiety levels and then repeating and extending the work for homework. Therefore, while we suggest the steps outlined below, other effective methods are viable at this stage. The stages of mirror/screen exposure are:

1. Ask the patient to stand facing the full-length mirror so that they can see their whole body, and to rate their anxiety level (usually close to 100% at this stage).
2. Ask the patient to describe their body, starting at the top of their head, and slowly working their way down to their feet. Stress that you want them to describe themselves objectively, as they see themselves in the mirror or screen now (rather than from memory or their imagined self-view), and then if they describe their body in a negative way, ask them to be more objective (e.g., "You say that you have fat cheeks, but how many centimetres across is your face at that point?").
3. As the patient describes their body, note any parts that they omit (e.g., ears, shoulders), so that you can ask them to describe that part as they scan their body a second time.
4. As the patient completes their description of a particular zone of their body (e.g., reaches their neck or their waist), ask them to rate their anxiety levels again. Do not be deterred if it takes about 20–25 minutes to start falling below 100% – that is often how long it takes for exposure to show major effects.

5. If the patient expresses reluctance to continue, stress that they have the option to stop, but that this would be just another safety behaviour, and it would mean that they will never overcome their anxiety and begin to appreciate their body if they back off now.
6. As you reach the patient's feet, get another anxiety rating, then ask the patient to do the same thing, going up the body this time and rating anxiety as they go along. By the time that they reach their head, there is usually an appreciable reduction in their anxiety ratings.
7. Repeat that process, but this time ask the patient to turn sideways on, so that they get a different view of their body (e.g., focusing on how their bottom and their calves seem to protrude). This might raise the patient's anxiety to close to 100% again, but this reduces more quickly as the patient goes down their body, teaching the patient that they are able to manage changes in perspective and the associated anxiety.
8. When the patient reaches their feet for the second time, with anxiety coming down again, we ask the patient to repeat the feet-to-head scan, but this time talking about the functionality of the body parts being described (e.g., Clinician: "What benefits do you get from your calves?"; Patient: "Well, I suppose that they help me to walk to work and for pleasure"). This approach is associated with further reductions in anxiety ratings.
9. After that second total body scan, we ask the patient to rate their anxiety one last time, then discuss the experience and the way in which the anxiety fell, despite their initial feelings about the task.

We then ask the patient to repeat the task of scanning their body for homework, but to do it in as many ways and places as possible. This diversity increases generalisation of safety learning (i.e., that viewing the body is safe, and that their body is acceptable), within the inhibitory learning model of exposure. We also encourage the patient to start acting "as if" they accept their body, as such counter-schematic behaviour can enhance the learning further. To support this, in the session, the clinician can have a sheet with a figure on it, and jot down the helpful comments that the patient makes (e.g., neutral descriptions, positive comments, functionality of the body), so that they can take it home to remind them during the homework exercises (see online skills video on https://sites.google.com/sheffield.ac.uk/cbt-an-20/videos).

Kendall et al. (2005) and others suggest that we should look for a 50% reduction in anxiety across the exposure session (e.g., if the patient's maximum anxiety rating was 90%, keep going until it reaches at least 45%). Such "within-session" effects are strongly desirable, so that the patient has immediate feedback on the benefits of exposure therapy. However, even if there is limited reduction in anxiety during the session, the homework exercises can ensure substantial positive between-session effects.

Following this session, the next session usually begins with a review of the exposure work and the patient's homework completion. If necessary, a further, shorter mirror exposure session can be conducted (given the faster level of anxiety reduction experienced), but often the patient's change in body acceptance is clear, and they do not feel the need for any repetition. Either way, we stress the importance of maintaining the homework and the counter-schematic behaviours before moving on to Phase 5.

10.10 Summary

This chapter has outlined the many different approaches to body image work that can be valuable in normalising body image, helping the individual to accept their body or treat it neutrally, thus reducing their risk of relapse substantially (Keel et al., 2005). As stated throughout, patients can have very different factors at work that maintain their long-standing body image disturbance, and it is important that the clinician should individualise the body image treatment accordingly. In reviewing the impact of the work with the patient as they go along, it can be useful for the clinician to present the patient's rationale for staying the same as "Theory A" (e.g., "If I keep reassurance-seeking/body checking/body comparison/seeking reassurance/mind-reading/avoiding, etc., that will make me feel safe in the short term"), while presenting the alternative as "Theory B" (e.g., "Body image feels important to me for a whole host of reasons, but my attempts to monitor/avoid it heighten this sense of importance, and that keeps feeding the anorexia nervosa, which keeps me so constrained").

Chapter 11

Phase 5 (Sessions 18–20 and beyond)
Ending and relapse prevention

This final phase in CBT-AN-20 is slightly longer than the comparable phase in CBT-T, given the need to ensure that the patient learns to practice skills and work on maintaining the benefits of therapy. The key elements are similar to those found in CBT for other disorders:

- Positive feedback on the benefits of the work conducted so far, to support self-efficacy;
- The development of an effective therapy blueprint;
- Normalising eating, to ensure that the patient can continue to progress without therapy sessions;
- Engaging others in support of the patient;
- Working on returning to or developing a life without anorexia nervosa;
- Follow-up sessions;
- Referral for any outstanding problems.

11.1   Enhancing self-efficacy

At this stage, it is very useful to remind the patient of how much work they have undertaken, and to stress how that work has been done by the patient themselves. Where the patient attributes the change to the clinician, it is important to pass that attribution back to the patient in a way that enhances self-efficacy, for example:

Patient: "Thank you – I could not have got here without you".
Clinician: "I appreciate that that is how you are seeing it right now, but what did I do, really? I have had one hour a week with you. You had 167 hours a week on your own, making this happen, facing your anxiety, and changing so very much as a result".
Patient: "But still, you were so helpful".
Clinician: "All I would say is that my job has been to coach you, and it's been up to you how to make use of these sessions. If you had not thrown yourself into all this change yourself, there is nothing that I could have done to make you

DOI: 10.4324/9781003594703-11

change. You have done a great job and look how far you have come. Now you get to face the future with a whole new set of skills to enable you to face everything that the world brings over the years".

Without such self-attribution for success, the patient is less likely to develop the self-efficacy needed to face challenges in the future. Furthermore, allowing the patient to take ownership over the changes they have made gives them yet another opportunity to leverage cognitive dissonance as a tool for maintaining treatment gains (e.g., "I've been the one to work so hard to recover; that affirms that I want to be recovered").

11.2   Therapy blueprint

Normally, at the end of Session 18, we will prepare a draft therapy blueprint with the patient, for discussion and refinement over the last couple of sessions. A blank is provided in Appendix A.29 for the therapist and patient to use. The blueprint is a tool to encourage the patient to reflect on their progress, and to plan for the future (see following sections). Such reflection and planning will assist with the development of self-efficacy and prevent relapse in the future. The key headers (and explanations) are:

- *What were my problems when I was first referred?*
  - This question is a reminder of how far the patient has come by engaging in therapy. It can be useful to remind the patient of just how ill they were and how poor their quality of life was before they engaged in therapy.
- *What has become more possible that seemed almost impossible before?*
  - Here, we are reorienting the patient to the gains of therapy – even those that are incremental.
- *What did I do to change, and what strengths did I harness to do so?*
  - This element reinforces the attribution for positive change to the patient, so that their self-efficacy is supported further.
- *What do I need to keep doing to stay well?*
  - Here we point to the fact that eating, as well as emotional and interpersonal changes, need to be maintained/practised ("When I'm well, I'm eating regularly and flexibly and treating my body with value and respect; I'm connecting with friends, noticing and understanding my feelings, and responding to them in healthier ways, etc."). This approach can be helpful for the patient to identify their top "must dos" that are part of staying well.
- *What changes do I still want to make, and how will I achieve them?*
  - Here, we point to the fact that getting out of the eating disorder is a start, but that the patient has a good amount of real life to build following the years of stifled development (e.g., completing studies, building relationships, employment, having children, etc.).

- *What might lead to a setback in the future?*
  - We ask the patient to consider and note what has caused them difficulties in the past, particularly the predisposing and precipitating factors (see Figure 5.1), and to consider what might be the early signs of such a recurrence (e.g., more evidence of the "anorexic voice" trying to influence choices of food or clothing).
- *What would be the symptoms of a setback?*
  - We use Freeman & Dolan's (2001) model of stages of change (see Section 3.9) and discuss the stages before relapse. We distinguish the complete setback of a *relapse* (returning to the eating disorder) from the notion of a *lapse* (where the person makes one behavioural slip, such as not eating their evening snack) and that of a *prelapse* (where the individual thinks about letting go of a recovery-oriented guideline, such as wondering whether they really need that snack – also known as a "permissive cognition").
- *How would I overcome the setback?*
  - In the event of a lapse or a prelapse, we ask the patient not to give up completely (e.g., abstinence violation leading to surrendering all changes, and hence to relapse). Rather, we ask them to treat the lapse or prelapse as an experiment, to give them a sense of control. For example:
    Clinician: "OK, so you missed/thought about missing that snack/completing your diary. Well, that might be because you are not going to complete a diary/eat totally predictably for the rest of your life, if you want to achieve a normal relationship with food. Do you know any people without an eating disorder who eat so rigidly? So now is maybe the time to experiment. How about not eating that snack for the next three days? If you start feeling hungry or hear that anorexic voice praising you, then it is too soon, and you can end the experiment and go back to eating that snack regularly. While if you don't get those urges, then you are eating well enough to be able to take that snack out, as long as you do not lose weight over the next few weeks".
    Again, the goal here is to enhance the patient's self-efficacy.
- *What if that doesn't work?*
  - This element is usually brief, consisting of a suggestion to seek further clinical help, and to do so promptly rather than getting caught up in the anorexic mindset again.

We ask the patient to hold weekly "self-therapy" sessions during the first few months of the follow-up period. We ask them to book 30 minutes each week to be able to reflect on their skills maintenance and their progress relative to the therapy blueprint, and to plan how they will use the coming week to support getting back on track, if necessary (see online skills video on https://sites.google.com/sheffield. ac.uk/cbt-an-20/videos).

11.3   Normalising eating

This topic has been detailed immediately above, where the patient identifies lapse and prelapse experiences. However, if the patient does not experience those urges to change, then it is worth the patient's while to plan experiments where they can normalise eating (e.g., having brunch rather than breakfast and lunch at the weekend; eating early if going out in the evening, then topping up when returning), so that they are not rigidly constrained by a food plan. This is an important part of rebuilding a confident and flexible relationship with food that is not constrained by anxiety or fear and that is not dependent on the "mechanical" eating that was so useful in getting the patient back to health. If the patient follows a religion that observes fasting periods, we will have asked them not to do so during therapy (often with support from a relevant religious authority), but we can encourage them to consider whether they want to return to that fasting pattern as an experiment at some point in the future.

11.4   Engaging others in support

Where appropriate, given their level of involvement in facilitating the therapy, we encourage patients to bring relatives and loved ones to the session where we review the therapy blueprint (just as we invited them to the assessment), so that they are better positioned to offer support if it is clearly going to be needed. Along with the patient, we stress that this is a fine line, where the family are being asked not to worry about small issues but to note and raise more threatening-looking situations (e.g., apparent weight loss; missing meals). We do this with the patient present, so that there is agreement about what the family and loved ones can raise as a concern. We also use this meeting as an opportunity to reflect on the positive changes that loved ones might have noticed, which again can serve to enhance the patient's self-efficacy and can reinforce to the patient that they don't need anorexia nervosa in order to be able to flourish in life.

11.5   Working on returning to or developing a healthy
life beyond anorexia nervosa

This is a further issue raised in the therapy blueprint. We want the patient to have normal, achievable (if delayed) life goals that are SMART (Specific, Measurable, Achievable, Relevant, and Time-bound) enough that the patient can value them (e.g., going out with friends regularly; qualifying as a lawyer at last; developing a relationship) and can identify progress towards them (e.g., spending sociable and fun time with peers each week; finishing that law degree; responding to people who show an interest in them). In addition to letting go of the anorexia nervosa symptoms, most patients describe that they measure recovery by their increased engagement in the world and associated quality of life. This newfound engagement comes not just from weight gain and improved brain functioning, but also through measurable reduction in anxiety and overvaluation of weight and shape that coincide with remembering, or newly discovering, non-eating-disorder–related interests, passions, and relationships that they choose to pursue.

To reinforce the benefits of therapy, we write an end-of-therapy letter to the patient. We include an example of such (Appendix A.12). In some cases, we also find it helpful to ask the patient to work on a diagram or picture that reflects what they are doing when living life beyond their anorexia nervosa, for discussion in the final session and for the patient to develop over time. We discuss this diagram at follow-up sessions to mark the patient's developmental changes and to emphasise the work that they have done and can continue to do (see Section 4.15).

11.6   Follow-up sessions

We recommend at least three follow-up sessions at one, three, and six months after the end of the 20 sessions of therapy. This time period could be extended to fit with local clinical practice, though we would not recommend fewer than three follow-ups. These are used to review maintenance of progress (e.g., how well has the patient maintained the skills that they learned in therapy, such as eating adequately?), and also to review the patient's progress in leaving the anorexia nervosa behind (e.g., re-establishing friendships; exercising for fun rather than weight control; and being more flexible and feeling more at ease in life, which are important markers of recovery). At the end of the 20 therapy sessions, we stress to the patient that we are hoping to see them at follow-up to be able to hear how they have continued to solve problems, rather than hearing that they gave up. Again, this is to enhance the patient's sense of self-efficacy, showing that we believe that they have the power to solve problems rather than returning to the eating disorder, and will continue to manage life's challenges in healthier ways.

11.7   Referral for any outstanding problems

At the first follow-up, we consider whether there are self-help methods that could be used to enhance changes that have been made. These might include further use of online resources for body image or for perfectionism or might consist of a recommended self-help book for working with social phobia, core beliefs, or other issues. A list of such resources is given in Appendix A.30.

At the second and third follow-ups, we review comorbidities that were present at the outset of therapy (e.g., depression, OCD, social anxiety, perfectionism). Often, these will have been substantially reduced by successful work with the patient's eating disorder. However, if they have not been reduced following the work on the anorexia nervosa, then we will make a referral to help the patient address the relevant issue (e.g., chronic OCD, trauma work) in a new course of therapy. Alternatively, if the clinician has the skills to work with that further problem, then they could offer a further course of therapy to address it, although drawing a clear distinction between the two therapies will be important to ensure that the patient can change track accordingly.

Chapter 12

Adaptations of CBT-AN-20

Although CBT-AN-20 has been designed to be appropriate to offer to most medically stable adults with anorexia nervosa, there are clinical scenarios where the core protocol can be adapted to suit specific groups of patients. In our experience, such adaptations are necessary when individuals (a) start treatment partially or fully weight-restored; (b) have atypical anorexia nervosa; (c) are adolescents; or (d) have low-weight avoidant/restrictive food intake disorder (ARFID). In this chapter, we detail the ways in which the CBT-AN-20 protocol can be adapted for each of these groups.

12.1   Partially or fully weight-restored

Some individuals present for treatment having already achieved partial or full weight restoration, but with many of the cognitive elements of anorexia nervosa still in place (e.g., preoccupation with eating, shape, and weight; active "anorexic voice"). Such cases include:

- Patients who are stepping down from higher levels of care (e.g., inpatient or residential care, partial hospitalisation/day programs, or intensive outpatient treatments), sometimes as the result of clinical decisions, sometimes due to financial constraints;
- Those transitioning from other types of treatment (e.g., family-based treatment);
- Individuals who have managed to make improvements on their own.

Diagnostically, these individuals might present with anorexia nervosa in partial remission, or they might meet criteria for atypical anorexia nervosa (see below). For individuals with a recent diagnosis of low-weight anorexia nervosa, it is important to consider such a case as being anorexia nervosa in partial remission, given their increased vulnerability to relapse (Eddy & Breithaupt, 2023). While the clinician might consider a therapy such as CBT-T if weight is fully restored and the remaining issues are circumscribed (e.g., body image alone), for many such patients the residual symptoms and needs will be extensive (e.g., lack of weight

DOI: 10.4324/9781003594703-12

acceptance; still experiencing the "anorexic voice"; still learning how to get their needs met without the eating disorder, such as feeling cared for). For individuals with these more complex and extensive needs, we find CBT-AN-20 to be a suitable therapy.

Naturally, there will be heterogeneity in patients' degrees of wellness in this partial recovery cohort. For individuals who have partly weight-restored but still have more weight to gain, CBT-AN-20 will look very similar to the core protocol (described in Chapters 7–11), with a focus in Phase 1 on continued weight regain and emphasis now on the patient taking ownership of that gain. If the patient is discharged from a higher level of care following full weight restoration, the clinician might wonder whether CBT-AN-20 is even necessary, as a good part of the treatment goal has already been achieved. However, we would advise that CBT-AN-20 remains highly relevant for this patient presentation. While the patient might be weight restored, this restoration is new and not yet durable. Weight maintenance is its own skill, which cannot easily be learned at a more intensive level of care (e.g., hospital or residential setting). For example, patients might have achieved weight restoration through a structured feeding program (maybe even tube feeding) or under parental supervision, all of which might have been necessary at the time but do not allow them the opportunity to choose to challenge their anxiety in the same way they could do in CBT-AN-20. In other words, they have not yet challenged the broken cognition that is at the heart of anorexia nervosa – that they will gain weight on a trajectory that is out of control. Instead, in higher levels of care, their food has been portioned out for them and overseen by a multidisciplinary team. As such, the patient has not yet had to actively challenge the "anorexic voice"; instead, they have been passively fed and can attribute the change squarely to the team and absolve themselves from the guilt of having gained weight. In CBT-AN-20, they will have to actively challenge the inevitable critique of the "anorexic voice" and take ownership of their eating and weight regain.

Bearing these clinical needs in mind, when partial or full weight restoration has already occurred prior to initiating CBT-AN-20, we recommend the following modifications to the core protocol, as illustrated in Figure 12.1 (in *italics*):

12.1.1   Assessment

The clinician should obtain records from any recent treatments to aid in history-taking.

12.1.2   Phase 1

Since at least some weight has already been regained, Phase 1 can be abbreviated (c. Sessions 1–8).

- Psychoeducation is still relevant. Although such patients are at a healthier weight, they are likely still climbing out of starvation mode, and this learning

| Phase 5: Ending and relapse prevention |

| Phase 4: Body image work *(begin earlier)* |

| Phase 3: Addressing emotional triggers *(begin earlier)* |

| Phase 2: Behavioural experiments: New foods and weight maintenance *(begin earlier)* |

| Progress review |

| Phase 1: Dietary change/exposure for weight regain/*maintenance* |

| Risk management; Therapy interfering behaviours; Alliance; Engagement/motivational work; Case Formulation; Measuring progress and outcomes; Ongoing review points |

| Assess | 1 | 2 | 3 | 4 | 5 | 6 | 7 | 8 | 9 | 10 | 11 | 12 | 13 | 14 | 15 | 16 | 17 | 18 | 19 | 20 | FU1 | FU2 | FU3 |

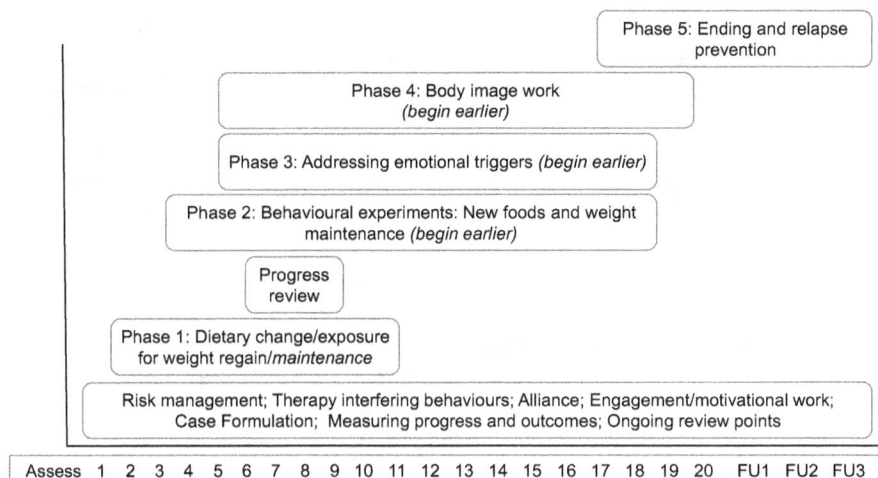

Figure 12.1 Modifications to CBT-AN-20 for patients who are partially or fully weight-restored (adaptations to core protocol shown in *italics*).

(e.g., about the Minnesota Starvation Study) remains important. Issues around body image and emotional factors are also likely to be important topics for psychoeducation. Patients might say that they have already covered this material when they were at a lower weight, but we advocate for a refresh as they are at a different point now, and the material might have a different meaning to them with more distance from acute low weight.

- If they still have further weight to gain, a weight regain plan will be needed.
- In reviewing prior treatments, most salient will be the patient's recent experience that has led to weight restoration and how this differs from CBT-AN-20. In addition to taking more ownership over food choices and weight gain, another possible difference (e.g., from hospital settings) is open weighing. Whereas the patient might have appreciated being shielded from the anxiety of knowing these numbers in the inpatient setting, in CBT-AN-20, open weighing will be critical to test weight predictions in the outpatient context to enable learning of weight stability or managed weight regain.
- When reviewing pros and cons of the anorexia nervosa and of leaving it behind, the clinician can help to highlight the pros of gaining weight that the patient has already experienced (e.g., increased energy, return of menses) and still wishes to realise (e.g., improved social connections). In the context of weight restoration, the patient might feel that they are already better, and so the cons of the eating disorder could feel farther away and less likely to return, making the patient less attentive to the need to work actively to maintain their progress to date. In such cases, the formulation becomes especially important, as the past relationship with anorexia nervosa might take on an increasingly idealised status, increasing the risk of relapse.

- The clinician can ask what the "anorexic voice" was like in the past treatment (e.g., hospitalisation, family-based treatment), and warn the patient that it may get louder now that they are playing a more active role in eating and recovery.
- Pause points for weight maintenance (see Phase 2, below) can begin earlier, but still not right away. The transition from a controlled eating environment to an *ad libitum* one is substantial, so patients will need to practice eating independently. That way, they can test that broken cognition – that eating freely will lead them to gain weight in a manner that is out of control. It will be important to allow the patient the opportunity to test that prediction for two or three weeks before introducing pause points.
- In the Session 6 review, the focus will still be on weight regain/maintenance, but evaluation of progress in reducing restrictive eating behaviours can take on even greater importance. If disability training/honest conversations are necessary, the potential need to return to the prior level of care (e.g., hospitalisation or family-based treatment) will necessarily be part of that discussion.

12.1.3 Phase 2

Again, because such patients are starting at or nearer to a healthier weight, the introduction of Phase 2 can begin earlier (c. Sessions 4–18).

- The patient might have been discharged from the hospital on a specific meal plan. While the meal plan can serve as a general guide, it is crucial that the clinician should not allow the patient to hide behind it as an excuse to skip the hard work of food exposure and behavioural experiments, which are aimed towards supporting the patient to build their confidence in flexible, healthy eating.
- We recommend moving to a more options-based eating plan, such as the REAL Food Guide (Section 4.3 and Appendix A.4), to enhance the patient's cognitive and emotional engagement with behavioural change.
- When creating feared and safe food lists, the clinician should help the patient to consider what environmentally relevant foods have been missing from their diet at that higher level of care. For example, the patient might benefit from including foods from local shops or restaurants, or the school or work cafeteria.

12.1.4 Phase 3

This focus on emotional and interpersonal factors can also start earlier (c. Sessions 6–19) and very much resembles that of the core protocol.

- While the patient may have started doing some of this work already, it will be important to highlight that when out of a higher level of care, they might experience more emotional triggers and mood fluctuations that simply did not occur in a controlled environment.

- Although the patient will have less access to immediate interpersonal support (e.g., 24/7 clinician access, parents) in the outpatient setting, they might also be better able to access emotion regulation and self-care tools that were not readily available in the hospital (e.g., the ability to spend time with a pet, or meet friends for coffee).

12.1.5   Phase 4

Body image work can begin earlier since weight is partly or fully restored (c. Session 6 onward), but it is likely to be based on different opportunities and constraints to those in the more intensive treatment setting.

- In higher levels of care, the patient might have been prevented from body checking (weighing, measuring, mirror checking). However, in the outpatient context, they will be surrounded with multiple opportunities to body check in the natural environment, and subsequent opportunities to realistically evaluate the impact of body checking on their mood and self-esteem.
- In the outpatient context, there will be more natural opportunities for body image exposure work (e.g., with mirrors and shop windows, and going out in public in tighter clothing).
- When designing surveys to evaluate patients' beliefs that they looked better before gaining weight, pre- and post-hospital photos might be a natural choice for hypothesis-testing.

12.1.6   Phase 5

The final phase will still focus on relapse prevention and will resemble the core protocol (Sessions 18–20).

- To enhance self-efficacy, the clinician should highlight the patient's agency and ownership of changes they achieved in the outpatient context, potentially contrasting that sense of personal responsibility with the experience of weight gain in the less controllable intensive treatment setting.

12.2   Atypical anorexia nervosa

Atypical anorexia nervosa (AAN) is defined in *DSM-5-TR* (American Psychiatric Association, 2022) as meeting all of the criteria for anorexia nervosa, except that despite significant weight loss, the individual's weight remains within or above the normal range. Although atypical anorexia nervosa is more common in community settings than anorexia nervosa itself (Harrop et al., 2021), atypical anorexia nervosa remains one of our least well-defined and understood eating disorder diagnoses, with a somewhat ambiguous definition and limited data on outcomes. It is however worth holding in mind that Keegan and Wade (2024a) found the odds of having a *good outcome from CBT-T at one-month follow-up were eight times less likely among patients with AAN than those with other disorders*, suggesting that recovery in this heterogeneous cohort of non-underweight patients is likely to require something other than CBT-T. Examples of presentations of atypical anorexia nervosa in the literature include (1) recent full threshold anorexia nervosa with subsequent weight regain (which we describe above as "anorexia nervosa in partial recovery"); (2) individuals who have restrictive eating, extreme weight and shape concerns, and mild weight suppression (but no recent history of low weight); and (3) individuals with premorbidly higher weight bodies who have precipitously lost weight but have not reached the threshold low weight for a diagnosis of anorexia nervosa. While the presentations of atypical anorexia nervosa are variable, the hallmark features unifying such presentations of atypical anorexia nervosa are restrictive eating and drive for thinness.

Individuals with a "partial recovery" presentation can be treated using the adaptations recommended above for those who are partially or fully weight-restored. In contrast, for those with a "mild weight suppression with no recent history of low weight" presentation, the clinician faces a choice point. In some cases, this presentation may be amenable to CBT-T (Kambanis, Graver, et al., 2025), which focuses on early dietary change, use of an inhibitory learning approach to exposure therapy, and similar approaches to body image. However, in most cases, CBT-T will not be enough and instead, the patient will benefit from CBT-AN-20's longer duration, anorexia-specific formulation; use of behavioural experiments to teach weight maintenance; working with the "anorexic voice"; and focus on emotional triggers for compulsive (rather than impulsive) behaviours. Considering the similarities and differences between the two therapies, clinical factors that could tip the scales in favour of CBT-AN-20 for this presentation include a higher degree of weight suppression, a more ego-syntonic relationship to the eating disorder, and/or high levels of compulsive behaviours (e.g., compulsive exercise) or personality features.

That leaves us with the "precipitous weight loss in a higher weight body" presentation. Such patients may have lost a great deal of weight, but their current weight falls in the normal weight or overweight/obese range because of a higher premorbid weight. These individuals show strikingly similar eating behaviour to those with full threshold anorexia nervosa (Jablonski et al., 2024), with commensurate severity of psychological symptoms and similar medical complications (Walsh et al., 2023). Often, body image concerns are even more pronounced in higher weight cases like this versus typical anorexia nervosa, as those with atypical anorexia nervosa have not reached the lower body weight that conforms with the societal ideal. One example of this presentation could be a patient whose care team has prescribed them medication or surgery to support weight loss due to medical comorbidities, but the person has lost more weight than is healthy and is now encountering eating disorder cognitions and behaviours. In such cases, we recommend proceeding with the usual phases and sessions of the core CBT-AN-20 protocol, with the following adaptations. Information for such patients and their loved ones is provided in Appendix A.31.

In summary, as a general rule of thumb, we are recommending CBT-AN-20 over CBT-T to give patients with the various atypical anorexia nervosa presentations a better chance of recovery.

12.2.1   Assessment

The patient's BMI will already be above 19 but will likely need to go higher. The clinician will need to liaise with the patient's medical provider and/or dietitian to determine a healthy minimum to work towards in treatment (Jhe et al., 2023).

12.2.2   Phase 1

- Psychoeducation about starvation very much applies, as the patient is in a calorie deficit and will likely be experiencing the psychological and physical manifestations of this biological state.
- When co-creating the formulation, it should be considered that the patient might never have realised their ultimate goal of an objectively low weight. In such cases, when discussing the idealised state represented by the earlier stage of anorexia nervosa, the clinician can also incorporate the perceived benefits and drawbacks of continuing to pursue that unrealised goal, and the extent to which predicted benefits are realistic and the drawbacks have been discounted by the patient.
- It will also be helpful to normalise the failure to achieve an objectively low body weight. While the patient might view this as a personal failing, it is helpful for the clinician to portray this as a good example of survival of the fittest, in which their body refused to go where Charles Darwin could not follow.
- The *individual* "anorexic voice" may be further reinforced by a *societal* "anorexic voice" (either felt by the patient or overtly reinforced by others) that encourages weight loss (and discourages weight gain) for individuals living in higher weight bodies. Both the individual and societal anorexic voices will need to be challenged, using the principles outlined in Section 4.9.

12.2.3   Phase 2

- In line with the societal "anorexic voice", the patient with atypical anorexia nervosa might be even more likely to push back on eating feared foods due to perceived stigma from others that they should not be eating high-calorie foods. Those beliefs about stigma should be treated as hypotheses and tested through surveys and/or behavioural experiments. The patient might believe that weight stigma beliefs are strongly held by everyone around them. To test that hypothesis, the patient could ask others to review photos of them at their premorbid weight and rate their agreement with statements such as: "This person does not deserve to be eating a slice of cake". The patient might predict that 100% of individuals will agree with this statement, while results show that only 20% actually do. Similarly, they could eat one of their feared foods at a café and evaluate their prediction of how many other patrons will stop and stare at them for more than five seconds or verbally admonish them for eating a slice of cake. While there might be one bullying patron, it is unlikely that everyone in the café will stop and stare. We can then use the survey here to ask the patient something like, "So two out of 10 people said you shouldn't be eating cake – do you want to live your life around the minority of people holding those opinions, or the majority who did not think that?"

12.2.4   Phase 3

- Individuals in higher weight bodies are at increased risk for discrimination. Negative comments, weight-based teasing, or other real experiences of weight bias can create emotional triggers that promote engagement in disordered eating, particularly if the target weight sits in the overweight range. In such cases, the clinician should validate the patient's experiences, and focus on how the patient can protect themselves from using eating disorder behaviours to cope (e.g., working with attributions regarding why others are critical in that way, such as it being due to the person being generally hostile or bullying; and working with seeing the bigger picture – that while some might hold critical views, that doesn't mean everyone holds those same views). Imagery rescripting of unpleasant memories of being bullied or criticised by others can be especially useful in Phase 4 when addressing body image.

12.2.5   Phase 4

- If a patient is at an objectively high weight, body image surveys that ask respondents to evaluate whether they are at an objectively high weight or larger than their peers will not be useful, as such statements are objectively true and will only reinforce the patient's concerns. Instead, as in CBT-T for non-underweight eating disorders, surveys will be more helpful if they evaluate the patient's *feared implications* of living in a larger body, and the associated stigma. For example, surveys could be set up to test the patient's fears that being at a higher weight means that others will see them as undeserving of food (see Phase 2), as unable to maintain friendships, or as undesirable to romantic partners. If in a survey, three out of ten people think the person is more attractive at the lower weight, the clinician could ask the patient whether they want to live their life around what those people think, or instead, go with what the majority think. The goal here will be to help challenge the patient's all-or-nothing thinking, helping them to recognise that while some people may believe they are more attractive at the lower weight, this is not universally true and may not be worth all the associated risks of low weight to please the minority of people. The use of the Body Neutrality handout (Appendix A.28) can also facilitate discussion related to compassionate body acceptance.

- There may be body image concerns that are specific to having lost weight from a higher weight body (e.g., excess skin) that can be incorporated into body image work.

12.2.6 Phase 5

- The relapse prevention plan should include a strategy for addressing weight-based discrimination and stigma, including from healthcare providers. For example, the patient might want to prepare in advance what they will say to a well-intentioned but misguided healthcare provider who recommends that they lose weight in response to irrelevant medical conditions, or that they should engage in potentially dangerous behaviours such as intermittent fasting.

12.3 Adolescents

International guidelines recommend family-based treatment (FBT) as the first line for adolescent anorexia nervosa (e.g., Academy for Eating Disorders, 2020), and we agree that whenever possible, FBT should be offered. However, while FBT can be helpful in facilitating weight restoration, it does not specifically address body image disturbance, and cognitive symptoms might remain following weight regain (Craig et al., 2019; Egbert et al., 2023). In these cases, CBT-AN-20 can be helpful as a next course of treatment (see above for using CBT-AN-20 in individuals who have weight restored). Furthermore, there are cases in which FBT is unacceptable, contraindicated, or ineffective (Dalle Grave et al., 2019). As FBT is resource-intensive, definitionally involving intensive parental participation, it can be challenging for some parents to undertake (e.g., in the setting of limited resources, other children, etc and some children will not want their family involved (Craig et al., 2019), so some families and individuals will opt for individual therapy. In other cases, FBT might be contraindicated, for example in the context of intrafamilial child abuse or significant parental discord. Individual therapy is not necessarily a lesser route. In a non-randomised trial, Le Grange and colleagues (2022) found that when adolescents were offered the choice between FBT and CBT-E, their treatment outcomes were similar. Therefore, when FBT is unacceptable or contraindicated, CBT might be an appropriate alternative, in the form of CBT-E (Dalle Grave & Calugi, 2020) or CBT-AN-20. For example, in a study of 49 adolescents with anorexia nervosa who were offered CBT-E, Dalle Grave and colleagues found that 71% of patients completed treatment and showed considerable weight gain and significant reductions in eating pathology and clinical impairment, demonstrating the efficacy of CBT-E for adolescents with anorexia nervosa (Dalle Grave et al., 2019).

Finally, some individuals with anorexia nervosa will be non-responders to FBT. The early change literature suggests that patients who will do well in FBT will have shown marked early progress. In contrast, if they have not gained 1.8 kgs by Session 4, then their chances of full weight restoration and recovery at the end of treatment substantially decline (Madden et al., 2015). At this point, their treatment team might advise they seek a higher level of care. However, if a higher level of care is unacceptable or infeasible, CBT-AN-20 can be offered as an alternative treatment.

When applying CBT-AN-20 to adolescents, we recommend the following adaptations:

12.3.1 Assessment

- First, and most important, is consideration of how to include caregivers. While significant others are often, but optionally, involved in CBT-AN-20 for adults, parent involvement is critical for the adolescent. Adolescents rarely operate independently – meaning that they rely on parents to purchase and often pre-pare foods, and they might depend on parents for transportation to therapy. Parents, in turn, are often the most invested parties in their children's recovery, and as such, they can play a key role in adolescent engagement in treatment. Furthermore, inclusion of parents can serve as an opportunity for the adoles-cent to share, showcase, and reinforce their learning. For some adolescents, parents will be involved only at key points in treatment (e.g., early progress review; creation of the therapy blueprint), while for others, parents might be included at the end of sessions around planning for the coming week to ensure they understand their patient-support role. The extent of parent inclusion should be determined with the patient (and parents) during the initial assess-ment and reviewed as necessary thereafter.
- In addition to the formal assessment with the adolescent, the clinician can include the parents in the initial evaluation to gather collateral data. This inclu-sion will enable the clinician to engage with the adolescent and parents to determine diagnosis, review illness and treatment history, and gather data on family structure, support, and resources relevant to treatment engagement.
- Including the parents in the introduction to treatment also allows the clini-cian to set the expectations for the course of therapy. Generally, for younger adolescents and for those who are more ambivalent about treatment, more fre-quent engagement with parents will be needed.
- Determination of expected body weight can be challenging in adolescents, who will be gaining weight and growing as part of healthy maturation. Review of individual growth charts (height, weight, and BMI centiles) and liaising with the paediatrician or adolescent medicine physician are critical in getting a sense of targets.

12.3.2   Phase 1

- Psychoeducation is done with the patient as usual, but parents can be brought in at the end of the sessions (as appropriate) to provide patients an opportunity to share information and consolidate learning.
- Parents are included in the early progress review (e.g., Session 6). When patients are doing well, this gives the parents an opportunity to share their impressions of progress and to reinforce positives they are seeing at home. When patients are not doing well, including parents in the review can give everyone an opportunity to brainstorm the next steps around intervention, which may include needing to move to a higher level of care.
- If disability training/honest conversations are needed (see Section 7.7), parents' involvement is two-fold. First, parents can help shape the intervention by providing information to help guide the clinician in delivering disability training (e.g., the patient will not be able to move away to college if not making progress). Second, alongside the patient, parents will be recipients of the disability training/honest conversation, receiving concrete and sobering information about what chronic anorexia nervosa will look like for their adolescent and for their entire family. Note that disability training/honest conversations with adolescents can feel challenging for the clinician, particularly as the patient's youth can make some of the long-term consequences seem farther off or less real. Having the parents present can help to drive home the real and immediate consequences of anorexia nervosa (e.g., staying home while peers achieve independence). Furthermore, parents will hold an image of their adolescent's full life trajectory *without the eating disorder*, and they can also help their child to achieve it. By contrast, some adult patients with anorexia nervosa – particularly those who have been chronically ill – will have already been off course for so long that it might be harder for their family or support people to see a clear path to return to premorbid functioning.

12.3.3   Phase 2

- Parents may be able to help with the planned eating exposures and experiments in Phases 1 and 2 by shopping for and preparing foods. They may be able to help the patient to identify foods that will be useful to test by reflecting back on foods the patient used to enjoy before the eating disorder onset, or on foods that are most relevant in the patient's day-to-day life.
- Some adolescents may wish to include their parents in planning for or conducting behavioural experiments during the week. Involving parents in the planning can help to keep the adolescent accountable.

12.3.4   Phase 3

• Parents are often acutely aware of adolescent mood fluctuations and might be able to help patients to identify core cognitions at the times and in the settings when mood deteriorates in everyday life and in interpersonal interactions.

12.3.5   Phase 4

• The clinician will want to enquire about patient body image as usual. For some older adolescents, this body image work will require no adaptations, while younger patients might benefit from including the parents in session to identify and plan personalised body image interventions.

12.3.6   Phase 5

• Parents are included in the creation of the therapy blueprint, giving the adolescent an opportunity to showcase their learning and demonstrate how they will take ownership of continuing and maintaining progress over time. Likewise, parents can help to reinforce this progress and to identify ways that they can continue to support the adolescent over time, as developmentally appropriate.

12.4   Low-weight avoidant/restrictive food intake disorder (ARFID)

ARFID is defined by avoidant and/or restrictive eating that can lead to a range of consequences, one of which is low weight, resembling anorexia nervosa. In the last decade, numerous interventions have been developed and are being trialled for ARFID. The best-studied approaches include cognitive-behavioural therapy for ARFID (CBT-AR; Thomas & Eddy, 2019), designed for individuals aged 10 and older, and family-based treatment for ARFID (FBT-ARFID; Lock, 2021) for youth aged 5–12 years old. While CBT-AN-20 has not been systematically evaluated for low-weight ARFID, it has clear value in weight restoration and challenging fears about food. CBT-AN-20 also has the advantage of offering some interventions not included in FBT-ARFID or CBT-AR – most notably body image work. While frank crossover from ARFID to anorexia nervosa (Kambanis, Tabri et al., 2025) or from anorexia nervosa to ARFID (Breithaupt et al., 2022) is rare, a subset of patients with ARFID do present with co-occurring weight and shape concerns (Abber et al., 2024). Weight and shape concerns in ARFID do not typically rise above community norms (Kambanis, Palmer et al., 2025), but some patients experience the emergence of clinically significant weight and shape concerns as they gain weight in treatment (Becker et al., 2020). Adaptations of CBT-AN-20 for low-weight ARFID are detailed below, as illustrated in Figure 12.2 (in *italics*). Information for such patients and their loved ones is provided in Appendix A.32.

```
                                              ┌──────────────────────────────┐
                                              │ Phase 5: Ending and relapse  │
                                              │         prevention           │
                                              └──────────────────────────────┘
                              ┌──────────────────────────────┐
                              │  Phase 4: Body image work    │
                              │         (optional)           │
                              └──────────────────────────────┘
                              ┌──────────────────────────────┐
                              │   Phase 3: Addressing        │
                              │   emotional triggers         │
                              │        (optional)            │
                              └──────────────────────────────┘
        ┌──────────────────────────────────────────────────────┐
        │ Phase 2: Behavioural experiments: New foods and weight│
        │ maintenance, increasing variety using experiments that test │
        │ ARFID-specific fears (sensory sensitivity; fear of aversive │
        │   consequences, or lack of interest in eating)       │
        └──────────────────────────────────────────────────────┘
                  ┌────────────┐
                  │  Progress  │
                  │   review   │
                  └────────────┘
        ┌──────────────────────────────────────────────────────┐
        │ Phase 1: Dietary change/exposure for weight regain, increasing │
        │      volume, starting with safe/preferred foods      │
        └──────────────────────────────────────────────────────┘
   ┌────────────────────────────────────────────────────────────────┐
   │ Risk management; Therapy interfering behaviours; Alliance; Engagement/motivational work; │
   │  Case Formulation; Measuring progress and outcomes; Ongoing review points │
   └────────────────────────────────────────────────────────────────┘
 ┌────────────────────────────────────────────────────────────────────┐
 │ Assess  1  2  3  4  5  6  7  8  9  10  11  12  13  14  15  16  17  18  19  20  FU1  FU2  FU3 │
 └────────────────────────────────────────────────────────────────────┘
```

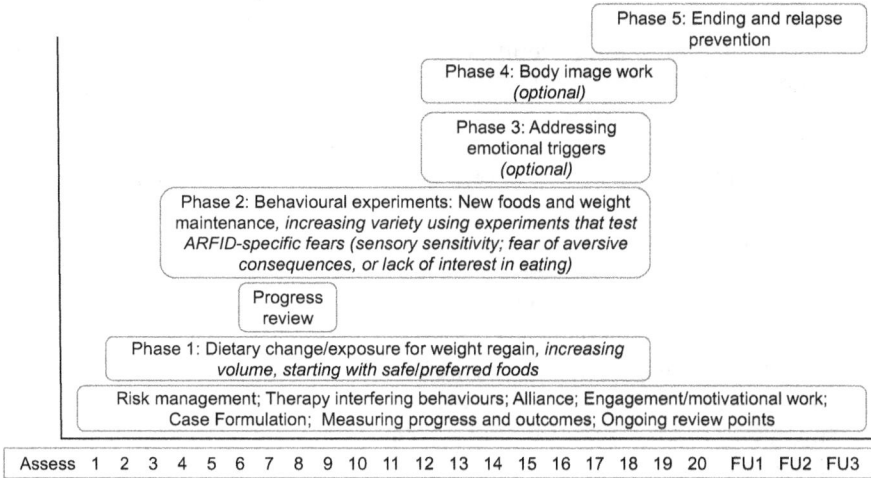

Figure 12.2 Modifications to CBT-AN-20 for low-weight ARFID patients (adaptations to core protocol shown in *italics*).

12.4.1   Assessment

• In addition to assessing for the typical eating disorder features, to aid in case formulation it will be critical for the clinician to determine which of the three clinical presentations are most salient for the patient with low-weight ARFID (i.e., fear of aversive consequences, lack of interest in eating or food, or sensory sensitivity), keeping in mind that patients can have more than one. Self-report instruments such as the Pica, ARFID, and Rumination Disorder-ARFID Questionnaire (PARDI-AR-Q; Bryant Waugh et al., 2022), can be useful to establish the baseline presence and severity of each ARFID presentation.

• To track weekly progress, the clinician should use a measure of ARFID symptoms (such as the PARDI-AR-Q) but might consider also adding the ED-15 in order to remain vigilant for the emergence of weight and shape concerns.

• Given the very young age of onset in ARFID, there might be no premorbid weight at the current height from which to calculate a healthy target weight range. The clinician should liaise with the patient's medical care provider to ascertain an appropriate healthy weight range that can be used as an interim goal, en route to finding what works for the individual patient.

12.4.2   Phase 1

• As in CBT-AR, we recommend that weight restoration begin with increasing the *volume* of preferred foods, rather than the immediate introduction of feared foods (which will require specific exposures in later phases of treatment – Thomas & Eddy, 2019). Supplement drinks, if tolerated, can be useful here.

- Weight predictions will still be necessary but will serve a different purpose than in the core protocol. In most cases, patients with ARFID will not need to test that broken cognition of gaining weight in an out-of-control fashion. However, what they do share with anorexia nervosa patients is a lack of appreciation of just how much food they may need to eat in order to see weight gain. For this reason, getting weight predictions will still be important, so that the patient with ARFID can receive immediate feedback on whether they have increased their intake enough to support weight gain.
- When discussing the pros and cons of the eating disorder, individuals with ARFID will typically show a less ego-syntonic relationship to their symptoms. Rather than viewing low-weight status as something to strive for, they might instead view weight gain as a desirable goal but as an insurmountable task. Others, who might have lived at a low weight throughout childhood, could struggle to find the motivation to commit to making consistent behavioural change. Salient "cons" might focus less on gaining weight or disliking their appearance and more on how scary, difficult, or upsetting it will be to change their eating patterns.

12.4.3   Phase 2

- After Phase 1 begins to address *volume* (i.e., difficulty eating enough food), Phase 2 will move on to address *variety* (i.e., difficulty eating enough different kinds of food). Asking the patient to commit to adding feared foods (e.g., adding a portion of meat to a meal) and to predict the likely impact on their weight (e.g., "I will gain half a kilo/a pound") will still be useful, if only to help the patient realise the magnitude of changes in eating that will be necessary to produce weight gain.
- Unlike with anorexia nervosa, the weight gain itself is unlikely to be distressing. To that end, food exposures and behavioural experiments should instead target feared predictions that are relevant for the patient's specific ARFID presentation. For example, if a patient with the *ARFID-lack of interest* presentation predicts that increasing portion sizes at a particular meal will result in unbearable feelings of fullness that will distract from daily activities, the clinician could ask them to increase the portion size of that meal daily for a week, rate their degree of fullness on a scale of 1–10 each time, and track whether they are still able meet their responsibilities (e.g., chores, work tasks) for the day, despite any physical discomfort. Similarly, if a patient with the *ARFID-fear of aversive consequences* predicts that eating a particular food will lead to vomiting, the clinician could ask them to add that particular food to a planned meal or snack every day for a week and record whether they vomit each time. (Of note, if the patient fears that a food could have fatal consequences, such as choking, the clinician might wish to offer that they can conduct the first food exposure together in session, but then quickly phase out the safety behaviour of the clinician being present.) Lastly, if a patient with the *ARFID-sensory*

sensitivity presentation would like to try a novel food but is worried it will be disgusting, the clinician could ask them to taste a small amount of that food every day for a week, increase the portion size each day, and record whether they are able to tolerate consumption of this novel food and whether the disgust declines with more exposures. As in CBT-AR, for the *ARFID-sensory sensitivity* presentation, we recommend that the patient themselves select the specific foods they would like to try.

12.4.4   Phase 3

- Emerging data suggest that, similar to individuals with other eating disorders, those with ARFID experience difficulties in emotion regulation (Stern, Graver et al., 2024). That said, individuals with ARFID show greater vulnerability to impulsivity than those with anorexia nervosa (Stern, McPherson et al., 2024). To that end, emotion work in Phase 3 will likely still be relevant, but might not need to focus as much on triggers for compulsive behaviours.

12.4.5   Phase 4

- As body image disturbance is not a core diagnostic criterion for ARFID, this module is likely be unnecessary in the majority of cases and could safely be omitted.
- However, given that a modest subset of individuals with ARFID experience clinically significant shape and weight concerns (Kambanis, Tabri et al., 2025), show crossover into frank anorexia nervosa (Kambanis, Palmer et al., 2025), or exhibit de novo shape and weight concerns in the context of weight gain (Becker et al., 2020), the clinician should be vigilant for the emergence of body image disturbance in clinical reports, backed up with careful monitoring of ED-15 scores where appropriate. In our clinical experience, body image disturbance is especially likely to present in patients who have had a life-long underweight status due to their ARFID and who come to realise only through weight gain that being low weight had become an implicit part of their identities.

12.4.6   Phase 5

- Phase 5 is similar to the core protocol, emphasising skills of relapse prevention.

12.5   Summary

With adaptations, CBT-AN-20 can be appropriate for a variety of clinical presentations on the anorexia nervosa/underweight spectrum. While some clinical presentations allow for the omission of entire phases of treatment (e.g., potentially omitting body image work for low-weight ARFID), other presentations benefit from adjusting the length of existing treatment phases (e.g., shortening Phase 1 for patients who are already weight-restored); making conceptual adjustments to existing interventions (e.g., addressing the societal "anorexic voice" in atypical anorexia nervosa); or placing more emphasis on involving parents or loved ones (e.g., to support adolescents).

In ballet, there is a stance called *fifth position* where the dancer is balanced evenly on both feet. Starting from fifth position, the dancer can transition into almost any step (leaps, turns) and travel in any direction (forward, backward, side). Similarly, the core CBT-AN-20 protocol can provide a secure jumping-off point to facilitate a variety of clinical adaptations. As we discuss in Chapter 13, nothing should be set in stone, as our patients will differ in their presentations and in their reactions to therapy.

Chapter 13

Final considerations for current and future therapists

Reflecting on progress in any difficult pursuit, comic book author Stephen McCranie famously quipped that "The master has failed more times than the beginner has even tried" (McCranie, 2014, p. 101). He could easily have been describing the development and delivery of treatments for anorexia nervosa. Having worked with hundreds of patients over the past several decades, and now supervising the next generation of junior colleagues, we can certainly attest that the development of CBT-AN-20 has been an iterative process that originated from our own initial missteps. In this penultimate chapter on final considerations for future therapists, we leverage our learnings from our mistakes and our successes to formulate our top tips for success in CBT-AN-20.

13.1 Tip #1: Believe that your patient can get better in half the time (and help them believe it too!)

Twenty sessions may seem like very few – especially for a disorder as entrenched and pernicious as anorexia nervosa. We used to offer longer treatments as routine but have been convinced by the evidence for other 20-session therapies for anorexia nervosa (e.g. SSCM and MANTRA), our initial CBT-AN-20 outcome data, and our clinical experience that a briefer CBT treatment can be equally effective. If you have any doubts about this, we hope you will borrow confidence from our team's recent open trial (Duggan et al., under consideration). In this study, we recruited 41 adults with anorexia nervosa from two National Health Service eating disorder services in the United Kingdom. Of note, these patients were of comparable eating disorder severity (with BMI between 15 and 19) to those included in prior studies of CBT-E (Fairburn et al., 2013). We evaluated benchmarks for recruitment, retention, and effectiveness based on existing efficacy and effectiveness studies for 40-session CBT for anorexia nervosa (Fairburn et al., 2013; Jenkins et al., 2019). Of the 41 patients, 54% ultimately completed the treatment, matching existing retention patterns for 40-session CBT in similar settings. Qualitative outcomes (Duggan et al., 2025) supported the acceptability of the therapy, with several patients providing positive feedback (see Chapter 14). There were strong to very strong effect sizes for improvements in eating attitudes, BMI, depression,

DOI: 10.4324/9781003594703-13

and anxiety, comparable with outcomes for longer therapies. These initial data suggest that CBT-AN-20 for anorexia nervosa is feasible, acceptable, and effective. Currently, we are working to replicate these findings across multiple sites in the United Kingdom, the United States, and Canada.

13.2   Tip #2: Your goal is to actively support the patient to get better, not get them to like you

Early in our clinical careers, we were taught that building rapport was the most important task of therapy. We were slower to push our patients to make change, for fear of upsetting them. We were too conventionally "nice". While we still agree that establishing a solid working alliance is critical for success in CBT-AN-20, and that clinicians should always be empathic and respectful, our experience and the evidence have led us to a different view on how to establish such an alliance. Graves et al. (2017) have used a meta-analysis to show that the working alliance (including agreement on therapeutic goals and tasks, as well as an affective bond between patient and clinician) is only weakly related to eating disorder outcomes, particularly for behavioural and cognitive therapies. In fact, *early behaviour change* predicts stronger therapeutic alliance at the end of eating disorder treatment and does so *over and above* the effect of early therapeutic alliance. Paradoxically, then, the most surefire way to establish a good alliance with your CBT-AN-20 patient is to push for early behavioural change.

Here is an example. In the early sessions of therapy, one of our patients initially balked at keeping self-monitoring records, increasing portion sizes, and conducting exposure to feared foods. The patient "jokingly" called the therapist "heartless" and "cold" for asking her to make so many changes simultaneously (e.g., stopping restricting, vomiting, and self-cutting). However, by the end of the therapy, when the patient was fully weight-restored and successfully refraining from purging and self-harm, she gifted the therapist a jar filled with slips of paper describing the aspects of the therapy for which she was grateful. Tellingly, these included "Caring about me", "Wanting a better life for me", and "Being on my side since Day 1". In summary, your goal is to get the patient better, rather than get them to like you. However, if you *do* get them better, they may end up liking you just fine.

13.3   Tip #3: Never worry alone

Anorexia nervosa – marked by rigidly maintained self-starvation that is defended by the illness at all costs – is scary and befuddling for patients, families, and clinicians alike. In this circumstance, one of the most important things we have learned as clinicians in this field is to never worry alone. This means that the best anorexia nervosa care is delivered when you, as a clinician, are also supported by a team. We would advise that it is critical for the CBT-AN-20 therapist to engage with a like-minded team of medical providers and a dietitian, if available, to ensure that providers are giving a unified message to the patient and to minimise the risk of splitting that can occur. For example, when we ask patients to make and then test weekly predictions about their weight through in-session weighing, we expect that some patients will resist or express increased discomfort. However, these elements will remain a mainstay of the treatment, a critical ingredient in testing their broken cognitions about weight. Given the unfamiliar nature of some CBT interventions, you may receive pushback from colleagues who are not conversant with the evidence behind the CBT-AN-20 approach. We have had experiences of well-meaning primary care or outside clinicians, unfamiliar with CBT, discouraging the patient from engaging in this work if it makes them anxious – an "error of kindness", as an old supervisor used to say.

Working as a part of a team who routinely practice CBT, and in particular CBT-T and CBT-AN-20, can go far in facilitating care within this model. For example, colleagues on our team routinely call on one another to participate in patient body image surveys and to practice role plays (particularly for challenging situations such as disability training). Utilising weekly team meetings to review cases, listen to audio files, and brainstorm together can be tremendously helpful. We have found that this peer support empowers us to help our patients challenge the "anorexic voice" and to be brave enough to apply challenging therapeutic tasks (insert the refrain here: "disability training/honest conversations", "open weighing", or "mirror exposure"). We appreciate that collaboration with colleagues can take many forms, be it through shared clinic practice as we have in our settings, informal discussion with other professionals, or formalised peer supervision.

Of course, "never worry alone" does not mean "do not worry at all". Indeed, our patients sometimes fluctuate between states of worry and concern for the dangerous consequences of starvation and being convinced by the "anorexic voice" to deny such concern. As clinicians, without thinking, we can very easily fall into the trap of failing to register a helpful amount of concern. The support of a team helps in our endeavour to maintain, communicate, and act upon an appropriate level of worry and concern.

13.4   Tip #4: Remember, your patient is not alone

As we all know, anorexia nervosa has a significant impact on everyone it touches – the individual, family members, friends, work colleagues, and more. During their course of the illness, the individual with anorexia nervosa has often narrowed their social circle as a cost of the illness. However, despite this, it is important to hold in mind the many ways in which this wider community can be a source of strength and support to the patient. The ancient proverb "it takes a village to raise a child" captures the essence of the importance of community in supporting those with anorexia nervosa in their recovery; whilst CBT-AN-20 might be seen by many as an individual treatment, we encourage you to always hold in mind that recovery occurs in an interpersonal context, and that working with significant others, whoever they are, and in fact leveraging those relationships, is likely to be an important part of treatment for most. Re-engaging with friends and family or forming new relationships can also be aspirational for those with anorexia nervosa. Engaging this wider community, whenever possible, can help to tip the balance towards a broader meaningful life without the eating disorder.

13.5   Tip #5: Don't take the "anorexic voice" personally

We have described at length how the "anorexic voice" speaks to the patient throughout the course of therapy, representing the mode where their eating disorder has taken a dominant role in their thinking. Sometimes, however, the "anorexic voice" speaks to the clinician as well. Collectively, in our time as eating disorder clinicians, we have been called not only "understanding", "supportive", and "helpful", but also "cold", "heartless", and "fat". While it is tempting to take such insults personally, we encourage clinicians instead to use this as an opportunity to peek into the patient's inner monologue. Sometimes, when a patient makes a particularly vicious comment about the clinician, they are reflecting back what the anorexic voice has been telling them about themselves all along. Psychodynamic theorists call this process *projective identification* – where a patient inadvertently projects their own feelings onto the clinician so effectively that the clinician themselves starts to feel them. While the clinician should always be open to feedback from the patient about what is or is not working in therapy, a surprising *ad hominem* attack should evoke a curious response on the part of the clinician, such as: "Does the anorexic voice say similar things about you?"

13.6   Tip #6: Early termination doesn't have to mean failure, and can even be therapeutic

In our initial CBT-AN-20 trial ('Duggan et al., under consideration), as well as in most trials of psychotherapies for anorexia nervosa (e.g., Fairburn et al., 2013), approximately half of patients do not complete the full course of therapy – whether they are discharged due to lack of engagement or simply choose to drop out. Clearly, this is not as good as we would hope. Future research is needed to identify predictors of dropout and non-response, and to develop and evaluate new interventions that can facilitate rapid response and in turn foster greater retention (Wade, 2023). Meanwhile, the current state of the science is that patient dropout is an inevitable part of being a clinician who treats anorexia nervosa.

In CBT-AN-20, the aim is to leverage potential or actual dropout as part of a therapeutic process, rather than as a mark of failure on either the patient's or the clinician's part. In the past, we too have let our therapies drag on during the acute stage of a patient's illness for several years without measurable change. At the time, we thought we were doing patients a favour by "hanging in there" and "not giving up on them". However, in retrospect, it is possible we were allowing them to remain stuck in their illnesses by *being in* therapy rather than *doing* therapy. Nowadays, while we absolutely continue to hold out hope that every single one of our patients can get better (whatever the duration or severity of their eating disorder), we know that this doesn't mean we need to meet with each of them indefinitely for weekly therapy sessions during that process. Instead, we ask them to come back when they are ready to engage more fully, or in some cases, to continue the hard work they had begun before stalling, now with a better picture of what working on recovery involves. In some cases, taking a pause from therapy, or being admitted to a more intensive level of care, is part of the journey.

CBT-AN-20 requires active participation from both the clinician and the patient. With some therapy experiences, there can be a sense, over the course of some weeks, that the patient is pulling away by not actively engaging, not completing homework, or not engaging in exposures. In such cases, rather than redouble efforts to push for change, we might serve the patient better by acknowledging this lack of engagement, being curious about it, and understanding it together, if possible, before deciding with them to discontinue treatment. In some cases, this will mean that the patient never really got started in treatment– they were *in* therapy but were not *doing* therapy. But for other patients, this will mean that they engaged more actively at the beginning, made some changes, and moved forward, but stopped shy of recovery. This latter case can be harder to terminate when the clinician hopes and pushes for recovery, but the patient is not ready for more and wants to settle where they are. We have learned that it is better to send patients off with hope – to acknowledge and celebrate the movement they have made by closing treatment and encouraging them to return to treatment when they are ready to make further change. As with the development of CBT-AN-20 itself, the treatment can be iterative.

This model fits with our research teams' longitudinal research findings, in which we see that, given time, most people with anorexia nervosa will improve and ultimately recover (Eddy et al., 2017), but that simply increasing treatment dosage does not predict better outcomes (Beintner & Jacobi, 2018). We like to underscore this finding to remind patients (and clinicians) that it is not merely being *in* treatment that helps patients move to recovery. Instead, the strongest predictors of outcome available to us are early change in active treatments (Real-Brioso et al., 2024) and past evidence of symptom interruption (Franko et al., 2018). These findings align with CBT-AN-20, in which we work for early change and use behavioural experiments to interrupt symptoms.

13.7   Tip #7: Collect data to contribute towards the advancement of future therapy for anorexia nervosa

We encourage readers to treat any therapy (including this one) as a stepping stone to future improvements. After all, the limited outcomes of all evidence-based therapies for anorexia nervosa (e.g., NICE, 2017; Solmi et al., 2021) can hardly be seen as satisfactory. As such, we anticipate treatment updates and revisions over time, and we encourage other teams to consider such changes based on their experience. We take a strategic approach to informing such updates and revisions – before we add to or revise the treatment, we need to be able to confirm that there is an evidence base to support that including those new elements is more effective than the original. Again, we encourage others to think the same way about CBT-AN-20 (and any other therapies); show that proposed changes are helpful to patients and theoretically coherent rather than simply doing them because they appeal to you as a clinician.

We will continue to keep collecting and examining data both on CBT-AN-20 and potential enhancements and alternatives. Of course, we encourage other clinicians to do the same with their own patients in private practice or in other clinic settings. Routinely collecting patient data during the course of CBT-AN-20 has two advantages, being immediately useful to the individual patient and serving the field longer-term as we grow our understanding of when, how, and for whom treatment works. Here are some ways of thinking about outcomes that we see as particularly important to follow as we move forward:

1. Mediators or mechanisms of change – how are people getting better, and can we supercharge it?
2. Does early weight gain predict later change across broader outcomes, for example, cognitions, emotions, behaviour, social engagement, quality of life, and so on?
3. Among patients who discharge prematurely from CBT-AN-20, who will return to treatment and on what timeline, and are they more likely to respond the second time around?
4. Are there situations or individuals where other evidence-based approaches to anorexia nervosa (e.g., CBT-E, MANTRA, SSCM, FBT, psychodynamic, or CBT-AR) might be more appropriate?

We will continue to collect these data to inform future versions of CBT-AN-20, and we hope that you will as well.

13.8   Summary

In closing, based on the iterative process of designing CBT-AN-20, our top tips for future clinicians include the following:

- Believe that your patient can get better in half the time (and help them believe it too!).
- Your goal is to actively support the patient to get better, *not* get them to like you.
- Never worry alone.
- Remember, your patient is not alone.
- Don't take the "anorexic voice" personally.

- Early termination doesn't have to mean failure and can even be therapeutic.
- Collect data to contribute towards the advancement of future therapy for anorexia nervosa.

Please keep those tips in mind as you deliver and develop CBT-AN-20 – you will be helping more people to access and benefit from an effective treatment for their anorexia nervosa.

Chapter 14

Summary and future directions

In developing CBT-AN-20 and writing this manual, we wanted to develop the therapy and to write the book that we wish we could have had access to when *we* first started working with patients with anorexia nervosa – in other words, a coherent treatment that has the potential to be effective, that is underpinned by clinician and patient experience, that is based on robust research, and that includes the most recent developments in clinical techniques.

14.1 Our own reflections

CBT-AN-20 is a flexible, patient-centred treatment protocol that is built on evidence-based principles. We are only too aware that everyone's journey is unique, and so throughout this book we have tried to highlight the importance of flexing the protocol to meet the individual needs of the patient, but without losing sight of the key phases of treatment, the core CBT skills available to us, and the overall aims of the therapy. At the heart of this book is our belief that those who develop anorexia nervosa *can* recover, however complex or long-lasting their eating problem. It is important that we retain that hope, standing alongside our patients at times when they find it hard to see and walk their own road to recovery.

Over the course of this book, we have highlighted the importance of holding in mind a holistic approach to treatment and recovery. We know that any effective CBT for anorexia nervosa involves working with a wide range of issues, including motivation, understanding the functional role of the illness, physical safety and nutrition, perfectionism, and self-criticism, to name but a few. We are also aware that developmental, physical, and systemic needs will vary over time, across the age range, and in different communities, requiring us to make individual-focused adaptations to treatment along the way. This understanding, combined with sound clinical skills and a therapeutic stance that fosters collaboration, compassionate firmness, and curiosity, are all key in supporting patients to re-build their nutritional health and potential to thrive in life, to be able to embrace the multiple parts of their self-identity, to show greater self-kindness, and to live a life consistent with their own values – ultimately building the strength to leave anorexia nervosa behind and to live with greater flexibility and freedom. These improvements in

DOI: 10.4324/9781003594703-14

health and quality of life impact not only the patients we work with but also their supporters and loved ones – the impact of effective therapy for anorexia nervosa is wide-reaching and profound.

It is exciting to see how research in the field of CBT and in eating disorders continues to generate new knowledge and evidence-based techniques. With that ongoing development of the field in mind, we hope that while this manual offers an up-to-date and useable guide, our website will be the place to visit for free downloadable resources and up-to-date adaptions as new evidence-based techniques emerge over time.

14.2   The final word on CBT-AN-20: The patient voice

Before we close this book, we wanted to share themes in the experience of patients who have completed CBT-AN-20, using example comments that those patients provided in our initial qualitative evaluation of the therapy (Duggan et al., 2025). They remind us of the effort that both patient and clinician have put into treatment, and the patients' experience of the process and outcomes of their own therapy journeys. We hope that they help to inspire you in your implementation and refinement of CBT-AN-20 as you work with your own patients.

The following themes and sub-themes emerged across patients who completed CBT-AN-20, each illustrated here with one or more typical patient experiences:

- The therapeutic relationship is very important, including both personal attachment and the focus on change:
  - "I had built a good relationship with [clinician], and her overall approach to my eating disorder helped me mentally and emotionally".
- The clinician's qualities matter:
  - "My therapist was never judgemental and always provided me with an answer to all my questions".
- How we communicate with our patients matters, and it can take time for us to earn their trust:
  - "I was originally pretty hesitant to open up, but as I became more comfortable, it felt easier".
  - "I was comfortable to talk freely with them. I felt heard and understood".
- The individual-centred nature of the therapy is critical:
  - "It was helpful to guide my treatment around what we both felt was benefiting me the most".
- Time-limited therapy is new to many patients, but valuable in creating focus on change:
  - "I was told I had to make improvements [by the progress review/Session 6] ... and that gave me the motivation to push through".
- CBT-AN-20 can have benefits compared to previous therapies:
  - "This was orders of magnitude better than any other therapy I've had".
  - "Miles better than any therapy I've received from any other services".

- It is clear therapy can be experienced as tough, especially at first:
  - "Sometimes I struggled to gain weight, and I was really stressed to be on the same weight for around two months eating more".
- But it is worthwhile in the longer term:
  - "It helped more than I thought it would. And I managed a lot more than I thought".
  - "I have noticed a significant shift in my attitudes towards food and allowing myself to challenge fear foods as well as my thought processes".
  - "It greatly helped me to regain valuable aspects of my life, including socially and professionally."
  - "I found the regular check-in on weight helpful to know I was on the right track".
- And finally, reflecting changes in the experience of CBT-AN-20 across the course of therapy, a theme of "tough but worthwhile" is combined in these quotes:
  - "Whilst it was very difficult at times, I'm glad I persevered".
  - "It was very difficult to have to put on weight and give up control of my eating, weight, and shape. They were what made me feel safe in the world and giving them up was extremely traumatic and distressing. It caused me to have suicidal thoughts. It's the worst experience I've had in my life. I couldn't even have imagined anything so awful before. Now I'm out the other end, it was absolutely worth it".

We find that final quote to be particularly telling. It should serve to remind us always that this is a challenging journey for the person with anorexia nervosa, but that it can ultimately be a hugely rewarding one. Experiences like suicidal thoughts in the face of giving up anorexia nervosa are common, regardless of the therapy – it is important to manage them to ensure the patient's safety, but without giving up on the prospect of recovery. We should also remember that it is also hard for the clinician to encourage changes when the patient finds them so hard. It is understandable that either the patient or the clinician might think "Maybe we don't have to push so hard for change" and allow the patient to remain more comfortable in the short term by not changing. However, as clinicians we always must remember that we are trying to help the patient to get out of a trap that they are likely to be stuck in for years or even decades (and might not survive) if we do not work with them effectively.

14.3 Conclusion

We are all working to ensure that the patient can achieve health, quality of life, self-efficacy, and happiness. If that means that in a few years' time the former patient cannot identify with that "anorexic voice" and cannot even remember their clinician's name, then it will have been a challenging but eminently worthwhile venture for the patient, their loved ones, and the clinician. So, we encourage you to use this manual and the associated resources to support patients with anorexia nervosa in moving on from their eating disorder. It will be a tough journey for all concerned, but the benefits can be life-changing.

We are grateful to the many therapists, patients, and researchers whose knowledge and expertise has gone into the development of the ideas and techniques that are included in this manual. The Acknowledgements give a glimpse of how many people have supported us in this work, showing that the development of an effective therapy is never the work of a few; it takes a whole village.

Appendices

The following materials are provided as Appendices to support the delivery of 20-session cognitive-behavioural therapy for anorexia nervosa (CBT-AN-20). Downloadable versions are presented via the website that supports this manual: CBT-AN-20 website (https://sites.google.com/sheffield.ac.uk/cbt-an-20). The website contains links to: CBT-AN-20 website (https://sites.google.com/d/1wk23BMhUXWBP3dVxq0akz8kmPXBQ-TMp/p/1J3qQ-QcDRU_iqemORb2r-36z88GswzUBG/edit?pli=1)

- Psychoeducation materials listed in the Appendices below;
- Clinician resources to support the therapist and supervisor;
- Other online resources, including single-session interventions that can be used to augment the therapy;
- Training videos that demonstrate the key skills needed in CBT-AN-20;
- Training details, for those who want to attend online or in-person sessions to support their skills and learning.

These materials can be copied or downloaded and used by patients, carers, services, clinicians, and researchers without charge, as long as they are acknowledged and are not used for commercial purposes or modified/translated without permission from the authors.

Appendix A: Psychoeducation materials and tools

Appendix number	Book section	Handouts (all available to download from the CBT-AN-20 website (https://sites.google.com/sheffield.ac.uk/cbt-an-20))
A.1	3.3	Growth mindset: Improving neuroplasticity
A.2	3.10	Goal-setting using WOOP
A.3	4.2	Controllable weight restoration
A.4	4.2	REAL Food Guide for anorexia nervosa
A.5	4.2	Traits (make your temperament work for you)

Appendix number	Book section	Handouts (all available to download from the CBT-AN-20 website (https://sites.google.com/sheffield.ac.uk/cbt-an-20))
A.6	4.2	Starvation effects
A.7	4.2	Long-term consequences of anorexia nervosa
A.8	4.2	Risks of compensatory behaviours
A.9	4.4.2	Formulation worksheet
A.10	4.4.3	5Ps Formulation (blank)
A.11	4.5.1	Case formulation letter
A.12	4.5.2	End of treatment letter
A.13	4.9	The nature of the "anorexic voice"
A.14	4.9	Full DIS-ED interview
A.15	4.11.1	The role of anxiety in anorexia nervosa
A.16	4.12	Behavioural experiment record
A.17	5.11	Information sheet for carers
A.18	5.12	Advantages of change, fears of change, and responses to fears
A.19	6.1	Therapy Checklist
A.20	7.2	Information for patients and carers on the nature and requirements of CBT-AN-20
A.21	7.4.1	Importance of carbohydrates
A.22	7.4.1	Blank energy graphs (sheet of eight, to cover a week)
A.23	9.2	Quick emotion regulation strategies
A.24	9.2	Emotional and interpersonal problems in anorexia nervosa
A.25	9.4.2	Core beliefs in anorexia nervosa
A.26	9.2	Flashcard: Identification of emotional triggers and reactions and core beliefs in anorexia nervosa
A.27	10.2	Body neutrality
A.28	10.5	Imagery rescripting for body image
A.29	11.2	Blank therapy blueprint for clinician and patient
A.30	11.7	List of useful resources for other problems
A.31	12.2	Handout for clients with atypical anorexia nervosa
A.32	12.4	Handout for clients with avoidant/restrictive food intake disorder

Appendix A.1: Growth mindset – Improving neuroplasticity

Growth Mindset

Are you stuck with your current thoughts and behaviours?

Not so long-ago scientists thought our brain and genes were fixed at birth and couldn't change. Over the last decade, science now shows us this just isn't true. What we now know to be true is that:

(1) Our brain is made up of tiny building blocks called neurons – about 100 billion of them. These neurons are constantly talking to each other and forming new connections. Our brain is evolving over our lifetime. We call this **BRAIN NEUROPLASTICITY**. We can promote neuroplasticity in many ways, which helps us learn new behaviours and change thought patterns. Having adequate nutritional intake is critical to support new connection-building between neurons.

(2) Your genes are like instructions for how your body works. Over your lifetime, these instructions can change based on what's happening around you. This is called the epigenome. Some things, like a healthy environment, can help 'turn off' bad parts of your genes, while bad environments can 'turn on' negative things in your genes, making them show up more. Not getting enough good food is one of the biggest things that can make these bad changes happen."

(3) Eating foods with complex carbs, like whole grains or vegetables, is really good for your brain and mental health. These foods release glucose (which is like fuel) into your bloodstream, helping your brain work better. They also help your gut stay healthy, which is important because a healthy gut can support brain chemicals that make you feel good, like tryptophan.

Everyone is a work in progress. We can all change for the better. By providing ourselves with helpful environments, we can learn new ways of thinking and doing. Each of us can grow into the person we want to be.

What are the environments that help our brain and genetic action support our efforts to change for the better?

Reading BOOKS: Brain scans of 8- to 12-year-olds showed stronger reading circuits in those who spent more time reading paper books than those who spent time on screens

Creative and visual arts help develop less frequently used brain areas: you don't have to be good at it, just enjoy the process of interpreting how you see the world into visual form

欢迎 स्वागत
WELCOME
BIENVENUE ようこそ
добро пожаловать
نر حبیب BEM-VINDO

Likewise, learning new **languages** develops new areas of your brain and forms new connections – even 10 minutes a day on a language learning app will help

Growth Mindset

Travel exposes you continually to new experiences and the need for problem-solving which helps form new brain connections

Learning and playing **music** exercises and develops new parts of your brain – again, you don't need to be any good at it!

Exercise also supports neuroplasticity and helpful genetic action

The practice of **divergent thinking** – different from your usual thought patterns – also stimulates neuroplasticity

Adequate nutrition is one of the most powerful ways to IMPROVE brain neuroplasticity, helpful genetic action, AND mental health

Brain activity is affected by even modest dieting; a young person's developing brain is particularly vulnerable.

Someone with a starved brain will struggle to make decisions, solve problems, regulate their emotions, and learn new behaviours.

A nourished brain and epigenome

A good place to start is that approximately 50% or more of total energy of your diet should come from carbohydrates. **Select at least 4 servings over the day** – examples of servings are below.

☐ ½ cup muesli	☐ 1 ½ cups Corn Flakes
☐ 1 cup Sustain	☐ 1 roll
☐ 1 cup All Bran	☐ 1 pita bread
☐ 1 cup Sultana Bran	☐ 2 slices bread
☐ 1 cup Just Right	☐ 2 fruit toast
☐ 1 cup cooked porridge	☐ 2 tortillas
☐ 1 ½ cups Special K	☐ 1 cup cooked pasta
☐ 1 ½ cups Rice Bubbles	☐ 1 cup cooked rice
☐ ¾ cup cous cous	☐ 1 cup mashed potato
☐ 1 cup cooked barley	☐ 2 medium potatoes
☐ 1 cup sweet corn	☐ 1 large, sweet potato
☐ 1 cup cooked quinoa	☐ 2 cups noodles

Want to know more about neuroplasticity?

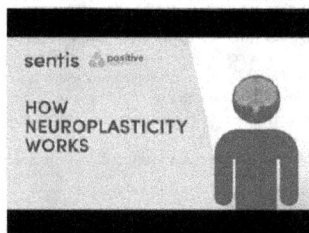

sentis ♦ positive

HOW NEUROPLASTICITY WORKS

Appendix A.2: Goal-setting using WOOP

Make a plan
And stop drifting

Ever felt like you were drowning?

It can be helpful to think about the experience of anorexia nervosa this way: Imagine you have fallen into a fast-flowing river. You know you are in danger of drowning, and when you emerge spluttering at the surface, you clutch at a log that is floating nearby. You experience a profound sense of relief and clutch to that log for all that you are worth. Slowly, you start to feel calmer. After some time has passed while you drift holding on to the log, you are feeling less comfortable, more cramped and constricted. You think perhaps it is time to try and get back to the riverbank. But it is not that easy. You are scared to let go of your log and doubt your ability to make it to the riverbank. More time passes and you know that to survive, you need to face the anxiety of letting go of the log and getting back to firm land.

You may have felt that the life you lived before developing anorexia nervosa was like that fast-flowing river. Whatever you were experiencing made you feel out of control and threatened. Anorexia nervosa was the log that initially saved your life, and you held on to it firmly. Now, however, it is getting in the way of you being able to live your life in the way that you want to, but you feel extremely apprehensive about letting it go. Who knows what will happen then?

The best way to leave the log is to decide on a plan and put it into action, navigating all the obstacles that might stop you from getting safely to the riverbank. Just letting go of the log and hoping for the best probably won't get you very far. You need to decide on the best route for getting where you want to go.

It is the same when you decide to walk away from anorexia nervosa. Just waking up one day and thinking "today is the day" is unlikely to get you far.

We will describe the best way to set short-term goals to increase your chance of a successful outcome, using WOOP: Wish, Outcome, Obstacle, Plan – see https://woopmylife.org/

Short-term goals

W is for WISH:

Take a moment to close your eyes. Picture yourself in a calm, safe place—a place where you feel secure and supported. Imagine yourself looking ahead over the next week like a path stretching before you. At the end of this path is your wish, something that will be happening differently in your life. What is it? Name your wish in 3-6 words, and then formulate this as a SMART goal:

- Specific - Define what will be accomplished and the actions to be taken to accomplish the goal.
- Measurable – what data will tell you that you achieved the goal?
- Achievable – choose something you think is probably within your reach but will stretch you.
- Relevant – choose a goal that maximises your progress against the anorexia nervosa.
- Time-based – we are looking at a goal that can be achieved and measured over the next week.

O is for OUTCOME:

Imagine yourself achieving this wish. Picture the scene in vivid detail—how does it feel to have achieved this? What does it say about you as a person?

Make a plan
And stop drifting

O is for OBSTACLE:

Picture a wall or barrier that appears on the path towards your wish. This wall represents something inside you—a habit, a fear, or a thought—that makes it harder to move forward. What words or images come to mind as you think about your main inner obstacle?

P is for PLAN:

Formulate "if (the obstacle) then (I will)" plans. Have a few to fall back on in case the first one does not work.

For example:

We know that when underweight, the goal of regaining nutritional health is much harder than people expect. You need to add what will seem like quite large amounts to your nutritional intake. This is because your metabolism becomes more efficient as you eat more and your body is prioritizing replenishing major organs in your body, including your brain, as well as bones.

Your **wish** might be to achieve better nutritional health. To make this a reality, consider a SMART goal. You might decide the first step to try is adding 4 servings of carbohydrates each day to your intake, at specific times of the day. You can find examples of servings in the Real Food Guide (Appendix 4 and CBT-AN-20 website).

Imagine the **outcome** at the end of the week if you can improve your nutritional health. What benefits might you observe across the areas of your life: thinking, relationships, health, mood, valued pursuits?

How would it feel to know that you had taken control from the anorexia nervosa? What would this say about you?

Consider the **obstacles** that might become apparent. One part of you wants to achieve this outcome but another part of you strongly objects – what is it saying?

Put into effect a **plan** – how will you respond to fears and how you can keep yourself focused on a helpful plan when you feel tempted to stop working on it?

Make a clear *'if-then'* plan that you can put into action if needed. What works best for you when you need to focus at times of high emotion and anxiety? e.g., 'If I'm tempted not to include the extra snacks in my meal plan, I will talk to my mum and remind myself that improving my health will mean I can get back to university.'

Long-term goals

It is also important to consider your *bigger picture goals*: what does recovery look like?

Picture where the road to recovery could lead you in 12 months time across the domains of your life: social, emotional, physical, intellect, spiritual, community engagement, work and study, hobbies. Think about the values you hold most dear - how can you use these to guide the decisions that you will need to make along the way? Which values have been sidelined by the anorexia nervosa and which of these do you want to revive? Consider the fast-flowing river and the issues that tipped you into anorexia nervosa in the first place – do these need to be tackled and how?

Appendix A.3: Controllable weight restoration

Restoring physical health
Controllable weight restoration

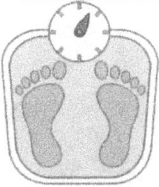

Why should you regain weight?

Often people with anorexia nervosa feel scared, angry, or dismissive of the idea of working towards a new healthy weight.

We can think about anorexia nervosa in many ways – including as a way of managing distress through food and the body, which involves becoming underweight or losing weight in an unhealthy way. Whatever the reason that people develop anorexia nervosa, if you've read our 'starvation' information sheet, you'll be familiar with how the resulting low weight and ways of losing weight affect our minds, bodies, and behaviours. Those effects can keep you locked into an eating disorder, unless directly tackled.

While it is true that recovery from anorexia nervosa is not just a matter of weight restoration, it is also true that it is absolutely *impossible to recover from anorexia nervosa without restoring weight.*

You might have lots of concerns about changes to your diet and weight. Taking time to identify and address those concerns before starting the process of making changes (and reviewing and updating this along the way) can be worthwhile. So, if you haven't already done so, in addition to reading the 'starvation' information and the 'anorexic voice' handout, we also recommend completing the 'motivation exercise' worksheet alongside the information provided here.

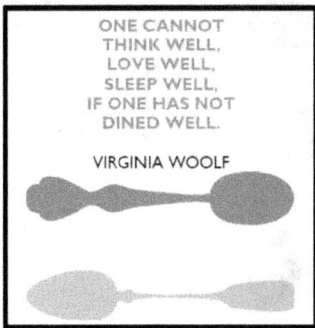

> ONE CANNOT
> THINK WELL,
> LOVE WELL,
> SLEEP WELL,
> IF ONE HAS NOT
> DINED WELL.
>
> VIRGINIA WOOLF

Rate of weight restoration

Lots of people with anorexia fear *uncontrollable* weight gain, so let's think about what to expect, and how to make that weight gain *controllable*, so that you know you will be able to stop when you get to a healthy place.

Planning initial changes:
It is important to discuss making changes with your eating with a healthcare provider, particularly if you have been restricting heavily or using laxatives (as sometimes physical monitoring and carefully planned changes are required).

Making initial changes:

When first making changes to behaviours that accompany the eating disorder and eating more, many people find that their weight increases quite a lot within the first few days. While this can be alarming, it is important to remember that this rate of change does not persist and is due to changes in food and fluid within the body (i.e., it has very little to do with body fat).

How much weight do I need to gain?

Your therapist can help you to work out what a healthy weight range for your body may be. It is never possible to be exact, but factors including your history of symptoms and eating disorder behaviours at different weights, age, height, sex, and the build of your family members (unless they also have eating disorders) can suggest roughly what a healthy weight for you might be.

After you become confident in your ability to restore weight, you might also choose to build in periods of maintaining weight before reaching a healthy weight, so that you know you can control the weight gain in the long term.

Successful recovery from anorexia usually involves aiming to restore an average of 1-2lbs (or 0.5-1kg) per week.

Unless you have previously been at a much higher weight, or have a complicating medical condition, then weight restoration is likely to take much longer than you expect. Research tells us that delaying weight restoration is likely to make therapy ineffective – as people who don't gain weight in the first 1-2 months don't usually respond to the therapy.

Restoring physical health
Controllable weight restoration

How to regain weight

Restoring an average of about 0.5kg (or 1lb) of weight requires eating about 500 additional calories per day, (i.e., *more than your current body needs to maintain weight*). However, that can vary, and the amount you need to eat to regain weight might be different at different times. If you are very active you might need to eat more to regain weight. And as the body starts to use energy in reversing the state of starvation, more food is required to simply maintain weight. Eating for weight restoration is often different to normal eating. It involves the challenge of learning to eat more than those around you (unless they are aiming to regain weight too).

So, what can you do to regain weight?

The simple answer is:

- eat more
- gain the weight that your body needs to be healthy, and
- learn how to feel in control and happy with yourself at a healthy weight

The more complicated answer is:

- face that fear about uncontrollable weight gain by eating more, and eating to a plan (see the REAL Food Guide)
- keep reminding yourself of all the problems that starvation has left you with
- learn that weight regain is slow, hard work (rather than uncontrollable and rapid)
- regain the weight that your body needs to feel healthy, and
- learn how to feel in control and happy with yourself at a healthy weight

In the end, you will need to decide between being at a lower weight and remaining with all the destruction of the anorexia nervosa or learning to accept a higher weight than you may wish to be while you live a fuller, more complicated but more satisfying life.

Where to find the additional calories needed for weight regain

After a few weeks of implementing a plan for normal eating, initial weight restoration is likely to stall. There are a few options for achieving the additional dietary intake required for weight restoration.

You will probably need to boost each of your meals and snacks. For example, you could choose energy dense options (e.g., cheese, nuts, chocolate), and ensure that you don't miss dessert.

Some people find energy dense drinks easier to manage. Using milkshakes (with high fat milk or milk substitute) with bananas and oats can be helpful.

If you are still struggling, you may wish to speak with your healthcare provider about whether they can prescribe or recommend meal supplements. Such supplements should be just that – additions to your regular meals and snacks to supplement them – not meal replacements.

Appendix A.4: REAL Food Guide (2025) for CBT-AN-20 Clinicians

(See the CBT-AN-20 website (https://sites.google.com/sheffield.ac.uk/cbt-an-20) for a copy of the shorter version for patients)

The REAL Food Guide (2025) for CBT-AN-20 Clinicians

Susan Hart, MNutrDiet, PhD
Conjoint A/Prof at ENRG (Eating Disorder and Nutrition Research Group), Western Sydney University
Caitlin McMaster, BSc(Nutr)(Hons), PhD
Sydney School of Health Sciences, Faculty of Medicine and Health, University of Sydney

The *REAL Food Guide*, first published in 2018, is a pictorial tool using core principles of nutrition with consideration of the beliefs and misinformation that are frequently endorsed by individuals with eating disorders (Hart et al., 2018). (REAL stands for *R*ecovery from *EA*ting disorders for *L*ife). The guide was designed primarily for clinicians working with people with eating disorders, to enhance knowledge about food choices and nutritional adequacy, and to provide effective support and advice. The guidance provided on food and eating by the *REAL Food Guide* is nutritionally adequate, meaning that meal plans for weight maintenance and weight regain will provide enough protein, carbohydrate and fat, essential vitamins and minerals to meet *most* individuals' needs. There are exceptions to this, as individuals may have preferences, dislikes, or nutritional needs requiring more or less food on an average day.

Several updates have been made here to the *REAL Food Guide for CBT-T Clinicians* to reflect more recent changes in food supply and sociocultural influences on dietary intake as well as emerging scientific evidence. The basis of the *REAL Food Guide* remains the same, however, as it is based on established nutritional science.

Using a framework to talk about food and eating allows a clinical team to be consistent, as well as to deliver a clearer and more tailored message than current public health nutrition messages (Hart et al., 2018). Additionally, research has shown that the nutrition and dietetic-focused skills that are valued by people with eating disorders include guidance about food portions (Yang et al., 2023). When all clinicians are comfortable having conversations about nutrition, and food decisions are not placed solely on the dietitian, the cohesiveness and functioning of the multidisciplinary team is enhanced (Brennan et al., 2025). While dietitians continue to provide expertise, therapists should actively engage in and support nutritional discussions (Brennan et al., 2025), which can be guided by this section. It is not intended to teach clinicians who are not dietitians to provide detailed nutrition intervention, write meal plans, undertake nutritional assessment, or be an alternative to seeing a dietitian. Rather, it summarises key messages on food and eating, tailored to the needs and concerns of people with an eating disorder.

When should I refer to a dietitian?

Evidence-based practice recommends the inclusion of nutrition and dietetic assessment, education, and intervention as part of the multidisciplinary management of people with eating disorders (Hay et al., 2014; Ozier & Henry, 2011). Dietitians help individuals define dietary problems and plan and implement appropriate nutrition interventions to address them with a person's physical, psychological, and nutritional recovery in mind (Heruc et al., 2020; Ozier & Henry, 2011). However, in real life there may be barriers to accessing dietetic treatment such as availability and affordability of care, waiting times for services, a perception that patients may not benefit from dietetic input or implement nutrition changes, or patients' willingness to attend dietetic services (Innes et al., 2017; Pomeroy & Cant, 2010). It is ideal that any clinician working with people with eating disorders has access to a dietitian to be able to discuss cases and their client's nutritional issues as well as to refer patients to when necessary (Waller et al., 2007). Indications for referral to a dietitian should include individuals with the following presentations:

- Pregnancy or breastfeeding;
- Preference for a plant-based diet, especially if vegan (British Dietetic Association, 2021);
- A comorbid medical diagnosis that impacts on food intake, for example, type 1 diabetes mellitus, gastrointestinal conditions such as Crohn's disease, food allergies or intolerances (including Coeliac disease), cystic fibrosis, and kidney disease to name a few;
- Taking medication that impacts on nutritional needs, appetite, or weight (e.g. anti-psychotic medications);
- Not meeting nutrition and weight targets in treatment;
- When progress has stagnated and the person with an eating disorder/family are not moving forward (Brennan et al., 2025);
- When there are transitions between different phases of treatment such as moving from weight restoration to maintenance (Brennan et al., 2025);
- Ongoing intake of a limited range of foods throughout treatment; and
- Avoidance of necessary skills and behaviours associated with eating, such as grocery shopping and preparing and cooking food.

Using the REAL Food Guide

The *REAL Food Guide* recommends *eating mechanically* (in addition to regular eating, as is considered best practice (Fairburn, 2008; Waller et al., 2007)) when a person commences treatment for an eating disorder. Although people with eating disorders usually experience difficulty in eating regularly, establishing structure with eating is a key component of achieving nutritionally adequate eating patterns, and forms the scaffold for recovery from an eating disorder. Eating mechanically refers to planning eating episodes ahead of time, relying on external cues to regulate eating (i.e. using a meal plan, setting an alarm, using a recovery app) and acknowledging internal cues such as hunger and fullness signals but not acting on them. Using meal plans and a structured approach to eating is most beneficial in the early stages of treatment for an eating disorder. As treatment continues toward recovery, individuals may rely less on meals plans and more on internal regulation of eating. However, guidance from the *REAL Food Guide* remains a benchmark to compare the adequacy of food choices.

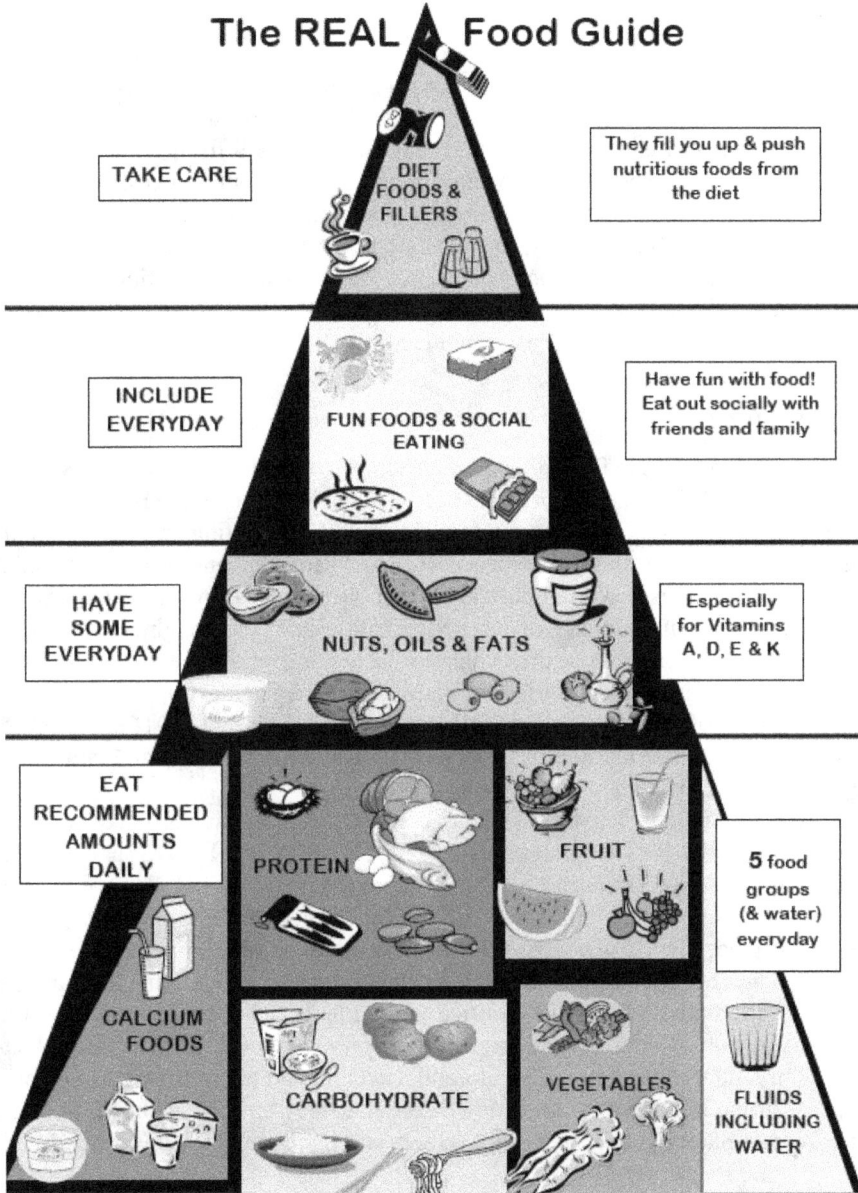

The REAL Food Guide

TAKE CARE

DIET FOODS & FILLERS

They fill you up & push nutritious foods from the diet

INCLUDE EVERYDAY

FUN FOODS & SOCIAL EATING

Have fun with food! Eat out socially with friends and family

HAVE SOME EVERYDAY

NUTS, OILS & FATS

Especially for Vitamins A, D, E & K

EAT RECOMMENDED AMOUNTS DAILY

PROTEIN

FRUIT

5 food groups (& water) everyday

CALCIUM FOODS

CARBOHYDRATE

VEGETABLES

FLUIDS INCLUDING WATER

Figure A1 The REAL Food Guide

There are four layers of the *REAL Food Guide*, with the bottom layer highlighting five core food groups (fruit, vegetables, carbohydrate, protein, calcium foods) and fluid. Additional layers provide recommendations on the inclusion of "nuts, fats and oils", "fun foods and social eating", and "diet foods and fillers". The recommended number of serves per day is an estimate of the minimum number of serves required each day for an adult older than 18 years to achieve nutrient requirements. It is a starting point, and some individuals may require more serves than is recommended below.

This section contains updates on nutritional issues based on recent literature, including consideration of plant-based eating, and emerging knowledge about influences on gut health with specific learnings for anorexia nervosa. *Plant-based* refers to a range of eating patterns that may include small to moderate amounts of animal products while also choosing proteins from plant sources. Integration of more plant-based choices into eating is increasingly normalised in our culture (Sullivan et al., 2024), not only for nutrition and health but also for ethical and environmental reasons (Hopwood et al., 2020). Some recommendations related to plant-based eating and gut health are easily integrated into the existing framework of the *REAL Food Guide*, and so are included here.

Calcium foods

This core group refers to foods that are rich sources of calcium, such as dairy products and calcium-fortified soy products. Most of the body's calcium is stored in the bones and teeth, with a small amount needed for blood clotting, muscle functioning, nerve conduction, and fluid balance. Having adequate dietary calcium to build strong healthy bones before middle age is the best way to prevent osteoporosis. Because of the consequences of restrictive eating and low weight, people with anorexia nervosa compromise their chance of achieving peak bone mass (Nagata et al., 2024). This places them at risk of diminished bone health (Lopes et al., 2022) and early onset of osteoporosis (or brittle bones) (Jagielska et al., 2016). Therefore, obtaining an adequate amount of dietary calcium is a key message and nutritional target for all people with eating disorders.

A lack of calcium-rich foods means compromising adequate intake of other nutrients essential for health such as protein, vitamins (A, E, B12, and riboflavin), and minerals (phosphorus, magnesium, potassium, and zinc). For people who choose not to have dairy products, calcium-*fortified* soy milk is the only recommended replacement. *Fortification* means that vitamins and minerals are added to the product to improve its nutrient content, and in Australia, guidelines advise that dairy alternatives should be fortified with at least 100 mg of calcium per 100 mL (Australian Government Department of Health & Ageing, 2013). Other plant-based dairy alternatives (e.g., rice, almond, coconut, and oat milk) are not recommended during treatment for an eating disorder as they have been shown to be an inadequate replacement for dairy, not only because they may not be fortified with calcium but also because they are lower in riboflavin, vitamin B12, iodine, and protein quantity and quality (Lawrence et al., 2025).

It is not recommended to choose fat-modified products as is suggested in many dietary guidelines for the general population, so "calcium foods" refer to standard, whole varieties. It is important to clarify with patients precisely what type of calcium food they are having. To demonstrate why this is important, it is necessary to have almost 2 cups of "light" milk or 2 ¼ cups of "skim" milk to provide the same nutritional value as one serve of standard milk.

Recommended serves of calcium foods per day Weight maintenance = three serves Weight regain = four serves
One serving size of calcium food 1 cup flavoured milk 1 ¼ cups plain, unflavoured milk 2 slices of cheese (each slice is size of your palm) ½ cup grated cheese ½ cup custard 1 cup flavoured yoghurt 1 cup plain, unflavoured yoghurt 1 cup Greek yoghurt 1 ½ cup of kefir 1 cup lassi
Plant-based choices (fortified calcium 200–300mg per serve or 100mg/100mL) 1 ½ plain, unflavoured soy milk 1 cup flavoured soy milk 2 slices of soy cheese ½ cup desserts made from fortified soy milk, e.g., custard

Protein foods

Protein is an essential macronutrient required to transport vitamins and minerals around the body, to provide the building blocks (amino acids) for growth and repair of body tissue, and to provide energy. Protein rich foods also provide iron, zinc, vitamin B12, and omega-3 essential fatty acids.

The *REAL Food Guide* recommends a variety of animal and plant-based protein foods each day. A simple method for achieving balanced meals at lunch and at dinner is to use *the Thirds Rule* (Figure A2). This means that on an average size plate, one third of the plate should be filled by carbohydrate foods, one third filled by protein foods, and one third filled by vegetables. For people with eating disorders, this might mean increasing the quantity of protein and carbohydrate but reducing the quantity of vegetables on the plate. Research has shown that intake of dietary iron can be low in people with eating disorders (Pettersson et al., 2021), so attention to an adequate intake of protein is an important target. Dietary iron found in plant-based protein sources (such as legumes) is not well absorbed by the body, so adding a vitamin C source to meals containing these foods can increase absorption of iron (Heffernan et al., 2017). Some examples of this in practice are adding fruit or a glass of juice to breakfast cereal or a serve of leafy greens with lentils to a main meal. Additionally, polyphenols from tea and coffee reduce the absorption of iron (Fuzi et al., 2017), so it is best if individuals following a plant-based diet avoid drinking tea and coffee with main meals, to enhance absorption of dietary iron when consuming these protein sources.

Recommended serves of protein foods per day Weight maintenance = two serves Weight regain = two serves	
One serve of protein foods	
Animal protein sources	Plant-based protein sources
Palm-size portion of chicken ¾ cup beef mince Palm-size portion of steak ½ cup canned salmon, drained ¾ cup canned tuna, drained Piece of white fish the size of whole hand 2 slices of cheese (each slice size of your palm) ½ cup grated cheese ½ cup ricotta cheese 3 eggs	1 cup chopped plain tofu ½ cup fried tofu 1 cup tempeh ¾ cup baked beans 1 cup chickpeas, kidney bean, lentils 1 full handful of almonds (~ 25) 2 tablespoons tahini 1/3 cup hummus 2 tablespoons peanut butter

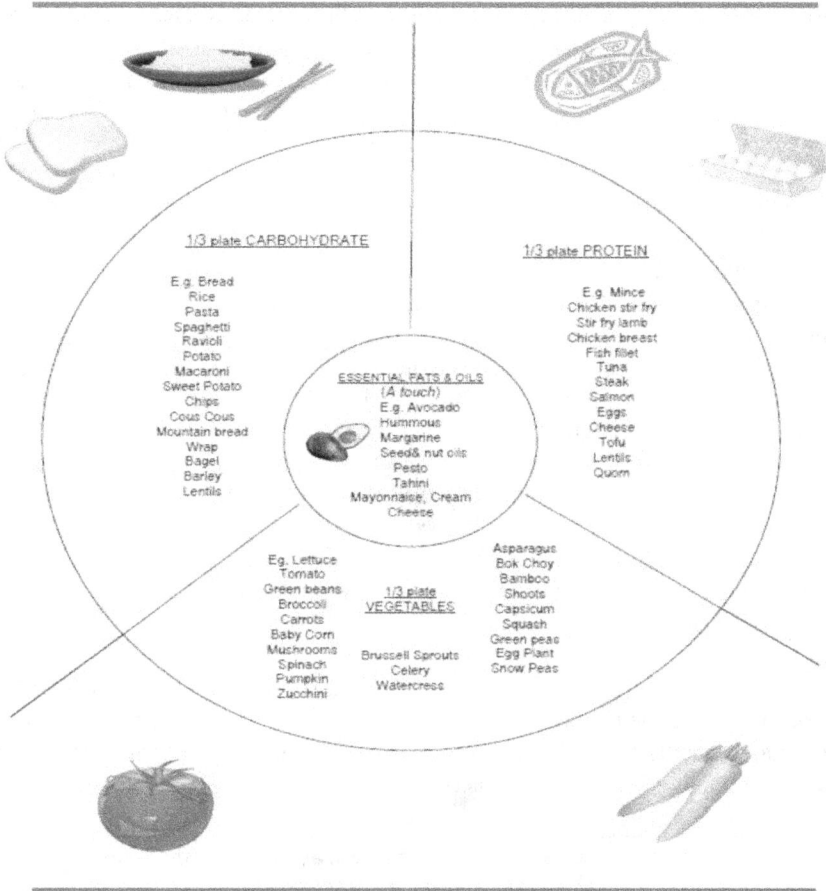

1/3 plate CARBOHYDRATE

E.g. Bread
Rice
Pasta
Spaghetti
Ravioli
Potato
Macaroni
Sweet Potato
Chips
Cous Cous
Mountain bread
Wrap
Bagel
Barley
Lentils

1/3 plate PROTEIN

E.g. Mince
Chicken stir fry
Stir fry lamb
Chicken breast
Fish fillet
Tuna
Steak
Salmon
Eggs
Cheese
Tofu
Lentils
Quorn

ESSENTIAL FATS & OILS
(A touch)
E.g. Avocado
Hummous
Margarine
Seed& nut oils
Pesto
Tahini
Mayonnaise, Cream
Cheese

E.g. Lettuce
Tomato
Green beans
Broccoli
Carrots
Baby Corn
Mushrooms
Spinach
Pumpkin
Zucchini

1/3 plate
VEGETABLES

Brussell Sprouts
Celery
Watercress

Asparagus
Bok Choy
Bamboo
Shoots
Capsicum
Squash
Green peas
Egg Plant
Snow Peas

Figure A2 Thirds rule for lunch and dinner meals.

Carbohydrate foods

This core food group refers to foods such as grains, cereal, rice, bread, pasta, and some starchy vegetables such as potatoes and corn. It is recommended that a variety of wholegrains and carbohydrate foods are included to achieve an adequate intake of energy, fibre, thiamine, folate, and iodine. *Variety* means choosing more than one food from this group over an average day. For example, a carbohydrate choice at lunch might be two slices of bread, and at dinner it could be one cup of cooked pasta. Additionally, variety over the week may mean that one night, rice is the carbohydrate of choice at dinner; one night it is potato; and one night it is spaghetti. A meal plan that has poor or low variety would be mean having rice every night of the week. When introducing a meal plan, the initial goal may be to include any source of carbohydrate at dinner. As treatment progresses, the goal may be to have a variety of choices as eating patterns improve.

The *REAL Food Guide* recommends that carbohydrate is included at breakfast (e.g., cereal and/or toast), lunch (e.g., sandwich or wrap), and at dinner (e.g., rice, pasta, potato). It is also included as a snack option (e.g., muesli bar, crackers) at least once per day. The amount of carbohydrate that is required is proportional to the amount of physical activity undertaken and whether weight gain is required. Individuals that are physically active will require a greater intake of carbohydrate to meet their energy and nutritional requirements than those who are relatively inactive.

During digestion, carbohydrate foods are broken down into glucose and absorbed into the bloodstream. Carbohydrate is needed for the body to function effectively, to provide fuel for the muscles and brain, and to stabilise blood glucose levels in the blood. The brain relies on glucose as its main fuel source to meet its energy demands. Inadequate carbohydrate intake can lead to tiredness, fatigue, dizziness, irritability, and low blood glucose levels. The effects of low blood glucose include blurred vision, difficulty concentrating, hunger, sweating, weakness, light-headedness, and confusion. As a result of malnutrition, people with eating disorders often have limited glycogen (the stored form of glucose) in their muscles and liver. When starting to eat more regularly and increasing the amount of carbohydrate in their diet, they will store some glucose in the liver and muscles as glycogen, which is packaged up with water. This may result in increases in weight of a few kilograms at the beginning of treatment, which often occur in a short space of time and do not align with the person's eating. This initial increase in weight is perceived as catastrophic for people with eating disorders, whose worst beliefs appear to be confirmed – that they will gain large amounts of weight by consuming even small amounts of food. An explanation of the role of carbohydrate and how it is stored by the body is useful at this time.

Recommended serves of carbohydrate (meals) per day Weight maintenance = three serves Weight regain = four serves	
One serve of carbohydrate (meals)	
Breakfast	**Lunch and dinner**
½ cup muesli/granola 1 cup cereal flakes 1 cup bran cereal 1 cup cooked oatmeal/porridge 2 slices bread 2 slices raisin/fruit toast 1 ½ cups puffed cereal (e.g. Rice Bubbles)	2 slices bread 2 slices of raisin toast 1 large slice sourdough bread 1 bread roll 2 dinner-sized bread rolls 1 cup cooked pasta 1 cup cooked rice 1 cup cooked quinoa 1 cup barley (cooked) 1 ½ cups cooked thick noodles 1 cup sweet corn 1 potato, baked or boiled (size of a fist) 1 ½ cups noodles thick (cooked)

Recommended serves of carbohydrate (snack) per day
Weight maintenance = one serve
Weight regain = two serves
One serve of carbohydrate (snack)
1 muesli bar
4 cups popcorn
1 crumpet + 1 teaspoon spread
1 slice bread + 1 teaspoon spread
1 slice raisin/fruit toast + 1 teaspoon spread
16 rice crackers
6 plain crackers (no spread)
3 large or 4 small crackers + 1 teaspoon spread

Carbohydrate foods are also an important source of dietary fibre, which refers to the edible parts of plants that are resistant to digestion by the body. Inadequate levels of dietary fibre contribute to constipation, while excessive amounts can contribute to bloating and early fullness. There is no doubt that adequate (though not excessive) dietary fibre is an important nutritional target for improving gut health, bowel function, and contributing positively to *gut microbiota* (Ruusunen et al., 2019). Therefore, aiming for small amounts of fibre in every meal or snack is recommended (Ruusunen et al., 2019). Gut microbiota refers to the system of microorganisms that exist in the digestive tract and is an emerging area of research in many areas of health, including in the cause and maintenance of anorexia nervosa symptoms (Jowik et al., 2021). Additionally, emerging research also proposes that *fermented foods* are energy- and nutrient-rich choices to support treatment in anorexia nervosa (Jowik et al., 2021; Rocks et al., 2021). Fermented foods refer to a wide variety of foods that belong in several core food groups, such as carbohydrates (e.g., sourdough bread), protein (e.g., tofu, miso, tempeh), calcium (e.g., yoghurt, including Greek yoghurt, feta, sour cream, kefir, lassi), diet fillers/flavours (e.g., fish sauce, soy sauce, balsamic vinegar, cocoa), vegetables (e.g., sauerkraut), and fluids (e.g., kombucha). While further research is needed, choosing fermented food options within different food groups is a simple principle that can be adopted within the existing framework of the *REAL Food Guide*.

Fruit

The *REAL Food Guide* recommends that a variety of different fruits of different colour are chosen each day to provide potassium, dietary fibre, vitamin C, and other beneficial nutrients. It is ideal to include fruit in different forms such as tinned, juiced, and dried fruits, which are nutritious and helpful to achieve adequate eating, especially early in treatment. On a weight maintenance meal plan, two pieces of fruit are recommended. For weight regain, four serves are recommended, with two of these serves coming from fruit juice added to lunch and dinner instead of having a glass of water. As a rule of thumb, having more serves of fruit is not recommended as it can be filling and push other foods from the diet, affecting the overall nutrient balance of the diet.

Recommended serves of fruit per day Weight maintenance = two serves Weight regain = four serves
One serve of fruit
1 orange 1 apple 1 pear 1 small or ½ large banana ¾ cup grapes 1 cup cherries 2 kiwi fruit 2 mandarins 3 plums 1 cup blueberries 2 cups strawberries# 2 tablespoons raisins or sultanas 6 dried apricot halves 1 cup tinned fruit, drained 1 cup fruit juice #Include strawberries occasionally as the portion can contribute to feeling full

Vegetables

It is recommended that people with eating disorders choose a variety of vegetables of different colours to provide vitamin C, folate, potassium, beta-carotene, and dietary fibre. It is important not to eat vegetables in excessive quantities as they are filling and push other nutritious food groups such as carbohydrate, fats, and protein foods from the diet.

Recommended serves of vegetables per day Weight maintenance = four serves Weight regain = four serves
One serve of vegetables
½ cup raw mushrooms 1 cup mixed salad ½ cup cooked peas 1 cup cherry tomatoes 1 fist-sized tomato 1 piece of cucumber the length of an index finger ½ capsicum 1 piece of carrot the length of an index finger Fermented vegetables, e.g. ½ cup sauerkraut

Fluid

Water is included as a core food group to emphasise that adequate hydration is an important component of daily nutritional requirements (Hart et al., 2018). Research has shown that people with eating disorders make fluid or drink choices are that are often related to eating disorder beliefs (Hart et al., 2011), from drinking excessively to drinking restrictively (Hart et al., 2005). Some people with eating disorders will restrict fluid intake to the extent that they put themselves at risk of dehydration. Others will drink large quantities of fluid to stop feelings of hunger, and to distract from the thought of food and eating. Generally, the kidneys will excrete any fluid in excess of requirements; however, it is possible to become water overloaded. Although this is rare, it has been reported in people with eating disorders (Santonastaso et al., 1998) and individuals who drink too much in a short space of time.

Recommended amount of fluid
Weight maintenance or regain = 1–2 cups of fluid at each meal and snack (1 cup = 250 mL)
The following drinks count towards fluid intake
Water Juice Tea and coffee Soft drinks Milk-based drinks Mineral water Iced tea Kombucha

It is important for fluids and drinks to be incorporated into meal plans in a structured way similarly to the way that food is planned. The *REAL Food Guide* recommends that people with eating disorders:

- Include one to two cups of fluid at every meal and snack each day (fluid includes water as well as milk, flavoured milky drinks, juice, tea, and coffee);
- Do not drink continuously from large bottles, which may encourage excessive intake;
- Do not drink fluid rapidly before the start of the meal;
- Do not drink to suppress appetite, i.e., if hungry, do not choose diet soft drink, tea, or coffee instead of eating;
- Drink fluids during or at the end of a meal if struggling with feelings of fullness;
- Are aware of the importance of drinking adequate fluid to replace fluid losses from excessive exercise or from purging behaviours.

Nuts, oils, and fats

The second layer of the *REAL Food Guide* describes "Nuts, Oils and Fats" to communicate that a healthy, balanced diet includes adequate amounts of dietary fats and oils, and foods that contain them each day (Hart et al., 2018). Foods containing essential fatty acids such as nuts, seeds, olives, and unsaturated fats and oils (e.g., sunflower, olive and sesame oil) are essential for good health, and emerging research is showing benefits far beyond just being an energy source in eating disorders (Ruusunen et al., 2019). It is recommended that one third of the total energy of the food eaten each day comes from dietary fat and oils (Australian Government Department of Health & Ageing, 2006). Fat-soluble vitamins are also provided by this food group, including vitamin A (for eyesight and healthy skin), vitamin D (for strong bones and teeth and the absorption of calcium and phosphate), vitamin E (a component of cell membranes), and vitamin K (involved in blood clotting). Low dietary intake of these vitamins and deficiencies of essential fatty acids have been documented in people with eating disorders (Allen et al., 2013; Chiurazzi et al., 2017; Jenkins et al., 2024; Pettersson et al., 2021). Vitamin D is a nutrient of interest for people with eating disorders (Jowik et al., 2021) and may be more at risk in people following plant-based diets (British Dietetic Association, 2021).

As demonstrated by dietary modelling and nutritional analysis (Hart et al., 2018), there are three important steps which should be recommended to people with eating disorders (regardless of whether they are required to gain weight or not) to achieve nutritional adequacy:

1. Include full fat dairy and calcium-rich foods, as individuals will be unlikely to meet their energy requirements if fat-modified varieties are chosen;
2. Include a spread or a source of fat/oil at each main meal; and
3. Include a fun food once per day (see below for details on this food group).

Recommended serves of nuts, oils, and fats per day Weight maintenance = two serves Weight regain = four serves	
One serve of nuts, oils, and fats	
Animal-based	**Plant-based**
2 teaspoons butter	1 teaspoon olive oil
3 teaspoons cream cheese	2 teaspoons margarine
3 teaspoons sour cream	2 teaspoons peanut butter
2 teaspoons mayonnaise	2 teaspoon tahini
	1 tablespoon avocado
	1 tablespoon hummus
	5 whole olives
	2 tablespoon almonds or 6 almonds

Fun foods and social eating

The third layer of the *REAL Food Guide* is for foods consumed when eating out or eating socially with others. These foods are included to assist with meeting energy requirements and to challenge beliefs that these foods should be avoided or removed from the diet for good health (Hart et al., 2018). It is also clinically important from a dietary and psychological perspective to include higher energy foods.

The *REAL Food Guide* recommends eating out and having social eating occasions at least two times per week. Social eating can be a daunting and challenging experience for someone with an eating disorder, and there are many eating situations that cause anxiety and stress such as banquets or buffets, shared meals with several dishes on the table, celebrations such as Christmas, cocktail parties with finger foods, and ordering from a menu where the portion size and ingredients are not listed. These situations can be challenging because of concerns about controlling or estimating portion sizes; monitoring how much has been eaten; exposure to feared foods; food hygiene issues; and spending money on food.

People with eating disorders also tend to isolate themselves socially because of their eating behaviour and their anxiety related to eating in a social situation. For example, they often perceive that people are looking at them when they eat or making judgements about what they are eating. To avoid the anxiety associated with eating these foods, they may avoid eating with their family, eat alone or in their bedroom, avoid social occasions such as birthdays, or avoid eating out in restaurants. This behaviour maintains dietary restriction and results in further social isolation. Eating away from home and in social situations is recommended so that people with eating disorders practice skills that enable them to expand the range of eating experiences they have exposure to and enable them to participate in social activities that involve food. Some experts recommend targeting eating-related anxiety by exposure to feared eating situations. These situations engage the person in challenging rather than avoiding their food fears and provide an opportunity to experience habituation of anxiety and the disconfirmation of the feared consequence (Becker et al., 2019; Steinglass et al., 2012). Our work with colleagues on implementing practical food groups into eating disorder treatment has shown that patients highly value skills that enable them to participate in social situations with peers, and this is a strong motivator for changing eating behaviour (Biddiscombe et al., 2018).

Recommended serves of fun foods per day
Weight maintenance = one serve
Weight regain = one serve
One serve of fun food
3 rich chocolate biscuits
4 chocolate coated biscuits
3 cream biscuits
4 wafer biscuits
5 plain sweet biscuits
1 medium chocolate bar (50–60g)
1/3 cup lollies or sweets
1 single serve bag crisps (50g)
3 scoops ice-cream
1 cupcake (bottom fits neatly into ½ cup)
1 muffin (bottom fits neatly into ½ cup)
1 palm sized piece of cake

Since the publication of the *REAL Food Guide* in 2018, the authors have had many discussions with colleagues and people with lived experience about the term "fun foods", with feedback that they are not "fun" and are potentially misnamed. Other naming options include "fear foods", "discretionary foods", or "higher energy foods"; however, no alternative has been found that suits all clinicians or people with lived experience. Due to the use of the term "fun foods" in the *REAL Food Guide* and for clarity about what this refers to, the authors are continuing with this term. The inclusion of these foods as both a dietary and therapeutic target remains essential for people with eating disorders (Becker et al., 2019).

Diet foods and fillers

The top layer of the *REAL Food Guide* depicts low energy foods, which may be used as a method of suppressing appetite and restricting energy for weight loss. Examples of the use of diet foods and fillers includes filling up on low energy foods, excessive use of artificial sweeteners, excessive quantities of fruit and vegetables, intake of low energy drinks such as water and diet soft drinks, and excessive intake of tea and coffee (Brown & Keel, 2013; Burgalassi et al., 2009; Hart et al., 2005; Schebendach et al., 2017). From a nutrition standpoint, these foods only become problematic when they make up a significant proportion of an individual's daily intake as they replace more nutritious foods in the diet. They may also keep people with eating disorders focused on dietary rules and restricting food, maintain fear of higher energy foods, and be counterproductive for weight restoration. The recommendation is not necessarily to eliminate these foods but to "be careful" regarding how they might affect overall dietary intake. Another group of foods that fit in this category are foods with a "health halo". These are foods where a significant health benefit is attributed to the food, making it more desirable as a food choice (Schuldt et al., 2012), such as choosing almond milk over dairy milk or only choosing foods labelled as organic.

Diet foods and fillers include:
Diet drinks and soft drink (e.g. diet cola, artificially sweetened beverages)
Foods labelled as "diet"
Artificial sweeteners
Artificially sweetened beverages
Chewing gum
Sugar-free sweets
Fat or energy modified foods
Excessive servings of fruits (especially lower calorie fruits such as strawberries)
Excessive servings of vegetables
Excessive use of sauces (e.g. sweet chilli sauce, tomato sauce)
Excessive use of salt and pepper

A note on veganism

A vegan diet is a type of plant-based diet where no animal products are included. Our analysis of vegan meal plans for both weight maintenance and weight regain in 2018 demonstrated that it is feasible to achieve nutritional adequacy with a vegan diet with careful planning (Hart et al., 2018). In recent years there has been a greater understanding about some individuals' preference for a vegan diet. Historically in treatment for an eating disorders, people who endorsed restriction of red meat alone may have been considered as engaging in another method of food restriction (O'Connor et al., 1987). As community values have changed with time (influenced by greater concerns about ethical and environmental considerations relating to food choices), so have clinicians' knowledge and consideration of dietary preferences among people undergoing eating disorder treatment.

The authors recommend that when working with people with eating disorders in an outpatient setting, those endorsing stricter plant-based diets should not be automatically excluded from treatment, and negotiating meeting nutritional requirements with a vegan-style meal plan may be appropriate when considered on a case-by-case basis. Accommodating dietary preferences in inpatient treatment is more complex (British Dietetic Association, 2021; Fuller et al., 2022). In an outpatient setting, a careful history should be taken by a dietitian exploring the motivation and timeline of following a vegan diet. Exploration of the individual's adherence to a vegan diet should be done in a way that is sensitive and non-judgmental, to allow for their beliefs to be respected but also challenged (McLean et al., 2025). McLean et al. (2025) also note that if clinicians do not attempt to understand individual dietary preferences, this may hinder people with eating disorders accessing evidence-based treatment due to having to choose between treatment and their dietary preferences. Additionally, some individuals with an eating disorder who followed a vegetarian or vegan diet felt they missed out on tailored education around how to follow a vegetarian or vegan diet post-treatment and during recovery, were not informed of comparable alternatives, and had lower treatment quality due to adhering to a vegetarian or vegan diet (McLean et al., 2025).

As a treatment principle, individuals who choose a limited number of foods should be encouraged to broaden their choices, and this applies for those who follow a vegan diet. Fuller et al. (2022) recommends that with appropriate expertise and planning, there no is reason why a vegan diet should not be well-balanced and meet the nutritional needs of any individual. The British Dietetic Association has also published a vegan version of the *REAL Food Pyramid*, which is recommend by the authors for more information (British Dietetic Association, 2021).

Sample meal plans

A nutritionally adequate meal plan will usually be more food than clients with an eating disorder have allowed themselves to eat, and initially they may doubt that this is an appropriate amount of food. Publications and recommendations written before 2015 were dominated by the direction of cautious introduction of food and in the initial stage of nutritional rehabilitation (Jowik et al., 2021). However, recent research supports the benefits of starting with a higher energy approach in the initial stages of treatment (Garber et al., 2021; Jowik et al., 2021). Barriers reported by people with eating disorders to following a meal plan that can be addressed include:

- It is too time consuming;
- Feeling that the whole day revolves around food, with less time for no-food activities;
- It costs too much money;
- It's inconvenient to stop other activities to plan, purchase, and prepare food;
- Initially, there is an increase in distress when following a meal plan and a perception that they feel worse, not better, by having a meal plan.

Table A1 Meal plan (including number of serves of each food group) for *weight maintenance*.

	Recommended serves	*Sample food choices*
BREAKFAST *Before 9 am*	1 carbohydrate serve	1 bowl cereal
	1 calcium serve	1 cup milk/tub yoghurt
	1 fruit serve	Fresh fruit/fruit cup/juice
	1 fluid	Tea/coffee
AM SNACK	1 fruit serve	1 apple
	1 calcium serve	1 tub yoghurt/2 slices cheese
	1 fluid	Tea/coffee/water
LUNCH *Between 12 and 2 pm*	1 carbohydrate serve	2 slices bread
	1 protein serve	1 chicken breast /beans/peanut butter
	1 fat/oil serve	1 tablespoon avocado/cream cheese
	2 vegetable serves	Grated carrot & lettuce
	1 fluid	1 cup water
PM SNACK	1 fun food	1 piece carrot cake
	1 fluid	Tea/coffee/water
DINNER *Between 6 and 8 pm*	1 carbohydrate serve	1 cup cooked rice
	1 protein serve	3/4 cup beef mince/tofu/lentils
	1 fat/oil serve	1 teaspoon sesame oil
	2 vegetable serves	Onion, capsicum, and beans
	1 fluid	1 cup water
SUPPER	1 fruit serve	6 dried apricot halves/banana
	1 calcium serve	1 cup hot chocolate
	1 fluid	Tea/coffee/water

Table A2 Meal plan (including number of serves of each food group) for *weight regain*.

	Recommended serves	Sample food choices
BREAKFAST	2 carbohydrate serves	1 bowl cereal
Before 9 am	1 fat/oil serve	2 slices bread + spread
	1 calcium serve	1 cup milk/tub yoghurt
	1 fruit serve	Fresh fruit/fruit cup/juice
	1 fluid	Tea/coffee
AM SNACK	1 carbohydrate snack	Muesli bar or 16 rice crackers
	1 calcium serve	1 tub yoghurt/2 slices cheese
	1 fluid	Tea/coffee/water
LUNCH	1 carbohydrate serve	2 slices bread
Between 12 and 2 pm	1 protein serve	1 chicken breast/beans/peanut butter
	1 fat/oil serve	1 tablespoon avocado/cream cheese
	1 vegetable serve	Grated carrot and lettuce
	2 fruit serve	1 orange
		1 cup juice
PM SNACK	1 fun food	1 piece carrot cake
	1 calcium serve	1 glass flavoured milk
	1 fluid	Tea/coffee/water
DINNER	1 carbohydrate serve	1 cup cooked rice
Between 6 and 8 pm	1 protein serve	3/4 cup beef mince/tofu/lentils
	1 fat/oil serve	1 teaspoon sesame oil
	1 vegetable serve	Onion, capsicum, and beans
	1 fruit serve	1 cup juice
SUPPER	1 fruit serve	6 dried apricot halves/banana
	1 calcium serve	1 cup hot chocolate
	1 fluid	Tea/coffee/water

Appendix A.5: Traits (Make your temperament work for you)

Make your temperament work for you

What is temperament?

Are you a party animal?

When we talk about temperament, we mean the type of person you are. For example, introvert versus extrovert, thrill-seeker versus harm avoidant, prefers order and neatness versus thrives on the unpredictable. There are some temperaments that seem to accompany anorexia nervosa. We are going to explore some here, including anxiety and harm avoidance, intolerance of uncertainty and obsessive-compulsivity, perfectionism and high self-criticism, flexible and big-picture thinking.

What causes temperaments?

Research shows that genes contribute to eating disorders, including anorexia nervosa. Genes cause temperaments. These temperaments show up in brain imaging studies, showing differences in the parts of the brain involved in eating in individuals with anorexia nervosa. These genes and brain networking can increase vulnerability to developing anorexia nervosa and can also play a role in maintaining it.

The good news

Unhelpful genetic action can be closed down and brains can be rewired when new behaviours are practised!

Science shows that people do change over the lifetime. We don't need to be trapped with the same old ways of responding to our temperaments.

Let's look at the typical temperaments that accompany anorexia nervosa, how they look in your life, and implications for changing your behaviour so you can make the trait work for you rather than against you.

Anxiety and harm avoidance

A personality trait characterized by excessive worrying over upcoming events; pessimism – expecting the worst to happen; shyness; and being fearful and doubtful. Avoidance behaviours, including avoidance of food, can be used to reduce anxious feelings.

Intolerance of uncertainty and obsessive compulsivity

A tendency to react negatively to uncertain situations or events. People with anorexia nervosa tend to need guarantees in life and may struggle to cope with unpredictability. Living a highly structured and ordered life and following rules can help people manage uncertainty. These rules can relate to food and/or how many times tasks need to be repeated to get them "just right".

Perfectionism and self-criticism

We know a lot about St Catherine of Siena (March 1347 – April 1380), an important theological writer who influenced papal and Italian politics. We also think that anorexia nervosa killed her at the age of 33. This is a quote from some of her writings which reflects the perfectionism temperament: "**Make a supreme effort to root out self-love from your heart and to plant in its place this holy self-hatred. This is the royal road by which we turn our backs on mediocrity, and which leads us without fail to the summit of perfection.**"

This quote reflects the multi-faceted nature of perfectionism. It values pursuit of black and white, all-or-nothing standards – in other words, it is either perfect or it is mediocre. The "holy self-hatred" is also part of perfectionism, a focus on perceived failure which leads to self-criticism (e.g., "I am a failure as a person"), and a tendency to overlook and undervalue things you do well.

Make your temperament work for you

Flexible and Big-picture thinking

Set shifting is the ability to figure out how to change your approach (being flexible) when something is no longer working. Anorexia nervosa is an example of *low* set-shifting. Refusing yourself nutrition may have worked initially in getting positive comments, dampening emotion, and enhancing your sense of control and self-worth. But things changed. Relationships were damaged, depression and anxiety seem constant, the eating disorder now controls you, and your self-esteem is worse than when you started. However, you feel helpless to respond in a different way to the changes.

Central coherence is the ability to see the bigger picture or general idea before diving into the detail. Low central coherence is where people's attention goes first to detail without stepping back enough to see the big picture. Like the saying – *can't see the wood for the trees.*

Anorexia nervosa loves the detail – the numbers on the scale, the calories in food. It makes it harder for you to consider yourself as a whole person.

Orchids and dandelions

Some people are dandelions – put them in any environment and they thrive. Some people are orchids – their environment needs to be carefully managed to allow them to thrive. You need to create the environments that help you enjoy the strengths of your temperament while minimizing the harms.

Making your temperament work for you

Create environments that help you get the advantages of your temperament while reducing the extremes that led you down the road to anorexia nervosa. Consider:

Instead of catastrophizing ("what if ...!" thinking), ask yourself: "What are the possible outcomes – best, worst and most likely? Am I jumping ahead of myself? How important is this in the scheme of things? Will it still worry me in one-months' time?"

People who have recovered from anorexia nervosa tend to eat the same food and amounts at the same time every day because they get anxious about food choices and gauging hunger and satiety. The Real Food Guide (Appendix A.4) has information about the amount, variety and flexibility required to find the "sweet spot" that maintains your nutritional health: this can become your new habit.

Focus your effort on achieving excellence rather than being perfect. Science tells us that not only does this lead to better mental health and social relationships, but it also means that people are *more* likely to achieve their valued goals. You can read more about this here: https://self-compassion.org/wp-content/uploads/2016/12/Self-Criticism.pdf. An 8-module evidence-based approach shown to decrease perfectionism and self-criticism, and help build self-compassion and self-worth can be found here: https://www.focusedmindsprogram.com/program-menu

Collect daily data on what you are doing that you would appreciate if other people did it – redirect your focus away from self-criticism to the detail of what is happening that tells you that you are good enough.

Work on flexible and big-picture thinking - you can find a workbook here: https://osf.io/2ua74. Think about ways to practice these skills every day in your life. Ongoing practice will make new connections in your brain that get strengthened over time.

Appendix A.6: Starvation effects

Starvation Effects
in anorexia nervosa

 A healthy body supports us to be at our best. In anorexia nervosa, physical health is severely impacted by nutritional and energy deficiency. This results in physical, psychological, emotional, and social suffering. The effects of starvation on our body and other areas of functioning are central to anorexia nervosa, though people often struggle to acknowledge this.

Starvation is one of the key symptoms of anorexia nervosa, and starvation effects underlie many of the negative effects of the illness. When you have anorexia nervosa, your body is in serious nutritional deficit, which means that you cannot function at anything like your best potential level. Not only do you not develop, but starvation means that you decline physically. Consider the following problems, which are all found in individuals with anorexia nervosa due to their being malnourished:

- *Physical:* Weakness; tiredness; cold intolerance; lack of energy and strength to exercise; loss of brain mass; bone deterioration; problems with your liver, heart, circulation, breathing, gastro-intestinal system, hair, and skin; stunted height growth; deterioration in reproductive, hormonal and menstrual function; food preoccupation, cravings and binge-eating; and more.
- *Psychological:* Poor concentration, memory, and attention; difficulty with 'big picture' thinking.
- *Emotional:* Unstable mood; depression; anxiety; angry outbursts; shame; guilt.
- *Social and interpersonal:* Isolation from friends, family and colleagues; loss of important friendships; deterioration of intimate relationships; loss of income, education and occupational potential.

All of this means you are left with poor quality of life, poor health, and limited ability to function in the world. Those around you might be worried about and uncomfortable around you. You could find yourself feeling controlled by your family, your loved ones, clinicians, and the like.

How do we know the problem is all about starvation?

There have been many studies examining the effects of nutrition and of the problems caused by starvation and the accompanying malnutrition. Two of the most informative are the Minnesota Study and the Dutch Hunger Winter studies. Interestingly, neither of these studies was designed to study anorexia nervosa specifically, meaning that they allow us to zero in on the effects of starvation itself.

Considering the Minnesota study, this was an experiment to determine the impact of starvation on healthy adults, in anticipation of widespread famine should the Axis powers win the second World War. It has taught us huge amounts about the effects of starvation on the human body. In this study, 36 men (conscientious objectors from the war who resided in the United States) were restricted to just 50% of their previous daily calorie intake until they had lost approximately 25% of their original body weight (very comparable to the weight loss in anorexia nervosa). So, what did starvation do to otherwise healthy people? It had all the physical, cognitive, emotional, and social/interpersonal effects outlined above. Several of the men even began to experience the unique thoughts and behaviors that we now consider the hallmark characteristics of eating disorders, including intense fear of weight gain, excessive exercise, and binge eating. This is particularly notable because prior to the study none of them had expressed a desire to lose weight. Rather, these symptoms crept up insidiously as unintended *consequences* of starvation.

Similarly, the Dutch Hunger Winter study documented the impact of the 1944-1945 Nazi occupation of the Netherlands when a German blockade cut off the food supply. For months, both adults and children were subsisting on just 500 to 700 calories per day.

Starvation Effects
in anorexia nervosa

Longitudinal research has closely followed the offspring who were either in utero or children/adolescents during the Hunger Winter. These studies have identified that, depending on the stage of gestational development or child age during the Hunger Winter, these offspring have gone on to experience an increased risk of a wide range of problems including cognitive impairment, lower educational attainment, schizophrenia, diabetes, obesity, and cardiovascular disease. In other words, much of what we understand as being features of anorexia nervosa are the *direct result* of starvation.

That means that if you want to get away from all these features of your anorexia nervosa, you will need to eat enough to overcome your starvation. That means eating enough to regain weight, to balance your nutrient intake, and to bring your body out of starvation.

Given all these problems of starvation, why do people keep restricting?

Initially, the feeling of self-control trumps all those damaging consequences – you might feel brilliant, at first. However, eventually, most likely within weeks or months, you are out of reserves, and your body starts to suffer and shut down.

If you want to understand that more clearly, think about other times that we run up deficits, and how it cannot last. Imagine that you are spending far more money than you have coming in. At first, you enjoy the spending. But then, problems stack up and you run out of reserves. That is when you feel terrible because you have huge debts that you cannot pay off.

So, why keep starving yourself when all those many and serious problems start taking over your life? Your answer to this might involve *fear* and *hope*:

Fear – Part of anorexia nervosa is the terror that develops about uncontrollable weight gain. So, you try to restrict to avoid that terrifying outcome.

Hope – The wish to be able to go back to the feeling when you first restricted – of being in control and being able to lose weight without all the negative consequences.

Remember

Starvation is a trap that keeps you locked into the eating disorder. It dulls your physical, social, academic and creative potentials, meaning that you are unable to be the real you. It might have felt great at the beginning but suffering and impairment increase over time.

But there is a way of reversing all those starvation effects – balanced nutritional intake for weight regain and learning how to maintain your weight. That is how so many people have escaped from anorexia nervosa, learning how to enjoy life in ways that feel so much more positive.

If you are interested in learning more about weight restoration or making the decision to work on this, you might find the handouts on the 'anorexic voice', 'restoring health' and 'advantages and fears of change' helpful.

Appendix A.7: Long-term consequences of anorexia nervosa

Long term consequences
of anorexia nervosa

There are numerous acute biological complications of starvation that can make getting out of the restrictive eating cycle difficult. But the consequences of anorexia nervosa are not only acute. Rather, they can develop into chronic physical illnesses and psychosocial problems. It is important that you and your loved ones should be aware of these long-term impacts, so that you can see what the benefits of getting out of anorexia nervosa could be for you. Below we highlight some of the major long-term consequences of anorexia nervosa:

Bone loss

Most bone mass builds during adolescence and young adulthood, which is often when an eating disorder first takes hold. One of the most common consequences of anorexia nervosa is bone loss (sometimes referred to as 'osteopenia' or 'osteoporosis', depending on the severity). Bone loss in anorexia nervosa is due to hormonal abnormalities and undernutrition. Low bone density can lead to fractures and, in the most severe cases, vertebral compression fractures, which can lead to pain, immobility, and height loss. While some bone loss will be long-standing, it can be partly reversed with weight restoration and treatment. The sooner you start to eat better, the sooner your bones can start rebuilding.

Grey matter loss in the brain

Grey matter is an essential tissue in our brain, making up the cell bodies of our neurons. Having sufficient grey matter is critical for thinking, feeling, and moving, so any loss of this tissue can cause problems in all these areas. In a recent structural brain imaging study from our team,[1] we found that adolescents and adults with anorexia nervosa had significantly lower grey matter volumes compared to healthy controls across nearly all parts of the brain – including the frontal, temporal, and parietal areas. The figure below shows the parts of the brain with lower grey matter volume in the anorexia nervosa group (compared to the healthy control group), marked in green, orange, and purple. On the bright side, several other studies have shown that grey matter loss can be reversed with weight restoration. So, eating for weight regain can have a real benefit for your brain.

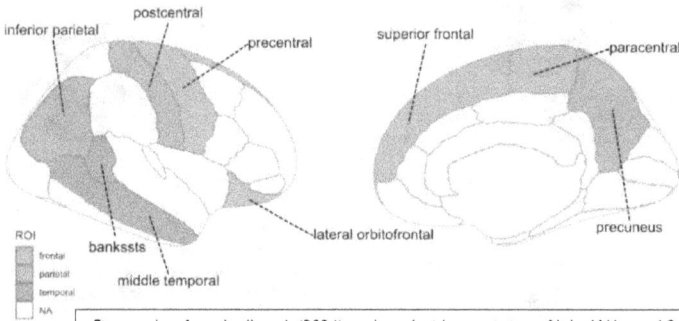

inferior parietal   postcentral   precentral   superior frontal   paracentral   lateral orbitofrontal   precuneus   bankssts   middle temporal

ROI
frontal
parietal
temporal
NA

Figure taken from Lyall et al. (2024), and used with permission of John Wiley and Sons

Long term consequences
Of anorexia nervosa

Fertility

One of the major consequences of restrictive eating is reduced levels of sex hormones, signaled by missed or absent periods or low testosterone in men. While some people continue to menstruate and can become pregnant, many people with anorexia nervosa have difficulty conceiving and carry an increased risk of miscarriage. The good news is that following the return of menses and eating disorder recovery, most people can ultimately conceive.

Gastrointestinal

One of the most common gastrointestinal problems that individuals with anorexia nervosa experience is delayed gastric emptying, where food stays longer and longer in the gastrointestinal tract as the body tries to squeeze out every calorie. This can lead to feelings of bloating, abdominal pain, and constipation. Ironically, these gastrointestinal side effects can make it even more difficult to consume as much food as the body really needs, keeping people trapped in a cycle of food restriction. However, working to restore normal eating can reverse this problem.

Psychosocial

In the early stages of the illness, individuals with anorexia nervosa often go through a 'honeymoon' phase, where they feel buoyed by their weight loss and experience a boost of confidence that enables them to more actively pursue relationships, education, and other goals. However, this honeymoon phase is short-lived. The truth is that, in the long term, most individuals with anorexia nervosa report feeling isolated, lonely, like a shell of their former selves. Fulfilling the unrelenting demands of the eating disorder can begin to feel like a full-time job that leaves little free time for pursuing meaningful relationships, educational goals, or hobbies.

As above, these effects are reversible with support and eating for recovery, even if it takes a while to decide what you want your future to look like.

Mortality

Anorexia nervosa is among the deadliest of any psychiatric illness. Research studies tell us that individuals with anorexia nervosa are five times more likely to die prematurely from any cause, and 18 times more likely to die by suicide, compared to individuals of similar ages without anorexia nervosa.[2] So, we should never underestimate the impact of anorexia nervosa on the individual, and we should focus on leaving the anorexia nervosa behind as soon as possible. Delaying recovery increases the risk of early death.

Summary

All these long-term consequences sound pretty horrible – and that is because they are. But please do not forget that they are all ones that can be reversed by eating for weight regain and health. This is why CBT-AN-20 is built around early changes in your eating and getting to a healthy weight.

Remember that giving yourself permission to have adequate nutrition will have a profound effect on improving the functioning of your brain and genes, as well as your body.

Taking care of your nutritional health will allow your body and mind to repair, recover, and move forward to support a life worth living.

1. https://onlinelibrary.wiley.com/doi/10.1002/eat.24168
2. https://www.sciencedirect.com/science/article/pii/S001044 0X14001862?via%3Dihub

Appendix A.8: Risks of compensatory behaviours

Compensatory Behaviours
The risks

What are compensatory behaviours?

Compensatory behaviors are what people with eating disorders do because they believe that this will make up for having eaten and consumed calories. As well as trying to compensate for perceived overeating, these behaviours can be an attempt to erase shame, anxiety, guilt or other "bad" feelings about the food eaten and the act of eating it.

We will talk about four specific behaviours and the associated risks: self-induced vomiting, misuse of laxatives, compulsive exercising, and chewing and spitting.

Self-induced vomiting

The most common risk of repeated vomiting is the damage that the gastric acid causes on your tooth enamel. It erodes and removes enamel - something that is not reversible. The damage is evident and visible, explaining why dentists can be the first people to pick up that someone has an eating disorder. This is why you should not brush your teeth after vomiting – use mouthwash instead.

Vomiting also causes damage to your digestive tract as gastric acid and food pieces are forcefully ejected. In the long-term, the digestive tract stops working properly. It loses touch with the ability to accurately signal hunger, or fullness. This is why even a small amount of food in the stomach can feel uncomfortable.

Of most medical concern is the imbalance in electrolytes (i.e., potassium, sodium) that vomiting causes, effects that can be fatal. Symptoms can include blood pressure changes, heart palpitations, seizures, and cardiac arrest.

People mistakenly believe that vomiting helps them get rid of all the calories they have just eaten. This is false. As soon as food enters your mouth and the saliva gets to work, the calories are being utilized by your body. This process continues as the food travels through your oesophagus and stomach. When you vomit, however much you have eaten, you retain a very significant number of the calories that you ate (two-thirds if it was a small binge, around half if it was a large binge). The longer you have been vomiting, the more efficient your body gets at holding onto calories. Your body is desperate to snatch nutrition for your safety and wellbeing. This is why vomiting becomes almost ineffective over time.

Laxatives

Laxatives can be extremely damaging and are completely ineffective at reducing calorie absorption.

The order of your digestive system is mouth, oesophagus, stomach, small intestine, large intestine (bowel), and then ejection from your body.

The issue here is that the food you eat gets absorbed in the small intestine. That is what the small intestine does, with the help of digestive juices released by liver, pancreas and gallbladder. By the time food waste moves to the final stop, the bowel, there are no calories left. But the bowel is what laxatives act on, meaning that those laxatives do not get rid of any calories.

You might experience temporary weight loss after taking laxatives – but this is due to catastrophic loss of fluid, which causes electrolyte imbalance. The body then builds the fluid back up as quickly as possible, which is why you can feel bloated.

Compensatory Behaviours
The risks

But laxative misuse carries even greater risks. In addition to ongoing intestinal bloating and discomfort, laxatives act as serious irritants to the lower levels of your digestive system. Laxative use reduces intestinal muscle tone, causing the bowel to become dependent on laxatives just to function at all.

Of most medical concern, complete paralysis of the large intestine can occur, requiring it to be removed surgically. While rare, we have known young people who have had to have an opening (stoma) made through the skin of their belly, and stools go through the stoma into a drainage bag outside the body (colostomy).

Once again, electrolyte imbalance from laxative abuse can cause palpitations, cardiac arrest and more.

These risks explain why in therapy you will be asked to cease laxative use immediately, or as quickly as possible. You might experience short-term discomfort, such as constipation or bloating. This can be quickly alleviated through natural means, namely a high fibre diet – wholemeal bread, high-fibre breakfast cereals, beans, fruit, vegetables, and 1.5 to 2 litres of water daily. Your general practitioner or dietitian can advise if temporary use of high-fibre supplements will be useful.

Compulsive exercise

This is when people feel they simply MUST exercise in the same driven way most days, to control weight. Even when injured they will continue to exercise, and they will start avoiding other important aspects of life (e.g., social engagements) because they prioritise exercise. People we have worked with look back on this level of exercise as being out of control and unenjoyable – a miserable experience. The greatest risk this form of compensation poses is injury, which can become long-term and disabling if the exercise does not cease. Working with your therapist, you will be able to examine new ways of exercising that promote health, better mood, and body appreciation.

Chewing and spitting

Research suggests that nearly 25% of people with eating disorders chew their food and then spit it out. Remembering that calories start being removed in the mouth, this means calories are ingested.

Vicious Cycles

Use of compensatory behaviours maintains the vicious cycle of the eating disorder. It is a self-harm behaviour where you punish your body and treat yourself as if you don't matter. If you don't believe you matter, then you won't prioritise nurturing your nutritional health. Therapy is about treating yourself as though you matter, even if you might not feel able to believe it yet and developing new coping strategies that will better help you achieve valued goals. Treating yourself in this way is the pathway to eventually starting to experience yourself as being worthwhile.

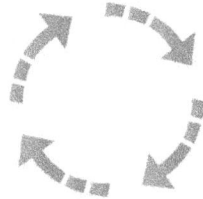

LIFE IS WAY TOO SHORT TO SPEND ANOTHER DAY AT WAR WITH YOURSELF.

Appendix A.9: Formulation worksheet (for patient)

Understanding my eating disorder

Developing a formulation

Spending some time thinking about how and why you developed anorexia nervosa and what keeps it going is an important part of recovery. It can help you to make sense of your experiences and is a good way to identify recovery goals and areas to focus on in therapy.

Together with your therapist you will pull together a shared understanding about why you developed an eating disorder, what keeps it going, and identifying pathways to change. We call this a 'formulation', and it can take into consideration a wide range of factors - biological /genetic, temperament, social, cultural and environmental. A formulation isn't static but evolves over time as new understanding emerges, so remember to update it regularly. Here we use the 5Ps approach which looks at the following areas:

Predisposing factors

We know that many factors can make someone vulnerable to developing an eating disorder. These might include difficult early life events that have influenced how you see yourself, your relationships and your place in the world. Personality traits can also play a role, but it's important to remember that many of these can also be your strengths! Think about your early life experiences and temperament. What do you think may have made you vulnerable to developing anorexia nervosa?

Precipitating factors

Think back to when you first made a conscious decision to lose weight. What was happening in your life at the time? Were you experiencing any life stressors, such as social or relationship difficulties, academic/work challenges, changes in mood? What do you think were your triggers? Did you experience changes in your weight or physical health? Had anyone commented on your eating, weight and/or shape?

Perpetuating factors (short term)

When you started to lose weight how did it make you feel? What changes did you first notice? Did your eating disorder initially help you manage any difficulties you were having at the time – think about things like self-worth, social/ emotional wellbeing, life transitions or emotions. Did it help you in your life? What were the positives?

Perpetuating factors (long term)

It is not uncommon for the relationship you have with your eating disorder to change over time. The factors that served to maintain your anorexia nervosa in the early days can be quite different to those that might be keeping it going now. What do you think keeps your eating disorder going in the here and now? Does it impact your sense of self-worth and identity? Have your relationships changed over time? Have you become disconnected from wider parts of your life? What's hard about letting it go?

Protective Factors (Strengths)

Think about the 'inner strengths' that you can draw on as you start to recover. Remember that some of your personality traits that you may have identified earlier can often be your strengths! If you find it hard to identify your strengths ask family, friends or loved ones for their thoughts. It is not uncommon to lose sight of strengths when you're in the depths of an eating disorder. How would others describe you? What were you like before you developed an eating disorder? Think about all the different parts of you. Also think about what support you can draw on to help you in your recovery. Who knows about your eating disorder? Who can you reach out to? Think about your personal strengths and the support networks that can support you in your recovery.

Understanding my eating disorder

Now summarise all this thinking in the diagram below. You can discuss this with your therapist.

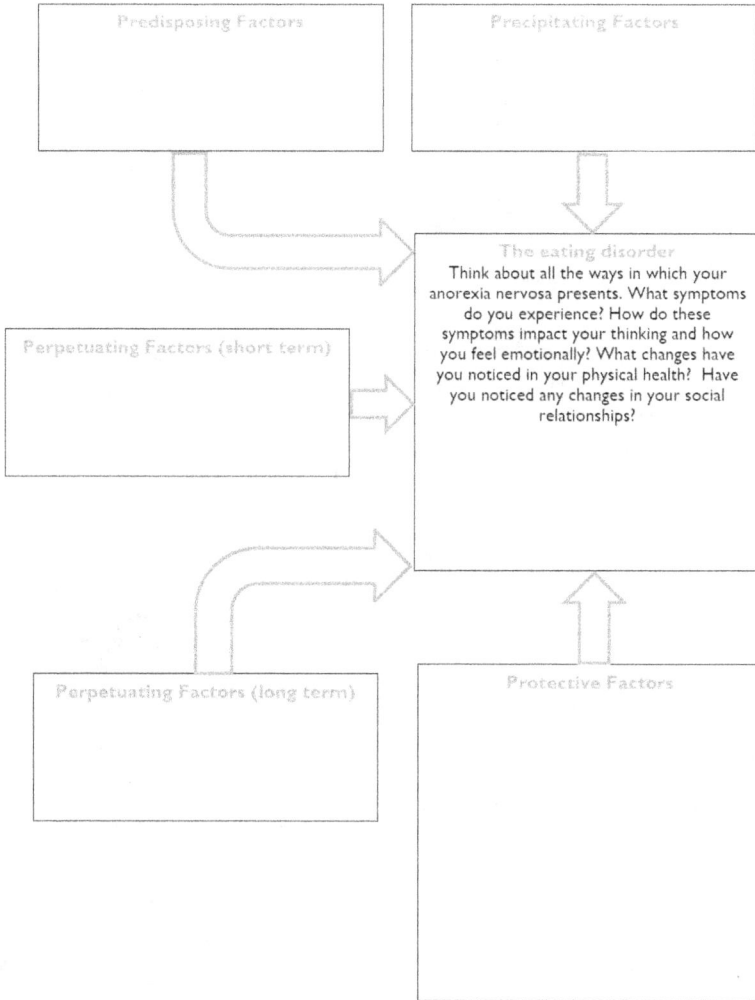

Predisposing Factors

Precipitating Factors

Perpetuating Factors (short term)

The eating disorder

Think about all the ways in which your anorexia nervosa presents. What symptoms do you experience? How do these symptoms impact your thinking and how you feel emotionally? What changes have you noticed in your physical health? Have you noticed any changes in your social relationships?

Perpetuating Factors (long term)

Protective Factors

Appendix A.10: 5Ps formulation (blank)

Developing a 5Ps formulation

Use this worksheet to help you understand why you developed anorexia nervosa and what keeps it going. Think about what initially kept it going (short term) as well as what keeps it going in the present (longer term). It can also be helpful to think about the strengths and resources you have that can support you to start to move on from your eating disorder.

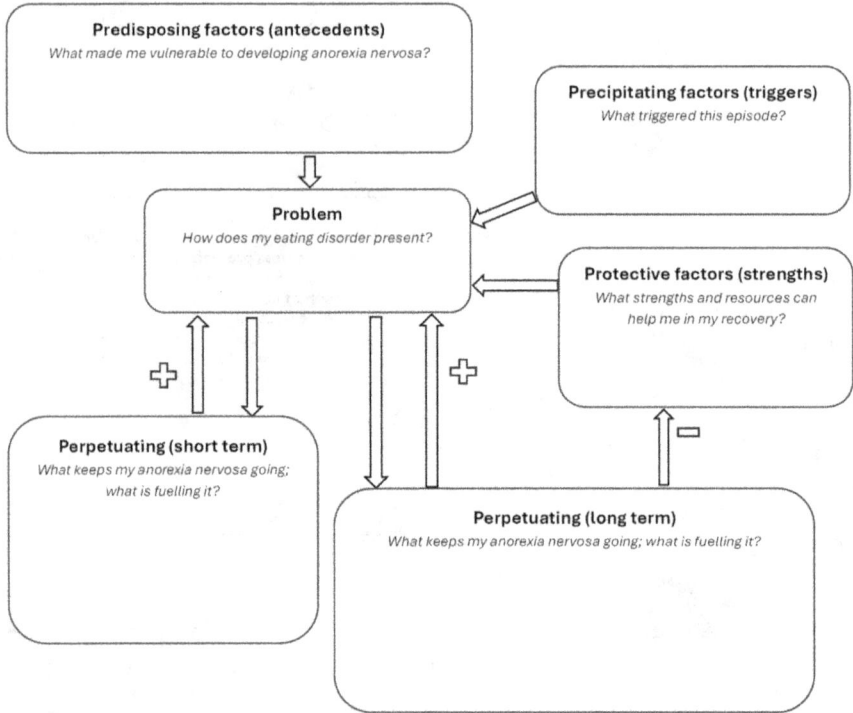

Predisposing factors (antecedents)
What made me vulnerable to developing anorexia nervosa?

Precipitating factors (triggers)
What triggered this episode?

Problem
How does my eating disorder present?

Protective factors (strengths)
What strengths and resources can help me in my recovery?

Perpetuating (short term)
What keeps my anorexia nervosa going; what is fuelling it?

Perpetuating (long term)
What keeps my anorexia nervosa going; what is fuelling it?

Note: '+' indicates 'enhancement'; '-' indicates 'reduction'.

Appendix A.11: Case formulation letter (example)

Dear Poppy

I'm writing this letter to summarise the work we have done together in the 8 sessions we've had so far. As I attempt to reflect the conversations we've had, please do let me know if there are bits which I have not quite understood, or things you would like to change.

I have valued your openness in sharing some of your early life experiences with me and I hope that through doing so we can start to make sense of why you developed anorexia nervosa. You spoke about how your eating disorder developed when you were a teenager and at the time you had some difficulties in your friendships at school, and when you later moved to college you found yourself desperately wanting to fit in and find new friends. Fuelled by your favourite social media, you started to focus more on your appearance – constantly thinking about what you could change about yourself to ensure that others would like you. Whilst this started with a general focus on style, over time you began to change your eating habits, as you became increasingly focused on needing to be "perfect" to be accepted by others.

We have spoken about how you felt miserable at school much of the time; you described yourself as a sensitive child who worried about academic work and friendships. You felt that no matter how hard you worked, the grades you got just weren't as good as you wanted. Relationships in your friendship group seemed to constantly change for no clear reason and you started to feel anxious about whether you would be the next one to be "axed from the group". You shared how a part of you didn't care if you were kicked out, but I have a sense that deep down you, like all of us, had a real desire to belong to something that was stable; to have friends, to feel cared for, and to connect to others.

When you moved to college you were determined to leave the boring and under-confident person you felt you were at school behind. We have reflected on how, when anorexia first came into your life, it gave you a sense of confidence and achievement; it felt good and gave you a way of feeling better about yourself. You were now in control. It also helped to numb difficult emotions, giving you some short-term relief from the relentless negative experience of feeling like there was something wrong with you. I wonder whether over time you internalised and blamed yourself for everything that was difficult in your life – developing a belief that it must be because there was something wrong with you. Perhaps these beliefs can start to change?

We have also spoken about your strengths: your hard-working nature and your willingness to listen and care for others. It feels like you are always one of the first to listen to a friend in need! We have also recognised those personality traits that can contribute to your current difficulties: your competitive nature and eye for detail. Whilst these are positive traits, they can also come at a cost, particularly when anorexia draws on them – having to follow strict rules about your eating and driving your mind and body into starvation has left you feeling short tempered, irritable, and tired. When I listen to you I can really hear how overwhelming this can all be for you.

One key maintaining factor that we have spent time thinking about is the strong sense of worthlessness that you feel inside. We've started to explore your "critical voice" and acknowledged that there is a part of you that can be very harsh towards yourself. We've also acknowledged that there are other parts of you – the fun part, the softer more compassionate part, and the excitable social part, to name but a few. I wonder whether these other parts have been crushed by your anorexia? Perhaps through our work together we can continue to think about ways in which you can connect with others whilst also "just being you"? I know in the past few weeks you've really drawn on your courage to take opportunities to meet friends, even though a part of you always wants to cancel at the last minute, but through meeting others you've seen that they do want to connect with you. Don't forget the text message from your friend who shared how much she enjoyed catching up. It feels like others have missed having you around. We've acknowledged that friendships can be valuable for lots of different reasons, and I would encourage you to continue to take opportunities to connect with others.

Poppy, I have been really struck by how positively you've embraced treatment despite finding elements, such as weight monitoring, difficult. You have shown so much openness and determination. Through drawing on these strengths you have been able to improve your eating despite those early worries about uncontrollable weight change. I wonder whether, though your weight chart, your body is sending you a message – that it isn't changing rapidly, but instead steadily improving its strength in a predictable way? You have also been open in sharing that changing your eating can leave you feeling guilty and greedy. I wonder if we can continue to work together to strengthen your confidence in allowing yourself to look after your body's nutritional needs.

When we first met you spoke about what recovery meant for you – you wanted to feel more confident in yourself, to have a job you enjoy, and to just feel freer in life. Well done for all the changes you have made so far – continuing to build on these will be an essential part of you moving on from your eating disorder and the grip that it has had on your life. I look forward to working through the next phases of treatment with you, where we will continue to work on building your confidence in your relationship with food, challenging your inner critic, and bringing together all the colourful and valued parts of you. I hope that over time you will continue to see and embrace life beyond your eating disorder.

With best wishes

Appendix A.12: End of treatment letter

Dear Martha

Now that you have completed your sessions, I wanted to write to share my reflections on the work we have done together over the past 6 months. It takes a lot of courage and commitment to work through the full course of treatment, so you deserve to feel proud of all that you have achieved and for sticking with it during the harder times.

When we first met, you shared that life had become overwhelming and every day felt like a battle. You felt fat despite being underweight and your "anorexic voice" had become increasingly critical and harsh – no matter how much you followed its rules, you were left feeling that you never got it right and just weren't good enough. Your physical and emotional health was suffering – you felt tired and tearful, and activities you once enjoyed, such as seeing friends and travelling, felt completely draining. However, despite the negatives, retreating into the predictable world of your eating disorder felt safe, but it was also an increasingly lonely and isolating place to live. Listening to you in those early sessions, I could really hear how difficult your life had become. I could also hear that there was a part deep inside you that just wanted to feel okay and have some fun.

During our early sessions, we talked about why you developed anorexia nervosa and what was keeping it going. You spoke about how at the beginning it made you feel good – it gave you a sense of control and achievement and became a way of managing the difficult emotions you were experiencing at the time. You also noticed that you'd often eat less when at home and we wondered whether over time this became your way of trying to communicate that all was not well? We talked about how others often don't understand the language of anorexia, and finding other ways of expressing your needs was going to be an important part of your recovery.

Since starting treatment, I have been so impressed with your perseverance and determination to move forward. Despite finding it difficult, you have always chosen to confront your fears, no matter how much anxiety this has caused you in the short term.

You have been able to show yourself greater "nutritional kindness" through increasing your intake and allowing your body to return to health. I remember how difficult it was for you to make those initial changes to your eating, but I can also remember how much better you started to feel. Now you eat for health and enjoyment, and continuing to build your confidence in eating flexibility and intuitively is a lovely next step.

During our last session we spoke about how, through treatment, you've been able to get to know the different parts of you, many of which had been crushed by your anorexia. You have been able to notice the "critical voice" within you and start to respond to it differently – showing yourself greater kindness and self-compassion. You are now much more able to look out for and appreciate the different parts of you – whether that's the competitive part, the fun part, the sad part, or the compassionate part. They are all valuable parts of you! Re-connecting with friends has also allowed you to see that others value you, and I hope your confidence in being with others continues to grow.

Stepping back from the "critical anorexic voice" has also allowed you to develop a more accepting and compassionate relationship with your body, where you can appreciate it for what it can do for you, rather than constantly criticising it for not being perfect. Through stepping back and letting go of the negative detail, you've become more flexible in how you think about your body, as well as many other areas of your life. Do re-visit the Body Neutrality handout if you need to and remember that *living* self-respect enables you to *feel* self-respect. I wonder if that internal belief that you deserve to look after yourself is starting to really grow?

I've also noticed how much better your mood is – now I see a smile! We've talked a lot about the importance of nutrition in recovery and the links between food, the brain, and emotion, and since improving your eating, you've really been able to develop your ability to notice and listen to your emotions in healthier ways – what are they saying you need in life? I've been struck by the positive responses you've had from others when you've taken a risk and been more open about how you are feeling.

When listening to you in recent weeks I have felt that you are really starting to live your life beyond anorexia – I was really impressed with how you made the decision to leave your job and find something different. That must have taken real courage, and your new job sounds much more enjoyable. I'm aware that anorexia is often born out of a need for control, but reflecting now I wonder whether it is you that is back in control? As you have mentioned, it feels like you now have more choice about how you spend your time – seeing friends, having a job, having more fun – these are all things you have in your life because you decided to move on from anorexia. It's been lovely to see you reconnect with so many of the other parts of your life.

I think it's important to remember how far you have come in your recovery – you've shown yourself that you can get your needs met in healthier ways. It is essential that you now continue to work on strengthening the progress you've made, working on further goals at your own pace. I would encourage you to regularly go back through your resources to remind yourself of all that we've covered. Over the coming weeks you may experience some difficult days or setbacks, and this is not uncommon. It doesn't mean that you are back at the start. Instead, think of it as an opportunity to reflect and learn – why is this happening now? Draw on your therapy blueprint and relapse plan to think about how to approach any challenges in healthier ways, without having to go back to an eating disorder.

Again, congratulations on all your hard work and successes during treatment. I am very much looking forward to meeting with you for our follow-up sessions over the next few months and hearing how things are going.

With best wishes

Appendix A.13: The nature of the "anorexic voice"

Rediscovering you
Giving a voice to all your parts

What is the anorexic voice?

It is not uncommon for people with an eating disorder to describe experiencing an 'anorexic part' or 'internal anorexic voice'. The idea that our mind has multiple 'modes' or 'voices' which together form an integrated personality is very normal and might be quite helpful e.g., allowing individuals to adapt to different situations and contexts. We all have many such parts to our personality – sometimes our social mode is more on show and at other times we might be more task focused. Some days our compassionate mind dominates and at other times we feel more anxious and isolated.

Over time the 'anorexic voice' disrupts the relationships between these healthier parts of self, becoming the dominant mode over time. This makes it hard for other parts to have a voice, integrate and thrive, and can get us stuck in rigid and unhelpful patterns. It is like the anorexic voice has a megaphone, overriding all messages from the other modes.

You may be familiar with this idea if you have seen the film Inside Out 2 – Joy, Sadness, Anger, Fear and Disgust have long been running a successful operation in Riley's mind, but during puberty Riley encounters new emotions, like Anxiety and Envy. Desperate to impress at a hockey camp, Anxiety takes over the controls taking Riley's life into places where she really doesn't want to go. Her life gets back on track when she learns to accept and balance all her emotions, including the more difficult ones, and this helps her to maintain a healthy 'sense of self'.

The evolution of the anorexic voice

Many people experience the voice as both protective and comforting, but also controlling and intrusive.

In the early stages:

The 'anorexic voice' is commonly seen as offering a solution – a way of resolving or managing difficulties related to self-worth, vulnerability, trauma, life transitions or intolerable emotions. Offering the promise of control over the complex and messy parts of life, relationships with the 'anorexic voice' are generally positive and eating disorder symptoms begin.

Domination comes next:

The voice becomes increasingly powerful. Eating disorder symptoms escalate, while motivation to stop this from happening is usually low. The voice is experienced as increasingly hostile and controlling, critical and isolating.

Then comes disempowerment:

The voice is now experienced as punitive and overwhelming. It dominates internal dialogues and undermines self-esteem and self-efficacy. It is almost in control, having drowned out the other voices inside you. Some people feel that their identity has been completely taken over and they doubt their ability to reclaim their life.

It is often at this point that people come into therapy, either because they want to, or because others who care about them have pressured them into it. It is typical for significant others to feel at this stage that they are losing their loved one, that person they knew has largely disappeared and they are desperate to find them again.

Rediscovering you
Giving a voice to all your parts

Taking back control and rediscovering your healthy 'sense of self'

Like tackling all difficult tasks, there is no one solution, but here are five strategies that will get you started on the path of reclamation:
(1) Understand the functions of the eating disorder – what needs did it meet in those early stages? – think about healthier ways to get these needs met that don't cause so much harm to yourself.
(2) Consider the advantages of using healthier means to meet your needs rather than relying on nutritional restriction, self-criticism and overcontrol.
(3) Actively work to reduce the biological consequences of starvation through improving nutritional intake.
(4) Develop more assertive and adaptive ways of responding to the anorexic voice.
(5) Give your multiple voices greater opportunities to be heard – embrace your complexity and multifaceted personality.

The functions of the eating disorder

Consider what needs the eating disorder is trying to address. What does it want for you? These represent valid and important needs in your life. Not something to be suffocated by the anorexia nervosa. List each of these needs, and brainstorm different ways of meeting these needs. The more the better! If it helps:
* think what you might say to someone else who was seeking advice on these ideas;
* sit down with someone else who can help you generate ideas.

Choose the ideas that seem a best fit for you and give them a try on as many occasions as possible. Work your way down the list to add as many alternative strategies to your life as you can.

Advantages
Make a list of the benefits of using different ways to meet your needs that support you instead of punishing you. As you try new strategies over time, your experiences will add to this list and show how much these changes can improve your life.

Eliminating starvation

Science tells us that our brains do continue to develop and change over our lifetime. Your best ally in reclaiming your healthy self is a fully nourished brain that is in peak condition for forming new connections between the neurons to help you learn and embed new behaviours. Whilst you can anticipate some 'push back' from the voice at first as you start to make these important changes, it is worth persisting as it will get easier with time.

Respond assertively to the anorexic voice

Speak back to the anorexic voice in a way that reflects your values. If you value showing compassion to others, consider a response to the critical anorexic voice that reflects this e.g., "I hear what you're saying - that it's greedy to eat more. I see it differently. I'm allowed to eat the food I like just like everyone else. It's good for me, so that's what I'm going to do". Remember you have a choice – the more you step back and stand up to the voice, the less powerful it will become.

Embrace the multiple parts of you

Keep a journal, celebrate any time when the healthier parts of you win, no matter how big or small they are to begin with. Take up practices that strengthen your healthy parts and do things that help these parts grow. Name these healthier parts, get reacquainted with complex beautiful you.

Appendix A.14: Full Dialogical Interview Schedule-Eating Disorders (DIS-ED)

Matthew Pugh

CITATION: Pugh, M. (2019). *Dialogical interview schedule for eating disorders.* Unpublished manuscript / protocol. London, UK.

Dialogical Interview Schedule for Eating Disorders (DIS-ED)

INTRODUCTION

The Dialogical Interview Schedule for Eating Disorders (DIS-ED) is a semi-structured approach to dialoguing with the internal eating disorder 'voice' or eating disorder 'self' (EDV/S).

The DIS-ED is inspired by a number of approaches, principally the Voice Dialogue method (Stone & Stone, 1988), as well as Psychodrama (Moreno, 1987), Ego State Therapy (Emmerson, 2003), and Talking with Voices (Corstens, Longden, & May, 2010).

The DIS-ED has three objectives. These are: 1). to help individuals better understand the functions, intentions, and origins of their EDV/S, 2). to encourage a decentred perspective on this aspect of the self, and 3). to create space for the emergence of more adaptive internal voices and new ways of relating to the EDV/S.

OVERVIEW

The DIS-ED is divided into four parts:

- Part one aims to explore the individual's experience of their EDV/S and put them at ease with the dialogical method.
- Part two aims to explore the content, origins, intentions, and relating style of the EDV/S through dialogue with this aspect of the self.
- Part three aims to help the individual 'step back' and observe the EDV/S from a decentred, metacognitive perspective.
- Part four aims to reflect on the process of dialoguing with the EDV/S and explore new ways of relating to these experiences.

Part two of the DIS-ED involves either direct or indirect dialogue with the EDV/S. Key areas of discussion during this phase of the DIS-ED include exploring the:

Functions of eating disorder voice / self:
- What is your role in this individual's life?
- What do you do for this individual?

Content of the eating disorder voice / self:
- What do you tend to say to this individual?
- How do you respond to this individual when they do a,b,c?

Origins of the eating disorder voice / self:
- When did you come into this individual's life? How do you come to be?
- Do you take after anyone this individual has known?

Intentions of the eating disorder voice / self:
- What's important to you?
- What do you want for this individual? What are your hopes for them?

Relationship between the individual and their eating disorder voice / self:
- How do you feel towards this individual? What's your relationship with them like?
- What is it like performing this role for this individual?

Underlying *feelings and concerns* of the eating disorder voice / self:
- What might happen if you didn't perform this role for this individual?
- What you want this individual to know or understand about yourself and your role?

Participant Background Information

Participant initials:...

Age:..

Self-described ethnicity:..

Eating disorder diagnosis:...

Self-reported length of illness:..

Current treatment (*type*): ....

Current treatment (*number of sessions*): - ....

Previous outpatient treatments (*number*):..

Previous outpatient treatments (*types*):..

Previous inpatient treatments (*number*):...

Implementing the DIS-ED

INTRODUCING THE DIS-ED

The DIS-ED begins with a brief introduction to the interview and its aims. Talking with internal voices and self-parts is not for everyone - engaging in the DIS-ED should always be consensual. Individuals are encouraged to discuss any questions or concerns about the approach before the interview begins.

Shall I begin by explaining the aims of this interview in a bit more detail?

Research suggests that many individuals experience an internal eating disorder voice. Other individuals describe experiencing not so much a voice, but rather a particular experience of the themselves linked to their eating disorder - what we might call their 'anorexic self' or 'anorexic part'. Internal voices and the experience of being made up of different selves, parts, or subpersonalities is very normal.

The aim of this interview is to simply get to know your 'eating disorder voice' or 'eating disorder self' better. We can do this by asking your eating disorder voice some questions. There are no right or wrong answers to these questions. I hope you will find this process of speaking with your eating disorder voice or self (EDV/S) very natural.

The interview is divided into three parts. First, I will ask you some very general questions about your experiences of your EDV/S. Afterwards, I will ask you to change seats and to speak from the perspective of your EDV/S. Last of all, I will ask you to return to your origin seat and reflect on what your EDV/S has said. I'll help guide you through this process.

Once we have completed the interview, we will take short break. After this, I would like to ask some very general questions about how you found the interview and the process of speaking with your EDV/S.

Do you have any questions?

Would you like to give it a try?

PHASE ONE - Exploring experiences of the EDV/S

The DIS-ED begins by exploring the individuals' general experiences of their EDV/S.

Would it be ok if we begin by talking a little about your EDV/S?

Example interview questions:
- Tell me about your experience of your EDV/S. What is it like?
- How does the EDV/S interact with you?
- When do you tend to experience the EDV/S?
- What do you think the EDV/S wants for you?

PHASE TWO - Dialogue with the EDV/S

Dialogue with the EDV/S involves the client speaking from the perspective of their EDV/S. Dialogues with the EDV/S can be either direct (inviting the individual to change seats and speak as their EDV/S) or indirect (inviting the client to convey, in the third person, what the EDV/S is saying).

> _DIRECT DIALOGUE with the EDV/S:_ If you feel ready, I'd like to speak with your EDV/S for a little while. All you have to do is change seats and speak as that part of your self. If at any time you want to stop, we can. Does that sound ok?

> _INDIRECT DIALOGUE with the EDV/S:_ I'd like to ask your EDV/S some questions. When I do, I'd like you to relay these questions to your EDV/S and to let me know how it responds. For example, I might ask you to say "hello" to the EDV/S on my behalf and to let me know what it says back.

Irrespective of whether dialogue is direct or indirect, the client is asked to place a chair representing the EDV/S somewhere in the room which feels appropriate and comfortable.

> Where would you like the chair for your EDV/S to be? [_Individual locates chair in the room_].

It can sometimes be helpful to check whether there is anything the individual would like to ask or explore with the EDV/S.

> Before we begin, is there anything particular you would like me to ask your EDV/S or things you'd like to know?

It is important that the interviewer communicates with the EDV/S in a manner which is respectful, curious, and non-confrontational. The EDV/S needs to feel secure and understood during dialogue. It can be helpful to think of the dialogue as being like getting to know an interesting stranger at a party.

> _DIRECT DIALOGUE with the EDV/S:_ I'd now like you to now change seats and to adopt the perspective of your EDV/s. [_Client changes seats_]. In this chair, I'd like you to speak as your EDV/S.

Sample interview questions for the EDV/S:

- So, [participant] is over here and you are his/her eating disorder voice.
- It's nice to meet you. What would you like me to call you?
- Tell me a bit about yourself. What's your role in this person's life? What do you do? (Function)
- What situations tend to bring you out? (Content)
  - How about when it comes to eating?
  - How about when it comes to the way this individual looks?
- What do you tend to say in situations like that? (Content)
- When did you first come into this person's life? Do you remember when you came to be? (Origins)
- What were your reasons for becoming a part of their life at that time? (Origins)
- Did you learn this role from anyone? Who do you take after? (Origins)
- What's it like playing this role for this person? Do you ever run into problems? (Relationship)
- How do you feel towards this person? How do you think this person feels towards you? (Relationship)
- Are you aware of any difficulties you might be causing this individual? (Relationship)
- Why do you do this for this person? (Intent)
- What do you want for this individual? (Intent)
- What's important to you? (Intent)
- What do you want for this individual? (Intent)
- What you think might happen if you weren't a part of this person's life? (Underlying feelings)
- What are you afraid of? (Underlying feelings)
  - What concerns / frustrates / saddens / makes you anxious? (Underlying feelings)
- What you think might happen if you weren't a part of this person's life? (Underlying feelings)
- If I could see you as you are, what would you look like? (Imagery)

The dialogue ends with the interviewer thanking the EDV/S for speaking and inviting it to share any parting words.

> Thank you for taking the time to speak with me today. It's been interesting getting to you know you better. Is there anything else that you would like to say or that I need to know before we draw this talk to a close?

PHASE THREE – Decentring from the EDV/S

The third phase of the DIS-ED invites the individual to 'step back' and observe the EDV/S from a new, decentred perspective (known as the 'witness state' in Voice Dialogue). The individual is first asked to return to their original chair and to separate from the EDV/S.

> I'd like you to return to your original chair now. As you best you can, leave your EDV/S in the empty seat and connect with your self again as you change chairs. [*Individual moves seats*].

Some individuals may need a little time to ground themselves when switching perspectives (e.g. stretching, attending to their breathing, walking around their chair, etc.).

> Let's take a moment to separate from your EDV/S by bringing attention to the breath. Find a rate of breathing that feels calm, soothing, and grounded. Focus on the experience of the air moving in and out of your body.

At this point, it is helpful to 'check-in' with the client and establish whether they have been able to separate from the EDV/S

> How are you feeling? Do you feel a little more separated from that side of your self?

Once the client has separated from the EDV/S, they are invited to stand beside the therapist, who then provides a summary of what this self has conveyed.

> Can you come and stand beside me? I'd now like to provide my understanding of what I have heard your EDV/S share with us…

Once a summary has been provided, the therapist draws attention to the decentred and observational nature of this new perspective.

> And now notice how, from this position, you can step back from the EDV/S and reflect upon it from more of a distance. [*Gestures to the empty chair*]. Witnessing what is happening between these parts of your self without needing to be involved.

The client then returns to their first chair.

PHASE FOUR - Reflecting on the dialogical process

The final part of the interview provides an opportunity to reflect on the dialogue and their impressions of the EDV/S.

Sample interview questions:

- What do you make of what the EDV/S has said?
- What do you make of the EDV/S intentions / what the EDV/S wants for you?
  - How does that fit with what you want for your self?
- Is there anything you would like the EDV/S to know or understand?
- Are there anything you want or need from the EDV/S?
- Is there anything you would like to say to the EDV/S?

Whilst the aim of this phase is not to facilitate a dialogue between the individual and their EDV/S, sometimes individuals will want to respond to their EDV/S directly. If statements seem to be directed at the EDV/S, rather than the interviewer, the individual can be invited to convey these to the empty chair ("Would you like to try saying that to your EDV/S?").

PHASE FIVE - Reflecting on the DIS-ED (*research purposes only*)

The participant is asked if they would like to take a break before discussing their experiences of engaging in the DIS-ED.

> You did a great job. Well done. Before we explore what your experience of talking with your EDV/S was like, would you like to take a break?

Wherever possible, the participant is encouraged to elaborate on their responses during the phase four interview (e.g. "Can you say more about that? Can you give me an example of that?").

Sample interview questions:

- How did you experience the interview? What stood out to you?
- What was it like to speak as your EDV/S?
- What was it like to respond to your EDV/S?
- How do you understand the EDV/S now? How do you feel towards it?
- How do you understand your eating difficulties after the interview?
- What was helpful or unhelpful about the interview we've had?
- What did you like or dislike about the process?
- What do you think you will take away from this experience?
- Overall, how would you describe your experience of this interview?

REFERENCES

Corstens, D., Longden, E., & May, R. (2012). Talking with voices: exploring what is expressed by the voices people hear. *Psychosis*, *4*, 95-104.

Emmerson, G. (2003). *Ego state therapy*. Carmarthen, UK: Crown House.

Moreno, J. L. (1987). *The essential Moreno: Writings on psychodrama, group method and spontaneity*. New York, NY: Springer.

Stone, H., & Stone, S. (1988). *Embracing our selves: The voice dialogue manual*. Novato, CA: Nataraj Publishing.

Appendix A.15: The role of anxiety in anorexia nervosa

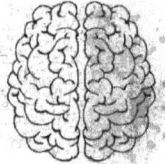

The role of anxiety
in anorexia nervosa

Anxiety underpins so much of what goes on in the eating disorders, making it important that you and your loved ones should understand it. That way, a lot of what your clinician is going to talk with you about will make sense, helping you to engage in cognitive behavioural therapy for your anorexia nervosa.

Remember that anxiety is not just central to your eating disorder, but it will also be central to a lot of other problems that you experience – social anxiety, obsessive-compulsive disorder, post-traumatic stress disorder, panic disorder, and more. So, learning how to address your anxiety in relation to anorexia nervosa can have many spin-off benefits when it comes to other problems that you might have.

Anxiety is a normal experience

Anxiety is a perfectly natural reaction to uncertain situations.

We all experience it. You will recognise it when you feel jittery (e.g., "My hands are shaking"), when you are not sure what is going to happen next (e.g., "Is that a friend at the door, or someone hostile", and when you try to work out how to manage the possibility of threat (e.g., "Should I run away or stand my ground?"). These reactions happen because we feel vulnerable to harm, which comes from a combination of our underlying traits (e.g., intolerance of uncertainty) plus our experiences of threats in the world.

Anxiety is about preparing for threats. When we are uncertain about what is going to happen, our body prepares so that we can either run away or face the thing that makes us afraid. So, when we are anxious, our bodies prepare for *fight or flight*.

So, your muscles tense, you feel sweaty, you look around you for threats, your heart races, etc. to make it possible to run away or fight back, according to the situation. Now that is useful when there is a <u>real</u> threat (e.g., if you encounter a big bear while out for a walk, then running away is an extremely good idea), but most of what we respond to is <u>perceived</u> threats that in reality will not do us any harm (e.g., however scared you might be of spiders, they are not normally in a position to harm you).

Anxiety and anorexia nervosa

Most importantly, if you have anorexia nervosa then you will likely be afraid of gaining weight in an uncontrollable way – of becoming huge, feeling your body growing and not having any control over the situation. In therapy, we will be testing out these anxious predictions so that you can understand how your body really works.

Overcoming anxiety in anorexia nervosa

So how do we get rid of anxiety? There are four ways – two of them take time but are good for you, while two of them are short-term but make things worse for you. Let's start with the positive, time-consuming ones:

1. Developing self-efficacy and a sense of safety
If we grow up in an unthreatening environment, we can still feel threatened/scared in the moment if something new comes into life (e.g., a scary moment in a movie), but we know that we are generally safe (e.g., we have seen many such moments, and they have never had bad outcomes for us), and the fear fades quickly. This is why most people are not concerned about eating a cupcake, for example, as they know it won't harm them.

The role of anxiety
in anorexia nervosa

2. Learning from exposure to the feared object
Exposure is a process whereby we spend time allowing the anxiety to fade, even after something that is objectively scary (e.g., we meet a dog who barks at us, and the dog takes a time to calm down and to be friendly). However, when we have sat with our anxiety for about 30-40 minutes, we learn that our anxiety subsides (due to biological changes). That way, we learn that anxiety is only a temporary state if we let it happen without trying to stop it. This is why we might worry if we will put on weight if we eat a cupcake, but if we eat that cupcake and sit with our anxiety until it fades, then we'll have no problem eating future cupcakes.

And now, the unproductive, impairing ways that we sometimes respond to anxiety (and which are so common in anorexia nervosa):

3. Blocking
When we experience anxiety, we can block it out by trying not to think about it. So, if a scary moment comes along, we run away from it straight away. That means that we feel anxious for a very short time, but because we run away from it, we feel calmer straight away. However, we then do not learn that the apparent threat was not real (e.g., someone who fears spiders might run away every time that they see one, but that means that they never learn that the anxiety fades anyway, through that exposure process). This pattern (behave in a way that gives short-term relief but that has long-term negative consequences) is called a *safety behaviour*. This is why we might eat a cupcake and then immediately make ourselves sick to deal with the panic of potentially putting on weight. And it means that we never learn that cakes do not make us gain huge amounts of weight.

4. Avoidance
Finally, we might try to avoid ever being in a threatening situation so that we do not feel threatened (e.g., constantly cleaning the house for fear of catching something that will make us ill). Again, as with safety behaviours, this will make us calmer in the moment, but more anxious over time, so that we must work even harder to avoid future risk of contamination. With anorexia nervosa, we see a pattern of efforts at avoidance of anything that is seen as a risk. That can involve restricting food intake to avoid any risk of gaining weight or exercising compulsively to avoid any risk of gaining weight.

What you need to know

What you and your loved ones need to know is that the avoidance and safety behaviours of anorexia nervosa will make you feel better in the short term. However, in the longer term, they will make you more and more scared of food and emotions.

That is why your clinician will be working with you to help you move away from avoidance and safety behaviours using exposure therapy (see number 2, above) so that you can learn that your anxiety will go down without using those unhelpful ways of coping.

It is time to face your fears, tolerate your uncertainty, and give yourself a chance at that better life.

Appendix A.16: Behavioural experiment record

Behavioural experiment record

Belief to be tested (Rate belief 0-100%)			
Experiment: What will I do to test the belief? When?			
Prediction: What exactly do I think will happen? How will I know whether it has happened or not? (Rate belief 0-100%)			
Alternative prediction: What else might happen? What have I got to gain? (Rate belief 0-100%)			
Outcome: What actually happened? Was the original prediction correct?			
Re-rate cognition: On balance, what is my view now? How do I rate the beliefs above in light of the experiment?			
Plan: What can I do now to further test the belief?			

Appendix A.17: Information sheet for carers

Information for carers
CBT-AN-20

What is CBT-AN-20?

CBT-AN-20 (Cognitive behavioural therapy for anorexia nervosa – 20 sessions) is a psychological therapy developed especially for anorexia nervosa. It has an early emphasis on getting started on the restoration of normal eating and healthy weight, as these are vital for recovery. Additionally, CBT-AN-20 helps your loved one to get a clearer understanding of anorexia nervosa and how it works for them. They will receive help to: build motivation to change (and keep going); improve their body image; manage difficult thoughts and feelings; and plan for a future free of the eating disorder.

Of course, both anorexia nervosa and recovery via therapy inevitably impact on you – the family and loved ones. This information sheet provides a few suggestions that you and your loved one might wish to consider and talk through together, to work out together how you can offer good support.

How can you help?

First, know that your loved one is lucky to have you. Not everybody has someone to share their recovery journey with, so they are already off to a good start with you on their side.

Everybody is different regarding the level and type of support they might want or manage, so it's probably best to try to discuss things with them now (and with their clinician, if your loved one decides to invite you to a session), and to keep checking in as things progress.

Support needs will change over time, so working out when to be proactive and when to step back is key.

Shopping, meal planning and preparation

Planning the timings and the content of three meals and two or three snacks each day is covered within CBT-20-AN from early on. If you have typically shopped and prepared meals for your loved one, please keep on doing this! Ask your loved one (or their clinician, if you are invited to a session) what changes you might make to ensure they are getting enough energy from any meals or snacks you prepare. The REAL Food Guide on the CBT-AN-20 website is likely to be what your loved one is using, so do look at that - it might give you some good ideas that you can share with your loved one.

In contrast, if your loved one has typically shopped for and prepared their own meals, this could be a good time to offer help as they learn new skills. Many people are surprised just how much food someone really needs to get to a healthy weight if they are malnourished.

Meal support

If you live with or regularly eat with your loved one, then you have probably noticed that mealtimes can be tense. Aiming to keep mealtimes calm and offering lighthearted conversation about things other than food is usually helpful. You could ask your loved one now if they would want you to acknowledge their struggle and efforts when you notice them.

CBT-AN-20 is different from other therapies for anorexia nervosa that you might have heard about, such as family-based treatment (FBT). While FBT is considered the first-line approach for young people with anorexia nervosa, it is not the right fit for all patients. FBT was not designed for adults, and the evidence shows that individual treatment can be equally helpful if the young person chooses it.

The key difference between FBT and CBT-AN-20 is that in CBT-AN-20, your loved one will be taking personal ownership of the changes in their eating. *In CBT-AN-20, your role is to support your loved one in learning to eat to increase their own self-efficacy (e.g., to increase the portions they eat), rather than to take charge of their eating yourself.*

Information for carers
CBT-AN-20

Food talk

It can sometimes feel like everyone's talking about dieting, which can heighten feelings of guilt for people working on recovery from anorexia nervosa. You can help with this by stepping away from diet culture, modelling a flexible attitude towards food (e.g., resisting the convention to label foods as good vs bad; healthy vs unhealthy; or as transgressions to be made up for). Reviewing and updating what social and other media you consume yourself might help with this.

Body talk

Restoration of a healthy body weight is crucial to recovery from anorexia nervosa. Your loved one might find this difficult at times. It might have been necessary to have expressed your concern about weight loss before your loved one asked for help. Now that they are working actively on restoring weight, conversations about weight are probably best kept to a minimum. If your loved one initiates conversations about weight, we recommend keeping the tone neutral (i.e., avoiding value judgements of 'good' vs 'bad' body sizes).

Reassurance

When we face anxiety-provoking changes, it is quite normal to want reassurance from those around us. However, the paradox of reassurance is that when it becomes repetitive it can actually end up fueling anxiety and keep people trapped in a never-ending cycle of anxiety and reassurance-seeking. If you notice this happening to your loved one, a more helpful alternative might be to show recognition of the painful feelings and trying to help in a different way.

What else might help can be very personal - you and your loved one might know what works for them, or this may be an opportunity to find out. Some people like hugs (and others hate them!). Or perhaps engaging in shared activity together (a puzzle, music, tv, connecting with nature or animals) might be you and your loved one's own joint way of taking the heat out of difficult feelings.

Don't lose sight of the person outside of anorexia nervosa

Recovery from anorexia nervosa is like a full-time job, and much of your support might center around the eating aspect of this. However, recovery from anorexia nervosa can also involve navigating independence, relationships, and identity. You have an important role to play in supporting or allowing your loved one sufficient space, trust, and respect to develop these import aspects of life outside of the eating disorder.

Managing painful feelings

It's that old cliché about having to put on your own oxygen mask before tending to the person next to you. We can all pick up on the feelings of those around us, and people with anorexia nervosa are sometimes particularly apt at this. When you respond from a place of relative calm, you'll be more able to help your loved one. Try tuning in, noticing any tension within your own body or breath and take a moment to release it, while aiming for your exhale to be a little longer than your inhale. It is hard to take in much verbal information when panicking, so keep things simple. Hold in mind that what you express through the feelings in your own body, flagged by your posture, tone and rate of communication, is important too.

Looking after yourself

Supporting a loved one in recovery from anorexia nervosa can be emotionally taxing. It can be terrifying to recognise the seriousness of your loved one's condition, and you might feel powerless to help. None of us are perfect, and sometimes it's hard to know whether you're getting it 'right' or 'wrong'. Don't lose sight of your own needs for support and understanding during this process. If your loved one is under the care of an eating disorder service, ask what carers' support they offer. You could otherwise look out for support groups in your local area or online. You might even wish to seek out your own therapy, too. The ideas on this website may be helpful: https://eatingdisorders.org.au/for-family-and-friends/living-with-someone-with-an-eating-disorder/

Appendix A18: Advantages of change, fears of change, and responses to fears

Think about the advantages of change – what makes you want to get better? Also think about any fears that might get in the way of you making the changes you want to make and how you might respond to these fears so that they don't get in the way of you moving forward in your recovery.

Advantages of Change	Fears of Change	Responses to Fears

Putting it all together: Summary statement I can use to help myself move forward in overcoming the eating disorder when times get tough:

Used with permission and based on the worksheet first presented in Cooper, M., Todd, G. & Wells, A. (2001). Bulimia Nervosa: A Cognitive Therapy Programme for Clients. London: Jessica Kingsley Publishers.

Appendix A.19: Therapy checklist

Therapist Checklist of Key Tasks across CBT-AN-20

Tick the tasks that you have addressed during each session and leave blank where you have not done the relevant task. The grey areas indicate times when it would not normally be used, but if it is relevant to the individual case then mark it there regardless. Discuss regularly in supervision/consultation, to monitor adherence.

Session	Assess	1	2	3	4	5	6	7	8	9	10	11	12	13	14	15	16	17	18	19	20	FU1	FU2	FU3
Across CBT-AN-20																								
Risk monitoring and actioning																								
Working with significant others																								
Progress monitoring (ED-15)																								
Outcome monitoring (EDE-Q7 pack)																								
Open weighing																								
Review of food logs/dietary intake																								
Agree planned changes to dietary intake																								
Starting therapy (Phase 1)																								
Engagement and motivation																								
Psychoeducation																								
Formulation																								
Working with the anorexic voice																								
Considering traits and thinking styles																								
Early treatment review																								
Review early engagement/progress																								
Working with barriers to change																								
Short augmentations																								
Disability training/honest conversations																								
Behavioural experiments (Phase 2)																								
Learning weight maintenance																								
Building food flexibility and confidence																								
Emotional/Interpersonal issues (Phase 3)																								
Working with schema level core beliefs																								
Working with emotions																								
Working through interpersonal issues																								
Working with attributional styles																								
Body image (Phase 4)																								
Psychoeducation/Body neutrality																								
Imagery rescripting																								
Surveys																								
Checking /Comparison																								
Mirror exposure																								
Ending and relapse prevention (Phase 5)																								
Therapy blueprint																								
Developing relapse plan																								
Building life beyond anorexia nervosa																								

Further explanation of terms and phases

Core skills: monitor and respond to changes in risk, collaboratively monitor engagement and progress, working to engage patients through adopting a therapeutic stance of hope, collaboration and curiosity, combining firmness and empathy in a way that promotes active engagement and recovery. Draw on the support of significant others as appropriate throughout treatment.

Starting therapy (phase 1): prioritize weight regain where necessary, balancing the need for progress with the need to explore ambivalence. Routinely review weight re-gain targets and eating plan, moving from weight regain to maintenance when the patient is at an agreed healthy weight level. Working with the anorexic voice and temperament/thinking styles such as intolerance of uncertainty, harm avoidance, overly detailed thinking styles, self-criticism and perfectionism to maximise understanding and engagement

Early treatment review: reinforce positives of change and if needed, work with barriers to change using motivational approaches such as increased focus on working with the anorexic voice and/or disability training. It may also include a short therapy augmentation that addresses a specific barrier to change, such as perfectionism (see Single Session Interventions) and/or increasing support from significant others. This stage may also involve safe planning of disengagement and next steps if appropriate.

Introducing new/feared foods (phase 2): encourage patients to do things differently/experiment with change, including facing feared situations (e.g., eating different differently, eating with others, not weighing themselves between sessions) and helping them to understand and learn from their experience. Building food flexibility and confidence.

Emotional and interpersonal issues: working with compulsive and impulsive behaviours, schema level core beliefs and emotional states, pro and counter schematic behaviours, and information processing and attributional styles. All aimed towards promoting a more balanced sense of self and healthier emotional and interpersonal functioning.

Body Image: working to reduce negative critical self-talk and encouraging body acceptance and/or body neutrality. Include psychoeducation (e.g., origins of body image concerns; perceptual distortions; impact of social media; body composition; role of emotional arousal; scheme for self-evaluation). Methods may also include behavioural experiments and strategic changes to behaviours, relabelling of feeling fat, and/or working with values and enhancing the importance of other domains for self-evaluation.

Ending and relapse prevention: including recognition of ending and patient becoming their own therapist, building self-efficacy; gradual handover of responsibility; normalising of slips and developing plan of how to get back on track; developing collaborative relapse prevention plan (including identifying early warning signs and possible future triggers for setbacks, as well as areas for the patient to continue to work on, taking a short- and long-term perspective).

Appendix A.20: Information for patients on the nature and requirements of CBT-AN-20

What does CBT-AN-20 offer?
What does it require of you?

A healthy body supports us to be at our best. Cognitive behavioural therapy for anorexia nervosa – 20 sessions (CBT-AN-20) is a psychological therapy developed especially for anorexia nervosa. While comparable in length to some other forms of recommended treatment, it is shorter than previous forms of CBT for anorexia nervosa.

Does CBT-AN-20 work?

Evidence to date says that CBT-AN-20 is as effective as other therapies and those completing treatment tend to report finding it both hard and worthwhile. We want to support you to make the most of therapy and feel the benefits of recovery as soon as possible.

What does CBT-AN-20 look like?

If you have anorexia nervosa, then you may be aware of some of the ways in which it changes how you feel and think, what you do, and how you are around other people. The emotional, psychological, social and physical factors are caused and maintained by a wide range of potential problems, but starvation is a critical element that you will need to address in treatment. So, eating enough to return to a healthy (for you) weight is going to be vital. All effective treatments for anorexia nervosa involve changing eating and working on controllable weight regain.

Evidence tells is that one of the best predictors of how much you're likely to benefit from treatment relates to how much you actively engage in change over the first few sessions. Given this we always review how treatment is going after about 6 sessions – this gives us an opportunity to review how you're finding therapy and whether it's helpful to continue. It's important that you work on making changes to your eating and weight from the beginning of therapy to give yourself the best change of benefitting from this treatment.

Phases of CBT-AN-20

This therapy comes in several overlapping phases and the length of each of these can be adjusted to suit your needs. These are the things you can expect to work on during the weeks ahead:

Staying safe. Given the physical and emotional effects of starvation, your therapist will always be keeping an eye out for your safety. Your responsibilities include being weighed and knowing your weight trend; having medical tests; talking about your mood. This helps ensure it is safe to continue with therapy. Your therapist might sometimes seem firm - that is always with your best interests at heart.

Monitoring change. As well as monitoring your weight, your therapist will also want to know how you are progressing in other ways – your mood, eating concerns, and behaviours. This is so that you and your therapist can be sure that therapy is helping.

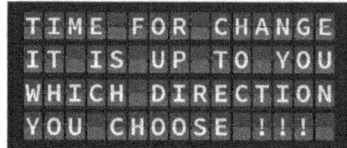

TIME FOR CHANGE
IT IS UP TO YOU
WHICH DIRECTION
YOU CHOOSE !!!

Understanding your individual journey. Early on in therapy, we will work with you on a personalised formulation – this is a map of the factors that drew you into anorexia nervosa, and that keep you stuck. This is needed so we can agree on the goals and approaches to change that are most suited to you.

What does CBT-AN-20 offer?
What does it require of you?

Working with factors that make you less motivated to change. Of course, if it were easy to let go of your eating disorder then you would have done that a long time ago. We often need to consider the factors that keep you holding onto your anorexia nervosa, despite all the ways in which it is having a negative impact on your life. Many people with anorexia nervosa talk about experiencing an 'anorexic voice', a part within themselves that starts out as a friend, but overtime becomes more of a bully, making it difficult to let go of restrictive eating – working with the 'anorexic voice' might be an important focus for treatment.

Psychoeducation/Handouts. An important part of helping you to move on from your eating disorder is to develop a good understanding of the nature and consequences of your eating disorder. It is hard to take the steps towards change if you do not understand why you developed anorexia nervosa and what keeps it going. It's also important to be able to see a way out. During treatment you will be given a range of handouts that will help you to understand the biology and psychology of anorexia nervosa. Taking time between sessions to read these is an important part of therapy. Your therapist will also work with you to help you get the most from these resources.

Changing your eating and working on getting your weight to a level that works for you. This is a part of therapy that you might find most scary and difficult. The fear that if you eat normally then you will lose control of your life, and that you will gain weight uncontrollably can make this part of treatment feel overwhelming. But changing your eating and regaining weight is a critical part of recovery and therapy will help you to learn that weight regain is not uncontrollable. Rather, it is a long, slow slog, that takes time and effort. And when you get to a healthy level, your therapist will switch to working with you to keep your weight stable.

Working with psychological and emotional issues. These are always important issues underlying an eating disorder and whilst some of these will resolve as you improve your eating, your therapist will be able to support you in understanding and working through your personal experiences and how they have influenced your thinking and feelings.

Working with your body image. Negative body image is something that nearly everyone with an eating disorder can relate to, and it will be important to work on the factors that affect your own individual experience of your body. The aim is to leave you able to appreciate your body, so that you are not constrained by how you see yourself. This is mostly later in therapy, so that your starvation and associated problems are reduced, allowing you to benefit from body image work.

Planning for a future without anorexia nervosa. Once you are free of your eating disorder, there is a whole future ahead of you – a future that you might have lost sight of. So, it is important that we focus on helping you to get back on track with the life you want to live.

Recovering from anorexia nervosa is undoubtedly hard work, but your therapist is here to help you. Those that have completed this treatment tell us that the effort is totally worth it for the prize of getting your life back.

Appendix A.21: Importance of carbohydrates

Why Carbohydrates
Matter in your recovery

When undertaking CBT-AN-20, you will notice that your therapist emphasises from the start a balanced diet (see handouts on Starvation Effects and the REAL Food Guide) to help you regain and maintain a healthy weight. A key part of healthy food intake is an adequate intake of carbohydrates.

There is a strong chance that you have heard carbohydrates being described as terrible for you, and that you fear eating them as a result. This might have come from hearing others talk about their dieting history, from online influencers, from faddy diets and many other places. Your brain might be telling you: "I don't need carbohydrates; I can do without them. They will just make me gain lots of weight". **Here are the facts.**

Brain and Body

Every part of your body needs carbohydrates continuously, to maintain basic processes (e.g., circulation; mobility), to support biological stability (e.g., bone growth), and to ensure that your brain functions and develops (see the Growth Mindset handout). Carbohydrates are also essential for balancing your mood, enabling you to feel happy and sociable. So, when you follow the rule, "Try to avoid carbohydrates", your capacity for thinking, your emotions, your relationships and your body all suffer.

The anorexia nervosa will argue that you can and should do without carbohydrates. Unfortunately, this is where things start to go wrong, because your body will disagree with that conclusion. And when anorexia and body argue you will be the one to suffer.

The upshot is that avoiding carbohydrates means that you are at risk of running out of energy, and that puts you at risk of overeating. Your body has a process called 'homeostasis', where it will try to restore your body to a healthy balance in vital nutrients – including carbohydrates. When you do not go along with that process, your body will get more desperate. You will start feeling the need for food, and the urge to eat will get stronger and stronger. This is human biology, and you cannot escape it.

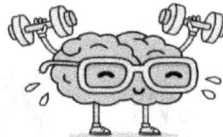

A simple way of looking at this is to imagine that your body is like a car. What would happen if you did not supply that car with petrol/gas or electricity? It would run down and would not work unless you topped up its fuel level. And then you would have to top up your supplies substantially.

In the case of binge eating, another way to understand that drive to eat carbohydrates is to imagine holding your breath under water for as long as you can. Over time the need for oxygen becomes stronger and stronger. When you finally bring your head out of the water you don't breathe normally at first, but rapidly gasp for air, as your body desperately strives to survive.

This is why the REAL Food Guide stresses carbohydrates as part of a balanced, healthy diet – because your body and brain need carbohydrates, whatever your social media or fad diet books might be telling you.

Why Carbohydrates
Matter in your recovery

How do I get back to eating in a balanced way?

First, understand that this will likely be scary at first – until you get used to it and the anxiety fades, then adding carbohydrates won't make you worry that you are going to eat and gain weight uncontrollably.

But it is important to remember that there will be positives too – people who add to their carbohydrate intake in this way soon find that they are happier, have more energy, can think straight, and socialise better.

Your body is using carbohydrates all the time – even when you are asleep. Your body takes a few hours to digest complex carbohydrates. So, you need to top up those complex carbohydrates every few hours by eating appropriate foods as part of your diet (e.g., bread, potatoes, pasta, rice, other grains). As you will see from the REAL Food Guide, it is recommended that eating three meals per day plus snacks is the best way for most people to get what their body needs. Each of those meals and snacks needs to contain carbohydrates to keep your fuel levels good. As a slow-burning fuel, the carbohydrates in starchy foods (e.g., bread, potato) are more effective than carbohydrates from fibre (e.g., vegetables), but both are better than simple sugars.

Of course, other foodstuffs are part of a balanced healthy diet – fruit, vegetables, fats, protein, and more. But the stress must be on 'balanced' and 'healthy', which means that trying to skip the complex carbohydrates will mean that your body will fight back, either shutting down systems (e.g., growth, concentration, hormones) or pushing you to eat in an uncontrolled way.

What if I decide that I can do without carbohydrates regardless?

First, be aware that this will likely be scary at first, but as you get used to it your anxiety will fade. It's not uncommon to worry that eating carbohydrates will lead to uncontrollable weight gain, but over time you'll be able to see that carbohydrates are not the danger that you fear. And you will begin to see the positives too...

The difficult reality is that you stay locked in the battle between the anorexia and your body, and you continue to suffer from all those starvation effects – health, cognitive, emotional, physical, and quality of life. Unfortunately, this is the difficult and often grim reality of your body's responses when your brain tries to do the impossible.

Just remember – your body has evolved over millennia to use and benefit from carbohydrates. No social media message or influencer telling your brain that you do not need carbohydrates is going to convince your body otherwise.

Appendix A.22: Blank energy graphs (x 8)

Blank energy graphs for you to complete over the coming week

This first graph is to remind you – when you are eating in a healthy way, the carbohydrates that you are eating will mean that your body remains in the 'comfort zone' throughout the day, as shown here.

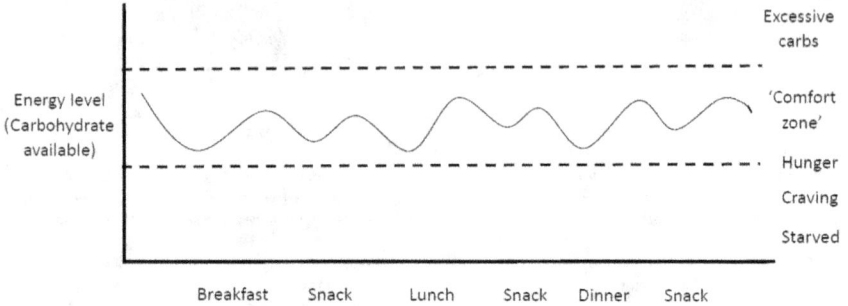

Please try to keep your carbohydrate levels in that comfort zone, by eating carbohydrates in that same sort of pattern (three meals, three snacks, with gaps of about two-three hours). The REAL Food Guide will help you to learn how to do that until it becomes routine for you. Keep the energy graph updated as the day goes by.

Day 1

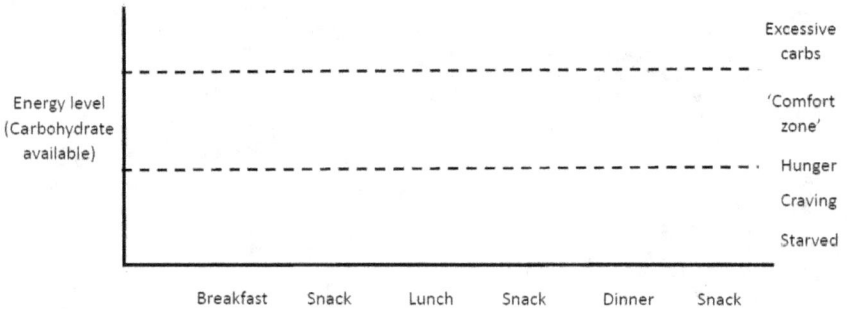

Day 2

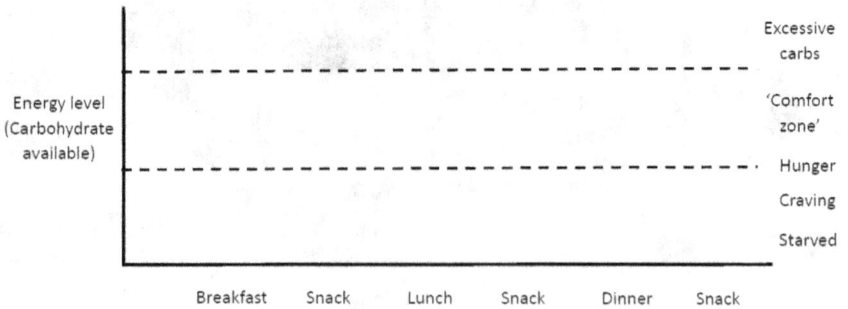

Day 3

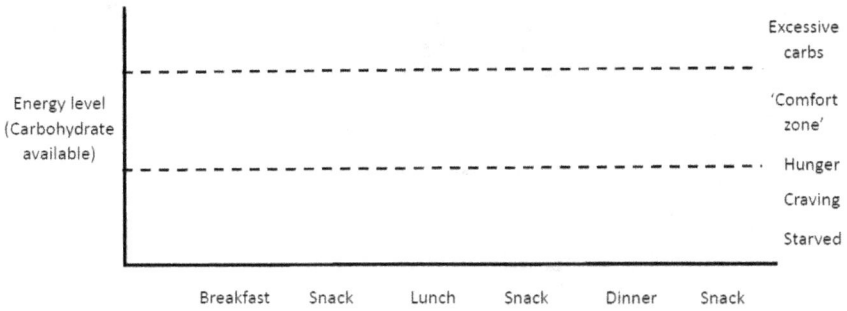

Energy level (Carbohydrate available)

Excessive carbs

'Comfort zone'

Hunger

Craving

Starved

Breakfast   Snack   Lunch   Snack   Dinner   Snack

Day 4

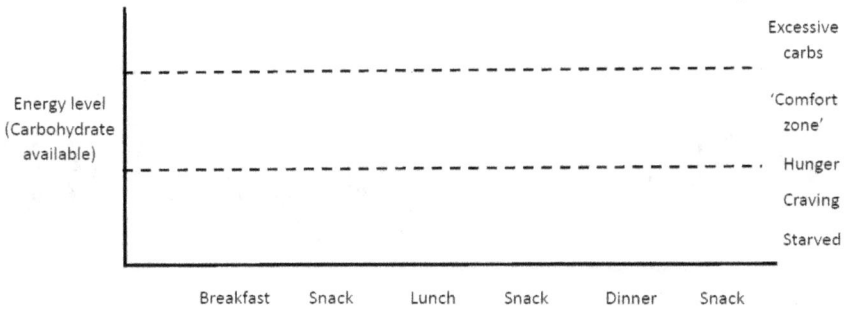

Energy level (Carbohydrate available)

Excessive carbs

'Comfort zone'

Hunger

Craving

Starved

Breakfast   Snack   Lunch   Snack   Dinner   Snack

Day 5

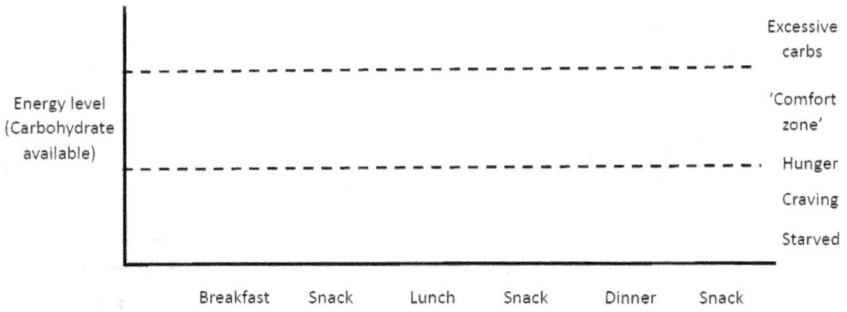

Energy level (Carbohydrate available)

Excessive carbs

'Comfort zone'

Hunger

Craving

Starved

Breakfast   Snack   Lunch   Snack   Dinner   Snack

Day 6

Day 7

Day 8

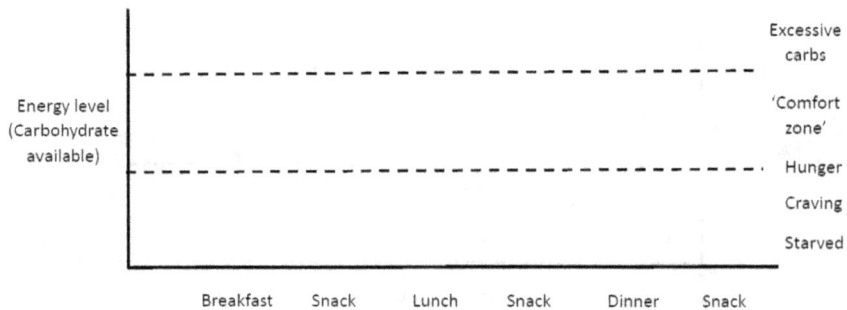

Appendix A.23: Quick strategies for emotion regulation

Emotion regulation
Quick strategies

Managing distress safely

Sometimes feelings can seem unbearable: this can be for several reasons. Some of us seem to have a genetic predisposition to experiencing feelings strongly. Some of us may have had past experiences where we have learned that certain feelings (or even feelings in general) are not safe or acceptable. And for some of us, a feeling in the present might activate an unresolved hurt from the past. Additionally, under-eating (particularly skipping the carbohydrates) and irregular eating patterns can also sometimes contribute to and be part of a wider pattern of dysregulation (a perceived inability to manage our emotional states).

Disruption to eating also impacts digestion, sleeping, and feelings. CBT-20-AN will help you to regulate the eating part of the picture, as well as working directly on any emotional distress that you experience for other reasons. Your digestion should improve because of this emotional stability. Building in scheduled and regular eating sometimes prompts consideration of your wider schedule, including sleep. Your emotional state might also become more manageable as a direct result of changes to your eating.

Emotional health involves being able to notice, differentiate between, and respond accordingly to our inner emotional worlds. When emotions feel overwhelming, unbearable, or almost impossible to safely survive, it can be helpful to ask two questions. First, how much of this feeling do you want to keep? Second, how can you safely get through this?

How much of this feeling do I want to keep?

Feelings convey important messages to us. We tend to have big feelings about things that matter to us. Sometimes though, and particularly in moments of panic, rage, or when feeling overwhelmed, it can be difficult to think clearly, to know exactly what that is bothering us, and to identify what we really need to do.

Surviving strong feelings is not about banishing them. Sometimes offering recognition to the hurting part of you can help - notice the emotional pain and plan to return to think things through once you've had the chance for things to sufficiently cool down. What important message is the emotion telling you?

How can I safely get through this?

Our body and mind have two complementary systems that help us to respond to perceived threats, and to manage a sustainable level of alertness. Our **sympathetic nervous system** becomes activated when we are feeling stressed - but our bodies cannot sustain this state for long. Our **parasympathetic nervous system** helps by slowing down our heart rate, resuming normal breathing, and restoring a relative sense of calm.

If you're someone who has previously used eating disorder behaviours or other potentially harmful ways of managing strong feelings, it might feel like anything else is a poor substitute. Please try to hold in mind that the aim here is not to eliminate the feeling, but to build curiosity in finding out what it takes to support your parasympathetic nervous system to kick in, so that it can lessen your distress and help it to become more bearable.

Emotion regulation
Quick strategies

Everyone is different in terms of what works for them, and some approaches might be better than others depending on the situation. We suggest a few ideas that you might choose to experiment with.

Breathing

Breathing in for 4 seconds, and out for 8 seconds – tracking your breathing by up tracing your index finger up and down your fingers on the other hand can help to stay focused.

Cold Temperature

Putting your hands in ice or cold water or taking a cold shower.

Relaxing your muscles

Tensing your muscles while breathing in and then relaxing while breathing out.

Music

Playing music that matches your current mood, or a preferable one (and if you want to sing or dance, go for it!).

Expressive Methods

Drawing, painting, writing, or creating in your own personal way – experiment with different levels of precision, messiness, and materials.

Gentle Movement

If you feel safe to go outside, moving around might help. Barefoot walking (if you have suitable weather and ground) can also be worth a try.

Connecting with Others

Calling loved ones or a helpline, contact with animals, nature, faith, and community might help, whether in person, online, or using pictures or mental imagery.

Self-soothe Box

Once you've got an idea of what sort of thing works for you, you might like to make a self-soothe box, this typically involves decorating an old shoe box and filling it with helpful items (e.g., pens, paper, other creative materials, sensory items), pictures and written prompts.

Roadblocks

Sometimes not liking yourself and feeling the need to punish yourself might get in the way of taking a pro-active approach to managing feelings safely. You might sometimes feel as if you need to suffer. This can create a negative cycle, leading you to associate harmful ways of coping with distress, and making you feel unconfident in your ability to manage. We urge you to give some of the above strategies a go and keep practicing them so that they become more automatic over time.

Please do discuss this work with your therapist, especially if you find it to be hard.

Appendix A.24: Emotional and interpersonal problems in anorexia nervosa

Emotional and Interpersonal
Problems in anorexia nervosa

Anorexia nervosa involves issues with eating and weight - problems that must be addressed to support physical safety. However, emotional and interpersonal problems often play a big role in anorexia nervosa too.

Emotional and interpersonal issues can change over the course of treatment

Early in treatment, emotional and interpersonal issues may center around topics such as low weight and how people react to the person's anorexia nervosa. For example, distress at weight restoration or disputes about mealtimes. However, there are sometimes other emotional and interpersonal problems related to anorexia nervosa.

Later in treatment, when weight has been fully or partially regained, other emotional and interpersonal issues may emerge. As you or your loved one become biologically stable and physically healthier, it is important to consider emotional and interpersonal issues. Often, emotional and interpersonal reactions will be positive. However, that is not always the case.

Emotional and interpersonal issues can change over the course of treatment

Sometimes, as the effects of restriction decrease, individual temperament begins to emerge and may need to be considered to leave anorexia nervosa behind. For example, some people might use the restriction and driven exercise elements of anorexia nervosa to avoid emotional experience, family interaction style, or social environment.

Restriction and driven exercise are relatively 'compulsive' behaviours, serving the function of preventing the feeling of emotions in the first place (in contrast to more 'impulsive' behaviours, such as binge-eating or vomiting, which block those emotions once already feeling them). That compulsivity can be linked to temperament – particularly for people who experience a lot of perfectionist traits.

Some examples:

a) The person who has always worried what others think of them might have been restricting their food intake to try to look acceptable in others' eyes: for fear of being judged negatively by other people. Here, we are looking at social anxiety, which might re-emerge when they are no longer restricting.

Their therapist might plan to work on 'social anxiety' with them, so that they are less concerned about what other people are thinking, and less likely to go back to restricting.

b) Someone whose childhood involved being teased might use exercise to avoid experiencing the shame of believing that they are unacceptable, and that others are judging them by their appearance or personality. They might feel that they can only cope with that shame by constantly working to be as thin and toned as possible.

Here, their therapist might work with them on being fair to themself and on their assumption that they were responsible for such shameful experiences, along with considering ways of reducing that shame so that they are able to exercise for health and fun, rather than compulsively.

c) The person who experienced a lot of criticism from their family in childhood or was shamed when expressing negative emotions might routinely self-criticise and suppress negative emotions. So, even when they have improved their eating and lowered their exercise, they become 'stuck', finding that no matter what they do, they still feel like a failure, and may be ashamed of or unsure of how to manage their negative emotions.

Their therapist might work with them on their childhood experiences, helping to re-evaluate beliefs about why family may have been so critical or intolerant of negative emotions (e.g., maybe it was not a reflection on the person's innate value, but about the family expectations or the circumstances that they were living in at the time).

Emotional and Interpersonal Problems in anorexia nervosa

What do I need to know to support the emotional focus of my therapy?

Emotions are perfectly normal, whether we see them as positive or negative. They are best seen as motivators (e.g., "If I am lonely, then why not message someone and meet up?"). Such feelings can arise from our interpersonal experiences in the past and be triggered by our interpersonal issues in the here and now. The negative emotions (e.g., shame, anger, anxiety, low mood, guilt) are more likely to be linked to your anorexia nervosa, as they are harder to face, leading you to avoid focusing on them (e.g., by restricting or exercising).

Your therapist is likely to want to help you to:

○ Understand where your negative emotions came from. While an individual's traits are relevant (e.g., tendency to be anxious), the most common theme in the origin of struggling with negative emotions is one of growing up in an environment (e.g., family, friends, school) where the expression of emotions was discouraged. It can be helpful to work with your therapist to understand your emotional experiences when you were younger.

○ Identify your current emotions and how they relate to your anorexia nervosa behaviours. For example, you might discuss keeping a diary to help you to understand why you did or did not eat at a particular time (e.g., was it related to how you felt about how other people were treating you at the time?). Learning how to understand your behaviours will help you to make critical decisions in the moment about whether you respond to your emotions using restriction/exercise or whether you challenge this urge, using healthier ways of responding instead.

○ Evaluate your beliefs about yourself and other people. For example, your therapist might help you to consider your understanding of who was responsible for your past negative experiences – considering whether it is necessary or helpful to be blaming yourself. For example, perhaps criticism of your weight was something that school bullies did to lots of people or was reflective of other ways in which you were disadvantaged which were not your fault. This new understanding will help you manage your emotional reactions in the future so that they do not result in negative consequences for you.

Thinking about your experiences and your feelings with your therapist might feel scary – as if you are breaking a rule. But it can be helpful to learn that you can think and behave differently around your emotions. So, give it a try, and watch what a difference it can make to respond thoughtfully to your emotions and your relationships with other people in this way.

"It's impossible," said pride. "It's risky," said experience. "It's pointless," said reason. "Give it a try," said heart.

Appendix A.25: Core beliefs in anorexia nervosa

Core Beliefs
in anorexia nervosa

What is a core belief?

We all have different 'levels' of thinking and beliefs. Normally, these help us to make sense of the world by making assumptions that we do not have to spend too much time thinking about (e.g., "The world is a pretty safe place"). However, when considering eating disorders and other psychological problems, those beliefs are likely to have become more negative.

In cognitive-behaviour therapy, we commonly refer to three different levels, which interact and feed into each other:

- Negative automatic thoughts – surface level beliefs that we are aware of at the time, and which we can reflect on without much effort (e.g., "I am late for my train").
- Conditional beliefs/dysfunctional assumptions – 'if...then...' beliefs that we can access if we think about it (e.g., "If I am late to get to work, then my boss will shout at me because I will miss that important meeting")
- Core beliefs/unconditional beliefs – personality-level beliefs about who we are, which we can find hard to access because we just assume them to be true so not open to alternative interpretations (e.g., "I am a bad person").

The stronger the core belief, the more we look for supporting evidence, and the more that we interpret the world in ways that support our core belief. Thus, this cycle of beliefs can become self-perpetuating.

How do core beliefs show up in eating disorders?

If we translate that to eating disorders, the pattern of linked beliefs can look like this:

- Negative automatic thought – "I am so fat" (despite any evidence)
- Conditional belief – "If I am fat, then no one will love me"
- Core belief – "I am unlovable"

The 'unlovable' core belief makes us expect that we will be rejected by others for many different reasons, including because of our size. This can often lead us to misinterpret situations and can drive our attention to focus on anything that says we might be overweight.

A lot of treatment for anorexia nervosa is about addressing beliefs about size and weight. For example, you might assume that your weight is rising uncontrollably, but elements of therapy (e.g., weight maintenance experiments; weight charts) can help you to address those unconditional beliefs (e.g., showing you that your certainty about uncontrollable, rapid weight gain may not be correct).

Negative Core Beliefs

These are beliefs about us or those around us that are:
- Based on negative experiences over time (e.g., being criticised, being teased, being abandoned by others).
- Difficult to change (e.g., simply trying to be 'logical' does not overcome them).
- Become stronger over time, as we look for evidence that they are true and ignore evidence that they are not true.

They include central beliefs that drive our emotions and hence our compulsive behaviours. Those central beliefs reflect our negative experiences and expectations about the world, such as:
- Abandonment – "Others will not be there for me".
- Defectiveness – "I am worthless and cannot get away from that".
- Vulnerability – "I am weak and at heightened risk of being harmed".

Core Beliefs
In anorexia nervosa

- Mistrust – "I cannot trust other people to be supportive".
- Emotional deprivation – "No one will be there to care for me".
- Dependence – "I am not competent to look after my own needs".

However, we also have compensatory beliefs, which reflect how we cope with having those negative central beliefs, and which also drive our compulsive behaviours, such as:

- Perfectionism – "In order to avoid being seen as a failure, I must do everything to the best possible standard, rather than letting it be 'good enough' to do the job".
- Emotional inhibition – "I cannot let anyone see my emotions or even show that I have them, because I will get no support or even be criticised for them".
- Social isolation – "Because I cannot trust others to be around, I must avoid other people".
- Subjugation/self-sacrifice – "I have to make myself useful, in order to keep people interested in me, even if my own needs never get met".

> *At its root, perfectionism isn't really about a deep love of being meticulous. It's about fear. Fear of making a mistake. Fear of disappointing others. Fear of failure. Fear of success.*
> Attributed to Michael Law

Core beliefs and emotion-driven behaviours in anorexia nervosa

Core beliefs are about more than size and weight in anorexia nervosa – they are also about emotions and how your emotions can trigger you into behaviours like restricting your intake, making yourself sick, or exercising compulsively.

Given the nature of the core beliefs, this can be an unconscious process. For example:

- Something in the world triggers your central belief (say, Abandonment is triggered by someone cancelling a social get-together).
- In turn, that core belief triggers an emotion (e.g., Anger).
- Add in that compensatory belief (Emotional Inhibition), and your avoidant behavioural reaction is to stay away from people completely or deny that you feel hurt.

The same applies to core beliefs that support avoidance behaviour related to the anorexia nervosa. For example:

- You get a mark that is lower than you expected in an exam, triggering a Defectiveness central belief.
- That makes you feel Ashamed.
- Your Emotional Inhibition compensatory belief makes you fearful of experiencing that shame.
- Your avoidant behavioural reaction is to exercise strongly whenever you can, to avoid that emotion.

Over therapy you will be identifying and examining your core beliefs and seeing which have played a role in maintaining your anorexia nervosa. It may be that some of these core beliefs which served a purpose in the past need to be "set free" and updated in terms of your current experience, allowing you to let go of using the anorexia nervosa to manage these unhelpful beliefs.

Appendix A.26: Flashcards: Identification of core beliefs and emotions in anorexia nervosa

By the time that you get to this part of therapy, you will be well experienced in keeping diaries, which will have focused on your eating and the thoughts that guided whether you ate or restricted. If you binged or vomited/took laxatives, the diary will have considered that too.

However, some eating behaviours can also be driven by your emotions, and the personality-level beliefs (core beliefs) that underpin those feelings. That is what we need to consider here, to help you identify and challenge those core beliefs and emotions.

When do I need to complete my core-belief/emotion diary?

You need to complete the diary when you first get the urge to use the behaviour, so that you can become aware of and challenge your thoughts and feelings at the time. That gives you a chance to choose whether you use the eating disorder behaviour or not.

The first two columns of the diary ask about your thoughts and your feelings. When you first start using the diary, you might find it hard to identify your thoughts and feelings. The reason that it can be difficult to recognise what you are thinking and feeling is that your eating behaviours stop you thinking the thoughts or feeling the feelings, so you find it hard to see patterns the next time round. The thoughts that are most likely to trigger binges are what are called 'core beliefs' – beliefs about who we are and how we routinely interact with the world.

How do I complete the diary?

The following tables list the type of thoughts/'core beliefs' and feelings/emotions that often trigger behaviours – especially restriction and compulsive/excessive exercise. Please follow these steps:

- Keep them available as 'flashcards', for when you decide to restrict, eat, exercise, binge, purge or use other eating disorder behaviours in a way that is inconsistent with recovery.
- When you are about to use such a behaviour, think about what thoughts and emotions might be driving that decision. If you cannot immediately label your core belief or emotion, use these labels and descriptions to suggest what your experiences might be.
- Put those core beliefs and emotions into your diary, marked with a '?' if you are not sure.
- Discuss them with your clinicians, to decide whether you are right and to help you identify your thoughts and feelings in real time.
- When you and your clinician have agreed on the likely core belief/emotion, place a tick against it, so that as you accumulate more experience of identifying that specific belief/emotion, you can start to learn your personal pattern of core beliefs and emotions.
- If you and your clinician identify feelings that are not on the flashcard already, add new ones at the bottom, to make it more personalised.

Getting to know your personal core beliefs will be very important for helping you and your clinician to make the intervention better for your individual needs.

Core belief/ thoughts	Definition	Tick each time identified
Vulnerable	Fear of harm or loss.	
Defectiveness	Lack of worth/self-esteem, and belief that others see me the same way.	
Mistrust	Belief that others are not trustworthy and will do me harm.	
Abandonment	Fear that others will abandon me, or will disappear and let me down when I need them.	
Emotional deprivation	Belief that no-one will be there to support or care for me.	
Social isolation	Belief that I am never going to have others who want to be around me or who I can rely on.	
Failure	Belief that I'm unable to succeed in tasks, relationships, etc.	
Dependence	Belief that I cannot succeed or get by without other people to support me.	
Poor self-control	Belief that I cannot control my behaviour.	
Perfectionism	Belief that I must always do my best, and even that is not good enough.	
Emotional inhibition	Belief that emotions are not safe to experience or express.	

Emotions	Definition	Tick each time identified
Angry	Feeling frustration, annoyance or resentment towards the world (at others; at myself).	
Anxious	Unsure about what is going to happen and whether it is a threat.	
Lonely	Experiencing sadness or distress due to feeling isolated and disconnected from others.	
Guilty	Feeling that I have done something wrong.	
Shame	A painful feeling of distress or humiliation that arises from the belief that you have done something wrong and others will judge you negatively.	
Sad/depressed	Feeling I've lost something or someone.	
Disgusted	Feeling extreme dislike or disapproval of a situation involving you and/or others, or the fear of contamination.	
Happy	Feeling excitement and arousal.	

Appendix A.27: Body neutrality

Body neutrality

Why do we care about our bodies so much?

Cavemen science!

Our hunter gatherer ancestors needed to compare to others for survival. For example, an early human might look at another and think "wow, they are really strong and I'm weak…. What are they doing differently and how can I do that too?". This might lead to crafting better hunting tools or foraging in a different area.
Comparing also helped early humans know where they fit in. It was important to be in a tribe for survival – protecting each other from threats, sourcing food together, and finding suitable mates. So, this makes sense! Comparison was essential for survival.

What about now?

Fortunately, we now don't need this old brain wiring. Comparison now is a trap, as it no longer helps survival. Rather, as they say, to compare is to despair.

The good news

We can change our brains! We can teach them to not spend so much time worrying about our bodies.

A possible solution? Body Neutrality

Body neutrality recognises:

1) Our feelings about our body change constantly depending on what is happening around us. So, our feelings are best mindfully observed without judgement.

2) A central focus on what our body allows us to do, and appreciating this will lead us to respect and care for our body.

3) Acknowledging that our self-worth encompasses both internal and external passions and isn't focused on our appearance.

Body neutrality means….

- It's okay if you don't love your body and it's okay if you do, these feelings come and go.

- Mindfully noticing all thoughts about our bodies, whether good, bad, or neutral, and allow them to exist without judgement.

- Our bodies change over time and all bodies have different features, abilities, and conditions and that is okay.

We understand there are many pressures you face to look a certain way. Unfortunately, society and mediums such as social media (TikTok, Facebook, Instagram) may treat people differently if they don't conform to a narrowly defined accepted body.

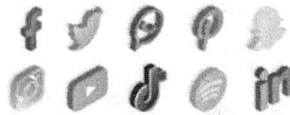

We know body neutrality can't undo this harm, but … we hope body neutrality offers a way to show compassion to your body and other's bodies despite this.

Body neutrality has also been presented as a more realistic alternative to loving your body and appearance, which might feel unachievable or leave us with a sense of failure if we are unable to achieve this goal.

Flinders University | Institute for Mental Health & wellbeing

Body neutrality

Body Neutrality in Action

1)   Notice the thought, feeling, or sensation and acknowledge you are thinking this. For example, "I notice I am having the thought that I hate my thighs".

2)   Acknowledge the thought without judgement. It's okay to have these thoughts/feelings/sensations, living in a world fixated on image of course you do!

3)   You might like to replace the thought with a more body neutral one. For example, "my thighs allow me move and do things I enjoy".

4)   You might like to list the things you appreciate about your body. For example, "my hands and arms allow me to hug my family" or "my lungs allow me to breathe in fresh air and replenish my body"

5)   Think about "What can you do to take care of your body so it can continue to achieve all those things you appreciate about it?" This might be nourishing your body with food from all food groups, moving your body in a way you enjoy, or allowing your body time to rest.

6)   Consider yourself as a whole person. The number on the scale or the image in the mirror isn't everything. Reflect on who you are as a complete human being and what your values are, your strengths, and the things that are most important to you (this might be friends, work, pets, hobbies etc.).

Practical strategies to practice body neutrality:

- Wear clothing that is comfortable and enjoyable.
- Give away any clothing that no longer fits or makes you feel good.

- Practice self-compassion – consider what you might say to a friend and use this as a starting point to speak kinder to yourself.

- Self-care activities – what ever you like that shows love and respect to your self and body (for example, having a bath, listening to music).
- Challenging any unhelpful body thoughts.
- Redirecting body conversations with others.
- Use of body neutral statements.
- Write a letter of gratitude to your body.
- Clean up your social media! Unfollow content that makes you feel bad about your body. You might follow body neutral content instead.
- Work on decreasing the time you spend in front of the mirror. Covering it up might help.
- Work on decreasing the number of times you weigh yourself or get rid of the scales completely.
- Engage in body activism (for example, write a letter to call out a body shaming advertisement).
- Find a community of like-minded individuals.
- Practice opposite action. Do the opposite of whatever your unhelpful thought is telling you!
- Acknowledge your strength, values, qualities.

Flinders University | Institute for Mental Health & wellbeing

Appendix A.28: Imagery rescripting for body image

Imagery Rescripting

Memories of early negative body image experiences

People with body image issues often say that memories of early negative appearance experiences, like being teased about how they look, can still affect how they feel about their body, even years later. These negative images can get 'stuck' in our minds.

We can't change what happened, but these past experiences don't have to impact our lives today.

With a 3-step strategy called 'imagery rescripting', we can look at those old memories in a new way, which helps us stop letting them affect how we see ourselves.

Step 1: *Think about the earliest event you can remember of an unpleasant body experience where you felt ashamed or embarrassed of your body or how your body looks.*

It could be something that happened to you when you were a child, or a teenager. Some examples are:

- being teased by your peers about how you look
- receiving negative/critical comments about your body or appearance
- feeling uncomfortable or insecure about your body when trying on clothes in a change-room, looking yourself in the mirror, getting ready with friends to go to a party, walking past a group of people who were looking at you, out in public.

Take a moment to close your eyes and imagine this earliest event as if it is happening right now. Please continue when you have a clear picture of this earliest event in your mind.

Now write down this event as if it is happening right now.

1. Write using "I" language (e.g., "I'm in the change room, trying on a pair of blue jeans. My friend is in the change room next to me also trying on clothes.")

2. Include as much detail as you can - what you are doing, who you are with, what you can see, how you are feeling, and what thoughts are going through your mind?

Step 2: Think about the same memory again. This time, when you close your eyes and **imagine** this event, imagine it <u>as if you were someone else watching the event happen from the outside, or on a screen.</u>

When you have a clear picture, write about this event in a few sentences as if it were happening to your younger self right now, but this time, write about what someone else would see if they were watching the event happen.

1. Write as if someone else is telling the story about you (e.g., if your name is Sarah, write "I see Sarah in the change room, she is trying on a pair of blue jeans. She's with her friend who is also trying on clothes.")

2. Include as much detail as you can, such as where Sarah is, what Sarah is doing, who Sarah is with, how Sarah might be feeling, and what thoughts might be going through Sarah's mind.

Some Tips on Writing

1. Use pen and paper to help increase formation of new connections in the brain that can embed new interpretations of an old memory.

2. Don't write to impress others, write openly and honestly. Don't overthink it.

3. You may experience some strong emotion while writing, but this will stabilise quickly.

Flinders University   Institute for Mental Health & wellbeing

Imagery Rescripting

Step 3: Think about the same memory one last time. This time, you are your younger self again (using "I" language), but <u>your wiser and kinder older self is with you in the room</u>. Your older self can get involved if you want them to. They can offer you kindness or provide new updated information based on what you know now, they can talk to you (or others) or do anything else that feels helpful and right in the situation.

Now, in a few sentences, write about this event as if it is happening right now, but this time, your wiser and older self is with you and can get involved.

1. Write using "I" language like you did earlier (e.g., "I'm in the change room, trying on a pair of blue jeans. My friend is in the change room next to me also trying on clothes.") but, when you talk about your older self, write it like you're telling a story about them (e.g., "older Sarah said...").
2. Include as much detail as you can, such as what you are doing, who you are with, what you can see, how you are feeling, and what thoughts are going through your mind.
3. Describe what your wiser and kinder older self does in the situation. Remember, they can offer you kindness or provide new updated information based on what you know now, they can talk to you (or others) or do anything else that feels helpful and right in the situation.

Wrapping it all up

*   Do this exercise three days in a row, take no more than 15 minutes on each occasion.
*   Note how the messages in the third step develop and change.
*   At the end of this exercise, write down in the notes section of your phone the key messages that came out of step 3 that make you feel differently about the old memory.

The evidence

Science tells us that when people use this imagery rescripting exercise, they experience increased body image acceptance and self-compassion. It is another example of how practising new styles of thinking can create new neuronal pathways in your brain, called neuroplasticity: https://www.youtube.com/watch?v=ELpfYCZa87g

Flinders University — Institute for Mental Health & Wellbeing

Appendix A.29: Blank therapy blueprint for clinician and patient

As you are coming to the end of therapy, we want you to remember all that you have done to get this far, so that:

1. You can see just how far you have come;
2. If you have any slips, you know how to get back on track;
3. You can use this memory to support you as you grow further.

Your clinician will discuss this document with you, but it is important that you spend time between sessions reminding yourself of all that you have done, too. So please keep adding to this document as you approach the end of therapy, and then use it in your "self-therapy" sessions and beyond, to keep you on the road to long-term recovery. The key areas to think about are as follows:

What were my problems when I was first referred?

What has become more possible, that seemed almost impossible before?

What did I do to change, and what strengths did I harness to do so?

What do I need to keep doing to stay well?

What changes do I still want to make, and how will I achieve them?

What might lead to a setback in the future?

What would be the symptoms of a setback?

How would I overcome the setback?

What if that doesn't work?

Appendix A.30: List of useful resources for other problems

The following list of weblinks details how the reader can access key resources that are cited in this book, and which are available online. We want the clinician and patient to be able to share these resources as early as possible, using these links, in order to support treatment. We also want to stress that there are wider sets of clinical resources for those with eating disorders via:

- The excellent Centre for Clinical Interventions (CCI) website – https://www.cci.health.wa.gov.au/Resources/Overview (in particular, their work on perfectionism, body image and much more)
- The Flinders University website, showcasing the interventions and evidence for single-session interventions and augmentations – https://www.flinders.edu.au/institute-mental-health-wellbeing/blackbird -initiative/nourished-mind
- The CBT-T website – https://sites.google.com/sheffield.ac.uk/cbt-t/resources?
- The Maudsley resources for carers – https://newmaudsleycarers-kent.co.uk/

Following CBT-AN-20, some patients will need further referral for other disorders that have not resolved. However, if there are outstanding issues that the clinician and patient agree might benefit from more of self-help approach, then the following books are excellent resources. The patient should be encouraged to remember just how much they have done to leave their eating disorder behind, so that they are able to bring their enhanced self-efficacy to the journey towards further recovery.

- Butler, G. (2016). *Overcoming Social Anxiety and Shyness: A Self-Help Guide Using Cognitive Behavioural Techniques*. Robinson.
- Fennell, M. (2016). *Overcoming Low Self-Esteem, 2nd Edition: A Self-help Guide Using Cognitive Behavioural Techniques*. Robinson.
- Gilbert, P. (2009). *Overcoming Depression: A Self-help Guide Using Cognitive Behavioural Techniques*. Robinson.
- Kennerley, H. (2014). *Overcoming Anxiety: A Self-help Guide Using Cognitive Behavioural Techniques*. Robinson.
- Shafran, R., Egan, S., & Wade, T. D. (2018). *Overcoming Perfectionism 2nd Edition: A Self-help Guide Using Scientifically Supported Cognitive Behavioural Techniques*. Robinson
- Veale, D., Willson, R., & Clarke, A. (2009). *Overcoming Body Image Problems including Body Dysmorphic Disorder*. Robinson.

Appendix A.31: Handout for patients with atypical anorexia nervosa

Atypical Anorexia Nervosa

Anorexia nervosa is diagnosed when someone is restricting their intake, is losing or has lost weight, has intense fears of weight gain, and has a disturbance in body image. All these symptoms result in starvation and impaired nutritional health.

The only difference between atypical anorexia nervosa and anorexia nervosa is that individuals with anorexia nervosa have a body mass index (BMI) less than 18.5 while individuals with atypical anorexia nervosa will have a BMI that is at or above 18.5, despite having lost a considerable amount of weight.

If you've been diagnosed with atypical anorexia nervosa, you may have the thought that because your weight is not below a BMI of 18.5, you are not "sick enough" to warrant treatment. We have a lot of evidence to show that your eating disorder is just as severe as anorexia nervosa in terms of many of the physical symptoms of starvation, and the eating disorder thoughts and behaviors that go along with it. The "atypical" label is a misnomer since atypical anorexia nervosa is more common than anorexia nervosa. On top of this, you might also have the additional burden of feeling that people around you— including some medical professionals—don't take your eating disorder seriously because you are less obviously under the weight that your body needs to be at. This way of being treated by others can even lead you to think that you need to lose even more weight to be 'thin enough' to deserve help.

We want you to know that you deserve this treatment and recovery just as much as anyone.

CBT-AN-20 will focus first on helping you to restore to a weight that is healthy for you. While we do not yet know what your body's healthy weight will be, we know that eating in recovery will mean you are making food decisions based on what you enjoy, when your body feels good, and when you no longer have symptoms of starvation.

One additional resource we recommend is *Almost Anorexic* (Jennifer J. Thomas & Jenni Schaefer, 2013, Hazelden Publishing). This book shares CBT strategies for individuals with eating disorders across the weight spectrum.

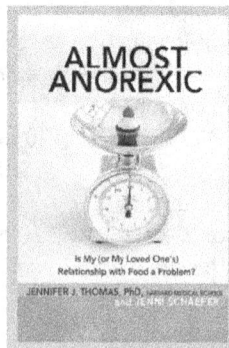

Appendix A.32: Handout for patients with avoidant/restrictive food intake disorder (ARFID)

Information Sheet for Individuals with
Avoidant/Restrictive Food Intake Disorder (ARFID)

Avoidant/restrictive food intake disorder (ARFID) is another kind of restrictive eating disorder. In ARFID, restrictive and/or avoidant eating patterns are usually related to (a) a lack of interest in eating and/or food, (b) a fear of aversive consequences of eating, or (c) sensitivity to tastes, textures, smells, or appearance of foods. Unlike anorexia nervosa, ARFID is usually not related to worries about gaining weight or getting fat. Indeed, individuals with ARFID often express a desire to be heavier, seeing themselves as too thin.

Lack of interest in
eating or food

Fear of aversive consequences

Sensory-based avoidance

Because ARFID is characterised by restrictive eating and/or avoidance of certain foods or food groups, like anorexia nervosa it can be associated with weight loss and starvation effects.

Cognitive-behavioral therapies are often used as a first line approach for the treatment of ARFID. CBT-AN-20 can be helpful, particularly for patients who have low weight or weight loss as a part of their ARFID presentation. In the beginning of treatment, the focus will be on helping you to get to a healthier weight. This will mean working on eating bigger volumes of foods that you already prefer or feel safe eating. Later in treatment, you will have a chance to practice increasing the variety of foods you eat to achieve a broader diet. As you expand your variety, you will work with your therapist to test your predictions about what might happen when you eat new foods, such as whether eating them will lead to intolerable fullness, really cause you to vomit or choke, or taste as terrible as you imagine.

One additional resource we'd recommend to support patients and their loved ones in understanding and working with ARFID is *The Picky Eater's Recovery Book* (Cambridge University Press, 2021), by Jennifer J. Thomas, Kendra R. Becker and Kamryn T. Eddy.

Appendix B: Other resources cited in this book

The following list contains links to tools and information that can be used by the clinician in delivering CBT-AN-20.

Sections where cited	Content	Link
Foreword; 1.6; 14.1	CBT-AN-20 website	https://sites.google.com/sheffield.ac.uk/cbt-an-20
3.5	Link: ED-15	https://cbt-t.sites.sheffield.ac.uk/resources
3.5; 4.7; 7.4.2	Therapy tracker	https://sites.google.com/sheffield.ac.uk/cbt-an-20
5.4	Medical issues to attend to in monitoring	https://cfih.com.au/wp-content/uploads/2017/01/Outpatient-Medical-Monitoring-for-Eating-Disorders-in-Adults.pdf
9.7.3	Psychoeducation on the functionality of self-criticism versus self-compassion	https://self-compassion.org/wp-content/uploads/2016/12/Self-Criticism.pdf.
10.6	NHMRC guidelines on appropriate exercise	https://www.health.gov.au/sites/default/files/documents/2021/09/physical-activity-and-sedentary-behaviour-guidelines-adults-18-to-64-years-fact-sheet_0.pdf

Appendix C: Single-session interventions and other brief interventions cited in the manual, to augment therapy

The following list contains links to single-session interventions (SSI) and other brief interventions that the patient can access to address specific issues that maintain anorexia nervosa in individual cases (e.g., perfectionism; self-criticism) over the broader CBT-AN-20 programme.

Content	Links
Single-session interventions (SSI)	
Self-worth: More than one piece	
Emotion regulation: Anchor in the moment: Learning to tolerate distress during tough times	
Negative body image: Flip the script: changing the way you see your body	
Self-acceptance: The bigger picture: Learning to accept yourself and see your worth	These seven single session interventions can all be accessed via:https://www.flinders.edu.au /institute-mental-health-wellbeing/blackbird -initiative/nourished-mind
Social isolation: Making meaningful connections	
Unhelpful thinking habits: Rewire your mind: changing unhelpful thinking habits	
Behavioural activation: Action brings change	
Brief interventions (4–8 modules)	
8-module CBT for clinical perfectionism (two versions, one for adolescents, one for ages 18 years and over)	https://www.overcomingperfectionism.com/ changing-your-perfectionism
Criticism and compassion (4 modules)	https://osf.io/xm95n/?view_only=cc0d5a4f566 c4de2b6f6061e784ebe3e
Social media curation (4 modules)	https://osf.io/vzajy?view_only=263cd3b98ef34 50e9b1975b94785fb6f

References

Abber, S. R., Becker, K. R., Stern, C. M., Palmer, L. P., Joiner, T. E., Breithaupt, L., Kambanis, P. E., Eddy, K. T., Thomas, J. J., & Burton-Murray, H. (2024). Latent profile analysis reveals overlapping ARFID and shape/weight motivations for restriction in eating disorders. *Psychological Medicine, 54*(11), 2956–2966. https://doi.org/10.1017/S003329172400103X

Adams, G., Turner, H., Hoskins, J., Robinson, A., & Waller, G. (2021). Effectiveness of a brief form of group dialectical behavior therapy for binge-eating disorder: Case series in a routine clinical setting. *International Journal of Eating Disorders, 54*(4), 615–620. https://doi.org/10.1002/eat.23470

Allen, K. L., Courtney, L., Croft, P., Hyam, L., Mills, R., Richards, K., Ahmed, M., & Schmidt, U. (2024). Programme-led and focused interventions for recent onset binge/purge eating disorders: Use and outcomes in the first episode rapid early intervention for eating disorders (FREED) network. *International Journal of Eating Disorders*. https://doi.org/10.1002/eat.24343

Allen, K. L., O'Hara, C. B., Bartholdy, S., Renwick, B., Keyes, A., Lose, A., Kenyon, M., DeJong, H., Broadbent, H., Loomes, R., McClelland, J., Serpell, L., Richards, L., Johnson-Sabine, E., Boughton, N., Whitehead, L., Treasure, J., Wade, T., & Schmidt, U. (2016). Written case formulations in the treatment of anorexia nervosa: Evidence for therapeutic benefits. *International Journal of Eating Disorders, 49*(9), 874–882. https://doi.org/10.1002/eat.22561

Allen, K. L., Mori, T. A., Beilin, L., Byrne, S. M., Hickling, S., & Oddy, W. H. (2013). Dietary intake in population-based adolescents: Support for a relationship between eating disorder symptoms, low fatty acid intake and depressive symptoms. *Journal of Human Nutrition and Dietetics, 26*(5), 459–469. https://doi.org/10.1111/jhn.12024

American Psychiatric Association. (2013). *Diagnostic and statistical manual of mental disorders* (5th ed.). American Psychiatric Association. https://doi.org/10.1176/appi.books.9780890425596

American Psychiatric Association. (2022). *Diagnostic and statistical manual of mental disorders* (5th ed., text rev.). https://doi.org/10.1176/appi.books.9780890425787

Andersson, G., Käll, A., Juhlin, S., Wahlström, C., de Fine Licht, E., Färdeman, S., Franck, A., Tholcke, A., Nachtweij, K., Fransson, E., Vernmark, K., Ludvigsson, M., & Berg, M. (2023). Free choice of treatment content, support on demand and supervision in internet-delivered CBT for adults with depression: A randomized factorial design trial. *Behaviour Research and Therapy, 162*, 104265. https://doi.org/10.1016/j.brat.2023.104265

Arai, M., Tonta, K. E., Erceg-Hurn, D. M., Raykos, B. C., Waller, G., & McEvoy, P. M. (2025). Eating-specific interpersonal difficulties: Changes and impacts on outcomes during ten-ession cognitive behavioral therapy for eating disorders (CBT-T). *International Journal of Eating Disorders, 58*(2), 362–371. https://doi.org/10.1002/eat.24336

Australian Government Department of Health & Ageing. (2006). *Nutrient reference values for Australia and New Zealand.* https://www.nhmrc.gov.au/file/3321/download?token =RHlu4kNJ

Australian Government Department of Health & Ageing. (2013). *Australian dietary guidelines.* https://www.eatforhealth.gov.au/guidelines/australian-guide-healthy-eating

Barakat, S., McLean, S. A., Bryant, E., Le, A., Marks, P., Touyz, S., & Maguire, S. (2023). Risk factors for eating disorders: Findings from a rapid review. *Journal of Eating Disorders, 11*(1), 8. https://doi.org/10.1186/s40337-022-00717-4

Beard, J. I. L., & Delgadillo, J. (2019). Early response to psychological therapy as a predictor of depression and anxiety treatment outcomes: A systematic review and meta-analysis. *Depression and Anxiety, 36*(9), 866–878. https://doi.org/10.1002/da.22931

Beck, A. T. (1996). Beyond belief: A theory of modes, personality and psychopathology. In P. M. Salkovskis (Ed.), *Frontiers of cognitive therapy* (pp. 1–25). Guilford.

Beck, J. S. (2005). *Cognitive therapy for challenging problems: What to do when the basics don't work.* Guilford.

Becker, C. B., & Stice, E. (2017). From efficacy to effectiveness to broad implementation: Evolution of the Body Project. *Journal of Consulting and Clinical Psychology, 85*(8), 767–782. https://doi.org/10.1037/ccp0000204

Becker, C. B., Zayfert, C., & Anderson, E. (2004). A survey of psychologists' attitudes towards and utilization of exposure therapy for PTSD. *Behaviour Research and Therapy, 42*(3), 277–292. https://doi.org/10.1016/S0005-7967(03)00138-4

Becker, C. B., Farrell, N. R., & Waller, G. (2019). *Exposure therapy for eating disorders.* Oxford University Press.

Becker, K. R., Breithaupt, L., Lawson, E. A., Eddy, K. T., & Thomas, J. J. (2020). Co-occurrence of avoidant/restrictive food intake disorder and traditional eating psychopathology. *Journal of the American Academy of Child and Adolescent Psychiatry, 59*(2), 209–212. https://doi.org.10.1016/j.jaac.2019.09.037

Beintner, I., & Jacobi, C. (2018). Are we overdosing treatment? Secondary findings from a study following women with bulimia nervosa after inpatient treatment. *International Journal of Eating Disorders, 51*(8), 899–905. https://doi.org/10.1002/eat.22894

Biddiscombe, R. J., Scanlan, J. N., Ross, J., Horsfield, S., Aradas, J., & Hart, S. (2018). Exploring the perceived usefulness of practical food groups in day treatment for individuals with eating disorders. *Australian Occupational Therapy Journal, 65*(2), 98–106. https://doi.org/10.1111/1440-1630.12442

Blackburn, I.-M., James, I. A., Milne, D. L., Baker, C., Standart, S., Garland, A., & Reichelt, F. K. (2001). The Revised Cognitive Therapy Scale (CTS-R): Psychometric properties. *Behavioural and Cognitive Psychotherapy, 29*(4), 431–446. https://doi.org/10.1017/ S1352465801004040

Bordin, E. S. (1979). The generalizability of the psychoanalytic concept of the working alliance. *Psychotherapy: Theory, Research & Practice, 16*(3), 252–260. https://doi.org /10.1037/h0085885

Breithaupt, L., Kahn, D. L., Slattery, M., Plessow, F., Mancuso, C., Izquierdo, A., Dreier, M. J., Becker, K. R., Franko, D. L., Thomas, J. J., Holsen, L., Lawson, E. A., Misra, M., &

Eddy, K. T. (2022). Eighteen-month course and outcome of adolescent restrictive eating disorders: Persistence, crossover, and recovery. *Journal of Clinical Child & Adolescent Psychology, 51*(5), 715–725. https://doi.org/10.1080/15374416.2022.2034634

Brennan, C., Green, G., Morgan, A., & Baudinet, J. (2025). The role of the dietitian within a day programme for adolescent anorexia nervosa: A reflexive thematic analysis of child and adolescent eating disorder clinician perspectives. *Journal of Human Nutrition and Dietetics, 38*(3), e70070. https://doi.org/10.1111/jhn.70070

British Association of Behavioural and Cognitive Psychotherapies. (2022). *BABCP standards of conduct, performance and ethics.* https://babcp.com/Standards

British Dietetic Association. (2021). *Practice guidance: Veganism and eating disorders (version 2).* British Dietetic Association.

Brown, A., McClelland, J., Boysen, E., Mountford, V., Glennon, D., & Schmidt, U. (2018). The FREED project (First episode and Rapid Early intervention in Eating Disorders): Service model, feasibility and acceptability. *Early Intervention in Psychiatry, 12*(2), 250–257. https://doi.org/10.1111/eip.12382

Brown, T. A., & Keel, P. K. (2013, 2013/05/01). What contributes to excessive diet soda intake in eating disorders: Appetitive drive, weight concerns, or both? *Eating Disorders, 21*(3), 265–274. https://doi.org/10.1080/10640266.2013.779190

Bryant-Waugh, R., Stern, C. M., Dreier, M. J., Micali, N., Cooke, L. J., Kuhnle, M. C., Wang, S., Breithaupt, L., Becker, K. R., Misra, M., Lawson, E. A., Eddy, K. T., & Thomas, J. J. (2022). Preliminary validation of the pica, ARFID and rumination disorder interview ARFID questionnaire (PARDI-AR-Q). *Journal of Eating Disorders, 10*(1), 179. https://doi.org/10.1186/s40337-022-00706-7

Burgalassi, A., Ramacciotti, C. E., Bianchi, M., Coli, E., Polese, L., Bondi, E., Massimetti, G., & Dell'Osso, L. (2009). Caffeine consumption among eating disorder patients: Epidemiology, motivations, and potential of abuse. *Eating and Weight Disorders-Studies on Anorexia, Bulimia and Obesity, 14*, e212–e218. https://doi.org/10.1007/BF03325119

Bulik, C. M., Berkman, N. D., Brownley, K. A., Sedway, J. A., & Lohr, K. N. (2007). Anorexia nervosa treatment: A systematic review of randomized controlled trials. *International Journal of Eating Disorders, 40*(4), 310–320. https://doi.org/10.1002/eat.20367

Campbell-Lee, D., Barton, S., & Armstrong, P. (2024). Higher-order CBT skills: Are there differences in meta-competence between trainee and experienced therapists? *The Cognitive Behaviour Therapist, 17*, e7. https://doi.org/10.1017/S1754470X24000047

Cardi, V., Leppanen, J., Mataix-Cols, D., Campbell, I. C., & Treasure, J. (2019). A case series to investigate food-related fear learning and extinction using in vivo food exposure in anorexia nervosa: A clinical application of the inhibitory learning framework. *European Eating Disorders Review, 27*(2), 173–181. https://doi.org/10.1002/erv.2639

Chen, E. Y., Cacioppo, J., Fettich, K., Gallop, R., McCloskey, M. S., Olino, T., & Zeffiro, T. A. (2017). An adaptive randomized trial of dialectical behavior therapy and cognitive behavior therapy for binge-eating. *Psychological Medicine, 47*(4), 703–717. https://doi.org/10.1017/S0033291716002543

Chua, N., Serpell, L., Burnett-Stuart, S., & Pugh, M. (2022). Interviewing anorexia: How do individuals given a diagnosis of anorexia nervosa experience voice dialogue with their eating disorder voice? A qualitative analysis. *Clinical Psychology & Psychotherapy, 29*(2), 600–610. https://doi.org/10.1002/cpp.2652

Chiurazzi, C., Cioffi, I., De Caprio, C., De Filippo, E., Marra, M., Sammarco, R., Di Guglielmo, M. L., Contaldo, F., & Pasanisi, F. (2017). Adequacy of nutrient intake in women with restrictive anorexia nervosa. *Nutrition, 38,* 80–84. https://doi.org/10.1016 /j.nut.2017.02.004

Clark, D. M., Canvin, L., Green, J., Layard, R., Pilling, S., & Janecka, M. (2018). Transparency about the outcomes of mental health services (IAPT approach): An analysis of public data. *Lancet, 391*(10121), 679–686. https://doi.org/10.1016/S0140 -6736(17)32133-5

Cohen, Z. D., Delgadillo J., & DeRubeis R. J. (2021). Personalized treatment approaches. In M. Barkham, W. Lutz, & L. G. Castonguay (Eds.), *Bergin and Garfield's handbook of psychotherapy and behavior change* (7th ed., pp. 667–700). Wiley.

Cooper, M., Todd, G., & Wells, A. (2001). *Bulimia Nervosa: A cognitive therapy programme for clients.* Jessica Kingsley.

Cooper, M. J., Wells, A., & Todd, G. (2004). A cognitive model of bulimia nervosa. *British Journal of Clinical Psychology, 43*(1), 1–16. https://doi.org/10.1348 /014466504772812931.

Cooper, P. J., Taylor, M. J., Cooper, Z., & Fairburn, C. G. (1987). The development and validation of the Body Shape Questionnaire. *International Journal of Eating Disorders, 6,* 485–494.

Cowdrey, N. D., & Waller, G. (2015). Are we really delivering evidence-based treatments for eating disorders? How eating-disordered patients describe their experience of cognitive behavioral therapy. *Behaviour Research and Therapy, 75,* 72–77. https://doi .org/10.1016/j.brat.2015.10.009

Craig, M., Waine, J., Wilson, S., & Waller, G. (2019). Optimizing treatment outcomes in adolescents with eating disorders. The potential role of cognitive behavioral therapy. *International Journal of Eating Disorders, 53,* 538–542. doi: 10.1002/eat.23067

Craske, M. G., Farchione, T. J., Allen, L. B., Barrios, V., Stoyanova, M., & Rose, R. (2007). Cognitive behavioral therapy for panic disorder and co-occurring mental health conditions: More of the same or less of more? *Behaviour Research and Therapy, 45*(6), 1095–1109. https://doi.org/10.1016/j.brat.2006.09.006

Crisp, A. H., Norton, K., Gowers, S., Halek, C., Bowyer, C., Yeldham, D., Levett, G., & Bhat, A. (1991). A controlled study of the effect of therapies aimed at adolescent and family psychopathology in anorexia nervosa. *British Journal of Psychiatry, 159*(3), 325–333. https://doi.org/10.1192/bjp.159.3.325

Cross, A., & Sheffield, D. (2019). Mental contrasting for health behaviour change: A systematic review and meta-analysis of effects and moderator variables. *Health Psychology Review, 13*(2), 209–225. https://doi.org/10.1080/17437199.2019.1594332

Cuijpers, P., Miguel, C., Ciharova, M., Quero, S., Plessen, C. Y., Ebert, D., Harrer, M., van Straten, A., & Karyotaki, E. (2023). Psychological treatment of depression with other comorbid mental disorders: Systematic review and meta-analysis. *Cognitive Behaviour Therapy, 52*(3), 246–268. https://doi.org/10.1080/16506073.2023.2166578

Dalle Grave, R., & Calugi, S. (2020). *Cognitive behavior therapy for adolescents with eating disorders.* Guilford.

Dalle Grave, R., Eckhardt, S., Calugi, S., & Le Grange, D. (2019). A conceptual comparison of family-based treatment and enhanced cognitive behavior therapy in the treatment of adolescents with eating disorders. *Journal of Eating Disorders, 7*(1), 42–42. https://doi .org/10.1186/s40337-019-0275-x

Dalle Grave, R., Sartirana, M., & Calugi, S. (2019). Enhanced cognitive behavioral therapy for adolescents with anorexia nervosa: Outcomes and predictors of change in a real-world setting. *International Journal of Eating Disorders, 52*(9), 1042-1046. https://doi.org/10.1002/eat.23122

de Boer, K., Johnson, C., Wade, T. D., Radunz, M., Fernando, A. N., Babb, J., Stafrace, S., & Sharp, G. (2023). A systematic review and meta-analysis of intensive treatment options for adults with eating disorders. *Clinical Psychology Review, 106*, 102354. https://doi.org/10.1016/j.cpr.2023.102354

Deacon, B., Farrell, N., Kemp, J., Dixon, L. S., Zhang, A., & McGrath, P. (2013). Assessing therapist reservations about exposure therapy for anxiety disorders: The Therapist Beliefs about Exposure Scale. *Journal of Anxiety Disorders, 27*, 772–780. https://doi.org/10.1016/j.janxdis.2013.04.006

de Jong, K., Conijn, J. M., Gallagher, R. A. V., Reshetnikova, A. S., Heij, M., & Lutz, M. C. (2021). Using progress feedback to improve outcomes and reduce drop-out, treatment duration, and deterioration: A multilevel meta-analysis. *Clinical Psychology Review, 85*, 102002. https://doi.org/10.1016/j.cpr.2021.102002

Delgadillo, J., Ali, S., Fleck, K., Agnew, C., Southgate, A., Parkhouse, L., Cohen, Z. D., DeRubeis, R. J., & Barkham, M. (2022). Stratified care vs stepped care for depression: A cluster randomized clinical trial. *JAMA Psychiatry, 79*(2), 101–108. https://doi.org/10.1001/jamapsychiatry.2021.3539

Delgadillo, J., de Jong, K., Lucock, M., Lutz, W., Rubel, J., Gilbody, S., Ali, S., Aguirre, E., Appleton, M., Nevin, J., O'Hayon, H., Patel, U., Sainty, A., Spencer, P., & McMillan, D. (2018). Feedback-informed treatment versus usual psychological treatment for depression and anxiety: A multisite, open-label, cluster randomised controlled trial. *The Lancet. Psychiatry, 5*(7), 564–572. https://doi.org/10.1016/S2215-0366(18)30162-7

Delgadillo, J., Deisenhofer, A. K., Probst, T., Shimokawa, K., Lambert, M. J., & Kleinstäuber, M. (2022). Progress feedback narrows the gap between more and less effective therapists: A therapist effects meta-analysis of clinical trials. *Journal of Consulting and Clinical Psychology, 90*(7), 559–567. https://doi.org/10.1037/ccp0000747

Diedrichs, P. C., Atkinson, M. J., Garbett, K. M., & Leckie, G. (2021). Evaluating the "Dove Confident Me" five-session body image intervention delivered by teachers in schools: A cluster randomized controlled effectiveness trial. *Journal of Adolescent Health, 68*(2), 331–341. https://doi.org/10.1016/j.jadohealth.2020.10.001

Dray, J., & Wade, T. D. (2012). Is the transtheoretical model and motivational interviewing approach applicable to the treatment of eating disorders? A review. *Clinical Psychology Review, 32*(6), 558–565. https://doi.org/10.1016/j.cpr.2012.06.005

Duggan, H., Rose, C., Turner, H., Cox, J., Ebbens, R., Southron, J., & Waller, G. (2025). How do outpatients experience 20-session cognitive-behavioral therapy for anorexia nervosa (CBT-AN-20)? A qualitative exploration. *International Journal of Eating Disorders*. https://doi.org/10.1002/eat.24528.

Duggan, H., Turner, H., Rose, C., Ruchpaul, E., Adams, G., Dursley, L., Ebbens., R., Gilbert, M., May, L., Melhuish, L., Mueller, R., Souissi, S., Webster, C., Williams, S., Yip, G., & Waller, G. (under consideration). Cognitive-behavioural therapy for anorexia nervosa (CBT-AN-20): Feasibility, acceptability, and preliminary effectiveness. *Cognitive Behaviour Therapy*.

Eddy, K. T., & Breithaupt, L. (2023). Atypical anorexia nervosa diagnosis should exclude those with lifetime anorexia nervosa: Commentary on Walsh, Hagan, and Lockwood

(2022). *International Journal of Eating Disorders, 56*(4), 838–840. https://doi.org/10 .1002/eat.23924

Eddy, K. T., Tabri, N., Thomas, J. J., Murray, H. B., Keshaviah, A., Hastings, E., Edkins, K., Krishna, M., Herzog, D. B., Keel, P. K., & Franko, D. L. (2017). Recovery from anorexia nervosa and bulimia nervosa at 22-year follow-up. *Journal of Clinical Psychiatry, 78*(2), 184–189. https://doi.org/10.4088/JCP.15m10393

Eisler, I., Simic, M., Blessitt, E., & Dodge, L., & MCCAED Team. (2016). *Maudsley service manual for child and adolescent eating disorders.* https://mccaed.slam.nhs.uk/wp-content/ uploads/2019/11/Maudsley-Service-Manual-for-Child-andAdolescent-Eating-Disorders-July-2016.pdf

Eisler, I., Simic, M., Russell, G. F., & Dare, C. (2007). A randomised controlled treatment trial of two forms of family therapy in adolescent anorexia nervosa: A five-year follow-up. *Journal of Child Psychology and Psychiatry, 48*(6), 552–560. https://doi.org/10.1111/j .1469-7610.2007.01726.x

Egbert, A. H., Gorrell, S., Smith, K. E., Goldschmidt, A. B., Hughes, E. K., Sawyer, S. M., Yeo, M., Lock, J., & Le Grange, D. (2023). When eating disorder attitudes and cognitions persist after weight restoration: An exploratory examination of non-cognitive responders to family-based treatment for adolescent anorexia nervosa. *European Eating Disorders Review, 31*(3), 425–432. https://doi.org/10.1002/erv.2968

El Ghoch, M., Calugi, S., Lamburghini, S., & Dalle Grave, R. (2014). Anorexia nervosa and body fat distribution: A systematic review. *Nutrients, 6*(9), 3895–3912. https://doi.org /10.3390/nu6093895

Erekson, D. M., Lambert, M. J., & Eggett, D. L. (2015). The relationship between session frequency and psychotherapy outcome in a naturalistic setting. *Journal of Consulting and Clinical Psychology, 83*(6), 1097–1107. https://doi.org/10.1037/a0039774

Fairburn, C. G. (2008). *Cognitive behavior therapy and eating disorders.* Guilford Press.

Fairburn, C. G., Cooper, Z., Doll, H. A., O'Connor, M. E., Palmer, R. L., & Dalle Grave, R. (2013). Enhanced cognitive behaviour therapy for adults with anorexia nervosa: A UK– Italy study. *Behaviour Research and Therapy, 51*(1), R2–R8. https://doi.org/10.1016/j .brat.2012.09.010

Fairburn, C. G., Shafran, R., & Cooper, Z. (1999). A cognitive behavioural theory of anorexia nervosa. *Behaviour Research and Therapy, 37*(1), 1–13. https://doi.org/10 .1016/S0005-7967(98)00102-8

Fetahi, E., Søgaard, A. S., & Sjögren, M. (2022). Estimating the effect of motivational interventions in patients with eating disorders: A systematic review and meta-analysis. *Journal of Personalized Medicine, 12*(4), 577. https://doi.org/10.3390/jpm12040577

Fforde, J. (2018). *Early riser.* Hodder & Stoughton.

Flückiger, C., Rubel, J., Del Re, A. C., Horvath, A. O., Wampold, B. E., Crits-Christoph, P., Atzil-Slonim, D., Compare, A., Falkenström, F., Ekeblad, A., Errázuriz, P., Fisher, H., Hoffart, A., Huppert, J. D., Kivity, Y., Kumar, M., Lutz, W., Muran, J. C., Strunk, D. R., ... Barber, J. P. (2020). The reciprocal relationship between alliance and early treatment symptoms: A two-stage individual participant data meta-analysis. *Journal of Consulting and Clinical Psychology, 88*(9), 829–843. https://doi.org/10.1037/ccp0000594

Fuller, S. J., Brown, A., Rowley, J., & Elliott-Archer, J. (2022). Veganism and eating disorders: Assessment and management considerations. *BJPsych Bulletin, 46*(2), 116–120. https://doi.org/10.1192/bjb.2021.37

Franko, D. L., Tabri, N., Keshaviah, A., Murray, H. B., Herzog, D. B., Thomas, J. J., Coniglio, K., Keel, P. K., & Eddy, K. T. (2018). Predictors of long-term recovery in anorexia nervosa and bulimia nervosa: Data from a 22-year longitudinal study. *Journal of Psychiatric Research, 96*, 183–188. https://doi.org/10.1016/j.jpsychires.2017.10.008

Freeman, A., & Dolan, M. (2001). Revisiting Prochaska and DiClemente's stages of change theory: An expansion and specification to aid in treatment planning and outcome evaluation. *Cognitive and Behavioral Practice, 8*(3), 224–234. https://doi.org/10.1016/S1077-7229(01)80057-2

Froreich, F. V., Ratcliffe, S. E., & Vartanian, L. R. (2020). Blind versus open weighing from an eating disorder patient perspective. *Journal of Eating Disorders, 8*, 39. https://doi.org/10.1186/s40337-020-00316-1

Fursland, A., Erceg-Hurn, D. M., Byrne, S. M., & McEvoy, P. M. (2018). A single session assessment and psychoeducational intervention for eating disorders: Impact on treatment waitlists and eating disorder symptoms. *International Journal of Eating Disorders, 51*(12), 1373–1377. https://doi.org/10.1002/eat.22983

Fuzi, S. F. A., Koller, D., Bruggraber, S., Pereira, D. I., Dainty, J. R., & Mushtaq, S. (2017). A 1-h time interval between a meal containing iron and consumption of tea attenuates the inhibitory effects on iron absorption: A controlled trial in a cohort of healthy UK women using a stable iron isotope. *American Journal of Clinical Nutrition, 106*(6), 1413–1421. https://doi.org/10.3945/ajcn.117.161364

Garber, A. K., Cheng, J., Accurso, E. C., Adams, S. H., Buckelew, S. M., Kapphahn, C. J., Kreiter, A., Le Grange, D., Machen, V. I., Moscicki, A.-B., Sy, A., Wilson, L., & Golden, N. H. (2021). Short-term outcomes of the study of refeeding to optimize inpatient gains for patients with anorexia nervosa: A multicenter randomized clinical trial. *JAMA Pediatrics, 175*(1), 19–27. https://doi.org/10.1001/jamapediatrics.2020.3359

Garner, D. M., & Bemis, K. M. (1982). A cognitive-behavioral approach to anorexia nervosa. *Cognitive Therapy and Research, 6*, 123–150. https://doi.org/10.1080/02619288.2014.875675

Geller, J., & Srikameswaran, S. (2006). Treatment non-negotiables: Why we need them and how to make them work. *European Eating Disorders Review, 14*(4), 212–217. https://doi.org/10.1002/erv.716

Geulayov, G., Ferrey, A., Hawton, K., Hermon, C., Reeves, G. K., Green, J., Beral, V., & Floud, S. (2019). Body mass index in midlife and risk of attempted suicide and suicide: Prospective study of 1 million UK women. *Psychological Medicine, 49*(13), 2279–2286. https://doi.org/10.1017/S0033291718003239

Gibbons, C. J., & DeRubeis, R. J. (2008). Anxiety symptom focus in sessions of cognitive therapy for depression. *Behavior Therapy, 39*(2), 117–125. https://doi.org/10.1016/j.beth.2007.05.006

Graves, T. A., Tabri, N., Thompson-Brenner, H., Franko, D. L., Eddy, K. T., Bourion-Bedes, S., Brown, A., Constantino, M. J., Flückiger, C., Forsberg, S., Isserlin, L., Couturier, J., Paulson Karlsson, G., Mander, J., Teufel, M., Mitchell, J. E., Crosby, R. D., Prestano, C., Satir, D. A., … & Thomas, J. J. (2017). A meta-analysis of the relation between therapeutic alliance and treatment outcome in eating disorders. *International Journal of Eating Disorders, 50*(4), 323–340. https://doi.org/10.1002/eat.22672

Grilo, C. M., Reas, D. L., Hopwood, C. J., & Crosby, R. D. (2015). Factor structure and construct validity of the Eating Disorder Examination-Questionnaire in college students:

Further support for a modified brief version. *International Journal of Eating Disorders, 48*(3), 284–289. https://doi.org/10.1002/eat.22358

Grilo, C. M., & Udo, T. (2021). Examining the significance of age of onset in persons with lifetime anorexia nervosa: Comparing child, adolescent, and emerging adult onsets in nationally representative U.S. study. *International Journal of Eating Disorders, 54*(9), 1632–1640. https://doi.org/10.1002/eat.23580

Grove, W. M., Zald, D. H., Lebow, B. S., Snitz, B. E., & Nelson, C. (2000). Clinical versus mechanical prediction: A meta-analysis. *Psychological Assessment, 12,* 19–30.

Hackmann, A., Bennett-Levy, J., & Holmes, E. A. (eds). (2015). Using imagery to work with upsetting memories. In A. Hackmann, J. Bennett-Levy, & E. A. Holmes (Eds.), *Oxford guide to imagery in cognitive therapy*. Oxford. https://doi.org/10.1093/med:psych/9780199234028.003.0009

Harned, M. S., Dimeff, L. A., Woodcock, E. A., & Contreras, I. (2013). Predicting adoption of exposure therapy in a randomized controlled dissemination trial. *Journal of Anxiety Disorders, 27*(8), 754-762. https://doi.org/10.1016/j.janxdis.2013.02.006

Harrop, E. N., Mensinger, J. L., Moore, M., & Lindhorst, T. (2021). Restrictive eating disorders in higher weight persons: A systematic review of atypical anorexia nervosa prevalence and consecutive admission literature. *International Journal of Eating Disorders, 54*(8), 1328–1357. https://doi.org/10.1002/eat.23519

Hart, S., Marnane, C., McMaster, C., & Thomas, A. (2018). Development of the "recovery from eating disorders for life" food guide (REAL food guide) - A food pyramid for adults with an eating disorder. *Journal of Eating Disorders, 6*, 6. https://doi.org/10.1186/s40337-018-0192-4

Hart, M., Hirneth, S., Mendelson, J., Jenkins, L., Pursey, K., & Waller, G. (2024). Brief cognitive behavioural therapy for eating disorders symptomatology among a mixed sample of adolescents and young adults in primary care: A non-randomised feasibility and pilot study. *European Eating Disorders Review, 32*(4), 676–686. https://doi.org/10.1002/erv.3075

Hart, S., Abraham, S., Franklin, R. C., & Russell, J. (2011). The reasons why eating disorder patients drink. *European Eating Disorders Review, 19*(2), 121–128. https://doi.org/https://doi.org/10.1002/erv.1051

Hart, S., Abraham, S., Luscombe, G., & Russell, J. (2005). Fluid intake in patients with eating disorders. *International Journal of Eating Disorders, 38*(1), 55–59. https://doi.org/https://doi.org/10.1002/eat.20155

Hart, S., Marnane, C., McMaster, C., & Thomas, A. (2018). Development of the "Recovery from Eating Disorders for Life" Food Guide (REAL Food Guide)-a food pyramid for adults with an eating disorder. *Journal of Eating Disorders, 6*(1), 6. https://doi.org/10.1186/s40337-018-0192-4

Hay, P., Chinn, D., Forbes, D., Madden, S., Newton, R., Sugenor, L., Touyz, S., & Ward, W. (2014). Royal Australian and New Zealand College of Psychiatrists clinical practice guidelines for the treatment of eating disorders. *Australian & New Zealand Journal of Psychiatry, 48*(11), 977–1008. https://doi.org/10.1177/0004867414555814

Heffernan, A., Evans, C., Holmes, M., & Moore, J. (2017). The regulation of dietary iron bioavailability by vitamin C: A systematic review and meta-analysis. *Proceedings of the Nutrition Society, 76*(OCE4), E182. https://doi.org/10.1017/S0029665117003445

Heruc, G., Hart, S., Stiles, G., Fleming, K., Casey, A., Sutherland, F., Jeffrey, S., Roberton, M., & Hurst, K. (2020). ANZAED practice and training standards for dietitians providing eating disorder treatment. *Journal of Eating Disorders, 8*(1), 77. https://doi.org/10.1186/s40337-020-00334-z

Hopwood, C. J., Bleidorn, W., Schwaba, T., & Chen, S. (2020). Health, environmental, and animal rights motives for vegetarian eating. *PloS one, 15*(4), e0230609. https://doi.org/10.1371/journal.pone.0230609

Hormoz, E., Pugh, M., & Waller, G. (2019). Do eating disorder voice characteristics predict treatment outcomes in anorexia nervosa? A pilot study. *Cognitive Behaviour Therapy, 48*(2), 137–145. https://doi.org/10.1080/16506073.2018.1476581

Innes, N. T., Clough, B. A., & Casey, L. M. (2017). Assessing treatment barriers in eating disorders: A systematic review. *Eating Disorders, 25*(1), 1-21. https://doi.org/10.1080/10640266.2016.1207455

Jablonski, M., Schebendach, J., Walsh, B. T., & Steinglass, J. E. (2024). Eating behavior in atypical anorexia nervosa. *International Journal of Eating Disorders, 57*(4), 780–784. https://doi.org/10.1002/eat.23886

Jagielska, G. W., Przedlacki, J., Bartoszewicz, Z., & Racicka, E. (2016). Bone mineralization disorders as a complication of anorexia nervosa - etiology, prevalence, course and treatment. *Psychiatria Polska, 50*(3), 509–520. https://doi.org/10.12740/pp/59289

Janse, P. D., de Jong, K., Veerkamp, C., van Dijk, M. K., Hutschemaekers, G. J. M., & Verbraak, M. J. P. M. (2020). The effect of feedback-informed cognitive behavioral therapy on treatment outcome: A randomized controlled trial. *Journal of Consulting and Clinical Psychology, 88(9)*, 818–828. https://doi.org/10.1037/ccp0000549

Jenkins, J., & Ogden, J. (2012). Becoming 'whole' again: A qualitative study of women's views of recovering from anorexia nervosa. *European Eating Disorders Review, 20*, 23–31. https://doi.org/10.1002/erv.1085

Jenkins, P. E., Morgan, C., & Houlihan, C. (2019). Outpatient CBT for underweight patients with eating disorders: Effectiveness within a national health service (NHS) eating disorders service. *Behavioural and Cognitive Psychotherapy, 47*(2), 217–229. https://doi.org/10.1017/S1352465818000449

Jenkins, P. E., Proctor, K., & Snuggs, S. (2024). Dietary intake of adults with eating disorders: A systematic review and meta-analysis. *Journal of Psychiatric Research.* https://doi.org/10.1016/j.jpsychires.2024.05.038

Jhe, G. B., Lin, J., Freizinger, M., & Richmond, T. (2023). Adolescents with anorexia nervosa or atypical anorexia nervosa with premorbid overweight/obesity: What should we do about their weight loss? *Journal of Child and Adolescent Psychiatric Nursing, 36*(1), 55–58. https://doi.org/10.1111/jcap.12394

Johns, R. G., Barkham, M., Kellett, S., & Saxon, D. (2019). A systematic review of therapist effects: A critical narrative update and refinement to review. *Clinical Psychology Review, 67*, 78–93. https://doi.org/10.1016/j.cpr.2018.08.004

Johnson, C. J., Linardon, J., Fuller-Tyszkiewicz, M., Williamson, P., & Wade, T. D. (2025). The impact of patient choice on uptake, adherence and outcomes across depression, anxiety and eating disorders: A systematic review and meta-analysis. *Psychological Medicine, 55,* e32. https://doi.org/10.1017/S0033291725000066

Joiner, T. E., Metalsky, G. I., Katz, J., & Beach, S. R. H. (1999). Depression and excessive reassurance-seeking. *Psychological Inquiry, 10*(3), 269–278. https://doi.org/10.1207/S15327965PLI1004_1

Jones, S., Raykos, B. C., McEvoy, P. M., Ieraci, J., Fursland, A., Byrne, S. M., & Waller, G. (2019). The development and validation of a measure of eating disorder-specific interpersonal problems: The Interpersonal Relationships in Eating Disorders (IR-ED) scale. *Psychological Assessment, 31,* 389–403. doi: 10.1037/pas0000666

Jowik, K., Tyszkiewicz-Nwafor, M., & Słopień, A. (2021). Anorexia nervosa—What has changed in the state of knowledge about nutritional rehabilitation for patients over the past 10 Years? A review of literature. *Nutrients, 13*(11), 3819. https://www.mdpi.com /2072-6643/13/11/3819

Kambanis, P. E., Graver, H., Palmer, L. P., Stern, C. M., Tabri, N., Dunford, A., Burton-Murray, H., Breithaupt. L., Wang, S. B., Rossman, S., Mancuso, C. J., Andrea, A. M., Waller, G., Freid, C. M., Eddy, K. T., Thomas, J. J., & Becker, K. R. (2025). Patterns of symptom change in behaviors and cognitions during 10-session cognitive behavioral therapy (CBT-T) for non-underweight eating disorders. *International Journal of Eating Disorders. 58*(7), 1392–1398 https://doi.org/10.1002/eat.24429

Kambanis, P. E., Palmer, L. P., Jhe, G., McPherson, I., Graver, H., Dalton, A. G., Ji, C., Asanza, E., Shabazian, L., Dunford, A., Breithaupt, L., Freizinger, M., Eddy, K. T., Misra, M., Micali, N., Holsen, L., Lawson, E. A., Becker, K. R., & Thomas, J. J. (2025). Frequency and predictors of shape/weight concerns and objective binge eating in avoidant/restrictive food intake disorder (ARFID). *International Journal of Eating Disorders, 58*(5), 986–992. https://doi.org/10.1002/eat.24398

Kambanis, P. E., Tabri, N., McPherson, I., Gydus, J. E., Kuhnle, M., Stern, C. M., Asanza, A., Becker, K. R., Breithaupt, L., Freizinger, M., Shrier, L., Bern, E., Eddy, K. T., Misra, M., Micali, N., Lawson, E. A., & Thomas, J. J. (2025). Prospective 2-year course and predictors of outcome in avoidant/restrictive food intake disorder. *Journal of the American Academy of Child & Adolescent Psychiatry, 64*(2), 262–275. https://doi.org /10.1016/j.jaac.2024.04.010

Keegan, E., Tchanturia, K., & Wade, T. D. (2021). Central coherence and set-shifting between nonunderweight eating disorders and anorexia nervosa: A systematic review and meta-analysis. *International Journal of Eating Disorders, 54*(3), 229–243. https:// doi.org/10.1002/eat.23430

Keegan, E., & Wade, T. D. (2024a). Early change predicts outcome in 10-session cognitive behavioural therapy for non-underweight patients with eating disorders: A secondary data analysis. *Clinical Psychologist, 28*(1), 70–74. https://doi.org/10.1080/13284207 .2024.2306934

Keegan, E., & Wade, T. D. (2024b). The role of readiness and confidence to change in the treatment of atypical anorexia nervosa and bulimia nervosa. *International Journal of Eating Disorders, 57*(4), 1020–1025. https://doi.org/10.1002/eat.23918

Keegan, E., Waller, G., Tchanturia, K., & Wade, T. D. (2024). The potential value of brief waitlist interventions in enhancing treatment retention and outcomes: a randomised controlled trial. *Cognitive Behaviour Therapy, 53*(6), 608–620. https://doi.org/10.1080 /16506073.2024.2351867

Keel, P. K., Dorer, D. J., Franko, D. L., Jackson, S. C., & Herzog, D. B. (2005). Postremission predictors of relapse in women with eating disorders. *American Journal of Psychiatry, 162*(12), 2263–2268. https://doi.org/10.1176/appi.ajp.162.12.2263

Kendall, P. C., Robin, J. A., Hedtke, K. A., Suveg, C., Flannery-Schroeder, E., & Gosch, E. A. (2005). Considering CBT with anxious youth? Think exposures. *Cognitive and Behavioral Practice, 12*(1), 136–148. https://doi.org/10.1016/S1077-7229(05)80048-3.

Kennerley, H., Kirk, J., & Westbrook, D. (2016). *An introduction to cognitive behaviour therapy: Skills and applications* (3rd ed.). Sage.

Kent, A., Waller, G., & Dagnan, D. (1999). A greater role of emotional than physical or sexual abuse in predicting disordered eating attitudes: The role of mediating variables. *International Journal of Eating Disorders, 25,* 159–167. https://doi.org/10.1002/(sici)1098-108x(199903)25:2<159::aid-eat5>3.0.co;2-f.

Keshaviah, A., Edkins, K., Hastings, E. R., Krishna, M., Franko, D. L., Herzog, D. B., Thomas, J. J., Murray, H. B., & Eddy, K. T. (2014). Re-examining premature mortality in anorexia nervosa: A meta-analysis redux. *Comprehensive Psychiatry, 55*(8), 1773–1784. https://doi.org/10.1016/j.comppsych.2014.07.017

Kindred, R., Bates, G. W., & McBride, N. L. (2022). Long-term outcomes of cognitive behavioural therapy for social anxiety disorder: A meta-analysis of randomised controlled trials. *Journal of Anxiety Disorders, 92,* 102640. https://doi.org/10.1016/j.janxdis.2022.102640

Klein, T., Breilmann, J., Schneider, C., Girlanda, F., Fiedler, I., Dawson, S., Crippa, A., Priebe, S., Barbui, C., Becker, T., & Kösters, M. (2024). Dose–response relationship in cognitive behavioral therapy for depression: A nonlinear metaregression analysis. *Journal of Consulting and Clinical Psychology, 92*(5), 296–309. https://doi.org/10.1037/ccp0000879

Knowles, L., Anokhina, A., & Serpell, L. (2013). Motivational interventions in the eating disorders: What is the evidence? *International Journal of Eating Disorders, 46*(2), 97–107. https://doi.org/10.1002/eat.22053

Lawrence, A. S., Russo-Batterham, D., Doyle, K., & Tescari, E. (2025). Time to consider more than just calcium? The impact on protein, riboflavin, vitamin B12 and iodine intake of replacing cows' milk with plant-based milk-like drinks—An Australian usual intake dietary modelling study. *European Journal of Nutrition, 64*(4), 1–17. https://doi.org/10.1007/s00394-025-03697-8

Langthorne, D., Beard, J., & Waller, G. (2023). Therapist factors associated with intent to use exposure therapy: A systematic review and meta-analysis. *Cognitive Behaviour Therapy, 52*(4), 347–379. https://doi.org/10.1080/16506073.2023.2191824

Lego, S. R., Raykos, B. C., Tonta, K. E., Erceg-Hurn, D. M., Waller, G., & McEvoy, P. M. (2024). Validation of the Interpersonal Relationships in Eating Disorders (IR-ED) Scale in an eating disorder sample. *International Journal of Eating Disorders, 57*(11), 2181–2193. https://doi.org/10.1002/eat.24259.

Le Grange, D., Eckhardt, S., Dalle Grave, R., Crosby, R. D., Peterson, C. B., Keery, H., Lesser, J., & Martell, C. (2022). Enhanced cognitive-behavior therapy and family-based treatment for adolescents with an eating disorder: A non-randomized effectiveness trial. *Psychological Medicine, 52*(13), 2520–2530. https://doi.org/10.1017/S0033291720004407

Linardon, J., & Brennan, L. (2017). The effects of cognitive-behavioral therapy for eating disorders on quality of life: A meta-analysis. *International Journal of Eating Disorders, 50*(7), 715–730. https://doi.org/10.1002/eat.22719

Linardon, J., Messer, M., Lee, S., & Fuller-Tyszkiewicz, M. (2019). Testing the measurement invariance of the Body Image Acceptance and Action Questionnaire between women with and without binge-eating disorder symptomatology: Further evidence for an abbreviated five-item version. *Psychological Assessment, 31*(11), 1368–1376. https://doi.org/10.1037/pas0000761

Linehan, M. M. (1993). *Cognitive behavioral treatment of borderline personality disorder.* Guilford.

Liu, C. I., Hua, M. H., Lu, M. L., & Goh, K. K. (2023). Effectiveness of cognitive behavioural-based interventions for adults with attention-deficit/hyperactivity disorder extends beyond core symptoms: A meta-analysis of randomized controlled trials. *Psychology and Psychotherapy*, *96*(3), 543–559. https://doi.org/10.1111/papt.12455

Lock, J. D. (2021). *Family-based treatment for avoidant/restrictive food intake disorder*. Routledge.

Lock, J., & Le Grange, D. (2012). *Treatment manual for anorexia nervosa: A family-based approach* (2nd ed.). Guilford.

Lopes, M. P., Robinson, L., Stubbs, B., Dos Santos Alvarenga, M., Araújo Martini, L., Campbell, I. C., & Schmidt, U. (2022). Associations between bone mineral density, body composition and amenorrhoea in females with eating disorders: A systematic review and meta-analysis. *Journal of Eating Disorders, 10*(1), 173. https://doi.org/10.1186/s40337-022-00694-8

Macdonald, P., Hibbs, R., Corfield, F., & Treasure, J. (2012). The use of motivational interviewing in eating disorders: A systematic review. *Psychiatry Research*, *200*(1), 1–11. https://doi.org/10.1016/j.psychres.2012.05.013

Macneil, C. A., Hasty, M. K., Conus, P., & Berk, M. (2012). Is diagnosis enough to guide interventions in mental health? Using case formulation in clinical practice. *BMC Medicine*, *10*, 111. https://doi.org/10.1186/1741-7015-10-111

Madden, S., Miskovic-Wheatley, J., Wallis, A., Kohn, M., Hay, P., & Touyz, S. (2015). Early weight gain in family-based treatment predicts greater weight gain and remission at the end of treatment and remission at 12-month follow-up in adolescent anorexia nervosa. *International Journal of Eating Disorders*, *48*(7), 919–922. https://doi.org/10.1002/eat.22414

Magill, M., Apodaca, T. R., Borsari, B., Gaume, J., Hoadley, A., Gordon, R. E. F., Tonigan, J. S., & Moyers, T. (2018). A meta-analysis of motivational interviewing process: Technical, relational, and conditional process models of change. *Journal of Consulting and Clinical Psychology*, *86*(2), 140–157. https://doi.org/10.1037/ccp0000250

Mandelli, L., Arminio, A., Atti, A. R., & De Ronchi, D. (2019). Suicide attempts in eating disorder subtypes: A meta-analysis of the literature employing DSM-IV, DSM-5, or ICD-10 diagnostic criteria. *Psychological Medicine*, *49*(8), 1237–1249. https://doi.org/10.1017/S0033291718003549

Mayer, L. E., Klein, D. A., Black, E., Attia, E., Shen, W., Mao, X., Shungu, D. C., Punyanita, M., Gallagher, D., Wang, J., Heymsfield, S. B., Hirsch, J., Ginsberg, H. N., & Walsh, B. T. (2009). Adipose tissue distribution after weight restoration and weight maintenance in women with anorexia nervosa. *The American Journal of Clinical Nutrition*, *90*(5), 1132–1137. https://doi.org/10.3945/ajcn.2009.27820

McClelland, J., Hodsoll, J., Brown, A., Lang, K., Boysen, E., Flynn, M., Mountfod, V. A., Glennon, D., & Schmidt, U. (2018). A pilot evaluation of a novel first episode and rapid early intervention service for eating disorders (FREED). *European Eating Disorders Review*, *26*(2), 129–140. https://doi.org/10.1002/erv.2579

McCranie S. (2014). *Brick by brick: Principles for achieving artistic mastery*. Self-published.

McIntosh, V. V. W., Robinson, P., Jordan, J., & Bulik, C. M. (2023). Specialist supportive clinical management (SSCM) and eating disorders. In P. Robinson, T. Wade, B. Herpertz-Dahlmann, F. Fernandez-Aranda, J. Treasure, & S. Wonderlich (Eds.), *Eating disorders*. Springer. https://doi.org/10.1007/978-3-030-97416-9_60-1

McKay, M. T., Cannon, M., Chambers, D., Conroy, R. M., Coughlan, H., Dodd, P., Healy, C., O'Donnell, L., & Clarke, M. C. (2021). Childhood trauma and adult mental disorder: A systematic review and meta-analysis of longitudinal cohort studies. *Acta Psychiatrica Scandinavica, 143*(3), 189–205. https://doi.org/10.1111/acps.13268

McLean, C. P., de Boer, K., Lee, M. F., & McLean, S. A. (2025). The treatment experiences of vegetarians and vegans with an eating disorder: A qualitative study. *Nutrients, 17*(2), 345. https://www.mdpi.com/2072-6643/17/2/345

McMaster, C. M., Wade, T., Franklin, J., & Hart, S. (2021). A review of treatment manuals for adults with an eating disorder: Nutrition content and consistency with current dietetic evidence. *Eating and Weight Disorders, 26*(1), 47–60. https://doi.org/10.1007/s40519-020-00850-6

Meehl, P. E. (1954). *Clinical versus statistical prediction: A theoretical analysis and a review of the evidence.* University of Minnesota Press. https://doi.org/10.1037/11281-000

Meehl, P. E. (1973). *Psychodiagnosis selected papers* (pp. 225–302, Chapter 13). University of Minnesota Press.

Meehl, P. E. (1986). Causes and effects of my disturbing little book. *Journal of Personality Assessment, 50,* 370–375.

Meule, A., Kolar, D. R., & Voderholzer, U. (2022). Weight suppression and body mass index at admission interactively predict weight trajectories during inpatient treatment of anorexia nervosa. *Journal of Psychosomatic Research, 158,* 110924. https://doi.org/10.1016/j.jpsychores.2022.110924

Miller, W. R., & Rollnick, S. (2013). *Motivational interviewing: Helping people change* (3rd ed.). Guilford.

Mills, R., Hyam, L., & Schmidt, U. (2024). Early intervention for eating disorders. *Current Opinion in Psychiatry, 37*(6), 397–403. https://doi.org/10.1097/YCO.0000000000000963

Monteleone, A. M., Pellegrino, F., Croatto, G., Carfagno, M., Hilbert, A., Treasure, J., Wade, T., Bulik, C. M., Zipfel, S., Hay, P., Schmidt, U., Castellini, G., Favaro, A., Fernandez-Aranda, F., Il Shin, J., Voderholzer, U., Ricca, V., Moretti, D., Busatta, D., ... & Solmi, M. (2022). Treatment of eating disorders: A systematic meta-review of meta-analyses and network meta-analyses. *Neuroscience and Biobehavioral Reviews, 142,* 104857. https://doi.org/10.1016/j.neubiorev.2022.104857

Mountford, V., & Waller, G. (2006). Using imagery in cognitive-behavioral treatment for eating disorders: Tackling the restrictive mode. *International Journal of Eating Disorders, 39*(7), 533–543. https://doi.org/10.1002/eat.20329

Murray, H. B., Tabri, N., Thomas, J. J., Herzog, D. B., Franko, D. L., & Eddy, K. T. (2017). Will I get fat? 22-year weight trajectories of individuals with eating disorders. *International Journal of Eating Disorders, 50*(7), 739–747. https://doi.org/10.1002/eat.22690

Nagata, J. M., Lee, S., & Downey, A. E. (2024). Addressing bone health in adolescents with anorexia nervosa—no bones about it. *JAMA Network Open, 7*(10), e2441719-e2441719. https://doi.org/10.1001/jamanetworkopen.2024.41719

National Institute for Health and Care Excellence (2017). *Eating disorders: Recognition and treatment.* NICE Guideline NG 69. Retrieved from https://www.nice.org.uk/guidance/ng69

Nye, A., Delgadillo, J., & Barkham, M. (2023). Efficacy of personalized psychological interventions: A systematic review and meta-analysis. *Journal of Consulting and Clinical Psychology, 91*(7), 389–397. https://doi.org/10.1037/ccp0000820

O'Connor, M. A., Touyz, S. W., Dunn, S. M., & Beumont, P. J. (1987). Vegetarianism in anorexia nervosa? A review of 116 consecutive cases. *Medical Journal of Australia, 147*(11–12), 540–542. https://doi.org/10.5694/j.1326-5377.1987.tb133677.x

Oettingen, G., & Cachia, J. Y. A. (2016). Problems with positive thinking and how to overcome them. In K. D. Vohs & R. F. Baumeister (Eds.), *Handbook of self-regulation: Research, theory, and applications* (pp. 547–570). Guilford.

Öst, L. G., Karlstedt, A., & Widén, S. (2012). The effects of cognitive behavior therapy delivered by students in a psychologist training program: An effectiveness study. *Behavior Therapy, 43*(1), 160–173. https://doi.org/10.1016/j.beth.2011.05.001

Ozier, A. D., & Henry, B. W. (2011). Position of the American Dietetic Association: Nutrition intervention in the treatment of eating disorders. *Journal of the American Dietetic Association, 111*(8), 1236–1241. https://doi.org/10.1016/j.jada.2011.06.016

Padesky, C. (1994). Schema change processes in cognitive therapy. *Clinical Psychology and Psychotherapy, 1,* 267–278.

Padesky, C. A., & Greenberger, D. (1995). *Clinician's guide to mind over mood.* Guilford.

Paphiti, A., & Newman, E. (2023). 10-session cognitive behavioural therapy (CBT-T) for eating disorders: A systematic review and narrative synthesis. *International Journal of Cognitive Therapy, 16*(4), 646–681. https://doi.org/10.1007/s41811-023-00184-y

Pennebaker, J. W. (1997). Writing about emotional experiences as a therapeutic process. *Psychological Science, 8*(3), 162–166. https://doi.org/10.1111/j.1467-9280.1997.tb0040

Pennesi, J. L., Johnson, C., Radünz, M., & Wade, T. D. (2024). Acute augmentations to psychological therapies in eating disorders: A systematic review and meta-analysis. *Current Psychiatry Reports, 26*(9), 447–459. https://doi.org/10.1007/s11920-024 -01519-y

Pennesi, J. L., & Wade, T. D. (2018). Imagery rescripting and cognitive dissonance: A randomized controlled trial of two brief online interventions for women at risk of developing an eating disorder. *International Journal of Eating Disorders, 51*(5), 439–448. https://doi.org/10.1002/eat.22849

Pépin, G., & King, R. (2016). Collaborative care skill training workshop: How Australian carers support a loved one with an eating disorder. *Advances in Eating Disorders, 4*(1), 47–58. https://doi.org/10.1080/21662630.2015.1081823

Pettersson, C., Svedlund, A., Wallengren, O., Swolin-Eide, D., Paulson Karlsson, G., & Ellegård, L. (2021). Dietary intake and nutritional status in adolescents and young adults with anorexia nervosa: A 3-year follow–up study. *Clinical Nutrition, 40*(10), 5391–5398. https://doi.org/10.1016/j.clnu.2021.08.014

Pomeroy, S. E., & Cant, R. P. (2010). General practitioners' decision to refer patients to dietitians: Insight into the clinical reasoning process. *Australian Journal of Primary Health, 16*(2), 147–153. https://doi.org/10.1071/py09024

Porter, C., Palmier-Claus, J., Branitsky, A., Mansell, W., Warwick, H., & Varese, F. (2020). Childhood adversity and borderline personality disorder: A meta-analysis. *Acta Psychiatrica Scandinavica, 141*(1), 6–20. https://doi.org/10.1111/acps.13118

Potterton, R., Brown, G., & Schmidt, U. (2025). "I thought if my parents got involved, then they'd make me get better": Emerging adults' experiences of support from family and friends during anorexia nervosa. *Journal of Eating Disorders, 13*, 80. https://doi.org/10.1186/s40337-025-01260-8

Prochaska, J. O., DiClemente, C. C., & Norcross, J. C. (1992). In search of how people change: Applications to addictive behaviors. *The American Psychologist, 47*(9), 1102–1114. https://doi.org/10.1037//0003-066x.47.9.1102

Pugh, M. (2016). The internal "anorexic voice": A feature or fallacy of eating disorders? *Advances in Eating Disorders, 4*(1), 75–83. https://doi.org/10.1080/21662630.2015.1116017

Pugh, M. (2018). Cognitive behavioural chairwork. *International Journal of Cognitive Therapy, 11*, 100–116. https://doi.org/10.1007/s41811-018-0001-5

Pugh, M. (2020). Understanding "Ed": A theoretical and empirical review of the internal eating disorder "voice". *Psychotherapy Section Review, 65*, 12–23.

Pugh, M., & Bell, T. (2020). Process-based chairwork: Applications and innovations in the time of COVID-19. *European Journal of Counselling Theory, Research, and Practice, 4*, 1–8.

Pugh, M., & Waller, G. (2017). Understanding the "anorexic voice" in anorexia nervosa. *Clinical Psychology & Psychotherapy, 24*(3), 670–676. https://doi.org/10.1002/cpp.2034

Qian, J., Wu, Y., Liu, F., Zhu, Y., Jin, H., Zhang, H., Wan, Y., Li, C., & Yu, D. (2022). An update on the prevalence of eating disorders in the general population: A systematic review and meta-analysis. *Eating and Weight Disorders, 27*(2), 415–428. https://doi.org/10.1007/s40519-021-01162-z

Radunz, M., Keegan, E., Osenk, I., & Wade, T. D. (2020). Relationship between eating disorder duration and treatment outcome: Systematic review and meta-analysis. *International Journal of Eating Disorders, 53*(11), 1761–1773. https://doi.org/10.1002/eat.23373

Ragnarsson, E. H., Reinebo, G., Ingvarsson, S., Lindgren, A., Beckman, M., Alfonsson, S., Hedman-Lagerlöf, M., Rahm, C., Sahlin, H., Stenfors, T., Sörman, K., Jansson-Fröjmark, M., & Lundgren, T. (2024). Effects of training in cognitive behavioural therapy and motivational interviewing on mental health practitioner behaviour: A systematic review and meta-analysis. *Clinical Psychology and Psychotherapy, 31*(3), e3003. https://doi.org/10.1002/cpp.3003

Real-Brioso, N., Estrada, E., Ruiz-Lee, A. L., Raykos, B. C., & Erceg-Hurn, D. M. (2024). Early response in people with anorexia nervosa receiving cognitive–behavioural therapy for eating disorders (CBT-ED): A latent change study. *Psychotherapy Research*, 1–16. https://doi.org/10.1080/10503307.2024.2432674

Reilly, E. E., Anderson, L. M., Gorrell, S., Schaumberg, K., & Anderson, D. A. (2017). Expanding exposure-based interventions for eating disorders. *International Journal of Eating Disorders, 50*(10), 1137–1141. https://doi.org/10.1002/eat.22761

Rocks, T., West, M., Hockey, M., Aslam, H., Lane, M., Loughman, A., Jacka, F. N., & Ruusunen, A. (2021). Possible use of fermented foods in rehabilitation of anorexia nervosa: The gut microbiota as a modulator. *Progress in Neuro-Psychopharmacology and Biological Psychiatry, 107*, 110201. https://doi.org/10.1016/j.pnpbp.2020.110201

Rose, C., Bakopoulou, I., & Novak, T. (2021). A case series of CBT-T in routine clinical practice. *International Journal of Eating Disorders, 54*(8), 1549–1554. https://doi.org/10.1002/eat.23566

Rose, C., & Waller, G. (2017). Cognitive-behavioral therapy for eating disorders in primary care settings: Does it work, and does a greater dose make it more effective? *International Journal of Eating Disorders, 50*(12), 1350–1355. https://doi.org/10.1002/eat.22778

Roth, A. D., & Pilling, S. (2007). *The competences required to deliver effective cognitive and behavioural therapy for people with depression and with anxiety disorders.* Department of Health.

Rowan, J. (1990). *Subpersonalities: The people inside us.* Routledge.

Royal College of Psychiatrists. (2022). *Medical Emergencies in Eating Disorders (MEED): Guidance on recognition and management.* CR 233.

Ruusunen, A., Rocks, T., Jacka, F., & Loughman, A. (2019). The gut microbiome in anorexia nervosa: Relevance for nutritional rehabilitation. *Psychopharmacology, 236*(5), 1545–1558. https://doi.org/10.1007/s00213-018-5159-2

Sala, M., Keshishian, A., Song, S., Moskowitz, R., Bulik, C. M., Roos, C. R., & Levinson, C. A. (2023). Predictors of relapse in eating disorders: A meta-analysis. *Journal of Psychiatric Research, 158*, 281–299. https://doi.org/10.1016/j.jpsychires.2023.01.002

Santonastaso, P., Sala, A., & Favaro, A. (1998). Water intoxication in anorexia nervosa: A case report. *International Journal of Eating Disorders, 24*(4), 439–442. https://doi.org/https://doi.org/10.1002/(SICI)1098-108X(199812)24:4<439::AID-EAT12>3.0.CO;2-4

Saxon, D., Firth, N., & Barkham, M. (2017). The relationship between therapist effects and therapy delivery factors: Therapy modality, dosage, and non-completion. *Administration and Policy in Mental Health, 44*(5), 705–715. https://doi.org/10.1007/s10488-016-0750-5

Schebendach, J., Klein, D. A., Mayer, L. E., Attia, E., Devlin, M. J., Foltin, R. W., & Walsh, B. T. (2017). Assessment of the motivation to use artificial sweetener among individuals with an eating disorder. *Appetite, 109*, 131–136. https://doi.org/10.1016/j.appet.2016.11.026

Schleider, J. L., Smith, A. C., & Ahuvia, I. (2023). Realizing the untapped promise of single-session interventions for eating disorders. *International Journal of Eating Disorders, 56*(5), 853–863. https://doi.org/10.1002/eat.23920

Schmidt, U., Startup, H., & Treasure, J. (2018). *A cognitive-interpersonal therapy workbook for treating anorexia nervosa: The Maudsley model.* Routledge.

Schuldt, J. P., Muller, D., & Schwarz, N. (2012). The "fair trade" effect: Health halos from social ethics claims. *Social Psychological and Personality Science, 3*(5), 581–589. https://doi.org/10.1177/1948550611431643

Serpell, L., Treasure, J., Teasdale, J., & Sullivan, V. (1999). Anorexia nervosa: Friend or foe? *International Journal of Eating Disorders, 25*(2), 177–186. https://doi.org/10.1002/(SICI)1098-108X(199903)25:2<177::AID-EAT7>3.0.CO;2-D

Shafran, R., Wroe, A., Nagra, S., Pissaridou, E., & Coughtrey, A. (2018). Cognitive behaviour treatment of co-occurring depression and generalised anxiety in routine clinical practice. *PloS One, 13*(7), e0201226. https://doi.org/10.1371/journal.pone.0201226

Silén, Y., Sipilä, P. N., Raevuori, A., Mustelin, L., Marttunen, M., Kaprio, J., & Keski-Rahkonen, A. (2020). DSM-5 eating disorders among adolescents and young adults in Finland: A public health concern. *International Journal of Eating Disorders, 53*(5), 520–531. https://doi.org/10.1002/eat.23236

Simpson, S., & Smith, E. (Eds.). (2019). *Schema therapy for eating disorders: Theory and practice for individual and group settings.* Routledge.

Solmi, M., Radua, J., Stubbs, B., Ricca, V., Moretti, D., Busatta, D., Carvalho, A. F., Dragioti, E., Favaro, A., Monteleone, A. M., Shin, J. I., Fusar-Poli, P., & Castellini, G. (2021). Risk factors for eating disorders: An umbrella review of published meta-analyses. *Brazilian Journal of Psychiatry, 43*(3), 314–323. https://doi.org/10.1590/1516 -4446-2020-1099

Solmi, M., Wade, T. D., Byrne, S., Del Giovane, C., Fairburn, C. G., Ostinelli, E. G., De Crescenzo, F., Johnson, C., Schmidt, U., Treasure, J., Favaro, A., Zipfel, S., & Cipriani, A. (2021). Comparative efficacy and acceptability of psychological interventions for the treatment of adult outpatients with anorexia nervosa: A systematic review and network meta-analysis. *The Lancet Psychiatry, 8*(3), 215–224. https://doi.org/10.1016/S2215 -0366(20)30566-6

Speers, A., Bhullar, N., Cosh, S., & Wootton, B. (2022). Correlates of therapist drift in psychological practice: A systematic review. *Clinical Psychology Review, 93*, 102–132. https:doi.or/10.1016/j/cpr.2022.102132

Steinglass, J., Albano, A. M., Simpson, H. B., Carpenter, K., Schebendach, J., & Attia, E. (2012). Fear of food as a treatment target: Exposure and response prevention for anorexia nervosa in an open series. *International Journal of Eating Disorders, 45*(4), 615–621. https://doi.org/https://doi.org/10.1002/eat.20936

Stern, C. M., Graver, H., McPherson, I., Gydus, J., Kambanis, P. E., Breithaupt, L., Burton-Murray, H., Zayas, L., Eddy, K. T., Thomas, J. J., & Becker, K. R. (2024). Difficulties in emotion regulation in avoidant/restrictive food intake disorder. *International Journal of Eating Disorders, 57*(11), 2156–2166. https://doi.org/10.1002/eat.24281

Stern, C. M., McPherson, I., Dreier, M. J., Coniglio, K., Palmer, L. P., Gydus, J., Graver, H., Germine, L. T., Tabri, N., Wang, S. B., Breithaupt, L., Eddy, K. T., Thomas, J. J., Plessow, F., & Becker, K. R. (2024). Avoidant/restrictive food intake disorder differs from anorexia nervosa in delay discounting. *Journal of Eating Disorders, 12*(1), 19. https://doi.org/10.1186/s40337-023-00958-x

Sullivan, V. K., Martínez-Steele, E., Garcia-Larsen, V., & Rebholz, C. M. (2024). Trends in plant-based diets among United States adults, 1999–March 2020. *The Journal of Nutrition, 154*(12), 3575–3584. https://doi.org/10.1016/j.tjnut.2024.08.004

Tatham, M., Hewitt, C., & Waller, G. (2020). Outcomes of brief and enhanced cognitive-behavioural therapy for adults with non-underweight eating disorders: A non-randomized comparison. *European Eating Disorders Review, 28*(6), 701–708. https://doi.org/10 .1002/erv.2765

Tatham, M., Turner, H., Mountford, V. A., Tritt, A., Dyas, R., & Waller G. (2015). Development, psychometric properties and preliminary clinical validation of a brief, session-by-session measure of eating disorder cognitions and behaviors: The ED-15. *International Journal of Eating Disorders, 48*, 1005–1115.

Thomas, J. J., & Eddy, K. T. (2019). *Cognitive-behavioral therapy for avoidant/restrictive food intake disorder: Children, adolescents, and adults.* Cambridge University Press.

Thomas, J. J., & McPherson, I. K. (2025). Elevating the discourse on the comorbidity and treatment of eating disorders and autism spectrum disorder: Commentary on Inal-Kaleli et al. and Nimbley et al. *International Journal of Eating Disorders, 58*(4), 673–676. https://doi.org/10.1002/eat.24363

Tobin, D. L., Banker, J. D., Weisberg, L., & Bowers, W. (2007). I know what you did last summer (and it was not CBT): A factor analytic model of international psychotherapeutic practice in the eating disorders. *International Journal of Eating Disorders, 40*, 754–757.

Tragantzopoulou, P., Mouratidis, C., Paitaridou, K., & Giannouli, V. (2024). The battle within: A qualitative meta-synthesis of the experience of the eating disorder voice. *Healthcare, 12*(22), 2306. https://doi.org/10.3390/healthcare12222306

Treasure, J., Smith, G., & Crane, A. (2007). *Skills-based learning for caring for a loved one with an eating disorder: The New Maudsley method.* Routledge.

Trivasse, H., Webb, T. L., & Waller, G. (2020). A meta-analysis of the effects of training clinicians in exposure therapy on knowledge, attitudes, intentions, and behavior. *Clinical Psychology Review, 80*, 101887. https://doi.org/10.1016/j.cpr.2020.101887

Turner, H., Marshall, E., Wood, F., Stopa, L., & Waller, G. (2016). CBT for eating disorders: The impact of early changes in eating pathology on later changes in personality pathology, anxiety and depression. *Behaviour Research and Therapy, 77*, 1–6.

Vall, E., & Wade, T. D. (2015). Predictors of treatment outcome in individuals with eating disorders: A systematic review and meta-analysis. *International Journal of Eating Disorders, 48*(7), 946–971. https://doi.org/10.1002/eat.22411

van Eeden, A. E., van Hoeken, D., & Hoek, H. W. (2021). Incidence, prevalence and mortality of anorexia nervosa and bulimia nervosa. *Current Opinion in Psychiatry, 34*(6), 515–524. https://doi.org/10.1097/YCO.0000000000000739

Vinchenzo, C., Lawrence, V., & McCombie, C. (2022). Patient perspectives on premature termination of eating disorder treatment: A systematic review and qualitative synthesis. *Journal of Eating Disorders, 10*(1), 39. https://doi.org/10.1186/s40337-022-00568-z

Vitousek, K. (2005). *Alienating patients from the "anorexic self": Externalization and alternative strategies.* Presented at the Seventh London International Eating Disorders Conference, London, April.

Vitousek, K., Watson, S., & Wilson, G. T. (1998). Enhancing motivation for change in treatment-resistant eating disorders. *Clinical Psychology Review, 18*(4), 391–420. https://doi.org/10.1016/s0272-7358(98)00012-9

von Ranson, K. M., Wallace, L. M., & Stevenson, A. (2013). Psychotherapies provided for eating disorders by community clinicians: Infrequent use of evidence-based treatment. *Psychotherapy Research, 23*(3), 333–343. https://doi.org/10.1080/10503307.2012.735377

Wade, T. D. (2023). Developing the "single-session mindset" in eating disorder research: Commentary on Schleider et al., 2023 "Realizing the untapped promise of single-session interventions for eating disorders". *International Journal of Eating Disorders, 56*(5), 864-866. https://doi.org/10.1002/eat.23930

Wade, T. D., Allen, K., Crosby, R. D., Fursland, A., Hay, P., McIntosh, V., Touyz, S., Schmidt, U., Treasure, J., & Byrne, S. (2021). Outpatient therapy for adult anorexia nervosa: Early weight gain trajectories and outcome. *European Eating Disorders Review, 29*(3), 472–481. https://doi.org/10.1002/erv.2775

Wade, T., Ambwani, S., Cardi, V., Albano, G., & Treasure, J. (2021). Outcomes for adults with anorexia nervosa who do not respond early to outpatient treatment. *International Journal of Eating Disorders, 54*(7), 1278–1282. https://doi.org/10.1002/eat.23508

Wade, T. D., Ghan, C., & Waller, G. (2021). A randomized controlled trial of two 10-session cognitive behaviour therapies for eating disorders: An exploratory investigation of which approach works best for whom. *Behaviour Research and Therapy, 146*, 103962. https://doi.org/10.1016/j.brat.2021.103962

Wade, T. D., Shafran, R., & Cooper, Z. (2024). Developing a protocol to address co-occurring mental health conditions in the treatment of eating disorders. *International Journal of Eating Disorders, 57*(6), 1291–1299. https://doi.org/10.1002/eat.24008

Wade, T. D., & Waller, G. (2025a). Ten generic competences to improve outcomes of cognitive behaviour therapy: Evidence, postulated processes and clinical implications. *Behaviour Research and Therapy.* https://doi.org/10.1016/j.brat.2025.104826

Wade, T. D., & Waller, G. (2025b). Transdiagnostic single session interventions identify rapid versus gradual responders and inform therapy personalisation before commencing therapy for eating disorders. *Cognitive Behaviour Therapy.* https://doi.org/10.1080/16506073.2025.2547977

Waller, G., Cordery, H., Corstorphine, E., Hinrichsen, H., Lawson, R., Mountford, V., & Russell, K. (2007). *Cognitive behavioral therapy for eating disorders: A comprehensive treatment guide.* Cambridge University Press.

Waller, G. (2017). Functional analytic model of anorexia nervosa and bulimia nervosa. In T. Wade (Ed.), *Encyclopaedia of feeding and eating disorders* (pp.403–407). Springer.

Waller, G., Cordery, H., Corstorphine, E., Hinrichsen, H., Lawson, R., Mountford, V., & Russell, K. (2007). *Cognitive behavioral therapy for eating disorders: A comprehensive treatment guide.* Cambridge University Press.

Waller, G., Kennerley, H., & Ohanian, V. (2007). Schema-focused cognitive behavioral therapy with eating disorders. In L. P. Riso, P. L. du Toit, D. J. Stein, & J. E. Young (Eds.), *Cognitive schemas and core beliefs in psychiatric disorders: A scientist-practitioner guide* (pp. 139–175). American Psychological Association.

Waller, G., & Mountford, V. A. (2015). Weighing patients within cognitive-behavioural therapy for eating disorders: How, when and why. *Behaviour Research and Therapy, 70,* 1-10.

Waller, G., Stringer, H., & Meyer, C. (2012). What cognitive behavioral techniques do therapists report using when delivering cognitive behavioral therapy for the eating disorders? *Journal of Consulting and Clinical Psychology, 80*(1), 171–175. https://doi.org/10.1037/a0026559

Waller, G., Tatham, M., Turner, H., Mountford, V. A., Bennetts, A., Bramwell, K., Dodd, J., & Ingram, L. (2018). A 10-session cognitive-behavioral therapy (CBT-T) for eating disorders: Outcomes from a case series of nonunderweight adult patients. *International Journal of Eating Disorders, 51*(3), 262–269. https://doi.org/10.1002/eat.22837

Waller, G., Turner, H. M., Tatham, M., Mountford, V. A., & Wade, T. D. (2019). *Brief cognitive behavioural therapy for non-underweight patients: CBT-T for eating disorders.* Hove, UK: Routledge.

Walsh, B. T., Hagan, K. E., & Lockwood, C. (2023). A systematic review comparing atypical anorexia nervosa and anorexia nervosa. *International Journal of Eating Disorders, 56*(4), 798–820. https://doi.org/10.1002/eat.23856

Wang, G., Wang, Y., & Gai, X. (2021). A meta-analysis of the effects of mental contrasting with implementation intentions on goal attainment. *Frontiers in Psychology, 12,* 565202. https://doi.org/10.3389/fpsyg.2021.565202

Wild, J., & Clark, D. M. (2011). Imagery rescripting of early traumatic memories in social phobia. *Cognitive and Behavioral Practice, 18*(4), 433–443. https://doi.org/10.1016/j.cbpra.2011.03.002

Wilson, G. T., Fairburn, C. G., & Agras, W. S. (1997). Cognitive-behavioral therapy for bulimia nervosa. In D. M. Garner & P. E. Garfinkel (Eds.), *Handbook of treatment for eating* disorders (2nd ed., pp 67–93). Guilford.

World Health Organization. (2022). *ICD-11: International classification of diseases (11th rev.)*. World Health Organisation. https://icd.who.int/

Yang, Y., Conti, J., McMaster, C. M., Piya, M. K., & Hay, P. (2023). "I need someone to help me build up my strength": A meta-synthesis of lived experience perspectives on the role and value of a dietitian in eating disorder treatment. *Behavioral Sciences, 13*(11), 944. https://doi.org/10.3390/bs13110944

Young, J. E. (1994). *Cognitive therapy for personality disorders: A schema-focused approach* (2nd ed.). Professional Resource Press.

Young, J. E. (1998). *The young schema questionnaire: Short form.* Available in electronic form at: http://.www.schematherapy.com

Young, J. E., & Klosko, J. S. (1993). *Reinventing your life*. Plume Publishers.

Young, J. E., Klosko, J. S., & Weishaar, M. E. (2003). *Schema therapy: A practitioner's guide*. Guilford.

Zhou, Y., Pennesi, J. L., & Wade, T. D. (2020). Online imagery rescripting among young women at risk of developing an eating disorder: A randomized controlled trial. *International Journal of Eating Disorders, 53*(12), 1906–1917. https://doi.org/10.1002/eat.23370

Index

For Product Safety Concerns and Information please contact our EU
representative GPSR@taylorandfrancis.com
Taylor & Francis Verlag GmbH, Kaufingerstraße 24, 80331 München, Germany

www.ingramcontent.com/pod-product-compliance
Lightning Source LLC
Chambersburg PA
CBHW051951270326
41929CB00015B/2617